Norma Procter – Her Life In Music

Dear Christina,

with love,

Norma Procter

Her Life In Music

By Lucy Wood

Typesetting and cover design by
The Book Typesetters
thebooktypesetters.com
us@thebooktypesetters.com
033 022 300 39

Published by Aswell House Publishing

First published 2021

ISBN 978-1-8382983-1-9

A note on the text

Norma Procter's archive, on which this book is based, is vast. However, there are contradictions regarding specific dates, particularly in Norma's diaries. Research has been carried out to establish accuracy within the main text, but the diaries are reproduced unedited.

Norma interchangeably refers to Grimsby and Cleethorpes as her hometowns, so both are therefore described in this manner, and text bracketed by [...] are additions to aid clarity.

Norma often made abridged notes, of incomplete sentences. The author has taken the occasional liberty of editing her words for the reader's comfort.

Contents

Chapter 1: Beginnings

It began with an envelope.

Norma Procter, a striking but shy teenager, nervously asked Kathleen Ferrier for an autograph. Ferrier was a British musical icon: a contralto who, once heard, was never forgotten. The Lancashire lass worked as a Post Office telephonist before achieving worldwide fame on the stage, and in the concert hall and recording studios. And here she was in Grimsby where Norma, herself an aspiring singer, lived and worked. It was an opportunity to meet her idol, and one Norma was determined not to miss.

'You have enjoyed y'self, haven't you?' Ferrier asked her. 'I've been watching you – come and say hello again won't you.' Norma was overwhelmed. She returned home that evening with Ferrier's autograph on a treasured Messiah score and with renewed focus on her own singing. Music was her passion.

Ferrier returned to Grimsby for more concerts and Norma always made sure to say hello, eventually finding the courage to ask if Ferrier taught to students. She had no time, she said, but scribbled a name and address on an envelope and handed it to Norma. This brief moment with Ferrier changed the course of her life. For that envelope took her directly to Professor Roy Henderson, a respected singer in his own right and, more importantly for Norma, an outstanding tutor – Ferrier's own tutor, no less.

Over a few short years, Norma was propelled from singing in local churches and concert venues to international success. The public adored her voice. Taking a seat to watch Norma perform was to embark on an emotional journey alongside her – she sang, yes, but *felt* the music too. For those fortunate enough to know her, she was loved for her wicked sense of humour and unerring dedication to music. Her social circle was a Who's Who of composers, conductors, singers, and musicians, and she kept her friends close. Intensely private, her personal and public life were separate – admittance to her privileged and small inner circle was the membership of a lifetime.

And what a life she had. Norma Procter travelled the world, performed with some of the greatest artists of the time and never once moved away from her family home in the northern town she loved so much. Hers was a life in music: a destiny, some might say, written in the stars as much as it was written on an envelope.

*

Mary Norma Procter was born on February 15, 1928, a daughter for John and Edith, and a younger sister for four-year-old Clarice Audrey. John and Edith had married in Grimsby in June 1922 and lived at number 245 Scartho Road. Later, they settled at number 194 Clee Road, Cleethorpes, where Norma lived for the rest of their life. As was family tradition, the children were known by their middle names, so the house was charmingly christened Nor-Dree and bore a proud plaque. 'Actually, it's Mary Norma Procter,' she wrote. 'Heaven knows why I was called by my second name, but then they didn't know what to call me – I was expected to be John Peter!'[1] Her parents were convinced she was a boy. When Edith gave birth to another girl, it angered John so much that he did not speak to his wife for six months – an indication of their somewhat turbulent marriage. John Procter was born in 1897. At ten years old, he earned half a crown a week as a telegraph messenger boy. Adulthood saw him become a fish merchant, trawler owner, hotelier, farmer and – famously – an owner of racing horses. Edith Clarice Hockney was born on July 12, 1897. According to Norma, Edith came from a wealthy family who did not approve of the match.[2]

Early childhood was full of simple pleasures for the young Audrey and Norma. At the private St. Giles School, they enjoyed lessons and playing with friends, and at home they were surrounded by music and beloved Airedale Terriers. 'Music has been the main interest and love of my life since before I can remember,' Norma wrote. 'My very earliest memories are being lifted onto a small kitchen table – I'd be about three years old – singing Jesus Bids Us Shine and Jesus Wants Me For A Sunbeam and other childish hymns I learnt at Sunday School. There was always music in the house, either by radio or gramophone records and I came from a musical family on both sides. Everyone sang… singers, pianists, organists, and a cellist long ago – just in an enjoyable amateur way and usually in church choirs and services, meetings and concerts, or around the piano. It was always hymns, ballads and songs, and from the Messiah and Elijah too.'[3]

Norma attended Wintringham Grammar School where, a few years later, the renowned singer Janet Baker was also taught. At a young age, Norma and her sister joined Grimsby Philharmonic Society and it was here she first met Alec Redshaw. He was musical director of the society, and a highly regarded musician and composer, and would later become one of Norma's life-long friends. 'People have asked many times – when did you first begin singing?' Norma recalled. 'My first public singing was actually on the Sunday School platform at our dear little Methodist church at Scartho village where we lived then, and later at Mill Road Methodist Church, in Cleethorpes. Audrey was four years older than me and already having piano and singing lessons. I'd begun having piano lessons aged five and to appease my own curiosity, insisted that I should also be allowed singing lessons too. For the sake of peace in the family home, I began! To mine and everyone's astonishment, I began winning prizes in many local and Lincolnshire competitive festivals, and singing lessons continued until I was thirteen years old, when at last they had to be given a rest to complete my school studies. There was nothing clever about me at school. I was a late developer all my life and still am!'[4]

American singer Marian Anderson was the first contralto to influence Norma. Similarly, Marian was interested in music from a young age and in 1955 made history by becoming the first black singer to appear at the Metropolitan Opera House in New York. 'She had a glorious voice,' she noted. 'Her amazing soul sound [was influential] when I was still finding it difficult to accept the great change in my own noise-box – from that piping sop to this "organ sound", as described by a Norwegian musician/producer, at sixteen years old! Bless her, she was very special in so many ways.'[5] She explained: 'I was sixteen when I began solo singing again and joined Mill Road Choir, and it was quite a shock to hear now this large low contralto noise after the previous piping soprano and although my music had completely taken me over, I adored the piano and still do. I had no idea or thought of becoming of a professional singer. Nor had I realised that those three years of rest had helped my voice change and mature naturally without force or damage by continually singing, just as when a boy's voice breaks at about that time and rest is essential for that change-over. I just carried on singing for pleasure and enjoyed duets with Audrey too.'[6]

After education, the world of work beckoned. A handwritten job reference, dated May 1945, described Norma as 'a good Christian and most admirable girl. I can commend her to any service which requires charm and understanding. [She is] most sympathetic and patient. She will make good in taking up responsibilities.' These virtues served her well. She took a job at Hope Street Clinic, in Grimsby, firstly as a dental nurse and then a nurse-secretary to an ophthalmic surgeon.

While Audrey enjoyed singing, she had no desire to become a professional. Norma, on the other hand, knew singing was in her heart but dared not dream of it being her career. At 18 years old, she performed in Handel's Messiah at Mill Road Church, Cleethorpes. The date was Sunday, December 1, 1946, performance time 2.15pm. Norma, singing as a contralto solo for the first time, appeared alongside soprano Dorothy King, tenor Charles Lang and baritone Wilfred Ingham. They were accompanied by the Cleethorpes String Quartet and organist Raymond Jones, and William T. Redshaw conducted. A newspaper cutting read: 'Old favourites and one new discovery will be appearing at the performance of the Messiah. Miss Procter is a young singer with a good voice and large range. This is her first Messiah role, and it is considered that she has a brilliant career before her.'

'Where it all began!' declared Norma in a handwritten note on the programme, '18 years old, my first Messiah. Thanks to dear Ruth Jackson who trained me for this performance.' The event was an important one. 'I suddenly realised what a wonderful message music had to give to the world,' noted Norma. 'This voice, I began to understand, was God's gift, not really mine and only lent to me for a while. What could I do about it? I had so little to offer but perhaps if I worked and tried hard enough, I could help spread the message, and so quietly then decided to dedicate my life, if possible, singing God's glorious gift of music.'[7] The performance was also significant because it attracted some notable support. In a letter to Norma's father, dated December 8, Ada Croft-Baker, a town alderman and important figure in the history of Grimsby and Cleethorpes, wrote: 'How I wish you could have heard your daughter sing in the Messiah. Her He Was Despised was a searching of the heart. I have never heard it so effective and I feel sure there is a great future in Norma in the singing world.' As a result of the letter, Norma's father bought her a Steinway grand piano.

★

By now Kathleen Ferrier was Norma's favourite singing idol. In that same year, 1946, she visited Grimsby to sing Messiah with Grimsby Philharmonic, and Norma was hooked: 'I was completely bowled over by the sheer beauty of this lovely face and voice, her personality and humility, and had no eyes for anyone else all evening, and her interpretation of He Was Despised was unforgettable.'[8] In another note, she wrote: 'This was the first time I saw and heard her in person in this glorious pre-Christmas concert, and was completely hypnotised by this beautiful looking lady. Just sitting on the platform in a lovely blue, silvery gown with a white fox collar was enough, but when she began to sing it was as if an angel was before us, in our midst – soul to soul and especially after He Was Despised. I have never heard anyone sing this aria as she did that evening, or since.'[9]

It was at this performance that Norma found the courage to ask for Ferrier's autograph. That first conversation left a lasting impression on the young admirer: 'At the end of the concert and totally unlike the very shy me, I went down for her autograph in my mother's pre-Christmas pressie – a newly bound copy of Messiah. She beckoned me forward and said 'You have enjoyed y'self, haven't you? I've been watching you – come and say hello again won't you.' I was so surprised but left the hall on cloud nine!'[10]

Ferrier was the great contralto of the era. Her warm personality endeared her to the nation, and she had an enviable worldwide career on the stage, in the concert hall and as a recording artist. She ironically nicknamed herself Klever Kaff, and during their later friendship, Norma took to calling her KK. Like the true fan she was, Norma kept diligent notes on the several concerts Ferrier performed in Grimsby.

The first was on October 9, 1943: two Elijah concerts with the Grimsby Philharmonic Society and Alec Redshaw for Mrs Churchill's Aid to Russia Fund. 'Then I seem to remember a concert with the Cleethorpes String Orchestra and Roland Leafe in the then Mill Road Church Sunday School Hall singing groups of songs – possibly 1944, though I have no actual date, only that she sang for an unbelievable fee of 5gns and hospitality!' she noted.[11]

There was a Messiah on December 1, 1945, and then Ferrier wore red on Valentine's Day 1946. In December that same year, when Norma first met her, she wore a blue and silver outfit to sing the Messiah with tenor Peter Pears and soprano Isobel Baillie. Tickets sold out in two days. The Grimsby Evening Telegraph said: 'Kathleen Ferrier gave a performance that was a lesson in voice expression, and Peter Pears accomplished a huge personal success with striking dignity in the opening Comfort Ye My People. The ease with which he reached his objective in subsequent arias gave an impression of graven serenity. Trevor Anthony (bass) sang with fire and vigour. But it was left to Isobel Baillie, displaying typical grace and charm, to capture the supreme moments of this evening, and out of a great performance her version of I Know That My Redeemer Liveth, following immediately on the Hallelujah chorus was perhaps the most moving. Even the audience deserved praise. The usual disturbances from the late comers were at a minimum, there was little coughing or talking during the performance, and, to avoid noisy rustling the pages of the scripts were turned over almost reverently in a practical and praiseworthy display of appreciation of a remarkable performance.'

Ferrier returned to Grimsby on April 24, 1947, with the Cleethorpes String Orchestra at Grimsby Central Hall. 'I was at that concert and spoke to Kathleen,' Norma noted. On December 4 and 5 the same year, Ferrier performed in the Messiah at the Central Hall alongside Isobel Baillie, Trevor

Anthony, and Alan Soulsby, with the Grimsby Philharmonic Orchestra. The second concert was notable because Baillie lost her voice. 'I was there when it happened,' said Norma. 'Kathleen, bless her, once again a wonderful and very clever KK just carried on singing. I think Peter Pears sang Come Unto Him – amazing – and in the meantime, Vera Burton was rushed over and stepped into the shock breach!'[12] Vera, a friend of Baillie's and a well-known singer in the area, was fortunately in the audience. Conductor Alec Redshaw, at Baillie's suggestion, promptly asked her to sing the third part of the performance. In Redshaw's book, Philharmony 1852–1977, he wrote: 'One thinks wistfully of that evening. She [Baillie] had had trouble with it [her voice] the previous evening and had warned us all that she feared the worst. Will her as we would "There were shepherds sadly but simply was not there", but Abiding In The Field was, no doubt, the only time it was sung in public by the beloved and glorious Kathleen Ferrier. Then too, Come Unto Him, as sung by Peter Pears, was another memorable experience.' The next concert was a recital at the Central Hall on November 16, 1950, with Phyllis Spurr. And, dressed in black velvet on January 14, 1952, a recital with Gerald Moore. 'Kathleen's unforgettable farewell,' reads one of Norma's archive notes.

At one of those early visits, Norma asked Ferrier for guidance on her own singing aspirations. She knew that leading baritone Roy Henderson took on pupils. She'd heard Elijah with the Grimsby Phil in October 1946, where Henderson performed without a score, and was immediately taken by his talent. 'My first concert seeing/hearing Prof,' Norma wrote. 'No score! Incredible portrayal of Elijah. Again, hypnotised.' Norma was nervous and modestly unsure of her own abilities, so approached Ferrier with trepidation: 'I always gladly went to say 'hello' [to Ferrier] as she'd asked, finally finding the courage to ask if she did any teaching herself. She hadn't the time, she said, but gave me on the envelope of her 25gns marked fee, Roy Henderson's – her Prof – name and details. Again, I was so shattered, as he was my original choice too. I still have that very precious envelope.'[13]

Without delay, a letter was duly sent to Henderson in Belsize Park Gardens, London. 'Dear Sir,' it read, 'I am desirous of extending my career as a singer and should be grateful if an audition could possibly be arranged at your studio. My age is eighteen years, and I am at present employed as a secretary to an ophthalmic surgeon. I have gained a number of prizes in festival work in my own town and surrounding district during my childhood. In December 1946, I sang the principal contralto arias in a local performance of Handel's Messiah. Some considerable time ago I spoke of my desire to Miss. Kathleen Ferrier, who advised me to get in touch with you. In anticipation I know [sic] await what I hope will be a favourable reply.'

A reply there was, and Norma was invited to audition. On a snow-clogged January day in 1947, she and her mother caught a train to London without saying a word to anyone. 'It seemed he already knew about me from Kathleen Ferrier and was impressed, tho' promised nothing – only very hard work and an enormous amount of learning,' she recalled. 'My classical repertoire was almost non-existent, to say nothing of the languages needed, and [all] whether I could control my tormenting unbearable nerves before a concert, and had the enormous stamina needed for a constant travelling minstrel.'[14] Endless hours of hard work lay ahead. Norma had much to learn, and she became an attentive student, amazed that she was being taught by the same tutor as her beloved Kathleen. Henderson – nicknamed Prof – suggested she move to London immediately, but the self-confessed home-bird instead travelled for lessons whenever she could afford it.

★

Roy Galbraith Henderson was born in Edinburgh in 1889. Singing was his calling and, while on early-morning sentry duty during the First World War, he would rehearse the ballad Simon The Cellarer, which he later became well-known for. He won 13 awards throughout his time studying at the Royal Academy of Music and began his professional career in 1925, when he substituted for another baritone in London. He had three weeks to learn the part and sang it from memory, a skill he instilled in Norma. Henderson's Covent Garden debut was in 1928, as Donner in Das Rheingold, and he debuted at Glyndebourne in 1934. His career continued in an upward trajectory for decades, becoming a professor at the Academy and retiring from the stage in 1952 but continuing to teach privately. He was Norma's only vocal teacher throughout her career. Norma looked forward to those journeys to London, and at Henderson's suggestion soon added the study of musicianship and piano to her schedule with none other than Alec Redshaw, his long-term friend who lived in Cleethorpes.

'Those weekly journeys to Prof were a wonderful way of being broken in, so to speak,' Norma recalled. 'It had never occurred to me to ask m'self first: do you like travelling? Do you like trains and planes? Hotels? Can you sleep in strange beds every other night? Eat meals at any hour of the day? Do you like living in a suitcase, endlessly packing and unpacking? Do you love people? Like writing letters? Have you plenty of patience, and always a real sense of humour? Loneliness? It soon became very clear to me all these things were very necessary for this life before even singing a note! Slowly, very slowly, I adjusted myself to this new life and completely different way of living for I had travelled almost nowhere, being very much the home girl.

Very slowly – for to my mind this is the only way. There are no short cuts in this career but learning all the time with the experience of each concert, conductor or accompanist… what to do and what not to do.'[15]

In time, Norma resigned from her job and her first year with Prof was spent working only on technique, breathing and exercises. The young woman had no idea what the future had in store and simply concentrated on improving her craft by learning from her idols: 'It was at the 1947 Edinburgh festival – the first since the war – that I heard [by radio] my first Mahler and perhaps most beloved, Das Lied von der Erde, with the greatest contralto Kathleen Ferrier and dear Peter Pears, and another great, the humble and beloved Bruno Walter. I was actually working in the kitchen and knew little of what it was all about – my German was very limited then – but by the end of Kathleen's Der Abschied, I was sitting in the kitchen corner with tears streaming down my face, and little thought that one day I would be trying to sing Mahler myself.' 'It was too much for m'ole heart-strings,' she noted in later life. 'I couldn't stop the flowing tears and was totally captured and overcome by Mahler's magical music forever. I eventually sang this very moving work. I still find it difficult to listen to KK's unequalled singing of this heart-rending work.'[16]

Norma's dedication paid off and the stage beckoned. She spent the summer of 1948 with the Glyndebourne Chorus and made her professional London debut in Handel's Messiah at Southwark Cathedral later that year. But this was not her first experience of public prominence. It had arrived earlier that year, entirely unwanted and out of her control, and Norma was mortified.

Chapter 2: Family

Norma's father was destined to be an entrepreneur. Born on November 12, 1897 to Frederick and Mary, he was part of a large family who lived at number 124 Duncombe Street, Grimsby[17] – not far from the Central Hall where Norma later performed as an artist. Frederick Procter married Mary following the death of his first wife, Sarah. John's siblings were Frederick (b. 1879), Annie (b. 1881), Charles (b. 1883), Joseph (b. 1885), Thomas (b. 1887) and Miriam (b. 1899). Thomas, an Able Seaman in the Royal Navy, was lost in action serving aboard HMS Aboukir in the North Sea in 1914. His body was never recovered for burial.

Young John did not waste time in making money. At 10 years old, he took a wage as a telegraph messenger boy. In March 1915, he lied about his age to enlist in the Army. He was 16 at the time but said he was 21. He served abroad and after demobbing became a clerk in the fish curer's office of A J Brown, on Grimsby Docks. 'I didn't know any more about fish curing than a fly,' he recalled later in a newspaper article, 'but inside five years I was manager, and in 1927, I left and went on my own in the fish curing business as the Supreme Fish Curing Company.'[18] He married Edith in 1922 and Audrey was born on January 30, 1924, followed by Norma four years later.

In 1935, he purchased A J Brown, creating what was at one point believed to be the largest fish-curing business in Britain. He acquired an Aberdeen-based trawler fleet and a farm near Brigg, and bought the The Shades Hotel, in Church Street, Spilsby, and The Lord Nelson Hotel, in Brigg. To say he was well-known in the area is an understatement, but it was his hobby of keeping racehorses that brought notoriety to the Procter family.

John purchased an eight-year-old Irish racehorse, Sheila's Cottage, within six weeks of hearing she was for sale. His intention was to race her in the Grand National. 'She is a wonderful mare,' he told a local journalist, 'and she is very fit. She will be ridden by Arthur Thompson, one of the best northern jockeys, who has ridden her every time she has run in England, and she has never fallen once. I think, and my trainer and jockey also think, she stands as good a chance as any in this year's race. We are trying all we can to have a Lincolnshire winner for the National this year. Half of Brigg will be at Aintree and I think I shall go crazy if she wins.'[19]

John had been interested in horseracing since childhood and long harboured the ambition to one day own a horse to race in the National. His dream came true, three years on from purchasing his first horse. His horses were trained by Captain Neville Crump, at Warwick House, in Middleham, Yorkshire, and it was at this stable where Sheila's Cottage, owned by Sir Hervy Bruce at the time, caught his attention. Crump had been training horses in Middleham for 10 years when Sheila's Cottage came along. She was bad-tempered and feisty, and difficult to train. But Crump, a straight-talking and loyal man, had great affection for her.

An article in the Lincolnshire Echo, dated February 1948, read: 'Mr Procter had a curious experience over his recent purchase from Sir Hervy, of Ballybrown. He bought her over the telephone while racing at Lingfield recently, and on the Monday when she won a selling race, it cost him 600 guineas to buy her in. Mr Procter said Sheila's Cottage was very unfortunate last year in her first attempt for the National. She went right round, only to be knocked over by a loose horse on the second circuit when going very well. He also has high hopes for his French horse, the five-years-old Prince Ki, who won on his first appearance in the country at Manchester on New Year's Day, and also won last Saturday. A yearling which Mr Procter bought for 1,000 guineas from Mr Clifford Nicholson at the Doncaster races has been named The Shades after the hotel of that name which Mr Procter owns at Spilsby. Other horses in his string at Middleham include Brig O' Nelson, Mainsail, which won at Hamilton Park, and Game Kid, which won at Ayr.'

When taking the photograph of Sheila's Cottage which accompanied the article, the photographer asked: 'Is she gentle?' Jack Douglas, head lad at Middleham, replied: 'I'm afraid she's a bit saucy. The mare has a mind of her own. She had a bite at a finger of one of the training staff during the week.' No doubt the horse's feisty nature appealed to John, perhaps akin to his own determination and endeavour. Meanwhile, Norma found it all rather embarrassing. In her diary entry for March 8 that year, she wrote: 'Masonic dinner (Field House). What a racket! Ghastly affair. I loathed it. Father turned up out of the blue. More embarrassment.'

*

Sheila's Cottage made the record books on Saturday, March 20, 1948 by winning the Grand National at Aintree – the first mare to do so since Shannon Lass in 1902, and only the twelfth in the entire history of the race.

It was extraordinary. Not only was Sheila's Cottage a mare, she was a 50-1 outsider. The thrilling race was played out before more than 500,000 spectators, an Aintree record. It was a competitive one, with many of the runners having already proved their worth in previous years.

It was a close-fought thing, ending in victory for jockey Arthur P Thompson, who won in a field of 43 runners by a length from Major D Vaughan's 25-1 First of the Dandies. The excitement at the course – and back home in Grimsby – was palpable. 'Her bravery and finishing power saw her overthrow First of the Dandies and relegate the horse to a hard-fought, one-length defeat,' wrote Stewart Peters in his book, The Grand National: The History Of The Aintree Spectacular. That afternoon's edition of the Lincolnshire Echo proudly declared 'Lincs horse wins Grand National' on the front page and reported a breathless account of the action. 'Sheila's Cottage won the Grand National this afternoon after an epic tussle with First of the Dandies,' said the article. 'The huge crowd – biggest since 1919 – yelled its excitement as the Lincolnshire-owned horse, prominent throughout the race, overhauled First of the Dandies on the final stretch to win by a length. Sheila's Cottage was 50-1. First of the Dandies started at 25-1 and Cromwell III, which was third, at 33-1. Silver Fame, which started favourite at 9-1, fell early in the race. The other Lincolnshire-owned horse, Gormanstown, entered by Mr Clifford Nicholson, of Gainsborough, was unplaced. There were 43 runners, and they were off to a perfect start, except that Musical Lad was left slightly.

'Housewarmer took the lead as the field swept towards the first jump. Then Lough Conn went into the lead. The first major disappointment for punters came when Silver Fame fell early in the race. Schubert, Sheila's Cottage and Cloncarrig were all jumping well at this stage. First of the Dandies then gradually drew to the front with Rowland Roy, Housewarmer and Happy Home all prominent. But Sheila's Cottage was jumping brilliantly and was soon among the challengers. Coming towards the home stretch she was lying second, and the race developed into a thrilling duel between the Lincolnshire horse and First of the Dandies.

'Gradually Sheila's Cottage overhauled, the horses raced neck to neck and then Mr Procter's gallant mare went forward to bring off one of the most exciting National victories for years. 'Immense crowds overflowed on to the course three-quarters of an hour before racing was due to begin, and the police requested them over the loudspeaker system to clear the course.'

The Grimsby Telegraph added its own take on the race. 'Shortly before the end of the race,' it wrote, 'she [Sheila's Cottage] did not look like she was going to be the winner. Another horse, Zahlia, jumped the second last fence and, full of running, looked a certain victor. But to the amazement of those watching, she suddenly veered off the course. The jockey, E. Reavey, had apparently got confused about the layout of the course. Sheila's Cottage was left to run home – the first mare to win the National for 46 years.'

John Procter's already firm reputation in Lincolnshire meant punters were pleased to back him for the National. The day before and on the morning of the race, bookmakers were inundated with punters from all over the county. A Grimsby bookmaker told the Telegraph after the race: 'The result is no good to Grimsby bookmakers. The local sentimental value attached to the horse's chances caused many people to back it. Most bookmakers would not be at all pleased with the result'. A bookmaker in Brigg said Sheila's Cottage had cost him a fortune: 'It was every other bet.'

Trainer Neville Crump told a reporter: 'I persuaded Mr Procter to buy Sheila's Cottage after Prince Ki (also owned by Mr Procter) had won at Manchester last November and he gave me 3,500 guineas for her. There was a doubt whether she would run because she was sore from a splint, but as the going was not too firm, I let her take her chance.' The last words went to John, who after the race declared to the Press: 'I am 50-years-old, but right at this moment, I feel 19.'

'A rangy, rugged mare with strength and courage, Sheila's Cottage was, by her trainer Neville Crump's own admission, a moody, angry individual but became the horse that really set the trainer's career alight,' wrote Peters in his book. 'For Crump, Thompson, and winning owner John Procter of Lincolnshire, it had been a thrilling Grand National – won by their horse in gritty but admirable fashion… her reward was retirement and a place at stud.' While jubilant scenes played out at Aintree, the streets of Grimsby were equally abuzz. The dozens of dock workers who'd taken a punt on the local horse were ecstatic at their winnings. John Procter was a hero.

★

Norma was 20 years old and mortified by the publicity the win brought the family. John's winnings were £9,500 and during that week alone he made a profit of about £19,000 from the bookies – a significant sum in 1948. He promptly purchased a Rolls Royce for £6,500 and gave £5 to every single pub in Grimsby, so regulars could have a round of drinks on him. He would light cigars with £10 notes. Norma was horrified by her father's behaviour and the attention he appeared to adore; the exact opposite of his shy, modest daughter who buried herself in music scores, and would later deal with her own fame by avoiding publicity wherever possible. When John left his wife Edith for a younger woman and moved out of the family home, Norma's heart was broken. It was an ordeal she never truly recovered from.

Her diary entries at the time reveal her inner thoughts:

> ***Friday, March 19:*** *Saw Grimsby Telegraph photo and first news of father's horse – terrible shock.*

> ***Saturday, March 20:*** *Grand National. What a dreadful shock – knew nothing about it. So ashamed and full of heartache and grief.*

> ***Monday, March 21:*** *Mother insisted we went to Mill Road. Arrived late – bus late – to be greeted by coughs and nudges, and whole congregation focused on me! I managed the first hymn but in the second, There Is A Green Hill, I burst into tears and ran out of the church and broke m'heart in the Sunday school hall. So ashamed and grief-stricken.*

She ended up being the go-between for her parents, sending messages from one to the other.[20] She also confided that when John gave Audrey away at her wedding in June 1948, he was blind drunk. If John Procter knew how anguished his daughter was is hard to say. But Norma was otherwise very happy. She was courting Frank 'Mitch' Mitchell, a local lad in the RAF, whom she'd promptly nicknamed Snogger. They met at a cricket match at Trent Bridge, and Mitch was 'the one' – the happy couple were set to marry.

Nor-Dree was a jolly, full place when he brought his equally handsome RAF pals to visit, and the family enjoyed entertaining. Not only that, Norma's singing career was about to take off. But she was ashamed of her father's conduct and carried it with her like a dead weight.

John enjoyed a charmed life in the months following the Grand National win. Soon afterwards, he was special guest at a boxing tournament in Scunthorpe and while the boxers were very well-received, by far the loudest cheer was reserved for John, who told the crowd: 'Look at me – the luckiest fellow in the world. How I did it I do not know.'[21]

The victory also propelled trainer Neville Crump's career to legendary status. He established his stables at Middleham as a National Hunt racing base, and his roll call of six horses jumped to almost 30. Sheila's Cottage remained, as ever, bad-tempered. Two days after the race, she bit off jockey Arthur Thompson's thumb. But there were no bad feelings: at the end of her life, she was buried at the bottom of Thompson's garden in Wexford.[22]

'The limelight was suddenly shone on the Procter family after the Grand National win,' said Nick Haste, Norma's nephew. 'John Procter milked the attention, and the fame went to his head. He had a Rolls Royce and a chauffeur and loved the high life. He lived a life of wine, women, and song, and he eventually left Edith and walked out of their family home.

'Obviously, this had a massive effect on Norma and my mother, Audrey. To this day I know the intrusion of the Press into their family life influenced Norma so much that she hated the Press with a vengeance and would have little to do with them when she could avoid it.'

★

More heartache came for Norma in November, when her father made front page news for a not so jubilant reason. The Lincolnshire Echo reported that police officers posed as guests at his Lord Nelson Hotel, stayed overnight and witnessed alcohol being served illegally. By now John was an even more prominent figure in the area, having become a Brigg councillor and chairman of the Brigg and District Licensed Victuallers' Association.

He appeared in court accused of supplying intoxicants outside of closing times to nine customers, and aiding and abetting his customers; in all, he faced a total of 18 summonses. Alongside him, his hotel manager and a barmaid were charged with aiding and abetting the licensee, and all nine customers were accused of consuming intoxicants outside of permitted hours. John and the barmaid pleaded guilty to five charges of supplying and not guilty to four, and the alternative charges of aiding and abetting were withdrawn. The hotel manager pleaded not guilty to all counts. Four customers pleaded not guilty, while the remaining five admitted the offences.

The case was reported in detail. Prosecuting, Mr T J Lewis told the court that normal licensing hours at the hotel were 10.30am to 2.30pm, extended to 4pm on Thursdays, and then 6.30pm to 10pm for evening service. Two officers had been deputed to book rooms at the hotel, posing as ordinary guests. Under instructions from superiors, the rooms were booked under the Ministry of Food and although the police denied ever actually claiming they were officials of the organisation, evidence was heard that they told other guests and John how they were in danger of losing their jobs with the ministry. John told the court that the men were 'scared to death'[23] and felt sorry for them.

At 4.55pm on October 28, a van with seven policemen inside pulled up outside the hotel and found it locked. One of the officers followed instructions to go to the front door and ask to be let outside to post a letter. The hotel manager obliged but when he spotted a policeman getting out of the van, he tried to close the door. The undercover officer deliberately dropped the envelope to keep the door open. While this was happening, two policemen climbed over a wall and entered the hotel through the back door. They found several men and the barmaid behind the bar, and seven glasses of beer scattered around the room. The men denied they were drinking, and the police departed – but left the two undercover officers at the hotel to see what happened next. Just before 6pm, the court heard that John told all those there: 'This is your story. You are guests of mine. I had asked you for tea.' One of the customers removed a wine glass from his Mackintosh pocket and replied: 'I think this is yours, John.' But he spotted an officer taking notes and immediately withdrew his remarks. Meanwhile, the hotel manager claimed he'd been unwell that day and was asleep, but the undercover officers confirmed it was he who opened the front door at 4.55pm.

In John's defence, the court was told that his generosity as a licensee was well-known. The hotel was a regular calling place on market day for farmers and merchants to have tea, and on this occasion, they were supplied with drinks while waiting for tea. Defence solicitor Daniel Brabin criticised the police for what he viewed as posing as Ministry of Food officials and for staying behind after the raid. He told the court: 'In this case, you have the pathetic circumstance of men not only pretending they are food officials but that they were going to lose their jobs, and another man in the hotel commiserating with them in their story of hardship.' John was fined £120, the barmaid £10 and several customers £10 also. The charges against the hotel manager were dismissed. Once again, Norma felt humiliated by her much-loved father's conduct. She simply could not understand why he behaved as he did.

Almost nine years on from this incident, John Procter became bankrupt. He attended a hearing at Boston Bankruptcy Court in 1957 without a penny to his name. Sheila's Cottage had been sold to settle a £100 debt and the Rolls Royce sold for £1,150, a fraction of the price he'd paid for it. The court heard how John was living in furnished rooms in Yarra Road, Cleethorpes, and had spent £58,000 in just one year. He told the court he wanted to obtain employment to clear some of his debts. In November 1958, he returned to the same court to secure the discharge of his bankruptcy. He was back working on Grimsby fish docks, earning £12 a week. Although she cared for him deeply, the incidents changed Norma's outlook on life.

Chapter 3: Engagements and Kathleen Ferrier

Back in 1948, Norma performed in the chorus of Glyndebourne Opera Company's Cosi Fan Tutte, in Edinburgh for three weeks of August. Her talent was noticed at the audition stage by Sir John Pritchard. Sir John signed a contract to conduct both Don Giovanni and Cosi Fan Tutte for just £25, and the fee also covered all the preliminary work, including choosing the chorus. He 'revealed an exciting find' in Norma. 'She looks nice and sings like an embryo Ferrier,' he said.[24]

An undated press cutting, headlined Cleethorpes Girl Is In The Opera, reported: 'On the stage of the King's Theatre, Edinburgh, next Monday, the first night of the Edinburgh Musical Festival's three-weeks' run, will be a 20-years-old opera singer Norma Procter, of Nor-Dree, Clee Road. Norma's story is almost too good to be true. It started 18 months ago when she sang contralto solos in Handel's Messiah with Mill Road Methodist Choir. An audition with BBC singer Roy Henderson led to weekly trips to London for tuition and last spring to a contract with the Glyndebourne Opera Company. Now her chief difficulty is learning Italian for Don Giovanni and Cosi Fan Tutte.' In the Fish Trades Gazette came a prediction: 'In Edinburgh now, rehearsing for an important part in the Edinburgh Music Festival, is Norma Procter, younger daughter of a family well known in fish-curing trade circles. Norma, possessor of a happy lilting voice, is appearing with the Glyndebourne Opera Company in a couple of Italian operas, the serious Don Giovanni, and the lighter Cosi Fan Tutte, both to be played in the original Italian. Norma is on the threshold of what is certain to be an important event in her life. That she will go far in opera and on the concert platform is the considered opinion of those who have heard her sing.'

The Glyndebourne cast that year was an international affair, with artists from Scotland and America among the company. The productions were praised as top-notch by the Press: 'A glance at the décor was sufficient to indicate that it is first-class. Windows to be used in Cosi Fan Tutte are an example of this. Their structure, and the beautiful curtains which adorn them, would do credit to an expensive Continental villa.'[25] 'It was a wonderful cast,' Norma declared. 'Paolo Silveri was a magnificent Don Rafael and Kubelik conducting!' Her contract stipulated that she must sing in English or Italian, 'and to dance, if required, in all performances, concerts, matinees or soirees given or organised by the management'[26] during her time in Scotland. Rehearsals began in Glyndebourne on August 3 and then switched to Edinburgh from August 11. Her salary was £8 a week, and each week contained seven performances.

She arrived at her lodgings in the city with Mary, a fellow chorus member: 'It was a huge Victorian house run by two maiden sisters, Misses Smith. There was no chance of getting smashed on whiskey or whatever with them, though I didn't drink in those days, as ever. Both were very dour and religious ladies who held prayer meetings there every Sunday afternoon (ghastly!). They were kind eventually, when they realised we weren't a couple of high kicker chorus gals!'[27]

She enjoyed it and returned in 1949, often sitting in the wings to observe the great singers of the day, however, opera was not for her: 'I knew at Glyndebourne it would never be mine – too much accent on production for me. Music was my love. Opera is so much more physically demanding than concert singing.'[28] Of Cosi Fan Tutte in particular, she remarked many years later: 'It's lovely music but the opera never really appealed to me – the plot and masses of recitations – though I sat for hours on a box in the wings looking, listening and learning, or trying to, but knew opera wasn't really for me.'[29]

But to all intents and purposes, her career was taking off. Already she'd sung with mezzo-soprano Janet Baker – later to become the world-famous Dame Janet – in a memorial concert in Grimsby on May 27, 1948. Baker, who attended Wintringham Grammar School in the town with Norma, was also on the up. In 1956, she came second in the Kathleen Ferrier Memorial Competition and, like Norma, was signed to the Ibbs & Tillett agency. In later years, when Norma was too unwell to perform at engagements or bookings, Janet took her place.

★

Meanwhile, Norma's friendship with Kathleen Ferrier was flourishing. Kathleen saw talent in the burgeoning singer and encouraged her professionally, as well as offering her home – a flat within Frognal Mansions, in Hampstead Heath – as a base for Norma in London. She was good company for Ferrier's father, William, known as Pop Ferrier, and her young housekeeper, Patricia (known as Paddy) Jewitt, herself a soprano and a scholarship student with Roy Henderson, when Kathleen was away from home. Always considerate, Norma was wary of imposing on their goodwill, but Ferrier did not see it that way. A diary entry for April 27, 1949, reads: 'Prof's. Stayed at Kath's with Paddy and Pop. She was wonderful. She'd returned from the continent. Troubled – not fair for me to be here. She and Paddy waved me off from Frognal Mansions 28th AM. I am staying in Lewes – Stabat Mater.'

'I often stayed overnight after a lesson… even sleeping in her bed to keep it aired!' Norma wrote. 'Kathleen encouraged a friendship between Paddy and I – typical, kindly, thoughtful Kath was concerned Paddy was alone at the flat when she was away and would she like a young friend to stay with her occasionally. To my great surprise, I was that very fortunate friend. I just couldn't believe my blessing and good fortune. I slept in the lovely music room divan/bed, close to Kath's wonderful £250 first prize Cramer piano she had won in a Daily Express competition in her teens, which she adored. She was a brilliant pianist too. Bless her, what enormous love and trust to allow another young, unknown contralto to share her private home and belongings, which truly tugged m'heart strings – tho' I told no one about [it] – only Prof and my close [people] knew. I used to have my hour's lesson with Prof. Paddy would come and collect me to [go to] the flat, and so save my having to catch the 4pm Kings Cross train to Grimsby.

'Once I was sitting in the hall at Prof's waiting for my lesson and could hear muted studio voices, when suddenly the door opened and there stood beloved KK, smothered in music and scores, and she dropped the lot! I rushed to help her and we both finished on the floor doubled up with laughter and music, and dear Prof wondering what we were up to. She looked so lovely in a brown suit and little white hat. I had to leave her – Prof was watching, but it made my day! It was priceless, loving laughter with a priceless, smiling singer. Oh, I could go on. "I live and love and die in a song" – her heartfelt quote, bless her. As for Win [Winifred Ferrier, Kathleen's sister], I just met her once at the flat with Pop and Paddy. She was poles apart from Kaff – a "hello" – but the voice and eyes again, and my intuition told me all. Paddy was wonderful to me. We had lots of laughter, and with dear Pop Ferrier, quietly reading or doing his crossword – one could see much of Kathleen's generous and kindly nature in him, bless him. Naturally, this could only be possible for a short but most memorable time, as we all began to go our various ways. Paddy decided a singer's life was not for her and married, living somewhere in Wales. Very sadly we lost touch over the years, but I have never forgotten her blessed goodness to me.'[30]

In 1956, Paddy sent a letter to her friend, thanking her for a small wedding posy and telegram, as Norma could not attend the ceremony. As is typical of Norma, in later life she would mention Paddy often, hoping she was well.

★

On Saturday, October 9, 1948, Norma made her professional London debut at Southwark Cathedral. Norma was nervous, naturally, but seeing familiar – and entirely unexpected – faces in the audience gave her confidence a boost. 'I was so knotted with nerves and as we were about to leave the vestry for this wonderful, vast cathedral, Dr. Cooke, the conductor, suddenly announced, "We are greatly honoured today – Kathleen Ferrier has just arrived for the performance",' Norma said. 'M'heart missed another beat from total surprise and shock, to find she had come with dear Paddy, to also hear her close friend Ena Mitchell, who was my soprano for the Messiah that unbelievable afternoon – when so desperately busy herself – but to find time to hear another Messiah – has never failed to amaze me. She gave a little wave and a very clever thumbs-up after O Thou That Tellest, another loving example of this amazing and adored lady, and matchless singer. She looked so lovely in a rare green corduroy velvet coat, and green hat with a gorgeous wobbly, wavy long feather, which caused much fun and laughter when we all met together after the performance. The provost of the cathedral then was the Rt Rev Canon Cuthbert Bardsley, a very close friend of Kathleen's whom I met and who later became the Bishop of Croydon and finally the Bishop of the newly-built Coventry Cathedral – a special friend to me, with his lovely wife, by then.'[31]

This day was a professional turning point for Norma. Her reputation spread quickly, and she was soon in demand around the entire country for festivals, oratorio performances and concerts. Leading concert agency Ibbs & Tillett[32] signed her up and so at last she embarked on the career she considered her calling. A November 1948 edition of The Gazette reported: 'Before a resplendent gathering of all sections of the trade, FISA [Fish Industry Sports Association] presented Grimsby's Norma Procter, an enchanting contralto, and Aberdeen's Mary Farquharson, the brilliant pianist who accompanied her. Singing a quintet of songs which fitted gracefully into the mood of the evening, Norma received not only the encores of the audience but also the professional approval of the band, whose rostrum she more than adequately occupied for many tuneful minutes. You see her in her gown of white net, young and gay… to these two people, FISA are greatly indebted for the enjoyment they gave.'

Professional engagements were coming in thick and fast. At the start of 1948, Norma had the foresight to begin keeping a diary – a habit which would last for decades. The entries during November and December are a multitude of Messiah performances. Thankfully, she was also fastidious in collecting archive material, and her first Messiah reviews are complimentary. 'Throughout the north, the annual performance of Messiah is probably the highlight of the year in Methodist churches,' an uncredited press clipping reported. 'It has become a tradition to hail each successive Messiah as greater than its predecessors – a tribute to the continued high standard.

'Miss Norma Procter used a magnificent contralto voice with the deepest sincerity, and while maintaining her richness of tone brought to her solos a moving delicacy.'

The South Yorkshire Times and Express's review of Rotherham Choral Society's Messiah was equally full of praise for Norma: 'Regardless of the number of times a season Handel's Messiah is presented by local choral societies, enthusiastic support can always be assured.

'There was superb singing by the contralto Norma Procter. She has powerful richness of tone and unfaltering notes served to enhance the poetical beauty of the music. These qualities were depicted in Then Shall The Eyes of The Blind, followed by the lovely air for contralto and soprano, He Shall Feed His Flock. Miss Procter's voice was heard again in her final air, He Was Despised.' And the Rotherham Advertiser said Norma 'displayed a particularly fine voice of ideal tone and moderation'. She was a success.

★

Back in Grimsby, the Press was behind its home-grown rising star. An uncredited cutting from one of the local newspapers heralded the coming new year as a bright one: 'Nineteen forty-nine promises to be a memorable year in Grimsby and Cleethorpes orchestras and choral music circles. From the point of view of purely local talent, however, one concert promises to be of more than passing interest. Four young Grimsby artists, Norma Procter, contralto, Fay and Rosalind Campey, violin and piano, and Janet Cotterill, piano, will give a recital at the Central Hall… Norma Procter is engaged by the Grimsby Philharmonic Society for their performance of Messiah in the autumn.'

Indeed, 1949 became another year of weekly lessons with Prof and professional engagements – including Norma's first official one with her beloved Grimsby Philharmonic Orchestra. It was, of course, Messiah: three performances at the Central Hall, the orchestra's home, performing alongside Ena Mitchell, Richard Lewis, Owen Brannigan and Willie Lang. She was paid 10 guineas for each concert. This cutting, uncredited in Norma's archive but probably from the Grimsby Telegraph and dated November 28, reveals her hectic schedule.

'For a town of its size, Cleethorpes has a large music-loving public. It has produced many first-class artists... a few days ago, I interviewed a young lady who has already made the grade and is becoming well-known all over England. Miss Norma Procter, of Old Clee, at 21, is a contralto of great promise and has already sung in oratorio in Hull, Seaford, Halifax, London, Nottingham, York, Birmingham, Huddersfield, Wigan, Newquay, Bournemouth, Chesterfield and Truro. Strangely enough, though she has had many successes, Miss Procter actually took up singing by chance. When she was very young her elder sister was taking singing lessons. "I didn't want to be left out, so I asked if I could learn too," she told me. After her first success in musical festivals when she was seven, the die was cast. She went from strength to strength and in a few years had a drawer full of awards.

'Now, she travels to London each week for a lesson from the famous Roy Henderson. When she decided to take up singing professionally, her success was immediate and since that day she has had many a triumph, particularly in those Yorkshire musical strongholds, Huddersfield and York. Though she faces audiences as part of her everyday life, Miss Procter told me she will never get over that nervous anticipation before a concert. Perhaps the most nerve-racking occasion came two years ago when she was asked to sing at Mill Road Men's Association. "I got to the hall late and was rushed out onto the stage," she said. "I had expected just a few people and when I saw that sea of faces, I nearly passed out".

'But there was no backing out. She sang a song. The applause came in waves, encores were demanded, and her first real public performance was over, a great success. Her biggest thrill, she told me, was singing in the Messiah at Southwark Cathedral. Miss Procter, though she has spent some time doing chorus work for experience at the famous Glyndebourne Opera, has no ambitions in the field of grand opera. She is essentially an oratorio artist, for there are very few good contralto roles in opera.'

As the year ended, Norma put more Messiahs under her professional belt, taking critiques in her stride and learning from them. The Hull Daily Mail's music critic, F.J.A., wrote in an article on November 14: 'It was a pity that the celebrity concert at the Queen's Hall on Saturday night was attended by such inclement weather. It reduced the size of the audience and caused sundry disturbing noises outside. The solo artists were Norma Procter, contralto, and Owen Brannigan, bass. Miss Procter is a singer with a good range of tone, generally free from the distressing "whoofy" quality of some contralto singers, as she showed in her first group of songs, all of which were by Handel. If one may commend one quality without condemning others one would praise especially her fine upper or mezzo range.

'Norma Procter's ringing top notes were again a feature of the solo part, and the Hull Male Voice Choir entered and proceeded for some time in really moving style... Alas! An unfortunate lapse in pitch spoiled what might otherwise have been a memorable performance. The light part-songs in the second half gave scope for a fine display of tone and technique. I felt that the Eriskay Love Lilt lacked the necessary tenderness, but Li'l Liza Jane was so full of fun and sparkle that we were more than compensated, and the repeat performance was fully justified.'

The Nottingham Journal, on December 10, reported: 'Carol concerts are popular everywhere at this season and Mr. Roy Henderson, who conducts at Nottingham Albert Hall tonight, promises "a very jolly evening" when the Oriana Choir and the Eastwood Male Voice Choir combine in an attractive programme. Mr. Heddle Nash, one of the soloists, is regarded as the finest lyric tenor this country has produced for at least a quarter of a century. With him is youthful Miss Norma Procter, a contralto, only 21 years of age, whose singing in the St. John Passion last April and later in St. Matthew Passion has led to many calls for her services.'

As the year drew to a close, Norma had little idea of what the new decade would bring. As ever, she stuck to her mantra of hard work, dedication, and more hard work, and looked forward to the future.

Chapter 4: Touring

The arrival of the new decade heralded the beginning of Norma's rise to international fame. Having proved her worth, she was a singer in demand. The early 1950s were a rush of engagements. By now she counted William Heddle Nash, Webster Booth, Gladys Ripley, Laelia Finneberg and Elsie Suddaby among others as contemporaries. But, as should be expected in a competitive industry, not everyone was friendly. Her diaries reveal tension, though infrequent, with some artists and colleagues.

She performed with Scottish soprano Isobel Baillie several times. Both were strong-willed and confident, and they experienced a personality clash. At a Messiah in Truro on January 26, 1950, Baillie was 'horrible' to her.[33] In fact, Prof had warned Norma about this possibility. She noted in her diary that the organisers were so pleased with her performance that they sent her an extra £10 on top of her fee. 'I was amazed!' she wrote. 'They were disgusted with I.Baillie.'[34]

It would appear that the passage of time did nothing to help. At a Messiah in 1954, Norma wrote in her diary that yet again Baillie was rude to her. But any such confrontations were outweighed by the friendships she made, and she was still courting Frank. Every birthday or important date was noted and lists of Christmas cards meticulously kept. Little notes are scattered throughout her archive, on scraps of paper or postcards, inside concert programmes, and on the pages bookending her diaries. It shows what importance she placed on the people she met and loved.

★

In October 1951, 23-year-old Norma's performance of the first section of Bantock's Omar Khayyam, alongside tenor William Herbert and baritone Gordon Clinton, was broadcast on the radio from Birmingham Town Hall. The concert was part of the city's Festival of British Music, with the City of Birmingham Choir and City of Birmingham Symphony Orchestra, led by

Norris Stanley. The hall was only half-full, much to the chagrin of the reviewers, who all praised the performance. By 1952, the inevitable comparisons to Kathleen Ferrier were made. 'The singer, Norma Procter, contralto, has one of the most beautiful voices I have ever heard,' enthused the music critic of the Fife Free Press & Kirkcaldy Guardian, on November 29, 1952. 'Trained by that prince of teachers, Roy Henderson, Miss Procter at once reminds one of Kathleen Ferrier, both in voice and appearance. Her voice is rich and full, but capable of the most delicate subtleties of technique and expression. It goes without saying that her breathing is perfect, for such flawless singing would be impossible without complete breath control. Her vowels are lovely and her articulation a model of clarity. The songs she chose displayed the extensive range of her voice and her beauty of tone throughout its entire compass. She opened with two well-contrasted Purcell songs, Music For Awhile and Man Is For Woman Made, followed by two Handel numbers, the exquisite Come To Me Soothing Sleep and the sprightly How Changed The Vision. Her second group consisted of four Brahms Lieder, again perfectly sung. What joy it is to hear singing of this kind, particularly when it is allied to great personal beauty and lively intelligence. Her programme ended with a modern or fairly modern group by Stanford and Parry. It does not take much foresight to predict a brilliant future for this lovely young artiste.'

Comparisons to Ferrier would have thrilled Norma, but one can imagine her shaking her head in denial. 'For me, Kath was so wonderful in every way,' Norma told journalist Fiona Clampin, many years later aged 84, for a feature Fiona was writing about Ferrier for a BBC music magazine. 'A glorious, unique voice and personality that was impossible to follow. There were immediate comparisons when I started out and people said to me "you're a second Kathleen Ferrier". They couldn't have paid a greater tribute, except it just wasn't true.'

★

Unbeknown to most, Kathleen Ferrier had cancer. In 1951, her performances were interspersed with a mastectomy and radiation therapy. The following year, she refused a series of injections, fearing her voice would be ruined. She sang her last Messiah that December and was also awarded a CBE.

At the start of 1953, she continued working, refusing an operation to remove her ovaries, again because of the potential impact on her voice. In February, she performed in Orpheus at the Royal Opera House, despite being weak from radiation therapy. During the second performance and while on stage, her left femur partially disintegrated. Quick-thinking cast members managed to cover her injury so she could continue singing. She even took her curtain call, and the audience were none the wiser. This was her final public appearance, and the two remaining performances were cancelled. Still, she kept the cancer a secret, publicly blaming arthritis. Even to her friends, she said it was a case of rheumatics.

'Kathleen and I kept in touch,' said Norma. 'Sometimes I saw her at Prof's, tho' she was constantly travelling worldwide, making an amazing name for herself and singing with the greatest conductors and musicians who all adored her and that glorious voice, and all the public admirers too. But we little thought on that unique and blessed visit to Southwark Cathedral in 1948 [Norma's London debut] that Bishop Cuthbert would be conducting her memorial service on November 24, 1953 only five years later, little realising how desperately ill she was becoming.'[35]

Norma – now signed to Decca – knew her heroine was in poor health but, like most others, not that she had cancer. Music publishers Novello & Company Ltd wrote to Norma on behalf of Sir Arthur Bliss on July 30, 1953, stating he 'has requested us to send you a copy of his scena for contralto and orchestra, The Enchantress'. Bliss wrote the work for Ferrier, who gave the first performance in April 1952. 'We hope you will find the work of interest,' the missive continued. Norma looked through the score – blissfully ignorant of Ferrier's dangerously failing health – but felt it was too much for her to handle. She did not try the work until ten years later. 'I must confess,' Norma noted in her diaries, 'I was a long time before even thinking of tackling it and its demands – far, far away. I remember looking through it in 1953 and strongly saying "I can't sing this incredible work!"'

Ill health in another performer saw Norma sing in the splendid surroundings of Westminster Abbey by chance. She took part in a performance of the Messiah by the Bach Choir, a charity concert in aid of the Abbey Appeal Fund, on Monday, July 6, 1953. Norma was called on at the last minute to take over from fellow contralto Gladys Ripley, who was taken ill. This was the last musical performance at the abbey before it was stripped of its Coronation setting. She noted: 'Reggie – Reginald Jaques, that special conductor, granted me to take dear Gladys Ripley's place when she sadly had to cancel health-wise. I was at home peeling potatoes, on the Saturday morning, and I caught the tea-time train to London.' 'Prof's birthday celebration,' notes her diary for that Saturday, July 4. 'Westminster Abbey rehearsal. Abbey still decorated with Coronation mantle.'

★

Kathleen Ferrier spent two months in hospital, missing her CBE investiture, and moved from Frognal Mansions to a ground-floor flat in St. John's Wood.

She lived there for seven weeks before going back into hospital for two operations, and her condition deteriorated further. 'When in London I was passing near the University College Hospital and took her a posy of deep pink roses and was amazed,' Norma recalled. 'Her private ward sister invited me in to see her. In spite of her problems, she was as lovely as ever and very excited to be going home in a few days, to a lovely new house and garden – but now with great walking difficulties. She wanted to know all about me – incredible! I little realised that was the last time I would see her.'[36] In a diary entry, Norma noted: 'I wonder how she could stand – let alone sing. It made me weep.'

As Kathleen grew weaker, she saw only her sister Winifred and close friends. She died aged 41, on October 8, 1953 – the exact date she had agreed to sing Delius's A Mass of Life at the Leeds Festival. It came as a huge shock to the public. Some industry insiders knew, and others had guessed the truth of the situation, but most had no idea and the inevitable news, when it came, was shattering. For poor Norma, the day began challengingly enough: 'Ibbs & Tillett rang, frantic. Dear Gladys Ripley, another lovely contralto who was also very kindly to young Norm, was very ill again, and would I deputise for her at Accrington Music Club the next evening – a joint recital with a special friend and brilliant young pianist, Clive Lythgoe. I spent the rest of the day making phone calls, programme preparations, trains etc, and I was so looking forward to hearing dear Denis Matthews, another brilliant pianist, at the Grimsby Central Hall that evening. I so adored the piano. I arrived late with a close friend for the concert and thought my mother and some of the audience looked strangely at me – but forgot – I so loved this wondrous piano playing and music.'

Winnie Osborne, a singer and assistant chorus master of Grimsby Philharmonic Society, was in the audience. She and her husband ran a farm in the Lincolnshire Wolds and became friends for life with Ferrier. 'Only at the end of the concert I saw Winnie Osborne, where Kathleen always stayed when singing in Grimsby, and I rushed to ask if she had any news of beloved Kath,' Norma continued. 'She had gone to see her in London, but it was too late, and Kathleen had died earlier that very day, and I had missed the six o'clock news. I just burst into tears and AR [Alec Redshaw] took me quietly aside, as I was to meet and have supper with Denis and him after the recital (I think he was staying at AR's). I was 25 years old but felt 2005! Denis M was wonderful and somehow I was given strength to go with him to AR's for a short time, tho' the thought of Accrington the next day was almost too much to bear.

'I eventually arrived there [Accrington] after a long, difficult cross-country journey but hadn't realised how close we were to Blackburn [Ferrier's childhood home]. Everyone knew her at the Music Club and were devastated by her death, but very kind and helpful to me – but I have never felt so second-hand, singing some of her arias and songs. Come To Me Soothing Sleep was one of my greatest tests of emotional control, and the most difficult of my career. I could only feel wherever she was, her loving spirit was with me and I must not let her down, or dear Gladys, who also died about two years later. I stayed in a little hotel and the manager was also very kind and helpful, but had little soothing sleep – before long it was time to be on m'travels the next day, and gradually try to learn to accept that awful guilty feeling – I should have been taken, not Kathleen.'[37]

Norma confessed that her memories of KK were 'deeply, emotionally draining'[38]. 'We all have our special memory of that Day of Sorrows,' she wrote. 'I was never told what her real illness was until almost then,' adding: 'She was so good and so kind to me – a unique voice and personality. I was stricken when she had to leave us so early in her life. I have many very special memories of her.'[39]

Ferrier's memorial service took place at Southwark Cathedral on November 24, and Norma attended alone. 'I travelled from Grimsby for the service,' she said. 'Southwark Cathedral thronged with many famous musicians, artists and ordinary people – just standing, who so loved and admired her. I returned home by train with a very sad and heavy heart. This world had lost an irreplaceable treasure. She was so lovely, and so good, kind, and helpful to young L-plated Norm. I can still see John Barbirolli at the service walking out down the main aisle in the final hymn with such heartache on his face and his eyes in agony. He could bear no more. As I looked around at the vast array of incredible world musicians, it never occurred to me that I might make music with some of them, one day.'[40] She added: 'There has never been another contralto voice to match hers nor her unique humble lovable and wonderful humorous personality since, what laughs we shared! I was devastated when she left us and owe her so much.'[41]

In the wake of Ferrier's death, the music industry looked to Norma as the natural replacement. Her first review in The Times, from December 1953, was of a performance of the Messiah with Goldsmiths Choral Union. 'The soloists … included a contralto, Miss Norma Procter, with a rich but admirably focused voice and sensitive musicianship,' the critic wrote. Ferrier's bookings were made years in advance and most were transferred to Norma, who felt under a great deal of pressure. She believed she would never reach her heroine's standard of singing and did not want any reflected glory. On a personal level, Norma was incredibly upset and found it difficult to overcome her emotions while singing pieces with close links to Kathleen. In truth, she never completely came to terms with her death, and a deep sadness remained with her for life.

On Christmas Eve, the eminent composer Benjamin Britten and his partner, the tenor Peter Pears, whom Norma sang with, got in touch. They asked her to learn the title role of Lucretia, in The Rape of Lucretia at the upcoming 1954 Aldeburgh Festival – the role Britten had chosen Ferrier for. But Norma did not accept, fearing she was not ready for it. Instead the part was taken by American mezzo-soprano Martha Lipton.

In an undated letter from Pears, it appears that Roy Henderson advised her against it.

Pears wrote: 'Indeed, I can quite understand what you feel about undertaking Lucretia at this moment, and although I am not sure that I entirely agree with the Prof, it is better to err on the side of caution in these things – young voices can all too easily come to harm by singing too big stuff too soon, and too much. But if you are not going to try Lucretia yet, my dear, I beg you not to do too many other things instead (Angels in Gerontius and such) and above all don't let Emmie Tillett overwork you – and insist on a good long holiday each summer. Musical life nowadays has got so that singers never have a proper holiday. We all ought to have two months off at least each summer, whatever temptations may pop up!' He added: 'Have a look at Ben's Canticle No.2, Abraham and Isaac, when you have some time!'

He also wrote to Alec Redshaw, lamenting her decision. 'I have heard from Norma and have written to her today – I quite understand her decision about Lucretia, though I don't entirely agree and certainly regret it. Still there it is – don't let's bother about auditions for the moment – she will be coming to Aldeburgh for the St. John Passion in June and can meet and sing to Ben then. I would rather like her to look at Ben's Canticle No.2 as there might be a chance of our recording it.'

Decca came calling too: they wanted her for the contralto part on a recording of the Messiah, with the London Philharmonic Orchestra conducted by Adrian Boult. Ferrier had long held the desire to record a complete version of the Messiah, ever since she herself first signed for Decca, and in 1946 the company promised her so as an incentive. She would have sung on this recording if she had been well. Instead, it became Norma's first recording ever and her first with Decca – so her first important commercial recording[42] – and she felt guilty that she was there instead of Kathleen. It was all too much for her. 'Difficult atmosphere and shattering experience,' she wrote in her diary of January 4, 1954, the day it took place.

Naively, she did not realise the other soloists would not be present and no one really bothered to put her at ease.[43] She was trembling with nerves but told herself she must do her best for Kathleen. When eventually the producers were satisfied with the recording, she was overcome with emotion and relief. Thankfully, Decca's head sound engineer, Jimmy Walker, gave her a reassuring hug, and congratulated her. 'I was desperately nervous, and I felt a sense of guilt,' she said. 'I was overwhelmed. I think my saviour was that the first take of He Was Despised [was used], which I so loved singing, and it was that aria which Kath had sung that so moved me at that first Grimsby Messiah concert.'[44]

She took pleasure in the whole recording experience, though. 'I enjoyed this new venture immensely but saw for the first time what really goes into making a record – something I had previously taken very much for granted. One particular memory: we were making a certain aria for the third consecutive time, and this appeared to be the best of all – and almost completed – when a cello string broke with quite a bang – and so we had to begin all over again. A good test on patience and humour. The different technique in recording and broadcasting also must be remembered – people are unable to see you, and so all visual expression has to be put into sound alone.'[45]

Two years later, she was invited to perform in Ferrier's hometown, a traumatic experience for young Norma. 'I sang in Blackburn for the first time after dearest Kaff's earthly farewell on Wednesday, December 16, 1956 – Christmas Messiah,' she recalled. 'Oh, I was so nervous, and my emotions were so difficult to control, let alone sing. But the Blackburn people were so wonderful and warm-hearted, and Kaff's blessed spirit was so close. It was a most moving, unforgettable Messiah. I have always been very guarded about personal memories for fear of using her name, bless her, in reflected glory.'[46]

To mark the 50th anniversary of Ferrier's death, Norma spoke to journalist Peter Chapman for the Grimsby Evening Telegraph: '[There are] so many special and wonderful memories to everyone fortunate to see and hear her many unforgettable concerts in the Grimsby area, where she was so loved and adored by everyone, especially those of us left still surviving. Bless her, dear Kathleen, [who] opened the door to my own humble singing career. There are incredible memories, stories, and wondrous laughter I could relate. All her generous goodness, love, and encouragement she gave to me until her cruel and tragic death, almost ten years to the day of her first Grimsby concert. There was no prima donna nonsense here. During those ten years she had captured the vast musical world with her divine voice, radiant, humble personality, and infectious northern humour. Her last recital in Grimsby was on January 14, 1952, with Gerald Moore, looking and singing even more radiantly in a beautiful black velvet gown, especially in Brahms' Four Serious Songs, though we little realised how close she was to the true meaning of those glorious poignant songs. For me, and thousands more, she was the greatest contralto and singer of the 20th century. A courageous human being – there will never be another Kathleen Ferrier.

Mercifully and gratefully, we have a wonderful collection of her fabulous recordings and her unique vocal spirit. Her blessed memory liveth forever: Gratias Deo!'[47]

In later years, Norma gave full support to the Kathleen Ferrier Society Bursary for Young Singers, urging them to discover 'the very special and rare find of a real contralto voice again'. 'It makes me very sad,' she noted in her archive, 'to see and hear, and understand, the demise, loss and almost death of this deep, unique and lovely sound. So many memorable and immortal composers wrote especially for this vocal sound, tone, colour and range, especially the lower register, and I must confess I am very grateful I came into this profession when I did, tho' I fully realise the whole musical scene has totally changed now. Enough! I have no wish to offend.' She added: 'I wonder what dear Prof and beloved KK make of all this.' Norma treasured a signed photograph of Ferrier, which took pride of place in her home. It read: 'To Norma – With my love and all the luck in the world.'. A pencilled note in her archive simply reads: 'I hope perhaps God will grant our meeting again in the next life.'

★

Nineteen fifty-four became a year of professional firsts for Norma. The Decca Messiah recording was followed less than a fortnight later by her debut appearance at London's Royal Albert Hall, which was to become her favourite venue in the city. It was a performance of Mozart's Requiem Mass, and Norma noted in her diary that it was the last performance there for distinguished English bass-baritone Keith Faulkner.

Meanwhile, Peter Pears remained keen for his partner, the composer Benjamin Britten, to hear Norma in person. On January 12, he wrote to Alec Redshaw. 'I have started the new year very badly,' he said, 'and all those days when you were going to be in London I was in bed with another ferocious cold. I would very much like Ben to hear her. I have a feeling that this winter is going to turn into the worst ever! Just a feeling in my bones! I hope they are wrong.'

That April, about six months after Ferrier's death, Norma's portrait filled the front cover of the Record News magazine. 'Norma Procter has one of the most beautiful contralto voices of the day,' the article declared, 'and, as an aside, she is even more beautiful than this excellent photograph shows her to be. She has signed up with the Decca Record Company, and her first recording of all was the contralto part in Handel's Messiah. A genuine North Country lass, quiet and charming, but with a fine sense of humour, she is a personality we hope to hear often on record now that she has made her debut.'

Norma's annotations suggest confusion over the reference to the North Country, and where she is described as beautiful, she has pencilled simply 'Never!' But secretly, she must have been thrilled at the recognition. Her career was going from strength to strength, and although she had performed yearly in her hometown, she had yet to appear as a solo artist in her own right in Grimsby.

This changed on March 4, 1954, when she gave her first solo recital at Grimsby Central Hall. It was presented by the Grimsby Philharmonic Society and she was accompanied by Alec Redshaw on his own Bechstein pianoforte. The programme included Handel, Purcell, Britten, Brahms and Parry. Her diary notes little of what pride she must have felt. Instead it reads: 'Pale blue water silk gown with Elizabethan collar decorated with pearls.' She soon began noting more regularly what outfits she wore to concerts, probably to avoid duplication. She considered dress an important part of her performance, and she turned to haute couture dressmaker Beryl Jordan for help. Her shop, at number 23 Beresford Street, Jersey, was a mecca for gowns and Norma thought it 'glorious'.

For many years, Beryl supplied Norma's stage costumes but, most importantly, they developed a strong bond of friendship which lasted for all of their lives. Bee or B, as Norma interchangeably called her, was kind and caring as well as talented, and Jersey soon became Norma's choice of holiday destination. They spent many a happy day sunbathing on the beaches and sampling local cuisine in the restaurants of St. Helier. As Norma's career grew, so did an important support network. In later life, she praised the 'many wonderful people and friends who helped me during those years and made my career possible' and expressed 'heartfelt gratitude for all their inspiration, encouragement and support.'[48] Beryl was, without a doubt, one of her best friends.

★

Another first followed shortly, on May 20. One of Norma's favourite pieces of music was The Dream of Gerontius, and she gave her first ever performance of the work with the 'most wonderful, inspiring' William Heddle Nash, at St. Paul's Church, Walsall. 'Organ only, which was at the rear of the church and the time lag was terrible – up a semitone!' she noted in her archive, 'but he encouraged me, like himself, to sing from memory and I never used a score in concert again. An amazing baptism to an amazing, glorious and unmatched work.' They both left their scores in the vestry. Shortly afterwards, on May 23, her diary notes a performance at the Albert Hall of Vaughan Williams's Five Tudor Portraits. Williams's Five Tudor Portraits, having first met the composer the year before when he conducted the Messiah at Dorking. A few days after the Albert Hall concert, on June 3, she performed Five Tudor Portraits again, this time with the LPO, and was surprised to see Williams in the front row with his wife, Ursula. 'Wonderful man,'[49] she wrote.

Meanwhile, reviewers continued to brim with praise for the young alto. Norma was one of four leading soloists at the Warwick Festival and crowned 'arguably the finest in this country' by the Warwick and Warwickshire Advertiser. She appeared alongside Jennifer Vyvyan, David Galliver and Richard Standen in an abridged version of the Messiah under the direction of Dr. Reginald Jacques, on May 29. 'Even in this company however,' said the reviewer, 'Norma Procter was outstanding, her singing of He Was Despised being almost unbearably moving.' Then there was her first London Gerontius on June 11, this time with an orchestra and choir, at the Royal Festival Hall; the third of four concerts celebrating the London Symphony Orchestra's jubilee of 1904–1954. She sang the part of the Angel and loved the 'wonderful' orchestral harmonies it involved.

And June 19, 1954, heralded Norma's first Aldeburgh Festival, a famous event in music founded in 1948 by Benjamin Britten, Peter Pears and the producer Eric Crozier, and known for its eclectic range of performances.[50] 'Terrified!' she wrote in her diary, of singing the alto arias in Bach's The Passion According to St. John, with Pears as the Evangelist. Later she recalled: 'Green with awe, fear, fright, and nerves, and well remember my first experience of Imo's [Imogen Holst] 'ballerina' conducting!'[51]

It was around this time that Norma was making firm friends among her peers. Jennifer Vyvyan was also from Roy Henderson's stable[52] and they'd sang the Messiah together in Grimsby, in December 1952 and 1953. Much later a joint recording of them both was released by Decca. Norma held great affection and esteem for Jennifer, and the feeling was mutual. In July 1954, the Fifeshire Advertiser reviewed a Decca recording of the Messiah on which Norma and Jennifer sang with tenor George Maran and bass Owen Brannigan. The reviewer praised Norma as an 'exquisite contralto… [she] has a lovely warm tone and is sensitive in performance… this Decca set has obviously been prepared with great love and care. It is fresh and vital, performed in excellent style and effuses an air of spaciousness and deep conviction. It is the set for a long time to come.'

★

The Proms are a major milestone in any singer's journey, and Norma's first ever was on Tuesday, August 17, 1954. She performed in Mozart's Requiem

Mass in C Minor, with Basil Cameron conducting. She gleefully noted in her diary that cellist Muriel Taylor and Margaret (Mable) Ritchie, who were also in the concert, were from Cleethorpes. Norma went on to appear at the Proms for more than two decades, notching up a total of 27 performances. 'I'm always in total disbelief that I used to sing in my much-loved hall,'[53] she later wrote. 'That glorious, unique and oh-so-loved hall. Memories! Memories! Or was it all a dream?!?'[54]

Next was her debut at the famous Three Choirs Festival, in Worcester, on September 5. Other soloists that year included Isobel Baillie, Gordon Clinton, Norman Walker and Roderick Jones, and Ralph Vaughn Williams premiered Hodie. She soon became a regular guest, performing works including Beethoven's Choral Symphony and Lennox Berkeley's Four Poems of St. Teresa of Avila. Her diary details the social side of such events:

Sunday, September 5: *Worcester. First 3 Choirs. Reception 8.45–11pm. Guildhall.*

Monday, September 6: *Elgar's The Apostles 11am with Bella Baillie. Lunch with Ald. Edwards 1.15.*

Tuesday, September 7: *Apostles 11.15am and 2.30pm. Buffet lunch at Willcocks.*

Wednesday, September 8: *Tea with Dean 4.15.*

Thursday, September 9: *Matthew 11.15–2.30. Lunch with Mayor.*

'Two newcomers to the festival have impressed all listeners by their quality,' declared the Yorkshire Post and Leeds Intelligencer's edition of September 11. 'Norma Procter is a contralto of rare and outstanding vocal gifts, who, one feels, is destined to make a great name.' Three days later, she was engaged by Decca to sing on her second record under her contract with the company – Elijah, conducted by Josef Krips. The recording took place at Kingsway Hall, London, over several days. 'Krips rather terrifying but here's hoping,' she wrote in her diary of September 13. Rehearsals followed and by September 19, she felt comfortable. 'Really beginning to enjoy working with Krips,' she wrote. 'Krips most helpful. I am learning lots.' Then, 'Krips calls me Miss Bellini', and 'Finished recording. Most exciting sessions.' In later life, she referred to it as 'the ole girl's Ace of Diamonds'. She said: 'I have an old recording which belonged to my aunt, but it's too worn and weary to listen to now, like its present owner! So full of scratches, pops, and squeaks too. Gosh, it makes me feel très ancient. I was a young thing in my mid-20s, and I wouldn't sing it like that now. Dear George [Maran, the tenor on the recording] was such a love. We met up many moons later in Darmstadt at the opera house where he was resident – when I was singing the Mahler 3rd Symphony. It was a lovely, brief reunion, towards the latter days of my career. He was just as kind and handsome, with lovely silver threads of distinction amongst the brown hair.'[55] 'Josef always called me Miss Bellini when we were recording,'[56] she added.

*

That December, after a long series of Messiahs around the country, Norma fell ill with flu. It lasted for days and she tried to rest at home between performances. The review of the Messiah in Leeds by Yorkshire Post music critic Ernest Bradbury must have been a balm to the frazzled singer. 'Among last night's soloists was Norma Procter, a contralto new to Leeds but not to London or the Three Choirs Festival,' he wrote. 'Her singing was finely accomplished, rich in tone and thoroughly musical. She is a singer of whom we shall hear a great deal more.' Norma was in demand, and Bradbury was right in his prediction. The world was about to see much more of her.

Chapter 5: Britten and Pears

By the mid-1950s, Norma was firm friends with Benjamin Britten and Peter Pears. She worked regularly with Peter at concerts, and soon their close friendship extended to include Ben, too. She spent her first weekend at their then home – Crabbe House, on the seafront at Aldeburgh, Suffolk – in 1954, the first of many visits until the couple moved to Red House. Now it houses Britten Pears Arts, dedicated to preserving material related to the pair and is where Norma's archive is kept. Playing with the couple's dog, a Dachshund called Clytie,[57] Norma was happy. She had followed her calling, and the public responded to her voice in ways she only dreamed of. Working with soprano Jennifer Vyvyan had blossomed into a close friendship, which Norma treasured greatly. She was in a golden circle of music and, to her contentment, found support, comfort, and – most importantly, in her eyes – friends.

Often, and inevitably, friendship mixed with work. Pears, writing in the mid-1950s, said: 'Norma dear, it was lovely having you here and I do hope your journey back was all right. You will be going off on holiday soon, so here is the programme which we suggest for Düsseldorf. Please let us have your reaction! I am enclosing a volume with the Schubert duet for you. Please note that on page 21 you go to tenor line and I go to yours. If it is still high for you, we can put it down into B or A minor. The two Schumann duets are I hope all right for you, with alterations in the first. Your first three Fs could be Ds. The second duet should be ok? You did say that you liked to sing Sehnsucht by Schubert, didn't you? We need one more light-ish Schubert song from you, and one Schumann (did you try Requiem?) – biggish one. Much love from Ben.'

Pears admired Norma, and he was very keen for their working lives to continue together. In May 1955 he wrote to Alec Redshaw, revealing the inner workings of staging performances and his whirlwind of a schedule.

'Yes, I did have a talk with Norma about Gerontius, and I must say that I am very tempted to have another shot at it,' he wrote. 'I did sing it two or three times years ago, and I remember that in Birmingham at any rate it was very well received, but I got a slight thing about the work and my voice not really being big enough, and refused to do it anymore. But if you like the idea of trying it with me, I would like to try it with you.

'Dates may prove a bit difficult I am afraid. We come back from round the world mid-March, and then come the usual round of Passions, and I have promised to go to Germany for some days in the week after Easter. After that we have been invited to go to Russia for three or four weeks from April 15th on an official visit. This has not yet been confirmed and anything may happen before then, but we have promised to go and do not want to miss it. Is it possible that our Gerontius could take place between the 9th and 15th, or is that too early for you? The Bartered Bride is on now, and I am stuttering away like mad. It is a sweet work, and the performance is fun, but perhaps not quite such fun as it ought to be. Anyway, I enjoy myself.'

It wasn't only Norma's peers taking note of her talent: the critics were, too. The Stage, in 1955, described Norma as a contralto 'surely destined to rank with the long line of singers whose names are linked with this country's special affection for oratorio.' Yet reviewers and her audiences never guessed that she suffered from crippling performance anxiety. The May 16, 1955 edition of the Lancashire Evening Post lamented the end of the Mary Wakefield Westmorland Music Festival, which concluded with an inspiring finale of the Messiah at St. George's Hall, Kendal.[58] It must have been an incredible event to witness. The enthusiastic reporter, credited as A.H.G, wrote: 'Every seat in the building was taken, the specially extended stage was packed with hundreds of singers and there was a full turn-out of the Westmorland Orchestra under John Hopkins, conductor of the BBC Northern Orchestra. The great choir sang with sureness, and blended remarkably well, the bass section being particularly rich and powerful.' Of Norma and Jennifer Vyvyan, A.H.G was full of praise: 'Both gave outstanding performances. Miss Procter's beautifully controlled signing in He Was Despised – one of the most expressive airs which Handel ever wrote – was quite memorable, while Miss Vyvyan's skill in the difficult runs in Rejoice Greatly, O Daughter of Zion and her sincerity in I Know That My Redeemer Liveth deserve the highest praise.'

May 20 saw Norma take her first ever trip abroad and experience flying for the first time. She travelled to Holland, performing at the Rio Grande in an afternoon concert on May 22 and the St. Matthew Passion the following day. 'V. nervous,' she wrote in her diary. 'Wonderful trip.' Then came Mozart's Requiem with Bruno Walter. She rehearsed at Maida Vale on May 28. 'Incredible man,' she wrote. 'Absolute love and poppet – so kind but what a genius and humility.'[59] The following day, the performance was broadcast on the BBC from the Royal Festival Hall. 'Incredible concert,' she said. 'He was a loveable and understanding genius.' In the score, she pencilled: 'This is the copy I used for the BBC performance with Bruno Walter conducting and Irmgard Seefried (sop), Richard Lewis (tenor) and Kim Borg (bass), the BBC Symphony Orchestra and Choir at the Royal Festival Hall. It was broadcast live and was Bruno's last London concert. A most wonderful man and conductor of such humble genius. He left a lasting impression upon me – never to be forgotten. We had to memorise the whole work – no scores allowed. Oh m'nerves! But it was one of my most memorable concerts. I was 27 years old.' Two days later she was back in the studio for Decca, this time with Alec Redshaw to record an album of folk songs. The session planned for the next day was cancelled though, as Norma was just too tired to do it justice.

Live performances continued apace, and she discovered a fan in the Yorkshire Post's chief music critic Ernest Bradbury. Leeds-born Bradbury critiqued for the Post from 1947 until 1984 and was known for not holding back on what he thought; many a singer quaked over his forthright views. But when praise was due, he heaped it in spades – and Norma was one of his favourites. Over the years, he consistently championed her. In a review dated September 8, 1955, of a concert in Hereford, part of the Three Choirs festival, he wrote that 'her remarkable contralto voice touched the edge of nobility and her whole eager, yet artistically restrained, performance was extraordinarily moving.'

Then for Norma it was back to Decca for recordings of the Messiah and Elijah, produced by Victor Olof, and to complete the folk song recording with Redshaw. Twenty-four hours later, she was on stage at the Royal Albert Hall for a performance of Choral 9th at The Proms.

★

Norma's working relationship with Benjamin Britten was at its height. Following Kathleen Ferrier's untimely death, the industry naturally looked to Norma – something she despised for many reasons. She felt it was disrespectful to her heroine and besides, she never – ever – thought of herself as anywhere near Ferrier's standard. Mostly though, Norma was still grieving for the woman she so admired and had been fortunate enough to call a friend. In fact, she mourned Ferrier all her life. Nevertheless, professionally, Britten turned to Norma. The contralto parts in his Spring Symphony and Abraham and Isaac, his Canticle II, had been written for Ferrier, and tragically she was not here to sing them. The canticle, a medieval mystery play, was premiered by Ferrier, Pears and Britten in Nottingham on January 21, 1952. Britten's plan was to record it with Norma, and so they booked Decca Studios, in London's Abbey Road.[60] A diary entry for Friday, October 7, 1955 reads: 'Decca A+I. Ben + Peter. 2pm–5pm.'

Norma, having put aside her reservations, was thrilled – here was a chance to perform a work she admired, and she would sing in Ferrier's honour. The trio met the day before[61] and attended the studios as planned, however, what they recorded is a mystery. Norma, Pears and Britten's diaries all confirm the appointment but nothing more. What research has revealed is that Canticle II was subsequently recorded sixteen months later, on February 25, 1957. Piecing the available information together, it is believed that the 1955 session was postponed because Britten wanted Dennis Brain, the British virtuoso horn player, but he was contracted to EMI at the time, and not Decca. It is supposed that the plan was to record all three of Britten's canticles in 1955 but cancelled due to Brain's unavailability.[62] So, skip forward to February 1957 and the trio resumed recording. They reconvened again on May 29 at Maida Vale Studios to record a version for the BBC, which was broadcast on June 9. And then the recording was beset by a tragedy. Dennis Brain, aged just 36 years old, died in a car crash that September, before Canticle III was completed. It was eventually recorded with Barry Tuckwell playing the horn, and it seemed to be progressing towards a release date. What eventually happened caused a rift between Norma and Britten, for she was replaced on the recording by a teenage boy.

★

John Hahessy was 14 years old. His musical career began at Westminster Cathedral as head chorister and he was a successful boy alto. Unbeknown to Norma, Britten – who dedicated his Corpus Christi Carol to the teenager – had Hahessy also record the part of Isaac. After the lengthy recording delays, it was Hahessy's version that was eventually released to the public, in 1961.

Norma was devastated. The work was closely connected to Kathleen Ferrier, and it was one of her favourite pieces of Ben's. But she was mostly hurt by the dismissive way she was informed. 'After a Wigmore recital with Ben and Peter – I seem to remember it was a Thursday evening, and on the following Saturday in Liverpool, as Peter and I were in a taxi en route for a rehearsal there – he broke the news that they had already recorded and released Abe and Ike with John,' she recalled, in correspondence to Decca many years later. Ben promised her that their version would be released at a later date. 'I so loved that work,' she added, 'though I felt deep down it never would be released and it never was, nor mentioned as I feared – sadly for me.' Her words masked a deeper sadness. She felt betrayed by

Britten, whom she considered a friend, and the incident soured their partnership.

Hahessy is now a tenor and performs under the name of John Elwes. In an interview with the Irish Times in 2013, he gave an interesting account of his association with Britten, which perhaps explains why Norma was ousted. Born in London to an Irish labourer father and British mother, he went into care, in part staying at Tapeley Park in Devon. This was owned by the family who established the Glyndebourne Festival, and five-year-old Hahessy impressed them with his voice. Aged eight, he joined the choir at Westminster Cathedral under tutor George Malcolm, a friend of Britten's. He told the newspaper: 'Whereas the Anglican choirs tend to iron out the roughness of boys and make them into angels, George took this and harnessed it and trained it. I think this is the kind of sound that Ben Britten liked – the ruggedness of children. Boys are noisy creatures.'

Britten visited the school and heard Hahessy, then aged 12, sing his Ceremony of Carols. A visit to Ben's London home followed, where he was asked to sing at the Royal Festival Hall, with Britten conducting. 'I remember giggling with Ben, not out of disrespect, but because he understood boy humour,' Elwes said in the article. 'There was the counter-tenor Alfred Deller, who started singing with a female voice and he had a beard. It was a giggling point for us.' The pair had an intense two years of working together. Elwes told the newspaper that at the time of the Abraham and Isaac recording, his voice had begun to deepen – exactly the type of tension Britten wanted in the high notes of the piece. He was rewarded with a book, a wristwatch, and a signed copy of the score. That Britten considered him his unofficial godson perhaps also explains why Norma's version was ditched. But she was greatly disappointed, and it remained a sore point forever more.

She wrote to Decca in 1999, enquiring of the original recording's whereabouts. 'Could you tell me whatever happened to a recording with Ben and Peter of Ben's Canticle No II, Abraham and Isaac?' she asked. 'I have checked my old '50s diaries and found a recording date at Decca Studios, Abbey Road, on Friday, October 7, 1955 – we three being Decca contracted artists, but it had to be kept 'on hold', as was Ben and Peter's already recorded Canticle I. We then had to wait before Canticle III could be recorded as Dennis Brain was already contracted to another recording company. Alas, as you know, Dennis was tragically killed before Canticle III could be completed. I hadn't the heart to ask what happened to that recording but often wondered. I suspect it was destroyed – unless by some miracle it is still somewhere in the Decca archives? It was a long, disappointing saga, though I was very glad for John Hahessy's opportunity.'

Later in life, she labelled the entire incident a 'disgrace'. 'They [Decca] knew nothing about it, and it was eventually found in the Decca archives,' she said. 'No further fee as so many people assumed – it was paid in 1955! – but heartfelt thanks that it was found. They [Ben and Peter] adored KK [Kathleen Ferrier], and I always thought what a rare and wonderful trio of twenty-twos they made – Kath 22nd April, Peter 22nd June, and Ben 22nd November [birthdays]. Unique, especially in their threesome recitals, and Abe and Ike, his most beautiful work, which was heart-aching, impossible to follow and years later. Aldeburgh [Festival] has changed – greatly – and Ben is now known to have been a "first class dropper" of many artists – enough Norm! – it is all so sad and doesn't belong with beautiful spiritual music, and joy and love.'[63]

Eventually, Norma's miracle was granted. The recording was finally heard in 2001, when it was included on Britten: The Rarities.

⋆

Back to 1955, and the praise kept coming. On October 14, she travelled to Ireland to perform The Dream of Gerontius with the Belfast Philharmonic Society in Ulster Hall, marking the society's new season. It saw the debut of Maurice Miles as conductor and was also a tribute concert to the late E Godfrey Brown, conductor of the society for 38 years. Northern Whig critic L.F.M.C. wrote: 'I last heard this work with Kathleen Ferrier as the Angel and if comparisons are inevitable, I hasten to assure last night's interpreter, Norma Procter, that her performance gave me real pleasure. Hers is a lovely voice with both purity and warmth and her insight stamped her an exceedingly gifted artist. May we hope for a return visit soon?' The Stage, in the following month, declared: 'Probably no music is dearer to the heart of Sir Malcolm Sargent than Handel's Messiah, and few conductors can have directed more performances. Recently at the Albert Hall he had 1,000 voices drawn from all over a dozen London choirs. The LSO played, and there was deserved praise for the up-and-coming contralto, Norma Procter, now gaining rapid recognition.' Such admiration was astonishing to Norma, who never managed to shake off a tendency towards self-criticism throughout her entire life. Yet the compliments – and scores of engagements – kept coming. She was a household name.

It was on November 15 that the artist Juliet Pannett saw Norma sing. She visited Croydon Civic Hall, near where she lived, to watch a lunch-hour recital – Norma's first ever, with Alec Redshaw accompanying her. The artist was so moved that she sketched Norma there and then. This eventually became a beautiful watercolour, for which Norma paid £5. Pannett had a distinguished career. She began painting at three-years-old and trained in Brighton, running a studio in Hove. She married, had children, and stopped painting but found it alleviated symptoms of depression from which she suffered, so resumed painting and the family moved to Croydon. Among her subjects were Field-Marshal Montgomery, Jean Cocteau, Louis Armstrong, Leonard Bernstein, Winston Churchill and several other Prime Ministers, the Royal Family including the Queen – and Norma Procter. She was awarded an MBE before she died in 2005, and both of her children are artists.

Norma treasured the painting and kept a copy of Pannett's obituary from the Daily Telegraph in her archive. In a letter of condolence to her children, Norma wrote: 'I noticed her sitting up in the gallery sketching away. Immediately after the recital I hurried over to see what she had achieved, being a great lover of sketching and painting m'self. I was so thrilled and amazed at what I saw. I straight away asked if it was possible to buy the painting when finally completed. Your mother, bless her, was so happy and surprised at my request. I especially remember her saying, "This is my first painting I have ever made of a literally performing artist". I was amazed and shattered, and so began her truly wondrous works of many musicians – singers, pianists, conductors, and many other notables. I was always so pleased to see her, mostly at rehearsals and afterwards at the Albert and Festival Halls – wherever – and we always had a quick chat whilst I marvelled at her amazing gift. To think my humble recital in Croydon perhaps began it all – for £5. Unbelievable! Many years ago, a BBC producer – sorry, I just can't remember his name – tried to persuade me to part with and sell my painting but I just couldn't/wouldn't.'

★

The rest of 1955 was spent in a long series of Messiahs around the UK, ending in Huddersfield and Birmingham. The Huddersfield concert was hard for Norma. She was told that her fellow contralto Gladys Ripley had died. Norma deputised for Gladys whenever she was poorly, and the news shocked her. 'Very difficult for me to sing,'[64] she wrote. Time, one would think, for a rest, but no. On New Year's Day 1956 she travelled to Edinburgh for a Messiah and evening concert. The first four months of the year saw her notch up 33 concerts, including two full Messiahs in one day in London and a performance in Antwerp before royalty.

Her diaries show that on May 5 she met Joan Sutherland, singing the Pergolesi Stabat Mater at Brecon Cathedral. She went on to enjoy a lifelong friendship with the singer and her husband, Richard Bonynge. 'Travel to Brecon,' her diary read. 'Met Joan Sutherland for the first time. Pooks (Adam), her son, four months old. Wonderful person and singer.' 'Joan was especially kind and helpful and, as with Kathleen, we shared some wonderful laughs together,' Norma recalled in later years. 'A sense of humour is a must in life generally, but certainly in this profession! I had many friends and acquaintances in the profession but my very closest or specials were scattered far and wide, and we constantly met up while I was on my travels.'[65]

On May 15 she wrote in her diary: 'Turned down Decca recording with Sir Adrian/LPO, arias, was supposed to have been for Kath. Prof disappointed.' Proof, then, that Norma – despite all her successes – felt below Ferrier's standard, something the Warwick and Warwickshire Advertiser's reviewer disagreed with. Her voice in The Dream of Gerontius, they said, was warm and radiant: 'This was angelic singing indeed.'

She managed to fit in a holiday to Guernsey where, no doubt, she met up with her friend Beryl Jordan but was soon hard at work again. August 7 saw her back at The Proms, under the baton of Sir Malcolm Sargent, performing Brahms's Serious Songs, and then Choral 9th in German on September 14. In October, she took a driving test and passed first time. It was the start of a love affair with the Mini. 'Driving test. Coo, I made it!'[66] she wrote. 'What a shock. Bought my first beloved Mini.' Not long after, she performed at Ilkley Music Club. It is nice to think she may have driven there. 'Gerald Moore told jokes in between songs – not my type, too sarcastic,'[67] she wrote. It is here we see the first mention of the names Brian and Frances, friends who attended the concert. In May 1955, she'd holidayed in Cumbria, at Sharrow Bay Hotel in Ullswater. Little did she know then what an important place of refuge it would become.

★

With its lakeside terrace and dining room with panoramic lake views, the tranquility of Sharrow Bay soothed and relaxed Norma. One can imagine how impressed she was: outside there were majestic peaks and fells to walk or climb, and inside offered comfortable lounges, fine food and good company. Sharrow was reputedly the first country house hotel in Britain when it accepted its first guests in Easter 1949. The pair behind it were Brian Sack and Francis Coulson, who joined forces to establish a hospitality powerhouse. Francis saw an advert for the property on the front page of the Manchester Guardian and moved in just four months after viewing it. His father paid the rent for the first year. At that time, the Lake District was not as popular with tourists as it is today and was not served by a motorway, but Francis forged ahead with his dream of opening it as a hotel. At first, there were five rooms and it cost just over one pound for bed, breakfast, dinner, and refreshments – including a hot chocolate at bedtime. It made about £20 profit in its first year.

Former RAF pilot Brian was working in a hotel in Hertfordshire and during Christmas 1951 he befriended two elderly customers who mentioned that Francis was looking for help. A meeting was arranged, and Brian joined Sharrow Bay in March 1952, with Francis cooking rich Edwardian menus and Brian in charge of front-of-house services. In 1956, while erecting a new sign outside the premises, they coined the term 'country house hotel'. They became partners in business and life, and Sharrow Bay was their lifelong passion, curating a homely atmosphere which led to an award-winning worldwide reputation. Celebrity guests included Sir Laurence Olivier, Sir Alec Guinness, Tom Courtenay, King Hussain of Jordan and JB Priestley, to name but a few. Francis and Brian were music lovers, so it was a delight for them to have Norma as a regular guest. Joan Sutherland stayed there, too. In later life, Norma spent much more time at Sharrow Bay in the company of dear friends. But for now, the stage demanded her attention.

★

Believing her voice was a God-given gift, Norma would sometimes donate her skills for free. On October 23, 1956, she and Alec Redshaw performed at St. Mary's Church, in Warwick, without a fee at a fundraiser. There is no review recorded but beforehand, the Warwick Advertiser wrote: 'If hard work spells success, then there should be no doubt of the financial outcome of the recital that Miss Norma Procter, the contralto, is to give. The hard work in this instance has been done by Mr and Mrs P.E. Dunkley, who are solely responsible for the recital and all the organising it has involved. It is thanks to their personal friendship with Miss Procter, which goes back over many years, that this distinguished singer, named more than once as the successor to the late Kathleen Ferrier, has agreed to come to Warwick and give her services at a time when she is in great demand.

'Those who heard her sing at the last two Warwick Festivals, at which she was soloist, will appreciate how fortunate is the town to have the opportunity of hearing her give a recital lasting an hour and a half. Miss Procter's gesture in coming here is a generous one, for a singer of her calibre, with engagements to fulfil in London and the country's larger cities, as well as on the continent, cannot lightly give her time to an effort of this kind. It shows remarkable generosity and willingness to meet a friend's request.'

In November she performed in Amsterdam, but complained she was too tired to sing well.[68] She spent New Year's Day 1957 once again in Edinburgh and made a Decca recording of one of Britten's canticles in late January. This was followed by her first visit to Spain, where she sang Elijah in German in Madrid under the baton of Ataulfo Argenta. 'He spoke no English, I no Spanish, so between us a little German,' she wrote. 'We poured our hearts into the music! Wonderful orchestra, choir and all!'[69]

Her second performance at Grimsby's Central Hall with one-time tutor Alec Redshaw was presented by the Grimsby Philharmonic on March 7. A cutting from the Grimsby Evening Telegraph read: 'Two people held a packed audience enthralled at the Central Hall last night. Norma Procter and Alec Redshaw, in a song recital, showed that two good artists can command attention and respect and move a gathering more deeply than a whole company of mediocre ones. The beauty and quality of Miss Procter's voice is too well known to need further elaboration. How well she justified local pride in her achievements. In Purcell's Mad Bess, she showed that she possesses dramatic ability as well. She was equally at home with a group of Lieder songs, and with folk songs. Alec Redshaw's part in the programme was more than that of an accompanist. His sympathetic and musicianly playing made this often-underrated role an important part of the evening's success. He also arranged three of the folk songs Miss Procter sang.'

On March 10, she embarked on a two-week tour of Scandinavia, performing in Naestved, Svendborg, Odense, Kolding, Aabenraa and Sandenburg. She complained of having a terrible throat and cough, and was drinking hot toddies to ease the symptoms. Norma flew home on March 23 to the news that her father was bankrupt and, worse still, it had been in the Press. 'Terrible publicity and trauma,'[70] she wrote. In mid-April, she performed the St. Matthew Passion with Joan Sutherland at Liverpool Cathedral. Afterwards the conductor, Sir John Barbirolli, held a party. 'Blue jokes galore!'[71] she remarked. The incident is elaborated on in the book Sir John Pritchard: His Life In Music, by Helen Conway. Afterwards, 'Hugues Cuenod, who had sung Evangelist and the rest of the men started telling dirty stories or limericks and she [Dame Joan] and Norma Procter were blushing to the roots of their hair.' Norma added: 'John Barbirolli was a fine conductor but had little thought for singers, with his fag smoke!'[72]

July came, and Norma was ready for a well-earned rest, so off she went to Jersey to spend some quality time with Beryl Jordan. They spent days on the beach, chatting and relaxing. After reluctantly leaving Jersey, she went to Prof's in London for a Proms rehearsal of Brahms's Four Serious Songs, where she 'broke down in tears'[73] because of the emotion of the piece. She didn't have long to compose herself. The Prom took place four days later, on July 29, with Sir Malcolm Sargent and the BBC Symphony Orchestra. 'Unbelievable reception from Promenaders,'[74] she noted. Inside a cassette recording of the occasion, Norma wrote: 'Sir Malcolm's superb orchestration. He always insisted upon the English biblical translation (Legwick Publishers). I once asked why not the original German, and he replied, "We don't read our bibles in German" – which was fair enough!'

August arrived, and she flew to Spain for Beethoven's 9th in German and no score, with bass Kim Borg. Then it was the Worcester Three Choirs, and more engagements – and now royalty was taking note of her. Inside a score of The Dream of Gerontius, Norma wrote: 'Sang to the Queen Mum at Haddo House, Aberdeen, on October 5, 1957. She was wonderful and we had tea after the performance. Amazing blue eyes – one forgot who she was! – so lovely and easy to talk to.' Then a season of Messiahs began, with a holiday to Torquay with her mother and another trip to Bee in Jersey thrown in for good measure. There was simply no stopping her.

Two UK Messiahs heralded the start of 1958, and a trip to Madrid to twice perform Messiah in German under the baton of Ataulfo Argenta. 'Just about to leave for concert,' she wrote, 'and zip in evening dress broke!'[75] A few days later she had lunch at the British Embassy and was due to give a recital too. Argenta was supposed to attend as a surprise but it was announced that he had died in a tragic accident the evening before at his home, from carbon monoxide inhalation. His last live concerts were the Messiahs with Norma on January 17 and 19. 'Decided to give the recital as a memorial,'[76] Norma noted.

Chapter 6: On The Road Again

Norma found Benjamin Britten's rejection of their Abraham and Isaac recording a bitter pill to swallow, but she continued to work with him and Peter Pears. She treasured her long-held friendship with Peter, and the fact remained that the trio complemented each other – onstage and off. While Norma was placid and focused before a concert and Peter retreated into yoga, sometimes Britten would be physically sick.[77] Peter would calm Ben down, and Norma would sit quietly aside, a relaxing influence in the room. And besides, as one of the country's leading contraltos, Ben needed her.

March 1958 saw them travel to Germany, in thick snow, for Norma's first public performance of Abraham and Isaac, in Cologne. She, Ben, and Peter also performed a recital in Dusseldorf. And her engagements away from Britten and Pears were continuously rolling in. She first performed Michael Tippett's A Child Of Our Time, about persecuted races, on April 1, 1958, with Shrewsbury School Boys Choir and Orchestra. 'This was a very difficult work for me – lovely spirituals,' she said. 'I was so nervous and shattered to find Michael Tippett was at the rehearsal and concert, but he was so kind and helpful. He had the most lovely blue eyes!'

With the disappointing Abe and Ike episode in their wake, it was time for Benjamin Britten to give something back. Norma's hometown of Grimsby staged the first ever all-Britten concert that spring – but the run-up was not plain sailing. Despite his profile as a unique composer with a unique tone, his work was not to everyone's taste. Grimsby Philharmonic announced the news of his forthcoming concert with excitement, but the public did not respond in kind. Expecting a rush of advance ticket sales, there were hardly any.

Alec Redshaw, writing in Philharmony 1852–1977, said these 'were hazardous times… it seemed to be a period of depression for music – possibly a delayed reaction to the unquenchable enthusiasm of the war years.' The inside cover of a programme for a Grimsby Central Hall concert in February held an honest declaration. 'A year ago, this Society offered to the public a concert performance of The Bartered Bride, a comic opera by Smetana which, some years earlier, had been tasted, and found palatable in all its stage glory,' it read. 'The majority of the public, however, were not disposed once again to enjoy the fun that abounds in this sparkling score. The performance was voted a brilliant one by the few who were there. Many of those who had not found it possible to attend the concert expressed their disappointment at having missed it. Their absence, alas, resulted in a loss of some £160, which had to be found by the Society from its own funds. Then, too, a large number of empty seats at Messiah last December brought about a further loss of almost £60.

'As would be expected, then, we find ourselves in a state of financial embarrassment. Yet, as ever, we are too proud to go a-begging. All we ask is that the public, who encouraged us in the first place to offer these concerts, shall continue to play their part by supporting us. Only with your unswerving support can we maintain the standard of solo artists to which you and we have become accustomed. At the moment we cannot plan ahead with confidence, as we could in the days before so many of our patrons acquired television sets. Meanwhile, we have ventured to promote a further concert of unusual interest, but about which many of you will be sceptical.'

This was, of course, a reference to the upcoming Britten concert. The Phil reported that people had been saying to members that they 'do not like Benjamin Britten'. 'This is the sort of statement we have been hearing since we announced our forthcoming Britten concert,' the piece in the programme continued. On what grounds is it made? It is more than likely that the average listener is puzzled, even baffled, when he hears any complex modern work for the first time… Human nature being what it is, his first reaction will be one of dislike, be the work by Benjamin Britten or any other contemporary composer. But the statement is unreasoned and unfair to the composer and to us. In our desire to introduce Benjamin Britten to Grimsby we have chosen a programme which is singularly attractive, consisting of a variety of pieces, all of which have a ready message for the ear of any listener.'

'It was gloom, gloom all the way,' said Redshaw. 'Many of the choir, then at a low ebb anyway, simply, as they say, "wouldn't wear it". Fear grew that the concert would be a disaster. Ticket sales were almost nil. The announced soloist was Peter Pears. At that time, he, Norma Procter and Benjamin Britten were in the midst of a long series of recitals together. Peter and I were due to perform the song cycle On This Island as part of our programme. It was an established fact that Norma Procter was the only singer who could pack our Central Hall for a recital. She was as concerned as anyone else at the general apathy. Since she was going to be in Grimsby at the time of our concert, she agreed that the programme should be changed, that she would join us so that she, Peter and I could perform the wonderful Abraham and Isaac canticle instead of the song cycle.

'This was announced in the Press and elsewhere. It made not the slightest difference. The concert was to take place on Friday, 18th April. I left on Monday 14th for an engagement in Liverpool. At that stage less than fifty seats had been taken for the concert. I reached home, having travelled overnight, at 6am on Thursday 17th to find a note which read, "Ben is coming. Everything under control". I was too exhausted to react to this or any other shock and collapsed into bed. The Grimsby Evening Telegraph was smartly on the scent. That night Benjamin Britten was front page news, complete with photograph.'[78]

What happened next is brilliantly described by Redshaw. 'Ben, Peter and I drove to the concert in Ben's car,' he wrote. 'As we turned into Duncombe Street from the south end we saw that the Central Hall end of the street was crowded with people. "What's going on?" said Ben. "They have come to see the monster who writes this terrible music" was my reply. 'The start of the concert was much delayed while these people were buying tickets and being shown to their seats. We had a splendid orchestra led by Martin Milner, who made a great impression upon Benjamin Britten, and was presently to become leader of the Hallé Orchestra. Saint Nicholas occupied the first half of the programme. It proved to be one (there have been others) of the Philharmonic miracles. At the end there was a silence that seemed an eternity. Then, not all hell, but all heaven was let loose. The applause reached almost hysterical proportions.

'After the interval came the Simple Symphony, conducted by Iris Lemare. By now the audience was ready for anything. They were not content to wait in the conventional way for the end of the work. They demanded – and got – immediate repeats of two of the movements. It was after this that officially I welcomed the composer. I said that he was unique amongst the great composers because he was, at the same time, the greatest accompanist in the world.

'My name was on the programme as one of the trio in Abraham and Isaac but I went on to say that, in the circumstances, I had not the slightest intention of taking part in this item. The concert overran its time by more than an hour. The audience, quite simply, would not let them go. In addition to the magic of the canticle, much of their current programme was lavished on us. Norma and Peter, of course, were looked upon as old friends but the audience virtually fell down and worshipped at the shrine of Benjamin Britten, entranced by his shy, little-boy charm and, so we thought, irrevocably converted to his music.'[79]

The concert was a triumph and remains a jewel in Grimsby's musical crown. But, as Redshaw recalled, there was more excitement to come. 'At midnight on the Thursday, the Mayoress of Grimsby, Councillor Mrs Florence Franklin, telephoned on the Mayor's behalf from the Town Hall to say that he and she would like to meet Mr Britten, and to ask if it might be possible for us to call upon them in the Mayor's Parlour. It was most difficult to find a mutually suitable time and it finally had to be after the concert, before the Mayor and Mayoress went on to another important social function. They were to be at the concert, not only in their official capacity, but out of the abiding interest in the cultural life of the town. In the event, and after one of the most stimulating conversations I have ever known, we all left the Town Hall at 1.30am.

'The very end of the story must be anonymous. At 4.30am, a Certain Very Important Person was stopped by a young police officer for speeding. With, perhaps, a special touch of charm, he told the officer that, a stranger here, it had not occurred to him that there would be a speed limit on such a magnificent road. He was cautioned, quite properly, and allowed to go. Perhaps if a young, personable, and ambitious police officer had been interested in music, the headlines in the Press that night might have read differently. This was the first all-Britten concert ever, anywhere, so he told us, and the overall picture of it reveals yet again that the Grimsby audience, once you have it in your net, can be as responsive and receptive as a London audience. But they do have something in common with trout.' Of this tale, Norma recalled: 'This really was a very special concert for Grimsby, and for me.'[80] A second all-Britten concert was held on October 22, 1964.

In an undated letter sent from the Hotel St. James in Paris to Redshaw, Peter Pears wrote: 'This is just a tiny note to say thank you to you for a very special occasion, on which you must be very sincerely congratulated. It was most courageous of you and I do so hope that you will feel that it was worthwhile both for yourself and for the town. Ben was most touched by the whole evening, enjoyed it thoroughly and was very glad that he came. Please do also thank Norma for being the sweet creature she is and singing Abe & Ike so beautifully.

'Our journey back [to London] was not without incident. At Southgate, the clutch gave up and we had to be towed in! However, it was repaired by next morning and we got down to Basingstoke on Sunday and had a v. pleasant concert in an old Tudor mansion. Then on Thursday we came on here and did the Schöne Müllerin last night – lovely audience. Tonight, there's the Spring Symphony and tomorrow we go onto Lyons and the South. It's heavenly here at the moment; I do hope the sun is also shining on you, Alec, wherever you are and will continue to do so.'

This correspondence was followed up on May 19th by a short note to Redshaw from Britten. 'It would be lovely to come to Grimsby again one of these days because, in spite of the police, we really did enjoy our visit enormously,' he said.

★

At Beverley Minster's Festival Of Music in May 1958, Norma was reunited on stage with Alec Redshaw once more. Hull Daily Mail music critic F.J.A. wrote, on May 2, that 'the size of the audience for the first concert of this year's festival… was evidence of the wide appeal of the singing of the internationally-renowned contralto Norma Procter, whose recital was such a feature of the festival last year. The programme on this occasion was, in the catholicity of its taste and its wide variety of period, indicative of Norma Procter's breadth of musicianship. The beauty of the voice, its even matching from note to note, and the ease which characterises the production, need no comment from me.

'The opening group was of unusual interest. Purcell's Here The Deities Approve was a fine example of breath control and was followed by the older versions of How Beautiful Are The Feet and Thou Art Gone Up On High from Handel's Messiah, originally written for alto voice. In the second group were the Four Mystical Songs of Vaughan Williams. All were notable for lovely interpretation… the gentle reverence with which Norma Procter treated these songs, as, also the other works in the programme was, in itself, a repulse to the hard and uncompromising authoritativeness which so often masquerades as interpretation.

'It is always a pleasure to hear an artist whose personality is wholly dedicated to revealing that of the composer. Stanford's A Soft Day had the authentic touch which depends so much on subtle vocal colouring of the words. Thanks are due to Norma Procter for singing James Lyon's charming I Sing Of A Maiden. It is always a mystery to me why this able and prolific composer should be so neglected. This song has a spiritual fragrance which is a musical extension of the content of the words.'

Several days later, the Manchester Guardian reviewed a performance of Gerontius in the city's Free Trade Hall, which was part of the Hallé Orchestra's centenary festival. 'His (Sir John Barbirolli) three excellent soloists, who like the choir all gave us the text with excruciating clarity, were Richard Lewis, in magnificent voice, Hervey Alan, splendidly sonorous if slightly inexpressive and Norma Procter, a more innocent and pure-toned Angel than we often hear in the part,' the article said. 'Dressed in pure white, and lacking only wings, she also looked very much like one – with rather incongruous effect between a Soul before his Maker and an Angel of Agony both in white tie and tails.' The review is marked in the margins by Norma with a series of exclamation question marks.

★

Her diary for June 21 reads: 'Aldeburgh Festival. Joshua. Lovely day. Quite enjoyed myself in Joshua. Out to tea with Peter and choir and lovely drive with him to Noye's Fludd. Ben the dear gave me his seat. Lovely drive back with Peter and quick look at Red House. Peter gave me sweet rose from garden.'[81]

At the Leeds Centenary Festival that October, they joined forces to present a programme of songs and duets by Purcell, Morley, Schubert and Schumann, and Abraham and Isaac. Her diary for October 10 read: 'Horenstein replaced Klempener, who set fire to himself smoking in bed.' A local newspaper critic wrote: 'Norma Procter's singing, always of gracious timbre, assumed, in this environment, an enchanting creaminess. Every syllable carried the gallery's considerable length so distinctly that listeners could have dispensed with the printed words.' Beforehand, the Yorkshire Evening Press joined Norma as she rehearsed. 'Time was when an afternoon at the home of the chorus master might have been a very discreet, finger-tips-together type of affair. This was vastly different,' the article read. 'After all, Herbert Bardgett hasn't become the most popular chorus master the Leeds Festival Chorus has ever had through being old fashioned. As we met in the lounge of his home in Cardigan Road, there was a very relaxed atmosphere. Baritone Geraint Evans was talking about rugby – his brother-in-law is famed fly-half Glyn Davies; tenor William McAlpine was on about his mother-in-law's Yorkshire pudding; soprano Jennifer Vyvyan, contralto Norma Procter and soprano Honor Sheppard were talking about Leeds as a shopping centre.'

Norma told the reporter: 'It's a wonderful shopping centre, if you find time to do any shopping in a week like this', adding that the festival was 'a great achievement for Leeds'. The reporter noted: 'On the way out, I heard the rattle of coffee cups. In the dining room was Mrs Elizabeth Bardgett, preparing for the interval. What's it like being married to a musical dynamo? 'Very pleasant,' she said in a voice which has almost lost the accent of her native Scotland. She likes these rehearsals at home – such a nice, friendly atmosphere. She must also like the atmosphere of the rehearsals elsewhere. She has attended all but two of the rehearsals for her husband's 300-strong Festival Chorus. Fortunately, she didn't have to make coffee for them!'

'A recital team without parallel in our land,' declared a headline in the Yorkshire Post of October 14. Norma's erstwhile supporter and music critic

Ernest Bradbury wrote: 'In the final work, Britten's own Canticle Abraham and Isaac, the three artists joined in a performance of singular beauty and conviction. We have marveled at Abraham and Isaac on many other occasions, and the listener loses none of its emotional force, or its striking musical invention, with repeated hearings. It is astonishing how Britten can make the most modest sequence of notes mean imaginative things; the miracle of it is Britten's own mingling of the stuff of music with the essence of his warm and full but absolutely self-sufficient sensibility. The Canticle made a deep impression on the large audience – as indeed did the whole recital.'

High praise indeed. That month Norma managed a short trip to Sharrow Bay and, as usual, her schedule was full, performing an astonishing number of concerts in her own right. Between her dates with Ben and Peter, she reunited with Sir Malcolm Sargent for a Proms performance of Brahms's Four Serious Songs. Then followed a raft of engagements up to the end of the year. Norma was a star, and a star in demand. February 1959 saw her travel to Antwerp to sing the St. John Passion, and then to Barcelona for Messiah. A live TV appearance of Brahms followed – and then a meeting with none other than Queen Elizabeth II.

The date was March 20, 1959, and the work was The Dream Of Gerontius. The performance was staged at Eton College School Hall, Windsor, where an audience of more than 600 welcomed the Queen, a patron of Eton Choral Society. Norma was a soloist alongside David Galliver and Roderick Williams, and she was presented to the Queen during the interval in the Macnaghten Library at the venue. 'Had the most awful large blind boil on my forehead,' she wrote in her diary. 'Looked and felt grim. In a beautiful Chanel satin and beaded dress.' 'Presented at the interval with other soloists and she [the Queen] never spoke a word?!' she added. 'Unbelievable comparison.'[82] That comparison is to the Queen Mother, whom she'd met in 1957. A report from the Windsor Express recorded the occasion somewhat more fondly than Norma: 'At the end of the performance there was a brief pause, followed by a burst of prolonged clapping. The soloists took their calls and then a member of the society, Miss Rosemary Gutteridge, came down from the platform and presented a bouquet to the Queen. The small crowd outside waved and clapped as Her Majesty came out of the hall into a chilly wind. As she drove away, the Queen smiled and waved back.'

With the arrival of warmer weather, Norma travelled to Cologne in May to perform in Handel's Alcina. 'Koln radio,' she wrote. 'Young Spanish sop who didn't know the work; Gutov, my German agent, phoned and I suggested Joan [Sutherland]. Joan and Ric arrived, to the rescue.'[83] Norma had only just been with Joan a fortnight before, recording for Decca in Geneva. 'Joan sang like a dream,' she added. The performance was recorded onto LP, and Norma was not happy with her own singing. 'My greatest disappointment is the "vorrei vendicari" contralto aria, which I begged to sing half as fast again, but [Ferdinand] Leitner, the conductor, wouldn't budge!' she recalled. 'I couldn't sing it so slowly... it's too slow and the tempo sticks. I used it many times later in recitals, and for agility exercises, at my tempo. Joan was wonderful and had to re-learn that large manuscript score with Ric coaching. She wore a gorgeous black velvet crinoline and after so many setbacks during that whole performance preparation, her zip gave way just before we were to go on stage. Amidst great giggles, I stitched her in, praying all night that the stitches wouldn't give way.

'Nicola Monti was a famous Italian tenor of that era – such a nice man – and I was horrified to find he'd learned the wrong part! But Fritz [Wunderlich, the German tenor who appears on the recording] was quite fantastic at the rehearsal and said, "Don't worry – I don't mind singing Ruggiero" and just got up and sight-read the whole part, off the cuff. Young Norm was quite shattered at this amazing feat. I adore his aria Sta Nell'Ircana – wonderful music and singing. I couldn't keep my toes still! Sad he died so young and tragically.[84] I sang two more performances of Alcina with Joan and Ric only, at Brighton Festival.'[85]

Meanwhile, back in Grimsby, Nor-Dree was bursting with life. It was home to Norma and her mother Edith, but also a focal point for Audrey and her family – now Audrey Haste, married to Norman, whom she met on a blind date, and mother to two young sons, Norman Paul and James Nicholas. In the Procter tradition, the boys were known by their middle names. Born in 1954 and 1958 respectively, the children were a delight to Norma. Audrey, Paul, and Nick (Norma called him Nicky Noo) stayed at Nor-Dree while Norman served in the RAF, and Norma took great joy in spending time with them.

When Norman – a navigator who was shot down twice during the war and flew Liberator planes – returned home, the family moved to number 9 Clee Crescent, a house so close to Nor-Dree that if they looked out of their bathroom window, they could wave at Norma and Edith in theirs.

'Norma was always excited to see us,' said Nick, 'and we would have lovely family get-togethers in Clee Road. My Nanna Edith was a great cook and made lovely food. Norma would often come back shattered but was always glad to get home and unwind in our company.

'I have very fond memories of meeting Norma at Grimsby Town railway station. She always greeted us with a big, warm smile, and loved the fact I had met her from her travels. She was away an awful lot at the height of her popularity, and the train service was limited in those days, so my dad and I used to pick her up from as far away as Sheffield or Doncaster.

'She loved coming home to Nor-Dree. Music was always a topic of conversation when we were in her company. She would tell us of all the wonderful concert halls she sang in, and the lovely people she met during her brilliant career.'

Time at home was nectar to Norma, an antidote to the exhausting and sometimes lonely business of travelling to perform. As she relaxed and took some much-needed time off, she had little idea of what challenges the following months, and the new decade ahead, would bring.

Chapter 7: Lucretia

It wasn't long before Benjamin Britten called on Norma to accept one of the most demanding engagements of her career so far.

Kathleen Ferrier sang the title role in the premiere of his The Rape of Lucretia at Glyndebourne in 1946, and he knew who to turn to for its revival at the Aldeburgh Festival in June 1959. Previous operatic chorus work stood her in good stead, but she had never before appeared in an operatic lead.

She was nervous, terribly so, once again stepping into a role her dear Kathleen had so competently fulfilled. Of course, her fears were unfounded; the magazine Opera branded her performance a 'personal triumph'. She played the part, it said, 'with extraordinary accomplishment and assurance'. She rehearsed for five days, recording for EMI for two days in-between. Her diary of June 18 reads: 'Lucretia dress rehearsal. V. nervous. Charles Mackerras [conductor] shouted at me at the beginning of my first scene due to wrong entrance of another singer. Completely threw me!' The performances took place over the following two days. 'Terrified!' she said. 'Still making our costume thru' the night.'[86]

The Stage described the production, with the English Opera Group, as 'impressive'. It wrote: 'Buffeted by an east wind more appropriate to the storm scenes in Peter Grimes than to the Appian Way, the Jubilee Hall at Aldeburgh housed a new production of Benjamin Britten's The Rape of Lucretia for one of the major events in the twelfth Aldeburgh Festival. In spite of the still not wholly convincing device of presenting a pagan tragedy through the framework of Christian faith and morals, represented by the solo male and female chorus, Britten's musical achievement is one of compelling power. Since it was first produced 13 years ago, a new generation of singers have acceded to parts which had become almost too closely identified with their originators.

'All but one of the cast this time are new – including a first appearance on any theatre stage for the concert singer Norma Procter as Lucretia – while

Charles Mackerras had not previously conducted the opera in England. Save for an unlucky accident to the oboe player's instrument mechanism, he obtained a fervent, well-shaped and moving performance. Miss Procter began hesitantly and rather woodenly in her dramatic movements as the beautiful and virtuous Roman wife for whom only death can wipe out the shame forced on her by the lustful Tarquinius. But notwithstanding an unfortunate make-up that gave her calm features a petulant appearance at variance with the character in emotional climaxes, she achieved a final scene of confession and suicide that forecasts a noble heroine if she can involve herself more deeply in the part.

Visually the opera was enhanced by a vivid and adaptable set by John Piper. This is kept down for the climactic scene in Lucretia's bedroom, softly lit from behind, as it might be shrouding it in the mists of history. The whole presentation, in fact, reaffirms that the opera must rank with Peter Grimes and The Turn Of The Screw as Britten's finest works for the lyric stage.'

A week or so later Lucretia was recorded for the BBC. The entire experience, she confessed, 'opened up a vast new world in music and made me realise why some operatic singers regard oratorio and concert work somewhat 'cold-blooded' – no make-up, costumes, scenery and movement to help tell the story – only yourself, your soul and voice.'[87]

★

After this, it was time for Norma to rest. She visited Bee in Jersey and was so tanned by the sun that when she came to sing on the first night of The Proms, on July 25, she needed no make-up at all.

Under Sir Malcolm Sargent and with Cyril Smith and Phyllis Sellick, she sang Elgar's Sea Pictures. It was televised, and she looked stunning in a turquoise gown that complemented her tan. Her favourite piece from Sea Pictures was On Sabbath Morning At Sea. 'I love this particular song for its great spiritual depth,' she wrote. 'One feels special moments of Gerontius and glimpses of his Pomp and Circumstance too. It's very moving to sing and wonderfully orchestrated.'[88]

A holiday in Sharrow Bay followed, then the Three Choirs Festival in Gloucester. On September 8, she struggled through a performance of Gerontius. 'Very ill,' she said. 'Carbuncles and boils on foot burst in concert.'[89] Two days later, she suffered a haemorrhage but managed to recover enough to travel to Brussels and Berlin for more concerts.

On December 2, she was the focus of the Woman's Hour radio programme on the BBC. It was a live broadcast and Norma was 'terrified.'[90] As usual though, she was well prepared and her comprehensive notes –

identical to those she would later use for her profile in a book in 1998 – served her well. She recapped how she loved music from three years old, sang through her childhood and teens and how, at 18, she sang her first solo alto during a Christmas Messiah. 'I realised what a wonderful message music had to give. It was God's gift,' her notes for the broadcast read. 'This voice was not mine, but only lent to me for a while. What was I going to do about it? Really, I had so little to offer, but perhaps if I worked and tried hard enough, I could help spread this message – and so it was that my own church opened the door into a new life.'

This new life was, on the whole, a delight. Norma was making a living from her passion, seeing the world and what must have felt heaven-sent – that she was held in great esteem by the profession she so loved. The roll call of conductors she worked with reads like a Who's Who of music: Bruno Walter, Jascha Horenstein, Rafael Kubelik and Leonard Bernstein to name but a handful. She recorded many great works on vinyl, including almost all the alto roles that Mahler ever wrote. It was her audiences, though, that remained her main motivation – a mantra which she carried throughout her entire, all-consuming career.

'There are countless things to cheer one on – the warmth from an audience for instance – what a wonderful feeling this is – to me almost like turning on an electric fire as you walk on to the platform. I love to watch reactions in an audience, and it is amazing what one can see and learn – yes, even when singing sometimes too!' she said. 'The rapt expression and attention of one face has often carried me through a heavy evening's recital. This contact between artist and audience is so important, and one reason why I prefer to memorise my work whenever possible – not for any self-glorification at all, but to me it gives a closeness which can otherwise often be broken by constant flickering over of pages and unnecessary movement. I hasten to say this is not always possible nor should always be expected – some artists are much more at ease with a score, and I think that in itself should be the deciding factor.

'I have little time for hobbies – but love needlework, pottering about the garden, and a favourite past time – exploring antique shops; also one day I hope to take up painting and dress designing again, which was a great love in my teens. People often remark how important dress is on the platform – and I heartily agree. I feel we owe this to our audience and take great delight in often designing and also choosing my dresses. Dressing up was one of my favourite games as a little girl, and I always get a great kick out of wearing a new dress, but quickly add, this takes second place when once on the platform – the music and its message are my only concern then.'[91]

During this time, Nor-Dree remained a stable haven to retreat to. She'd managed travelling to London for her lessons with Prof, and later for tutoring in German Lieder with Hans Oppenheim, so saw no need to change. 'It proves it is not essential for an artist to live in London,' she said, 'although I must confess very careful planning has to be made with journeys and wardrobe on long tours, and it does entail considerable extra travelling – but for me it is worth it all, if only to have a few hours at home to really relax.'[92]

Her mother, sister and brother-in-law were her biggest supporters. But what of a special someone to share her life with? Way back in 1948 – January 9 to be precise – Norma had met the man she was going to marry.[93] Local lad Frank Mitchell, known as Mitch, was in the RAF. She first encountered him at Trent Bridge during a cricket match. 'Never really a cricket fan or gal,' Norma confessed, so it was fate that she was there and so was Mitch. Her lessons with Prof were progressing, and people were requesting that she sing at concerts. This was a very happy time for hard-working Norma, and her diaries show how content she was with Mitch. She nicknamed him Snogger and made delighted notes every time he was home. Her 1948 diary read:

> ***Friday, January 9:*** *Met Frank! / Mitch.*
>
> ***Friday, May 14:*** *Snogger home. Wizard!*
>
> ***Wednesday, May 19:*** *Back again! Crumbs!*
>
> ***Saturday, May 22:*** *Mitchell's away – America.*
>
> ***Friday, July 9:*** *Snogger home. London.*
>
> ***Wednesday, July 28:*** *Snogger – Bury!*
>
> ***Tuesday, August 24:*** *Snogger home in Grimsby.*
>
> ***Saturday, August 28:*** *Snogger going to Buckden.*
>
> ***Thursday, September 16:*** *Snogger home!*
>
> ***Saturday, October 2:*** *Frank's birthday.*
>
> ***Friday, October 29:*** *Snog home!*
>
> ***Friday, December 17:*** *Snogger home!*

Her 1949 diary is similarly peppered with excited comments. In June that year, Mitch finished college and Norma notes that he went for an interview. In August he travelled to Edinburgh to be with Norma while she performed in the Glyndebourne Chorus. In June 1950, Mitch returned to school for a short while. On January 9, 1951, the anniversary of their meeting, Norma blithely comments: 'Three years not out!' On their fourth anniversary, Mitch gave her a book – More Than Singing by Lotte Lehmann – and inscribed it with five kisses. They were a happy couple, but external forces began to work on them. Mitch's family disapproved of Norma's career choice, disliking how much travelling she had to do, and did not want them to marry. In her early diaries, he is last mentioned on Tuesday, October 21, 1952. 'Mitch away' is all Norma wrote.

'She'd nearly bought the hat,' said Dawn Stewart, one of her closest confidants, 'and everyone in both families were very happy at first. But that was until Frank's family realised how hard-set Norma was on a career in music. Frank wasn't bothered so much, but his family didn't like it. Norma, realising this, made her choice although it broke her heart.' This open opposition, combined with Norma's yearning for music, took its toll. Sadly, they went their separate ways – and there and then, Norma decided on the single life.

Brief mentions of Frank in correspondence during her older years suggest he was her one true love. What a decision she faced: choosing music, and what was undoubtedly going to be a prolific career, over Frank – with whom she was deeply in love. Here was someone to share her life, to marry and begin a family of their own. After their relationship ended, she consciously chose not to marry or have children. She confided to friends how it hurt her to leave behind her much-loved nephews while she travelled for her career. She adored Paul and Nick, and the wrench of leaving them when she had to go away proved almost too much to bear. Leaving her sister's children was hard enough, so how would she cope if they were her own? It would be too painful and unfair.

'She knew in her heart that she had to sing and decided to put that first, and it was a rule she stuck to from then on,' said Dawn. 'She'd say, "I am never in one place long enough to have a relationship." Norma used to speak of Joan Sutherland, of how lucky she was to have her husband, who happily went with Joan around the world.'

On April 8, 1958, Frank married, and Norma was pleased for him. 'Mitch's wedding,' her diary reads, 'Lovely, bless them both with all happiness.' 'He died quite early on in life, though,' Dawn continued, 'and Norma said, whenever we spoke about him, "Well, I would have been on my own anyway". Because of Frank's and her brother-in-law Norman's connection to the RAF, Norma loved the organisation and supported it throughout her entire life. If Norma confided in anyone about her romances, they have kept their silence. Through her diaries and throwaway comments here and there, we know she did have relationships but any more than that was under wraps. We have photographs of her with who we assume are boyfriends, but that's all we know.'

Nick Haste, Norma's nephew, told how his aunt was very fond of Mitch. 'She chose to further her career,' he said, 'and it broke Mitch's heart. It was said that she would have to be selfish and hard, and it wouldn't have been fair on him, with all the travelling and demands her career would entail. I was given the impression from Norma in her later years that she had made a mistake in not marrying him. If she had married, she would have had someone to love and share more special times and ease the burden of life. She knew this and so did all the family.'

Having chosen music over marriage to her serviceman beau, Norma was acutely aware of the sacrifice she had made, and so channelled her huge capacity for care, love and kindness into friendships that lasted lifetimes. She had made a choice. Music was everything.

★

The 1960s arrived with its usual flurry of Messiahs. Winter progressed to spring with BBC recordings and public concerts, including a refugee fundraiser in Aberystwyth. In early May 1960, her diary records a recital in Beverley with Britten and Pears. 'Becoming more difficult,' she wrote. Norma was beginning to feel restless about their working relationship. Although she forgave Ben for his behaviour over the Abe and Ike recording and they had since performed for a long time as a trio with great success, the way Ben had treated Norma still stung, and his temperamental nature was beginning to grate on her.

Two days after the Beverley recital, she sang Britten's Spring Symphony at Haddo House, Aberdeen, with Ben and Peter in the audience. There was a gap of two more days and then another Haddo show, this time the St. John Passion with Peter, and Ben watching on. Despite things 'becoming more difficult', in Norma's words, they were still on strong form. Indeed, they were preparing for the Aldeburgh Festival, returning with two nights of The Rape of Lucretia, again with the English Opera Group, on June 18 and 20.[94] But Norma, although by now the consummate professional, admitted to being nervous about the shows – and she'd begun feeling unwell again.

★

Before Aldeburgh, she was reunited with friend and accompanist Alec Redshaw for the third time at Grimsby's Central Hall. Britten was on the programme, along with Purcell, Handel, Mahler, Wolf, Schumann, Schubert, Warlock and Head, and works arranged by Redshaw himself, including Go Down Moses, Steal Away, Peter Go Ring-a Dem Bells, Nobody Knows The Trouble I've Seen and I Got A Robe. The following day, the Grimsby Evening Telegraph of May 13, 1960, joyously declared: 'Every time Norma Procter sings in Grimsby, she leaves us more deeply impressed by the power and magic of her art, which seems to grow in splendor from year to year. A packed audience gave her a well-earned ovation at the end of her recital. This fine singer must surely be reaching her zenith. That lovely contralto voice has now a full maturity which makes it pure joy to listen to. Those of us lucky enough to be there can say we have heard a great singer at her best. Miss Procter's technical mastery and fine musicianship, of course, appeared in every note she sang. Relaxed and natural in manner, she makes it all seem so easy, but what long devotion to the hard work of her craft it must represent. The range of her work is astonishing. Full of fun in folk songs, tenderly reverent in spirituals, fiercely dramatic in Handelian opera, her touch never falters. And her warm personality dominates the hall. Alec Redshaw, whose work at the piano gave her just the firm but discreet support every soloist hopes for, appeared not only as an accompanist. The original and successful arrangement of five spirituals which formed the final group was his work, and he was warmly applauded for it. Miss Procter and Mr Redshaw put us in their debt.'

★

Norma's years of personal sacrifice, dedication and practice were paying off.

At Aldeburgh, critics praised Norma's 'vocal dignity' in the role of Lucretia. But there was a difference in this year's run. Norma had to wear 'a rather brassy blonde wig as Ben couldn't bear to see me again in brunette – Lucretia was dark, as quoted in the text'[95] and the Press did not fail to pick up on it.

A cutting from an unmarked newspaper of June 19, 1960, read: 'The composer conducted a strong and mellow performance… weighing the notes at the full sonorous value, contemplating the drama in the music instead of attacking it. The Rape of Lucretia was Britten's first chamber opera, and he was still treating his twelve players as a small orchestra rather than as a duodecimet of instrumental soloists… every word, every note, from the stage was audible. The contemplative character of Mr Britten's interpretation seems to stem from Lucretia herself, and Miss Norma Procter now has the histrionic as well as the vocal dignity to sustain her part as that of a protagonist; her singing radiates the natural goodness of Lucretia, and when, to the doleful wailing of the cor anglais, she confesses her sin to her husband before killing herself, Miss Procter is profoundly moving. Lucretias have previously been dark-haired but this year Miss Procter assumes a wig with the blond shade of her own hair.'

And this from the East Anglian Daily Times, published the following day: 'It was a magnificent performance in every way, Peter Pears and Judith Pierce as the chorus creating immediately from the opening a highly charged atmosphere and general level of execution maintained to the end. The orchestra played brilliantly and there was a fine team of soloists, with a few new personages. Norma Procter again took the role of Lucretia and gave a performance which has gained considerably in depth and tension since her stage debut in this part last year. In fact, her appearance in the second act constituted one of the most moving and accomplished pieces of tragic acting for quite a long time and when the final curtain came down, we felt we had witnessed a taut and highly integrated performance fully representative of the composer's genius.'

Norma must have been pleased with the reaction to Lucretia, especially as no one knew she was feeling unwell. On June 26, six days after Lucretia's second night, she caught the train from Aldeburgh to London for an appointment at a private clinic. A date was immediately set for two days' time, for Norma to go under the surgeon's knife for a tonsillectomy. On the Monday, she met with her agent Emmie Tillett and the following day, returned to the clinic. 'Op. V. ill,' she wrote. 'Terrible time. Lost over a stone in weight and pints of blood. Never given a transfusion which I so needed.'[96] The operation was performed by Joan Sutherland's specialist, Sir Ivor Griffiths, and it was on Joan's advice that Norma underwent it. 'Afterwards I joined Bupa!'[97] she blithely noted.

Her recovery was long and tiresome to a hard-working singer: she didn't return home to Grimsby until July 6, during which time she noted that Prof had visited her. On July 20, she travelled to Switzerland and spent a fortnight there. Very little was said about this time in her diary, only that it was a 'terrible time' and 'two weeks of hell.'[98]

In the meantime, plans had to be made for when she was able to return to work. A Montverdi concert, directed by Raymond Leppard, was being organised for October 11 at London's Royal Festival Hall with Norma, Elsie Morison, Hughes Cuenod, Duncan Robertson, Max Worthley and Joseph Ward. Emanuel Hurwitz was to lead The English Chamber Orchestra. A handwritten letter from Leppard, dated August 20, read: 'My dear Norma, so very glad you are going to sing in the Monteverdi concert in October.

Will you do the Great Messenger scene in L'Orfeo (we only do acts 1 and 2). I am making a completely new edition, but the vocal score has the right vocal line except that note values have been halved. I have copied it out again with the original note values – it makes more sense that way. In [L'Incoronazione Di] Poppea, I would be grateful if you would sing the Lament of Ottaria and the wonderful lullaby of Poppea's nurse, Arnalta. I enclose a rough translation to save you trouble. Perhaps we could meet in the fairly near future to go through it and set things a bit. The simplest thing would be if you could let me know when you might be in town and I will try to arrange to be there. Love Raymond.'

For now, though, Norma was recovering. She visited Bee in Jersey, enjoying the summer sun and all that the island had to offer. And then it was time for her to sing again. On September 11, she took part in a recorded Prom rehearsal at Maida Vale. 'V. nervous. First real sing since tonsillectomy. Three-month break! Never told anyone.'[99] The Prom, Alto Rhapsody, was part of Henry Wood's Promenade Concerts and took place at the Royal Albert Hall on September 13. Norma performed Rhapsody by Brahms with the BBC Men's Chorus and the London New Music Singers, conducted by Sir Malcolm Sargent. 'Sir Malcolm was wonderful,' she said. Coincidentally, the programme notes were made by Julius Harrison, who gave Norma her first ever award for singing at the Cleethorpes Music Festival when she was aged seven in 1935. 'A lovely bronze medal and I still have it,' Norma recalled in a jotting on the programme. 'Everyone was shattered, especially little Norm.'[100]

★

In November, she rehearsed with American-born conductor and violinist Yehudi Menuhin. 'So nervous,'[101] she noted. 'Yehudi was so lovely to work with, and kind, as was his wife Diana.'[102] It was for a late-night charity concert with Peter Pears of Abraham and Isaac. It took place on November 18 at the Royal Festival Hall at 11pm, in aid of Christian Action's Defence and Aid Fund for South Africa. Ben, of course, was in attendance. She stayed overnight at St. George's Hotel in Holland Park, that weekend recording Spring Symphony for the BBC. On Ben's birthday, November 22, she was back at Kingsway Hall with Decca, recording the same piece of work. By then, what was to be the biggest point of her career so far came calling. It was time for Orpheus.

Chapter 8: Orpheus

One can only guess how shattered 'little Norm' felt when she began rehearsing for her operatic debut at Covent Garden. She was taking the title role in Gluck's Orpheus, and it was to be her only appearance for The Royal Opera. This was the most high-profile role of her career to date and Norma was unwell again. Imagine her state of mind as she stepped into the role her beloved Kathleen Ferrier had performed eight years before – the very role that was to be Ferrier's last. Orpheus held deep emotional connections for Norma, and she rehearsed in the very same robe Ferrier wore for her performances, her name tag still inside. On November 21, she wore the robe for a photo call at the famous venue. 'Met Jimmy Gibson, chief rèpètiteur, an absolute sod! I hated him,'[103] she wrote. Rehearsals officially began on December 6, and Norma worked hard to learn the role in-between performing her usual stint of Christmas Messiahs.

It is unsurprising, then, that she became run-down and suffered from an attack of hives. She had regular adrenalin injections to ease the symptoms but was in great pain. She made it home for Christmas on December 24. 'So ill,' she said. 'Crazy with urticaria. Saw Doc again for double injection – all the time trying to rehearse.'[104] On Boxing Day, she was back in London for more Orpheus rehearsals. She continued to have a 'terrible time with Jimmy – a swine and a bully,' she wrote in an archive note. 'I couldn't do anything right. Broke my spirit.' She was 'distraught and unhappy at Covent Garden'[105] and had a long talk with Peter Pears about the situation. Worse still, ongoing foot problems meant she was struggling to cope with navigating the high banks of steps on the Orpheus set. 'I loved the music but not the production. I was very unhappy, not well, and my one real comfort was Kathleen's robe… which I wore throughout all the many rehearsals to prepare and cope with the long-skirted robe I was to wear, and never-ending steps on the set,' said Norma. 'It was her love and spirit within her robe which cheered and urged me onwards.'[106]

New Year's Day 1961 offered no rest for Norma. She attended a music call with Louis de Froment, the conductor. Rehearsals continued in earnest, and the general dress rehearsal took place on the morning of Friday, January 13. 'No audience,' noted Norma. 'Terrible media session on stage after performance. Houston Rogers v. kind. He took "Orpheo" photos.'[107] Opening night was on the following Monday, with the BBC in attendance to broadcast it. Norma's feeling post-show was perfectly clear. A note in her archive read: 'What a ghastly night! I knew I was right and should never have attempted this glorious piece. Wasn't ready for the stage. George Harewood [a former director of the Royal Opera House] so rude and flaming mad – first on set after curtain calls. I was wrung out and shattered. Perspiration pouring out of me.' A note in the back of her diary elaborates. 'God were it now I'd have told them to stuff it! BBC too – Orpheus 1st night – so nervous and terrible atmosphere. [George] Harewood so rude. Lovely Louis de Froment, Orpheus conductor, so kind but hated the set up. Wonderful man.'

She received mixed reviews from London critics. They praised her singing but were less complementary about her acting skills, an area Norma openly admitted was a weakness. It was, after all, singing she loved, not acting – and opera, unfortunately, required it. The Stage wrote: 'Norma Proctor [sic] was making her Covent Garden debut as Orpheus and, judging from the ovation she received at the end, there was no doubt of her success. Her voice has a rich, even timbre in all registers, except for a slight deterioration of quality on the highest notes. During the first act her grief was under control and her performance lacked real dramatic bite. In the later scenes, however, her singing grew in emotional intensity until the climax was reached with a truly superb Che Faro in the last act. The complete success of this opera… depends ultimately on the singer of the title role, and so the Covent Garden Opera can congratulate themselves on having found a worthy successor to the past exponents of this role, making this both a welcome and successful revival.'

Norma's erstwhile supporter, the critic Ernest Bradbury, said in The Yorkshire Post that Orpheus was 'one of her finest artistic achievements' and acknowledged the emotional strain she was under. The report, under the headline 'Debut that had Ferrier memory', read: 'Tonight's presentation at Covent Garden of Gluck's Orpheus was called a revival, but it was of necessity something more than that. It will be eight years next month since that ill-fated production whose second performance was also the last given by the late Kathleen Ferrier. There could have been no stomach for a revival in any shorter period of time and there had, in any case, to be a voice capable of replacing that of Ferrier. Miss Norma Procter, another Northerner (she misses Yorkshire status by having her home at Cleethorpes, over the border) has in recent years done much that was formerly associated with Kathleen Ferrier, notably the recitals with Benjamin Britten and Peter Pears: but she has won this position by being blessed with a voice that – shall we say? – comes nearer than that of any other of our day to Ferrier's.

'This must be both a pleasure and a hardship to Miss Procter. It can have been no easy task to make her debut playing against the memory of that last legendary Covent Garden Orpheus; even the programme carried a gramophone recording advertisement of the work with "the superlative Kathleen Ferrier." It is therefore as well to put that other performance temporarily out of mind, and to hail this new performance with a new conductor (Louis de Froment) and a new producer (Colin Graham) as something special in its own right. As for Miss Procter, she made the most telling effects by the simple, unassuming sincerity of her playing, by splendid articulation and by her pure tonal feeling for Gluck's lines. She is on the stage almost the whole time, yet her poise, like her singing, never faltered for a moment: this must surely be regarded as one of her finest artistic achievements to the present time, and the audience recognised this warmly at the end. Before this there had been some restraint on both sides of the curtain, maybe because the work was being broadcast – not always a good thing on a first night. But the audience threw restraint to the winds at the end, giving Miss Procter the ovation she had undoubtedly earned.'

Quick to support a home-grown star, the Grimsby Evening Telegraph published a round-up of national reviews. 'The Covent Garden debut last night of Grimsby's Norma Procter in the exacting title role in Gluck's Orhpeus had a mixed reception by London critics,' it reported. 'Most of them praised her singing, but found her acting less satisfactory – understandably so, since Miss Procter has earned her reputation on the concert platform and last night's role was only her second in opera. The Times, however, found both singing and acting admirable. Miss Procter and Miss Elsie Morison (Eurydice), they say, suggested two real human beings, one noble and restrained, the other deeply passionate and vulnerable. Martin Cooper, Daily Telegraph, said Miss Procter's voice was "admirably firm and evenly developed, though lacking expansion at the top and at present rather monotonous in colour". But, he says, as a debut in a notoriously testing role, hers was an "exceptional performance".

'For Andrew Smith, Daily Herald, Miss Procter's "rich and mellow voice" was just right for the role and "she maintained a golden flow of song". "But", he adds, "she has still to learn the tricks of operatic acting. For me she was a voice only, not an integrated character". Says Charles Reid, Daily Mail, "The new Orpheus was young and comely and, although she had had little but platform experience hitherto, went through the acting motions intelligently and with some grace. The tessitura of the part, however, seemed a bit high for either her comfort or ours. Certain upper phrases, including her crucial opening ones, were undeniably tart."

'Noel Goodwin, Daily Express: "She has a deep, rich contralto voice, but as yet it does not have enough warmth of human feeling. Nerves understandably muted the effect of her first arias last night as Orpheus mourns the death of Eurydice and resolves to quell the Furies of Hell to regain his beloved. But in the last great lament, when Eurydice dies a second time, the tears every listener should suffer refused to spring." In The Guardian, Philip Hope-Wallace wrote: "In her musicianly and stately assumption of Gluck's Orpheus, this splendid contralto voice seemed to have found a new and more vibrant glow. The firmness remains but the cloying element has gone. Some of the singing in the third act was expressive as well as merely beautiful as sound. But the projection of the character is somewhat muted."

To the Press, she put on a brave face. 'A really memorable night. I just can't describe how wonderful it was,' she told the Grimsby Telegraph, explaining how telegrams and letters of congratulations poured in before the performance, mainly from her musical friends in Grimsby and Cleethorpes. 'People have been so wonderful. And the reception from the audience… I just can't describe how I felt. Such a mixture and confusion of feeling.' 'I really don't see myself as Delilah or Carmen,' she said in another interview, this time with The Daily Herald. It wrote: 'At 32, good-looking Miss Procter has been singing professionally for ten years and stands high in the ranks of our younger artists. She believes that singers should get as wide an experience as possible and hopes for more opera work. But she has no intention of deserting the oratorio platform.'

And here lay the rub: Norma did not want to act on the operatic stage. In fact, she did not want to act at all. The concert platform was her natural home. But the role certainly did its job in terms of publicity. The magazine Music and Musicians featured Norma on the front cover of the January 1961 issue, and wrote a feature about her life and career to date. The same issue featured Louis de Froment too.

'Music has been the main interest of Norma Procter since before she can remember,' the magazine declared. 'Today Norma's voice is in demand from many quarters. Constantly travelling but still making her home in Grimsby, she has little time for anything except the demands of her career.

'Most top-rank musicians, whether singers or players, find it necessary to leave provincial homes and live in London. Norma has found that it is not essential, and still goes home to Grimsby between her engagements. Home is still her headquarters, where she can join even if only for a few days at a time the mother who helped her with encouragement and understanding when early difficulties appeared. Every summer, usually the off season for many artists, she tries to have a good rest, both physically and vocally. "Too many concerts and too much travelling can be tiring, and if I am tired my voice sounds tired".'

In separate correspondence, she commented on receiving unexpected praise. 'The wonderful surprise of flowers at the end of a concert never fails to give me a thrill – and I love too the peaceful and perfect setting of a church or cathedral with its quietness and no applause at the beginning or end of the concert,'[108] she said. 'Then there is the little thank-you at the end of a concert which always means so much, especially when you feel perhaps it hadn't gone so well. I must tell you a lovely remark passed on to me by the president of a society. One of the choir members stopped him after the concert and said: "Bye, it were worth a bring-and-buy sale to 'ave 'er!" – and that really made my evening.'[109]

These interviews and snippets offer a useful portrait of Norma's public life at this time, keeping private the grief and unhappiness she felt through the entire run at Covent Garden. According to Norma's diary, Orpheus was performed seven times – on January 16, 18, 21, 24 and 30, and February 1 and 2 – and she received £50 per show. 'I paid hotel and all expenses,' she said. No doubt she was grateful to see friendly faces in the crowd of January 21, when her sister Audrey and brother-in-law Norman made the trip from Grimsby to watch the production. At no point did she reveal that on January 26, with more performances to go, she fell ill with a dreadful bout of gastroenteritis. And, to add to her woes, she had a procedure on January 27 where her sinuses were drilled. Poor Norma was physically and emotionally drained.

On the final night, she was surprised by some kind words from a theatrical legend. 'Sir John Gielgud very kindly passed at the back of the stage where I was standing alone,' she wrote. 'I was feeling very alone and unhappy – he so surprised me, and with that wonderful gentle/kindly voice said, "I'm so sorry not to see your performance of Orpheus but I'm very involved with Britten's A Midsummer Night's Dream". He was directing/producing its London premiere, which followed my performance. I shall never forget this kindly word and greeting, and wished he was producing Orpheus. We then found ourselves in different cars at the traffic lights in The Strand and he gave me a wonderful smile and wave. A very special gentleman.'[110]

And her diary drips with glee on February 3, when she returned home, exhausted. 'Thank God,' she said. 'Vowed I'd never sing opera again on stage and never did, except for Mahler's Song of the Earth ballet years later at Covent Garden with Nureyev, who was wonderful to me.'[111]

Chapter 9: The 1960s

The despised run of Orpheus was over, and Norma happily returned to concert work and recordings. But her body was run-down. Suffering from flu and voice problems, she cancelled work from March 3 until after Easter but soon returned to the stage around the UK and abroad, including Copenhagen and Cologne. In July, she appeared on a private recording of Gerontius, conducted by David Willcocks, at Kings College in Cambridge. August 10 was a Prom of Mozart's Requiem Mass, followed by a Prom of Britten's Cantata Academia five days later. On August 28, she stayed at Red House, Britten and Pears's home in Aldeburgh, and was ill with gastroenteritis. September saw her back at the Three Choirs Festival, in Hereford, and on the 14th she travelled to a festival in Ulm to perform an Abe and Ike recital with Ben and Peter, and Bach's cantatas. 'Very ill with flu bug – throat specialist,' she wrote. 'So ashamed, ill again!'[112]

The situation wasn't about to get any better. On November 2 she was star soloist at a Grimsby Philharmonic Society concert with a string orchestra led by Fay Campey, but bad health plagued her throughout November and December. She was suffering from boils and carbuncles, and her resistance was low. She came down with a cold and embarked on a series of injections with an osteopath for her foot. 'Sang in agony with left foot,' she said, of a performance of Messiah at Coventry. 'Standing on one leg! V. ill. Arrived home in agony at 3am with Norm [brother-in-law]. Crawled on knees upstairs.'[113] Three days later, she was admitted to St. Hugh's Hospital in Grimsby by ambulance. Norma had developed osteomyelitis, a nasty bone infection. 'Raging pain in left foot,' she noted. 'Couldn't walk or put foot to the ground. Nothing shown on x-rays for three weeks. Blood count rose to 120/130. Foot in plaster below knee. Two needlings – four-hourly injections – one million units of streptomycin (became a pin cushion). Shadow at last on x-rays. Hellish pain. Pethidine injections and tablets. Allergic to morphine.'[114]

With her foot cast in a heavy plaster, she travelled to Cologne in mid-December for Christmas Messiahs. 'Hellish painful days,'[115] she commented. And her predicament did not escape the Press's notice. Engagements in Israel were cancelled, much to Norma's regret. A newspaper in her hometown reported how she was staying in St. Hugh's while being treated for a leg infection. The article, published on December 20, said: 'Miss Procter was to have broadcast tonight, as one of the soloists in a performance of Messiah by Huddersfield Choral Society, conducted by Sir Malcolm Sargent. On Friday, she was due to fly to Israel, and would have been singing in Jerusalem on Christmas Day.'

Norma's inability to perform appalled and upset her in equal measures: she hated letting people down and was never happier when singing. On Christmas Eve, she was very ill with 'rigours' and felt poorly over the entire festive period. She was unable to work between Christmas and New Year. The foot plaster was removed on December 30. 'X-ray shows trouble at last,' she said, relieved. 'Op for Monday AM after talk with Mr Holdsworth, Sheffield consultant.'[116]

So, 1962 began for Norma on the operating table at St. Hugh's, where 'wonderful' orthopaedic surgeon Nick James attempted to fix her left foot. The right side, he told her, was so full of puss that he described it as a 'mass of butter.'[117] 'Osteomyelitis critical and lucky to have my foot at all,' she noted. 'What bliss when I came round; that hellish three weeks of pain had stopped, thank God.'[118] The night before her departure from St. Hugh's, a mole was removed from her left forearm and sent for analysis. It was bad news: Norma had skin cancer.

The first half of 1962 was hard. She endured six-hourly injections for her foot problem until early March and often complained of being in pain with spasms. She took up painting to pass the time, but these were 'dark days.'[119] Two operations were carried out for the cancer: the first with local anaesthetic and the second fully under, her foot still in plaster. She had a consultation with Sir Stanford Cade, Kathleen Ferrier's specialist, and the latter operation was carried out by Mr James, who had operated on her foot. It took him four hours to remove all body moles and perform a skin graft.

Needless to say, Norma's engagements were cancelled, and support from her friends now was crucial. Joan Sutherland, on hearing of her bed-ridden status, sent a Decca LP of highlights of her Lucia to keep her company. Towards the end of May, Norma escaped to Sharrow Bay for a few days before having her plaster removed. Her first proper walk since January occurred on May 27 to the back door, but the right side of her foot was paralysed and her left side was arthritic, with a permanent scar from the surgery. Worse still, although she was wearing surgical stockings, her big toe was now in a permanently upright position. She was in pain, uncomfortable too, and could not find any suitable pairs of shoes.

Rehabilitation still ongoing, her first concert of the year was Haydn's Imperial Mass and Britten's Cantata Academia at Cambridge Guildhall on June 13. The following day, she performed at Aldeburgh. But her foot flared up again, and in July had an appointment in Sheffield with a consultant. 'Decided against Russia tour and for half of left big toe to be cut off,'[120] she said. Within days of the appointment, the procedure – her fifth operation – took place, again performed by Mr. James. On August 26, she resumed lessons with Prof and her first public sing since the summer took place on September 2 at Walsall. 'What agonies!'[121] she declared. Feeling very unwell, she sang at the Gloucester Three Choirs Festival, followed immediately by Prom rehearsals with Sir Malcolm Sargent. She wrote: 'Sir M made a wonderful welcome speech for me.'[122] The Prom itself, on September 14, was the Coronation Mass and Mozart's Choral 9th. Norma had 'terrible trouble'[123] climbing the stairs at the venue. In fact, it would take Norma three years to walk normally again, and even then, her left foot would be forever weak.

With a tour of Russia cancelled, she slowly returned to the concert platform, including a few days in Berlin to perform Bach's B Minor. She was still having trouble walking and standing yet ploughed on with her usual raft of Messiahs in the run-up to Christmas. At Huddersfield, on December 17, she was sent home by Sir Malcolm because she was so ill, and her final Messiah of the year was cancelled. 'I must mention Norman, my brother-in-law, with real gratitude for the many hundreds of miles he has driven me on my travels,' she said once. 'In mid-December 1961 and until September 1962, a long spell of ill health kept me out of the profession when sadly I missed tours in the USA and Russia and was never given the opportunity to return again, thanks to an un-named agent, but I re-learned the true and important priorities in life during that time. Good health had always been and still is top of my priority list; there is no price upon it. I turned down Far Eastern/Australian tours due to lack of stamina and missed concerts in Canada and Japan also because of clashing dates elsewhere. I was very fortunate in having a wonderful band of specialists, doctors and nurses to whom I owe my life, and heartfelt gratitude.'[124]

★

The new year of 1963 brought good news. Norma accepted an offer to perform Sir Arthur Bliss's The Enchantress. Bliss had sent her the score – which he had written for Kathleen Ferrier – ten years earlier, hoping she would find it of interest. Back then, Norma hadn't felt confident enough to handle the work but now the time had come, though 'fearfully'[125] on her part, at a BBC studio concert. She rehearsed in London before travelling to

Glasgow to perform with the Scottish Orchestra and conductor Norman Del Mar on January 24. 'Truly shattered by its demands,'[126] she said, adding: 'Stayed with Norman Del Mar – very kind but I was terrible company.'[127]

Her ailments were understandably affecting her spirit and mental health as well as her body, and it was becoming harder to keep them private because she was turning down work, only singing when she truly felt up to it. Joan Sutherland, writing from New York on February 10, said: 'Dear Norm, thank you for the note and I'm so sorry you don't feel up to doing Cornelia – more for yourself than the fact of having you with us,' she wrote. 'I do hope that you will feel better once the warmer weather comes. It has been such an awful winter and no help to you, I'm sure. You must do what you feel you can and take things slowly until you feel really fit. Is there any possibility of your coming to the villa this summer? I feel it would do you so much good. Do think about it dear and we will fix dates during the time we are in London – May and June. Things here have been hectic since the long silence, but now begin to settle to a jog trot, thank heavens! The weather has been up and down. However, the kiddies are loving it – I can see them over in Central Park from my window, skating. Our little apartment should be ready soon – or I'll want to know the reason why! It is beginning to look quite nice. Lots of love to you from the both of us and looking forward to seeing you again. We'll be back in about 12 weeks now.'

In March, conductor Dean Dixon asked Norma to sing in Frankfurt, but she felt too poorly to accept. In early April she flew to Cologne to sing the St. Matthew Passion with Gunter Wand conducting but was 'very sad and lonely – could hardly walk'.[128] Despite her obvious distress, she continued to sing when she could, around the UK and in Copenhagen, alongside singers including her friend Jennifer Vyvyan and with conductors such as Josef Krips. On June 25, she sang Gerontius with the Bach Choir. 'Lovely welcome back, bless them,' she wrote. 'Singing is such a battle; one is always having to sing about the things one is trying to forget or longing for and can't have. But we try to press on. Why? And what for? I don't know but am grateful.'[129] Then to Aldeburgh that weekend: 'Music In England. Victorian ballads. Quite an ordeal but a lovely welcome too.'[130]

A short break in Jersey followed, then The Proms came around again. On August 14 she performed in Alto Rhapsody by Brahms, her last Prom with Sir Malcolm Sargent. 'He was wonderful as he cleverly supported and cradled my right arm in his left arm as we had a long walk round the platform arena,' she said in her diary. 'My left foot and balance were very unsteady. It was a memorable reception from the beloved Promenaders!' The following day she rehearsed Britten's Spring Symphony for the upcoming Edinburgh Festival and suffered a 'ghastly dysentery attack.'[131] She caught the 4pm train back home to recover in time for her next Prom on August 19 – The Enchantress. 'What a day!'[132] she exclaimed.

She flew to Edinburgh the very next day to sing Spring Symphony and spent a few days in the city before a recital of Abraham and Isaac with Britten and Pears. 'Very ill and low,' she said. 'Afternoon train home.'[133]

Her glowing review in The Scotsman of the trio's performance must have secretly thrilled her, in the context of Britten's abrupt dismissal of their Abe and Ike recording. It wrote: 'Miss Procter is the perfect Isaac, catching all the pathetic overtones – particularly the moving little breathless phrases just before the climax – fitting her voice admirably to the strange tenor-contralto synthesis which represents the voice of God, and subtly catching the poetic naivety of the Chester Miracle Play from which the text is taken.'

Unfortunately, her health was yet to pick up. 'Went off feeling like death,'[134] she said, of a Three Choirs performance in Birmingham on August 30. Yet she refused to give in. On September 2, she sang with bass John Carol Case in the premiere of Mary of Magdala, a cantata for contralto and bass solo written by Sir Arthur Bliss, in Worcester Cathedral as part of the Three Choirs Festival.

Norma noted that no scores were allowed during the concert, and that it was also performed in Birmingham and Hull, and that a Prom was mooted but was never confirmed. Speaking of The Proms, she was back at the Albert Hall on September 12 for Spring Symphony, and soon came down with a terrible cold. She recovered enough in time for September 29, when she performed El Pessebre in English with Pablo Casals at London's Festival Hall, noting it was a 'very remarkable occasion with a lovable, humble genius'.

Norma's breathless schedule of engagements continued for the rest of the year. She travelled to Zurich in November with Ben and Peter, where she and Peter performed Christmas oratorios. During her usual December Messiahs, she complained of feeling unwell and, unusually for her, spent an entire day in bed between shows.

★

The year 1964 began with Messiahs and recordings, and in March a tiring overnight trip to Hanover, then Madrid and Cologne. 'Feeling lousy,'[135] she confessed. Following a concert in Wigan on April 4, she wrote in her diary: 'Felt so ill and dreadful. Almost collapsed on arrival home at front door.'

That summer she was back at Aldeburgh for Orpheus, before flying to Tel-Aviv. Her archive contains a copy of a letter she sent to an unnamed recipient[136] dated July 16, while she was staying at the Samuel Hotel. Norma wrote: 'Thursday – I think! 11.30am (10.30am to you). Hello – well we made it. I'm pinching myself so hard, I really can't believe this is me! Am sitting on my own little balcony with a wonderful view of the town and sea. The waves rush in like a team of white sea stallions. Had a good flight – Boeing – enormous great jet. I stopped 40 minutes at Amsterdam, and then direct over Munich, Innsbruck, Crete and here. Only three kilos overweight and allowed two because of Ron's underweight. Travelled together from air terminal, which was nice company. We were met and brought here by car. It seems we have five concerts, three in Tel-Aviv, one in Jerusalem and one in Caesarea – isn't that wonderful – tho' I won't believe it 'til I've actually done it! Have sent a cutting to Mummy. We sing in the old Roman amphitheatre in Caesarea – reconstruction, restoration etc by the Rothschilds – we open the first concert next Wednesday. First concert Tel-Aviv 19th, 20th, Jerusalem 22nd, Caesarea 23rd or 24th, Tel-Aviv 25th, so you see it's a busy week. Just been invited to British Ambassador's for lunch on 21st – help!

'Am taking it easy today. It's très, très hot and perspiration's pouring out of me – also from temperature too, but I'm alright and taking codeine and Achromycin as instructed – so grateful for the latter as it will help with mi' mouth and arm even tho' I'm one big ache with everything now. But by [the time] this reaches you, I should be much better, so don't worry. Can't begin to explain my feelings as I sit here. It seems incredible to be singing in the actual places where our Lord and St. Paul (Corinthians) moved and lived – and my cup is fairly full! There were such moving scenes at the airport; some of these poor souls meeting up with families for the first time in their lives and others for many years. One old boy in the plane had waited 51 years to see his sister. Everything comes to him who knoweth how to wait!'

★

It was after a Prom concert that Norma found a lump under her left armpit.

The date was August 12. She sang Britten's Cantata Academia and was happy because Bee, her pal from Jersey, was in town. 'Found problem after Prom,' she said. 'Deep shock.'[137]

She arranged to see Sir Stanford Cade at Westminster Hospital, but not before singing in another Prom, Mahler's 8th with Sir Charles Groves and Bee an encouraging face in the crowd. She underwent a biopsy and on September 13, and Sir Stanford confirmed her worst fears. It was lymphatic cancer, and she had a 50/50 chance of survival. Glands were removed, and the six weeks of radium treatment she endured meant she would never be able to have children.

'Very lonely days but had to be,' she wrote. 'Very few people knew or were told of the cancer, on Sir Stanford's advice. I blamed any problems on the foot. Weight rose to 13 ½ stone.'[138]

Within two weeks of the treatment ending she returned to singing, her first performance being a Messiah at York with Wilfred Brown. By this time, she was also a sought-after judge at festivals and academies. 'Felt grim,' she noted, at a judging session on November 19. Her determination to power through her illness is astonishing. She went on to perform 13 more Messiahs in the run-up to the new year, travelled around the UK in January and to Madrid in February to sing Song of the Earth three times with Jascha Horenstein ('Wonderful!' she noted in her diary), treating herself to a first-class flight home.

More recordings took place, including for the BBC and a Messiah with Sir Malcolm Sargent, as did trips to Cologne, Frankfurt, and Lyon. She holidayed in Jersey before The Proms, this year the Choral 9th, and followed this with a relentless schedule of concerts around the UK and in Copenhagen and Frankfurt. Not once in her diary for 1965 does she complain of feeling ill. Unfortunately, 1966 did not begin so well.

*

January 7 and Norma found herself in Edinburgh for Gerontius but 'felt so ill.'[139] Less than a week later, she was at Grimsby's Central Hall for a Messiah: 'I looked ghastly, like a barrage balloon – so ashamed.'[140] In rehearsals for an upcoming performance of Das Lied with Jascha Horenstein, she noted that her upper register had completely gone. The concert occurred on January 25, with the Royal Philharmonic Orchestra at the Odeon Theatre, Swiss Cottage, London. 'I was so very ill,' she recalled, in a diary note. 'I had no strength to lift the voice, as I had for the three performances with Jascha in Madrid in 1965. I knew it was hopeless. I was so depressed and disappointed because it was a work I loved so much.' The following day, she again teamed up with Horenstein for Song of the Earth. 'Disaster for me – very ill but an incredible crit from The Guardian,' she said. 'My voice no longer obeyed.'[141]

The newspaper wrote: 'Happily, we had a contralto soloist, Norma Procter, who came closer to matching Kathleen Ferrier's unique interpretation than any other singer I have known. The voice itself is extraordinarily like, particularly in the register at the bottom of the treble stave where so many of Mahler's most expressive phrases lie. Like Ferrier, Miss Procter is able to control the tone colour with precision, stilling her vibrato on such a phrase in the final song as The World Now Sleeps, or later catching the tenderness which Mahler prescribes for the soaring phrase "I journey to my homeland".'

The Guardian's critic, then, was full of praise. But Norma, who to herself sounded terrible, knew her voice was growing weaker. She was in an ironic situation: she was at the height of her career and fame, known around the world for her smooth contralto sound, and esteemed peers were desperate to work with her. Mary Plumstead wrote the music for The Song of The Cross for Norma; composers were writing just for her. It must have been hard, both professionally and personally, to do battle in secret but she soldiered on. Two days after Horenstein's concert, she travelled to Geneva despite feeling 'a bit grim again.'[142] March 16 saw Norma sing with The Royal Liverpool Philharmonic, conducted by Sir Malcolm Sargent, in Leeds Town Hall. It was Norma and Sir Malcolm's first concert together following his own bout of illness and an operation, and the pair shared a big hug.

Concerts in Barcelona followed. In early April she met Leonard Bernstein and his wife for the first time at a rehearsal for a performance of Mahler's 8th under his baton. 'He was wonderful and gave me a lift in his chauffeur-driven car to The Savoy where I was staying,' Norma said. 'He was very troubled with chorus problems – don't know their work!'[143] The concert, on April 17 at the Royal Albert Hall, was televised and Princess Margaret was in the audience.

Norma then travelled to Hamburg and fulfilled singing engagements around the UK. By May, she was preparing to sing at Covent Garden – five years on from Orpheus and despite having vowed she'd never do so again. She was contractually obliged to take part in the Royal Ballet's production of Kenneth Macmillan's Song of the Earth/Das Lied with a cast that included Rudolf Nureyev, Antoinette Sibley, and Lynn Seymour. She and Bee went to see the ballet on May 20, her only chance to watch and listen to the performance from the stalls, with an orchestra, before the first performance on June 25. 'Disgraceful,'[144] is her dismissive one-word-only comment. Norma came down with a cold in-between but continued to perform and record until the opening night. 'He [Nureyev] was so kind and supportive to me,'[145] she said, adding in her diary: 'No orchestral rehearsal allowed. Terrible! Piano rehearsal only. Swarowsky conducting; very angry. Frankfurt Ballet Orchestra played more wrong notes than I've ever heard in Das Lied. I did sing many Orpheus concert performances later, some in German and Italian, but for me I came to this profession for the music, not production, and there were many more operatic singers suited to the stage than I.'

That summer, following a show in Rotterdam, she reunited with Britten and Pears to perform the St. John Passion. Ben conducted the performance and Norma was devastated because she could barely sing. 'Concert nearly broke me,'[146] she confessed. Undeterred, after a break to Jersey, she undertook a tour of Hanover, Louisenhof, Ghent, Tournai and Ulm, while also making more recordings. In October she sang at the reopening of the Teatro Real in Madrid, in the presence of royalty, with an 'awful stomach.'[147] In December, she fell ill with flu but managed to sing in Dusseldorf. Christmas came and went, and the new year began with the Messiah in Glasgow, followed by an overseas trip to Wuppertal and Hanover. She was back by January 14, to perform the Messiah in Grimsby.

Throughout the 1960s, she performed nine times – including three other Messiahs, in 1960, 1962 and 1966 – with the Grimsby Philharmonic, a society with a place in her heart. Critic Frank Whitmarsh, reviewing this 1967 Messiah for the Grimsby Evening Telegraph, wrote: 'Few singers seem to achieve a new perfection every time one hears them. One of those who has this rarest of qualities is Norma Procter. It was a well-sung performance all round, and the bass, John Shirley-Quirk, was especially outstanding. Jean Ward Skerrow, soprano, and Robert Tear, tenor, sang competently, and with a clear freshness and care. If the more mature artists outshone them, they are not blamed for it. For at least one (perhaps prejudiced!) listener, however, all this served but to accentuate the profound and immensely moving art of Miss Procter. She and Handel had the evening between them. And this is not just a matter of that cream-golden voice, and the relaxed ease and maturity of her singing. It is something deeper. No singer I have ever heard can so distil the very essence of this immense work. She seizes its very heart of meaning and reveals it to us. When she sang Oh Thou That Tellest, it was with joy leaping in her voice. He Shall Feed His Flock had an unbelievable tenderness with no trace of sentimentality; and He Was Despised was all pain. Some singers can turn even an act of worship into a performance. Miss Procter turned a performance into an act of worship.'

February brought her first concert with Karl Richter and she continued working. A bout of gastric flu knocked her for six in Bavaria but there were no cancellations. She forged ahead and travelled to Copenhagen, Barcelona, Madrid, Koln, Bielefeld, Stuttgart and Leonsberg. Her schedule was literally exhausting, and there was no sign of it letting up.

★

'Wot a night!'

Three short words in Norma's archive summed up her opinion of what's best described as an interesting performance on April 20, 1967. The Grimsby Philharmonic Society choir was preparing for a joint concert with Hull Choral Union of Missa Solemnis (Beethoven), with the Royal Liverpool Philharmonic Orchestra. Norma's fellow soloists were Rae Woodland, Ronald Dowd, and John Homes. Alec Redshaw recalled:[148] 'The plain fact was that both choirs were by then ready to do battle with the mammoth work, but neither choir was quite big enough in itself to do full justice to the sheer physical magnitude of it. Quite apart from its spiritual and musical content, it requires almost more skill and stamina than any other choral work, including the Mass in B Minor.

'Norma Procter, as contralto soloist, performed a life-saving act of historic renown when another soloist was unlucky enough to flounder, for she virtually recomposed the music and brought it back to its chartered course.'

Norma elaborated on the event in a handwritten note: 'Fatal Hull/Grimsby performance – somehow I rescued it! There was total confusion. The choir was singing against the orchestra, and only the orchestra was correct. I listened hard. Everyone stopped and I found myself singing where I came in and sang the chorus line. The chorus mercifully picked up from me!' Interestingly, her diary entry for this performance reads: 'AR very rude. Performance almost fell apart. Shattered! I saved the day!' No more was written, so we will never know what took place between herself and Redshaw.

Ever up for a challenge, she agreed to sing at the World Peace Conference in Geneva on June 29 under the baton of Pablo Casals… in Catalan. 'Only had two or three days to learn it,' she wrote. 'No one spoke Catalan at the BBC World Service so [record producer] Walter Legge's daughter taught me over the phone. I wrote down and learned it phonetically. It was very frightening – all the other soloists spoke Catalan fluently and were Spanish. Wonderful Casals again and his lovely young wife.'[149]

From there she travelled to Basel to sing. During the concert, a front filling fell out of a tooth and Norma was patched up by a local dentist. She travelled on to Jerusalem and then Frankfurt, where she first met Rafael Kubelik. There she also met Elsie Morison for the first time since they performed together in Orpheus at Covent Garden; Morison had married Kubelik in 1963. 'He was such a wonderful man and musician, of great integrity, courage and humility,'[150] she said.

The summer saw Norma's usual schedule of engagements, including recordings in Heilsbronn and a performance of the St. John Passion at the Arnsbach Festival. A holiday in Jersey, then off to Copenhagen, Madrid, Carmona and Santander, and some UK dates throughout September. Towards end of the month Norma spent eight days in Germany, then came down with flu but soldiered on, travelling to Vienna, Luxembourg, Gothenburg, Rotterdam and The Hague. The year headed to a close with the usual Messiahs and Christmas concerts. No wonder on December 23 Norma wrote in her diary: 'Home. Praise God!!'

★

The early part of 1968 saw no let-up in her schedule. She travelled to Essen, Berlin, Zurich, Koln, Rotterdam, Barcelona, Madrid, Sweden and

Nuremburg, and on May 30 she embarked on a long and tiring Italian tour, taking in Trieste, Ravenna, Verona, L'Aquila, Bergano, Treviso and Trento. 'Hellish trip,'[151] was all Norma had to say about this. She caught a flu, only just making it to Glasgow for a performance of Britten's Spring Symphony before departing for Munich, which was a 'wonderful trip.'[152] Sweden next, then a holiday in Jersey, followed by more concerts and a Spring Symphony Prom on August 8, then to the Three Choirs in Gloucester and Flanders Festival, in Belgium.

She made it home for a few days, then flew to Baden to perform Karl Amadeus Hartmann's Symphonie with the Sinfonieorchester des Sudwestfunk [Southwest German Radio Symphony Orchestra], a public concert broadcast on the radio. Ernest Bour conducted, of whom Norma had little to say: 'A very difficult man, for a very difficult score. Poor communicator!'[153] The exhausting schedule continued into the autumn: Hanover, Dusseldorf, Munich, Amsterdam, and back to Munich on November 2 for Deutsche Grammophon recordings. She also performed in Lincoln at a memorial concert for her dear Sir Malcolm Sargent, who had died in 1967, and then at the Royal Festival Hall, where Prince Charles and Princess Anne were undercover in the audience.

The year went by in a flash; it was Messiah time before she knew it. December 19 saw her perform Orpheus in German, which was 'very difficult to learn after English.'[154] A day later she flew to Zurich, making it home by Christmas Eve. But there was no rest to be had – there was a piece of music to learn for a recording on January 6. 'Study Nicholas Maws Scenes and Arias. Very difficult piece. No Christmas – or cards written. Too busy learning Mr Maws's work. Horrible!'[155]

In January 1969 Norma flew to Lisbon, staying in the Hotel Miraparque, for performances of Messiah. 'Suitcase broken into and jewellery stolen. Très ill,'[156] she wrote. Later, she flew to Munich to record Mahler for Deutsche Grammophon and then to Lausanne, Frankfurt, Vienna, Barcelona, Koln and Gothenburg for concerts. The majestic Norwich Cathedral was the setting for a performance of The Dream of Gerontius on May 10 with Peter Pears, accompanied by the City of Birmingham Symphony Orchestra and the 250-strong University of East Anglia choir, conducted by Philip Ledger. It was the first performance of Gerontius in the city in a decade. A somewhat wrinkled and uncredited newspaper clipping from Norma's archive noted: 'The audience of more than 1,000, including Benjamin Britten, spread into the presbytery and transepts. Not for a long time has such superb heart-stirring singing been heard locally as in the partnership between Peter Pears and Norma Procter. Both sang from memory and with total commitment. The result was a vivid enactment by Mr Pears of all the emotions of the deathbed scene in Part I, while Miss Procter, with her true contralto timbre, poured forth a stream of beautiful tone, embodying the calm presence of the Guardian Angel.' The much-thumbed press cutting is marked with Norma's handwriting as being 'one of my most memorable of Gerontius, with Peter.'

But the newspaper report missed out on a juicy detail about the afternoon rehearsal. 'I suddenly looked down from our slightly raised platform to see the cathedral mouse bobbing his head and running up and down the ornamental metal opening in the floor. I nearly jumped a mile!' she wrote. 'I told Peter – who was short-sighted and couldn't see it! – and amid much laughter, promised "if that little creature clambers up here, especially tonight in my long robe, regardless, I shall climb on my chair!". Needless to say, so wonderful was the atmosphere during the performance I completely forgot about our little friend – more concerned to see Ben and all the Aldeburgh Festival regulars sobbing on the front rows.'[157]

★

After a gap of more than two years, she made a triumphant public return to Lincolnshire on June 6 for a special recital at Market Rasen Methodist Church, accompanied by Alec Redshaw. The programme contained Purcell, Handel, Schubert, Dvorak, Elgar, Head, Stanford, Warlock, Ireland. The Grimsby Evening Telegraph's Frank Whitmarsh reported in the following day's edition: 'It was worth waiting for! Norma Procter's first recital in her native county for more than two years was a wonderful occasion. We knew, at Market Rasen Methodist Church last night, that we could expect a renewal of well-remembered pleasures. But memories fade.

'As soon as she started singing, one realised with a shock that one had really forgotten just how good a singer she was. What we heard was that cream-and-honey voice, with its dazzling range and quite startling power, now in the high tide of its glorious maturity. It was an experience to be grateful for. The voice was used, in twenty different ways, with consummate musicianship. It was a catholic and varied programme which she and Alec Redshaw, who accompanied, gave us. It ranged from Purcell and Handel, through Schubert, Dvorak and Elgar, to Peter Warlock – and Alec Redshaw. One was left wondering if there was anything at all Miss Procter could not sing? She even reconciled me (well, almost) to a horrid little sloppy Stanford piece, Johneen. Whether this was worth the skill and feeling she gave it is a matter of opinion, but it showed her versatility if nothing else.

'Any good singer is more than a voice, but it is particularly true of Norma Procter that one doubles one's enjoyment and understanding by watching as well as listening. Tenderness in Music For A-While, high tragedy with Dido, deep religious feeling in Handel, Dvorak and spirituals – how these things go with that wicked sense of humour which comes out in folk songs is her secret. But all are there, coupled with that unbelievably relaxed and easy delivery which is the deceptive fruit of years of dedicated effort, and the sign of complete mastery.

'For her last group, Miss Procter sang some negro spirituals which had been arranged by Alec Redshaw. Sung with just the right degree of restrained feeling, these showed Mr Redshaw's work to be both original and discreet – of an individual character, but well-mannered music which gave proper precedence to the singer. Called back again and again for encores, Miss Procter in one of them achieved a real tour de force. Leaving the rostrum, she stood on the floor within arm's length of the front rows to sing, very softly but with ringing sincerity, If There's Anybody Here Like Weeping Mary. It received what is perhaps a singer's final accolade – a measurable spell of utter silence at the end before the applause welled up and rolled over her.'

On June 24, she recorded Bach's Cantata 169 at a public concert in Gouda 'with a brilliant organist in a wonderful cathedral church. It was later broadcast in 1970 by the BBC, with permission of Netherlands Radio.'[158]

⋆

December 1969 was bitter-sweet. She travelled to Lisbon for two performances of Les Noces for the Portuguese radio, but she was 'broke in heart.' The intensive treatment she endured for lymphatic cancer had taken its toll. 'I had to sing these concerts because my voice could no longer sustain Das Lied Van Der Erde, which Bernard Haitink had asked me to deputise with him at the R.F.H [Royal Festival Hall] – the one work I longed to sing with him and was never able to sing again', she recalled. 'I was broken-hearted because I was unable to sing this glorious work anymore. I last sang the work at Covent Garden in June and July of 1966, the ballet version, with Nureyev dancing the first performance. He was so wonderful to me, as were all the dancers and [Hans] Swarowsky conducting (first met him in Rio de Janeiro). Les Noces is not my work, especially in comparison with Das Lied.'[159]

The decade had been hard on her: she kept treatments a secret and performed as much as her body allowed. Other, less spiritually strong people might have given up on such a demanding career, but not Norma. She carried on because she had so much more to give.

Chapter 10: Private Matters

At the beginning of 1970, Norma was only 42 years old but felt like she owned the body of an ailing pensioner. 'Swarowsky asked for me to sing Das Lied concerts in Vienna with the Vienna Philharmonic in the beautiful Musikverein hall, and again had to turn down another wonderful offer of this special work,' she said. 'Always fated with this Mahler work that I perhaps loved the most, and too much – the first Mahler I ever heard. I sang three memorable concerts of it (in Madrid in 1963, and a bad performance with Jascha Horenstein in London in 1964, then in 1966) but it was impossible – treatment took its toll.'[160] To the public and her contemporaries, nothing was wrong. Like Kathleen Ferrier, she kept everything private.

Ibbs & Tillet issued a publicity brochure promoting Norma's virtues: 'Possessing a voice of unusual beauty which developed at an early age, Norma Procter studied under Roy Henderson and Alec Redshaw and rapidly made a name for herself throughout Great Britain. Her first London appearance was at Southwark Cathedral when her success was so immediate that she was soon singing in all the principal music centres and appearing at the leading music festivals in this country. Her success in Great Britain was quickly noticed abroad and now she is constantly in demand for engagements in Scandinavia, Holland, Belgium, Germany, Austria, Switzerland, and Spain. Music festivals abroad at which she has appeared include Santander in 1957, Vienna in 1958 and Berlin in 1959. At the Aldeburgh Festivals of 1959 and 1960, Norma Procter appeared in the production of The Rape of Lucretia, and in January 1961 she made her debut at Covent Garden, singing the title role in Gluck's Orpheus. She was one of the soloists in Bach's St. John Passion at the 1961 Aldeburgh Festival. Apart from her many public appearances throughout Europe, she is well known for her frequent broadcasts, both in this country and in Holland and Germany. She has recorded in Switzerland and Germany, and among the records she has made in Great Britain for Decca are those of the Messiah and Elijah and Britten's Spring Symphony. Among the highlights of her career she treasures a memorable performance of the Mozart Requiem conducted by Bruno Walter.'

It is a successful roll call by anyone's account and ill health notwithstanding, Norma was not ready to give up – although she knew it might not be long before her hand was forced.

The Seventies began with that staple of the season, the Messiah at Grimsby Central Hall, one of her regular engagements with the Grimsby Philharmonic Society. She performed alongside Elizabeth Simon, Gerald English, John Holmes and Derek Garside, and the Manchester Mozart Orchestra. In April, she returned to Hull City Hall with the Phil and Hull Choral Union for Mass in B Minor Bach. This time, she performed alongside Hazel Holt, Wynford Evans, Donald Bell, Fay Campey, John Barrow, Michael Jeans and John Bimson, and the Manchester Mozart Orchestra. During the first half of the year, she recorded Delius's Mass of Life, travelled to Munich, Stockholm, Skovde, San Sebastian, Amsterdam, the Isle of Man, Holland, Paris, Dusseldorf and Zurich, and suffered from flu in June. 'Flu returned, and terrible worries with recording (top notes),' she wrote. 'Throat specialist advised not to sing.'[161] She ignored this advice and recorded for Deutsche Grammophon with Karl Richter. 'Beginning of the end with Karl,' she wrote. 'Terrible recording – hopeless!'[162]

Shortly before a much-needed break to Jersey at the end of July, Norma recorded Mahler's Symphony No.3 for the Unicorn record label with Jascha Horenstein. After the holiday, she travelled to La Comina for performances of Missa Solemnis and Beethoven's Choral 9th but she was poorly again: 'Gastric flu. Came back vomiting, and diarrhoea all way back on the plane.'[163] There was a 'magnificent'[164] Prom with Vaughan Williams on August 26, followed by autumn trips to Amsterdam, Lausanne, Rotterdam, Brussels, Antwerp, Paris and Barcelona, and a tour of Germany too.

Norma paired up with Bernard Haitink at the Royal Festival Hall on November 19 and 22 with the London Philharmonic Orchestra for performances of Mahler's Symphony No.3 in D Minor. The concert was mentioned in a biography written about Haitink, of whom Norma was very fond. 'It mentioned the critics' general acclaim of his great conducting and for him, it was one of his most memorable concerts. It was for me too. Everyone was totally overwhelmed,'[165] she said. The What Love Tells Me movement, she added, 'was always too much for me – try as I would, I could not stop the tears falling.' More trips to Germany followed. She was so busy that she had to remember small domestic details by writing them down in her diary. 'Wash hair,' she reminded herself, on December 6.

The first half of 1971 saw Norma travel to the familiar stomping grounds of Malmo, Vienna, Munich and Madrid. On June 29 and 30, she sang at the opening of Amsterdam's Concertgebouw, which is renowned for its superb acoustics. Norma replaced an alto singer who had fallen ill and rushed over from London with her passport in hand. July 23 saw her sing on the opening night of The Proms. On August 2, she performed in a Prom to celebrate Sir Arthur Bliss's 80th birthday. Sir Adrian Boult conducted the London Symphony Orchestra and the programme featured Things To Come, The Enchantress and Music For Strings.

'Walking on – green with fright inside! – but wearing a red gown – Sir Arthur [Bliss] insisted it must be very appropriately red!' she noted in her diary. 'This concert was a most memorable occasion with Sir Arthur there of course, and the work [The Enchantress] was given a great reception. Sir Arthur came on stage to receive well-deserved applause and he presented me with a lovely bouquet, and there was a party afterwards. Somehow the work didn't take off with the Press or with recording companies. He was very enthusiastic about the performance and sometime later when a friend approached him for me to record the work, he gave his blessing but was told it was already listed to be recorded by another nameless, very well-known mezzo later, when she had the time – but who, in fact, never made the recording. Such has been my bad luck with this wonderful scena; not even Kathleen [Ferrier], for whom it was written, was given the opportunity to record this work. I knew it was a winner.' Norma, ever one for adding to her vast archive, made friends with professional sound engineer W H Troutbeck, after he was recommended to her by the well-known conductor Edmund Rubbra. He spool-recorded many of her performances for the BBC, including The Enchantress concert.

Listening back to it, she heard a mistake. Writing to a friend, she exclaimed: 'To discover with horror my slight rearranged text mistake! Tho' totally unaware in the performance. By then I was away… with the fairies!? Or the Gods!? Don't know if you've ever seen the mighty score or text. Very interesting hearing the orchestral and vocal balance – oh so many changes I would now make, if I could. Sir Adrian, bless him, sat throughout the evening, having by then very painful bone problems. I could then and can now fully understand his painful plight.'

In later years, a record company declined the offer to transfer her cassette onto CD because the quality was too poor. It remained a sore point for Norma, who unsuccessfully tried other avenues. Unsurprisingly, recordings of The Enchantress were eventually made and are available today.

★

At the 1971 Proms, Norma sang Maher's Symphony No.3 on August 16 and Britten's Spring Symphony on August 19. By August 30, she was in Bern,

Switzerland, for a Brahms concert. 'I wanted to sing in English, but Max Rostal refused to let me and decided not to sing Sapphische Ode as rehearsed,' she wrote. 'Not an easy concert/atmosphere. Great surprise to find a v. distinguished face at front of the audience – Rudolph Kempe [the German conductor] and wife. Never seen or met before. We all had supper together after the concert.'[166]

A month later, she sang the Messiah in Strasbourg Cathedral under Karl Richter's baton. 'Fabulous cathedral!' said a delighted Norma. 'The largest – couldn't see the far back of the building.'[167] Then to Barcelona and Madrid, on stage at the Teatro Real for the International Music Festival. She kept a translation of an eloquent article from an uncredited local newspaper. 'We are so used to Norma Procter's art standing out among the soloists in numerous cantatas and oratorios that we could not imagine her in a specialisation as different as is that of a Lieder singer,' it read.

'It is in this facet that we have just admired her in the festival. The voice of Norma Procter, so extraordinarily abundant, of dramatic and demure timbre, with a tendency to meaningful bottom tones, we find is not at variance with romantic lyricism. Of course, the famous artist began her programme with five arias from the opera-cantata repertoire; three by Purcell and two by Handel, and where she was particularly convincing because of the perfection of their style, because of the sobriety of the virtuosity dominated by exemplary schooling. But it is also true that she knew how to acquire temperate and exquisitely ductile expression for the Four Serious Songs by Brahms and, above all, to translate in a particularly admirable form five very beautiful Lieders of Schumann, meaning that after the interpretation of these works, no one could say that Norma Procter was not an ideal singer for chamber concerts without the support of an orchestral background.

'In the rest of the programme, the concert confirmed her capacity to adapt herself to different styles. Four spirituals, admirably harmonised by Redshaw, were sung with expressive conviction, without the abandon that seems inherent in this type of music. We again found more open phrasing, although equally beautiful, in the three encores of English songs with which the artist responded to the lavish ovations.'

Not forgetting her local supporters, on November 13 she performed in Songs of the Sea for the Grimsby Philharmonic Society, at the town's Central Hall, in a programme which included the premiere of Robert Walker's Three Sea Songs, dedicated to Alec Redshaw and written with Norma and the Phil in mind. She performed with Robert Bateman and The Capriol Orchestra of London. A cutting from the Grimsby Evening Telegraph read: 'A young composer is fortunate if he has such an artist and such a choir to launch his work, but the benefits were by no means one-sided. Since Robert Walker is organist and master of the choristers at St. James's, Grimsby, and remembering that tag about prophets in their own country, let us waste no time in making it clear that this was real music. The ovation the composer received from the audience afterwards had been thoroughly well earned.'

And the engagements kept coming. 'Home,' she wrote in her diary of December 23, after concerts in Amsterdam and The Hague. 'Worn out!' The pattern of work was becoming familiar by now, and 1972 began with trips to Hanover, Frankfurt, Israel, Luxembourg, Amsterdam, Madrid, and Gothenburg. By March, she was complaining of a bad throat, which developed into laryngitis. 'No voice – terrible,'[168] she commented.

At the end of May she travelled to Aldeburgh to rehearse for a wine and song evening of Schubert. It was her first Aldeburgh concert for eight years. 'I knew it would be my last,' she noted in her archive, 'which it was.' By now, her relationship with Benjamin Britten had irreparably broken down. 'Rehearsal evening at Red House,' she wrote in her diary of June 1st. 'Terrible atmosphere with Ben.' And then, on June 21: 'Last Aldeburgh concert. Terrible atmosphere.'

Although Norma had somewhat repaired her relationship with Britten following the Abraham and Isaac disappointment, things never quite returned to harmony. Eventually, perhaps inevitably given Britten's famously hot-and-cold temperament, their friendship petered out, despite her close attachment to Pears. Not one to dwell, Norma jetted off to fulfil engagements in Grenada, Madrid, Munich, Rome and Dornstadt, as well as around the UK.

That year also saw her perform recitals with Vienna-born pianist Paul Hamburger.[169] Norma described him as 'very special' and 'a wonderful friend, a brilliant musician/accompanist.' Commenting, many years later, on a memorial concert held in his honour at the Guildhall School of Music and Drama, in correspondence to his family, Norma said: 'A lovely programme and so worthy of dear Paul and his wondrous talents, evoking many memories for the somewhat short time I was able to work with him. My only regret is that I did not make contact long before our recitals began together in 1972 when he was head/chief accompanist of the BBC Radio 3 recital programmes – and sadly, our last recital in 1975 – then finally a "prelude" LP recording of Brahms, Mahler and English ballads in 1976.

'I spent many memorable hours at the Netherhall (Gardens) flat with dear Clare and Paul. I rarely listen to my old recordings – the L plates never come off – only loom larger!! – but at that time I had my own engineer and so can listen to all Paul's magical accompaniments during our memorable session together. We always kept in touch and I wrote as always last Christmastide to Somerset, but hearing nothing, assumed he was making another rapturous return to Vienna – teaching masterclasses and passing on his remarkable talents.'

★

Norma spent 1973 in a similar way to the years that had gone before: travelling internationally and around Great Britain. She continued recording and judging singing contests, including the Franco Vinas Competition in Barcelona in November. In March 1974, she recorded Mahler's Kindertotenlieder with 'dear ole' Norman Del Mar. Years later, after finding a cassette of it, she recalled: 'It was made on his birthday – a live concert at the Cardiff BBC studios with the BBC Welsh Orchestra. I'd forgotten about it. It's very beautiful, but [they are] very moving songs to sing, and I've remembered since that I was feeling somewhat vulnerable emotionally that day.

'My mother was very ill, and I had other problems,[170] tho' fine during the performance. As the applause broke, through my very deep involvement with that amazing music and texts, as I took my curtain call, I was totally unable to control the tears streaming down my face! It was the first time it had happened to me with such uncontrollable feelings – goodness knows what the audience thought, the orchestra and everyone! I am ashamed to say it's happened again as I've re-lived it all, just listening. I especially loved the second song, where the children's eyes have now become stars, and, of course, the last song, and that peaceful, haunting, and lovely lullaby. Very difficult and demanding musically/vocally but glorious to try and sing/perform!'[171]

Easter 1974 saw Norma floored by grief at the early death of Jennifer Vyvyan. The soprano died aged 48, having, like Kathleen Ferrier, kept a health problem a secret from everyone but her husband and her diaries. Hers was a respiratory illness, a terrible development for a singer. But she never retired; she simply kept going until she was taken. Having both emerged from Roy Henderson's stable and performing together frequently, Norma and Jennifer's bond was close. 'My very dear Jennie, my special and closest singer and friend,' she wrote. 'Her eventual husband became my accountant. Very sadly she died. Her son, Jonathan, was just seven.'[172]

A day after Jennifer's funeral, Norma sang the Messiah with the Royal Choral Society. Jennifer should have been singing with her. One can only imagine how Norma felt, especially as her own health was worsening. In July, she went under the surgeon's knife once more – this time to have a benign lipoma the size of an orange removed from her left side, at St. Hugh's in Grimsby. Thankfully that same month also brought a wonderful surprise, when Norma was appointed an honorary member of the Royal Academy of

Music. She attended a ceremony on July 25 at Dukes Hall, presided by The Rt Hon The Lord Boyle of Handsworth, where guests enjoyed a tasty luncheon and musical performances. She said it was 'a proud and happy day in my career' and 'one of the loveliest surprises I have ever received.'[173] 'I was deeply touched that you should think and consider me a worthy fellow member of this great academy,' she told the gathered guests, reading from a script she wrote and later stored in her archive. 'Believe me, I shall always remember this day with humble gratitude.'

And the year also gave Norma one of her most treasured memories. She was privileged to sing Rule, Britannia! at the Last Night of the Proms, in her favourite London venue, the Royal Albert Hall.[174] She described her effort as 'humble.' 'Incredible,' she said, 'and as always, I look[ed] down on that sea/ocean of people in that beloved hall in total disbelief… how I was given the courage and strength to just walk out there, let alone try to sing! My Prom Angels did it – or was it another dream?!'[175]

★

Norma, with years of experience behind her, was eternally in demand. Unbeknown to anyone but her closest circle, bad health continued to plague her. That October, she was back in St. Hugh's, Grimsby. She had requested a hysterectomy but instead underwent dilation and curettage. 'It helped but affected singing latterly,'[176] she said. True to form, she continued singing, travelling to Madrid in November to perform Mahler's 3rd. At rehearsals, she wrote: 'Gerd Albrecht, Berlin Opera director, wonderful conductor and person. Wanted me to sing Erda in Wagner's Das Rheingold in Madrid but no, I said, sorry. Later on, the opportunity to sing the same part at Bayreuth. Opera just not me! Lovely Teresa Berganza came to congratulate me, and would I teach her the Mahler. What a humbling, shattering request. So amazed!'[177]

Time marched on, treading familiar ground and familiar venues. She sang The Dream of Gerontius at Lincoln Cathedral on June 28, 1975, a day after returning from engagements in Zurich. It was her last performance in the county of Lincolnshire. 'Psalm 119, verse 54 was on a plaque in the side chapel in the cathedral, where I waited throughout part one of Gerontius, in total terror and tiredness from previous concerts, and travelling from Zurich the previous day,' she recalled. 'Archdeacon Dudman quoted the psalm and verse for me whilst in the chapel.'[178]

Norma was very spiritual and had a particular affinity with angels. Her home was decorated with many angel ornaments, and the notelets she sent to friends often depicted angel designs. In later years, the frequency of references to angels increased and she would almost always sign off with an affectionate 'Angels Guard Thee'. She found great comfort in her faith and insisted that angels watched over her, putting her good fortune and luck down to their presence. It is apt, then, that she was an angel in Gerontius, and praised for her angelic singing.[179] After all, Norma believed her voice was a gift from God. It was there to be shared, and so she carried on singing for as long as her voice allowed.

*

In December 1976 Benjamin Britten died aged 63. His funeral was held at his beloved Aldeburgh. Gramaphone magazine published a tribute to him, written by John Culshaw from Decca, a label with which Norma recorded, among other works, Britten's Spring Symphony. 'He was only really at peace in Aldeburgh,' it read. 'The Red House really was peace: a large, rambling place secluded from the town, to which various extensions and conversions had been added to over the years. To be a weekend guest there was to relax completely. He loved good food, and the best food of all was at The Red House because it was fresh, like fish straight out of the sea with vegetables from the garden.'

Norma had experienced that hospitality many times. There are no notes in her archive on her thoughts of Britten's death, nor is his date of death recorded in her diary. One imagines it shocked Norma, despite their artistic differences. She was not yet at the time of life where one expects friends and peers to expire, but she had already experienced that sort of heartbreak in spades. In later years, she told how the news of colleagues dying made her feel melancholy, wistful for a past that could never occur again. But older age was a long way off, and despite her own ill health, Norma still had plenty to give.

The year ticked by into 1977 and here there is slight confusion in Norma's diaries. On January 8, she remarked on her last ever appearance in Grimsby [at this point, Grimsby was in the county of Humberside, not Lincolnshire]. The town's Philharmonic Society staged a gala performance of Messiah, and Norma sang with Elizabeth Harwood, Richard Lewis and Raimund Herincx. 'Never again!' she wrote in the diary entry. 'No one else knew but sitting on the Central Hall platform, I decided I couldn't and wouldn't go through such a prelude of anguish or sing in Grimsby again, and never did.' However, an entry in her diary on Saturday, January 14 the following year notes that she sang the Messiah in Grimsby. 'Terrible ordeal,' it says. 'Last time I sang in Grimsby. Mother very ill.'

Nonetheless, Grimsby remained forever important to her. She never moved away, or moved to a new house even, and was never drawn to London like her peers, preferring to escape to normality. Her archives for around this time mention little: she vomited just before a rehearsal in London on February 26 and was admitted to hospital the following day. In July, she attended a Royal Garden Party: 'Terrible! Bored stiff! Alone all the time.'[180]

Norma must have felt surrounded by illness. Her sister Audrey was unwell, and her friend from Jersey, Beryl Jordan, was admitted to hospital. Then her father died on September 28. John Procter had bowel cancer and had been treated at hospital in Grimsby. Her diary entry simply reads: 'Daddy died. Halle Cantata Academia rehearsal.' She cared for him very much but remembered keenly how he deserted the family and – being such a private person – how his public behaviour embarrassed them. She never turned him away, though, and although their relationship was strained, she loved him and nursed him during times of bad health.

Norma was not there when he died. He was cremated in Grimsby on October 3. 'Went alone,' she wrote. 'Sobbed m'heart out as they sang.'[181] His death was another huge blow for Norma, and there was yet more heartache to come. Just days after her father's passing, Alec Redshaw died. Her long-term accompanist, as well as mentor, supporter, and friend, was gone too.

Redshaw's career in music was prolific. After studying in London with Frank Moore, he started out as an accompanist and conductor of the Cleethorpes Festival Choir. Soon he became a sought-after teacher and conducted The Grimsby Choral Society. He was the Grimsby Philharmonic Society's choral director from 1934 until his death and conducted the Hull Choral Union from 1959 to 1974. Like Norma, he was a keen supporter of the Central Hall, Grimsby's premier concert venue, and remained loyal to the area despite travelling around the UK and Canada to adjudicate at music festivals. In 1962, he co-founded the Everyman Club of Great Grimsby, and managed The Redshaw Singers, formed after the end of the war. It is fair to say his contribution to local life equalled that of music.

Ironically, in the early years of their partnership, Norma wanted nothing to do with him. When she began weekly singing lessons in London with Roy Henderson, he demanded that she also studied musicianship and piano in Grimsby. He was long-term friends with Redshaw and recommended him, but Norma's reaction was along the lines of: 'Oh no! Anyone but Alec Redshaw!' She simply did not like him but as time went on, they made friends and performed together many times.[182] In later life, Norma kept a framed photograph of him in her music room. 'I studied musically with Alec, never vocally,' Norma explained. 'I always travelled to London to Roy Henderson for my vocal work, but Alec and myself had a great rapport musically and he used to accompany me. We worked very hard together indeed.

'His life was all music. He had very little time for hobbies. I first met him betwixt 18 and 20, and very strangely in a way, because I didn't particularly want to work with him. Because of not making my career base in London, Roy said, "Well you have to work with Alec Redshaw" and I said, "Oh, anyone but Alec Redshaw, please!" But we became very great friends and great colleagues. I owe a great deal to both profs, as I call them, as each were individuals – one with his musical background and the other for vocal training… finishing off, putting the finishing touches to a performance, song or whatever.'[183]

The talented musician died in a nursing home in Cleethorpes following an operation and short illness. The funeral was held at St. James's Church [now Grimsby Minster] on October 6, followed by a service at Grimsby Crematorium. Respected journalist Peter Chapman, writing in his Odd Man Out column in the Grimsby Evening Telegraph, said his loss was a 'profound shock'. 'One is suddenly faced with the realisation that there is just nobody to replace him,' he said. 'This is some measure of our good fortune in having had him among us for so long… a musician who "ought" to have left the neighbourhood 40 years ago if what had concerned him was his own career. Many young unknowns whom he invited to sing in Grimsby went on to become nationally and internationally famous – people like Kathleen Ferrier and Dame Janet Baker.

'But it was not only budding professionals he helped. One of his most amiable traits was to be seen in the real, active, and quite uncondescending support he would give to anyone or any society making a real contribution to music in the town. "This chap's doing some awfully good work," he once said in a muttered aside at a concert given by a small chapel choir under an amateur conductor. Many professional musicians would not have admitted its existence; Alec was there as a paying customer. He had his faults. He could be spiky and awkward to deal with, and he could hurt people's feelings. Much of this, however, was due to a sensitivity which was in itself so easily hurt that it had to defend itself. He was a kindly man of great abilities, and a very fine musician.'

Throughout her career, Norma repeatedly credited Alec Redshaw, alongside Roy Henderson, for her successes, expressing gratitude whenever she could. Life went on, she knew that, and one imagines she sang with Alec in mind at her concerts that winter.

★

The year 1978 flew by in a rush of concerts and recordings. She noted just one illness in her diary: a bout of flu in August, which was treated with antibiotics. The following year followed a similar pattern. Her diary of July 14 notes that she performed her last Dream of Gerontius – 25 years on from her first. It reads: 'Croydon. Terrible nerves! Fairfield Hall. Silver grey. Last Gerontius.' It was one of her favourite works to perform. Indeed, she was fortunate to have once made a private recording of a performance at Kings College, Cambridge, which she treasured. 'Wonderful acoustics,'[184] she noted. In later life, she fondly recalled once again the 'unique and memorable' Gerontius on June 19, 1954 in Aldeburgh Parish Church, with Norma singing the alto arias and Peter Pears as the Evangelist, and the Royal Marine Band, conducted by the great Col Vivian Dunn in the Marine Chapel at Deal. 'Incredible playing and atmosphere – but all brass instruments!' she said. 'I missed the strings and wondered what Elgar thought as he looked down upon us all?! An all-brass Gerontius was a new and unforgettable experience for me.'[185] She was now at a time in her life and career where there were very few new experiences left. She was showing no signs of slowing down, though, and the new decade soon arrived.

Chapter 11: David Cregeen

Sunday, February 10, 1980 was the last time Norma performed with Peter Pears. They sang at Paisley Abbey in the St. John Passion. 'Tho' 70 years plus, he was still in very fine voice – tho' I knew my vocal days were numbered,'[186] she said.

Her diary for 1980 reveals a quieter schedule. There are various recitals but significantly fewer in number. She met with her friend Bee in London and visited Brian and Francis at Sharrow Bay, the Lake District retreat so important to her.

In 1981 she met another person who became one of her close friends, the British sculptor David Cregeen. A Manxman, he was educated in England, Canada, and Scotland before going to the University of Edinburgh and Edinburgh College of Art, graduating in 1976 with a master's degree and a Master of Philosophy. He then moved to Florence where he completed his training as a sculptor at the Accademia di Bella Arte and the Scuola di Nudo. On his return to the UK he spent several years collaborating with London's leading contemporary dance company, Ballet Rambert. The work from that period formed the basis of his first solo exhibition.

An early commission of that time was to sculpt a posthumous portrait head of Wing Commander Guy Gibson of the 617 RAF Squadron, The Dambusters. Gibson was shot down over Holland and the commission was from the former members of the Dutch Resistance as an expression and symbol of their profound gratitude for the part played by the RAF in the liberation of Holland. It was presented to members of the 617 Squadron Association by the mayor of Rotterdam at a ceremony in the city in 1980.

In 1982 Cregeen was awarded the Grollo d'Oro in Treviso, Venice, in 1982 for his sculpture The Chosen Maiden, inspired by Rambert's revival of the ballet The Rite of Spring. In 1983 he took part in an exhibition in New York entitled Britain Salutes New York where he was introduced to the curator of Dr. Arthur M. Sackler's collections, Lois Katz, and then to Dr.

Sackler, whose remarkable collections were at the time being shown in the Edinburgh Festival over a number of years. Dr. Sackler commissioned him to sculpt a portrait of his wife Jillian and then himself, following which he invited Cregeen to undertake the prestigious commission which Dr. Sackler named Faces In History, which was to sculpt twenty of the world's most outstanding people drawn from differing walks of life. Dr. Sackler died in 1986, within a year of launching the project. However, it was continued by his widow, through one of the foundations her husband had established, and Faces In History has since remained an on-going feature of Cregeen's professional life.

Some of the portrait heads sculpted from life for the project were taken from the world of political and religious leadership, and have included Queen Elizabeth II as Head of The Commonwealth, Pope John-Paul II, President Nelson Mandela, President Mikhail Gorbachev, the Dalai Lama, and Margaret Thatcher, Baroness. From the world of science and the arts are the double Nobel Laureate Professor Linus Pauling, Professor Stephen Hawking, and Sir John Gielgud.

Dr. Sackler was an American psychiatrist, art collector, philanthropist, and benefactor to many museums, among which, with his wife, he endowed the Arthur and Jillian Sackler Gallery at the Royal Academy of Arts in London. Cregeen sculpted Dr. Sackler's portrait head in 1983, undertaken one year after he completed his portrait of Norma. The first of the edition of the larger-than-life bronze is at the National Portrait Gallery in Washington DC. In her catalogue to a retrospective exhibition of Cregeen's work in New York, Lois Katz described this portrait head: 'The finished portrait reflects Sackler's intensity, his intelligence and his vision.... Cregeen has captured the liveliness and complexity of Sackler's personality. Determination and scholarly intensity are expressed by the thrust of the chin and the high forehead. But it is the eyes that reflect the man in life, they look into the future and sparkle with the pleasure of its challenge.' Norma's copy of the catalogue, which was entitled David Cregeen: A Retrospective Exhibition, is annotated with her pencilled comments.

In 1985, Dr. and Mrs Sackler, alongside Norma and others, became patrons to the London exhibition and UK tour of Humanism In Contemporary British Sculpture, in which Cregeen took part.

In an interesting musical link, the sculptor's maternal grandmother's first cousin was the composer Herbert Howells, with whom Norma worked at the Three Choirs Festival in Gloucester Cathedral. And there was another coincidental link, with Kathleen Ferrier. Cregeen's father loved her recordings, and regularly played them in the home when David was a child living in Canada.

'I remember speaking to Norma about Herbert Howells and telling her the story of how as a young teenager and already seen as having remarkable musical ability, he was seated next to Ralph Vaughn Williams in a performance of The Dream of Gerontius at Gloucester Cathedral,' said David. 'Apparently the boy was so clearly moved by the music that Williams shared his score with him and became his mentor. I spoke of my own love of that particular oratorio and learned that it was also one of Norma's.

'She considered Howells's finest work to be Hymnus Paradisi. I told her that I understood from my great uncle (my grandmother's brother) that he wrote it while staying with his and their cousin on a Howells family farm in the Wye Valley, where I and my family later stayed regularly during my childhood before we moved to Canada. The farmhouse dated back several hundred years – very beautiful and still belonging and run by those cousins.'

Both Norma and David participated in the Mannanan Festival on the Isle of Mann in 1981. Norma's diary entry for June 27 reads: 'Isle of Man Messiah. Rehearsal 11am. Met David Cregeen, sculptor, who asked to sculpt my head!!'

'I was sitting in the front row and was completely captured and inspired by her – the combination of her voice and her expression as she sang,' David recalled. 'I was seated next to the theologian Father Harry Williams, who regularly came to the festival. He was tutor to the Prince of Wales when he was at Cambridge University. I turned to him at the end and said, "That was really amazing. What a head! I would love to sculpt her." "Then let me introduce you," he replied, and we went into the vestry where, having introduced me, he said to Norma, "And David wants to sculpt you". After some words together, she said, "Alright, we'll organise it" and we did. That combination of facial expression and the voice has always been a very powerful inspiration for me.

'Norma's exceptionally warm character as I experienced her was something very special. What's also interesting is that she told me later that she had been very conscious of the intensity of my gaze on her at the time, during the performance. Even now it's unforgettable, with the depth of feeling and particular resonance in her voice as she sang, especially the lines in He Was Despised. I can hear her now. I tried to convey that in my portrait head of her. It was the last night of the festival, one of her last formal concerts, and my first major solo exhibition.'

The next time he saw Norma was March 7, 1982, when she sat for him.

'I was living and working near Islington where I had my studio,' he said. 'When the taxi drew up, the driver who brought Norma turned around in his seat and asked if she was sure it was the correct address, no doubt because the exterior of the building looked rather dilapidated. He apparently said to her, "Will you be alright madam?"

'We often laughed recollecting that comment. My studio was on the third floor of the building and when I say it was dilapidated it certainly was, but I was sharing it with good and interesting people.'

This first sitting lasted about an hour and a half, during which David began work on the head immediately, using clay and an armature (the framework for the sculpture).

'Norma was very perceptive and commented on how, like a singer, a sculptor uses the whole of the body while working. Although I hadn't really registered this, I realised it is of course true that one works from the toes up, with all the energy going into the shoulders. Speaking of movement there are, for me, strong parallels between the movement within a sculpture and the movement of music. We discussed how, as with the conversation within music, so too there is that internal conversation within sculpture, only in a different form.

'Artistically, in the creative act, one draws on a different side of the brain and one's feelings and experiences. Before each performance Norma explained to me how she would prepare through quiet contemplation. Similarly, before a sitting I prepare myself psychologically and, of course, in the work I become wholly absorbed to the extent that, on one occasion, amusingly, I was working on a large sculpture of the whole figure and with a live model who was posing in the nude. It was a particularly hot day and I had to keep spraying the clay to keep it malleable. I was so absorbed that I confused the person modelling with the sculpture and to her surprise I started to spray her instead of the clay figure.'

Norma visited the studio for a second sitting on April 18. It was a busy time for Cregeen. He had other projects to complete, and he was also restoring a former church hall into both a residence and a studio. He took Norma to see the building as it was being completed.

'It was in Waterloo behind the OXO Tower, in Roupell Street,' he said. 'We had a final sitting there and I can still see her making her way very carefully down the stairs from the 'maisonine' floor that I had built. She had difficulty coming down them and it was the first time I realised she had this difficulty in walking as a consequence of an earlier illness and, as she explained, one she'd had to manage throughout her professional life.'

David having made the first cast, Norma asked for a second, which she gave to her friends Brian and Francis, at Sharrow Bay.

'We did the work over quite a long period of time, and with a number of sittings when she was in London,' said David. 'She was very interested in the work and paid a lot of attention while I was doing it, as in fact did the Queen Mother whom I was to sculpt some years later. That was a commission from Middle Temple where she was an Honorary Bencher, a position she particularly enjoyed. It was to commemorate her 90th birthday.

'Through the world of music, Norma's professional friendship with Benjamin Britten and Peter Pears, and the Aldeburgh Festival, she met the Queen Mother on a number of occasions. The Queen Mother's very close great friend was Ruth, Lady Fermoy, who started the King's Lynn Festival. Lady Fermoy was also a close friend of the Countess of Harewood, later Marion Thorpe.'

Norma and David spoke a great deal about the music profession, including Norma's great fondness for Bernard Haitink and Yehudi Menuhin. Norma is mentioned in a book by Simon Mundy on Haitink, and she annotated her personal copy, marking passages about concerts in which she performed. She and Menuhin had a lot in common, especially their shared emotional and warm personalities.

David spoke of how he met Menuhin. 'It was in connection with a proposal which Menuhin endorsed for me to create larger-than-life posthumous portrait heads of the two assassinated leaders of Egypt and Israel, Anwar Sadat and Yitzhak Rabin, to be placed together as a contribution to the peace process in the Middle East. Following our discussion concerning this proposal and my work, I made some drawings of him and from these I went on to create a portrait head of him for Faces In History. This meeting at his London home was only two or three months before he died. About a month after that meeting, we met by chance outside Peter Jones in Sloane Square. We had a short chat and he explained that he'd gone there to buy a Valentine's present for his wife.

'Norma loved my head of her. Through those sittings we would cover a lot of ground as we talked, both personal and professional. I prefer my sitter to talk. It helps with understanding character, but it was particularly special in Norma's case as it laid the ground for that very close friendship which was to last for the rest of her life. We always kept in close contact, usually by telephone. As with any sensitive artist she could feel what other people felt and thought, including, of course, in the voice. In her case this was both in her character and in her training.

'I remember explaining to her that when I started sculpture and was working with my hands in the clay, it felt like I'd come home. She told me how it had been the same with her singing. The depth of experience from her professional life was so interesting to hear. When I first met her, I was struck by the presence she conveyed while at the same time there was something so human and unpretentious.'

In early 1984 arrangements were being made for the exhibition Humanism In Contemporary British Sculpture, which was to take place at the Royal Festival Hall in London. Cregeen was one of the five sculptors taking part and he asked Norma if she would be one of a small group of patrons. She agreed. A member of the organising committee, Raymond Lokker, wrote to thank her, and when David asked her if she might like to suggest others to give their support to the project she became actively engaged, writing to her friend and musical associate Marion Thorpe, who was by then the wife of the former Liberal party leader Jeremy Thorpe. At Marion's suggestion, she wrote to Peter Pears. The final list was Princess Margareta of Romania as the Principle Patron, Sir Peter Pears, Lady Trehane, the Rt Hon Jeremy Thorpe, Mrs Marion Thorpe, Norma, and, through David's work in New York, Dr. and Mrs Sackler, Mrs Theodate Johnson Severns, the sister of the leading American architect Philip Johnson, and film producer John Roche.

Norma kept a copy of the letter she wrote to Marion. As the daughter of the leading musicologist Erwin Stein (a pupil and later the great authority on Arnold Schoenburgh), Marion herself had an early professional life as a concert pianist. Benjamin Britten was a close family friend and neighbour of the Steins in London when Marion was a teenager, and Britten's early musical career was steered by her father. Marion later became a co-founder of the Leeds Piano Competition and was closely involved with the Aldeburgh Festival. Through Britten, Norma became a close friend of Marion and was a frequent visitor to Harewood House. She correctly realised that Marion would respond warmly to David, and she and her husband subsequently became friends. They stayed with David on several occasions at his home and studio on the southern coast of Turkey in the antique city of Side, a place where Menuhin had also visited some years earlier.

Norma's initial letter to Marion about the exhibition read: 'We all feel we would love to have such talented people as you both are, especially artistically, to share in this project.' The impassioned plea to the couple worked and on Marion's recommendation, Norma wrote to Peter Pears: 'A fine young sculptor friend of mine and his friend are arranging an exhibition… we so wanted Marion and Jeremy to be patrons and are over the moon that they have accepted. Marion ended her letter with 'Perhaps Peter should be a patron too?' It had occurred to me, but I didn't want to trouble you. However, we should love to have you share in this project. Think about it… here's hoping the answer will be yes!'

It was, and Norma's bronze portrait head was shown along with other work in Humanism In Contemporary British Sculpture. The exhibition was sponsored by the Greater London Council in association with The Save The Children Fund UK and was opened at London's Royal Festival Hall by The Rt Hon Jeremy Thorpe on April 24, 1985, prior to a UK tour.

'A year after my finishing my portrait head of her, I started travelling to New York,' David recalled, 'but through that whole period we kept closely in touch through cards and telephone conversations.'

David cites the Scottish portrait painter Beatrice Huntington as one of his greatest professional influences. She was also the wife of the Scottish colourist William MacDonald; Spanish MacDonald, as he was called.

'In 1906 at the age of sixteen,' he said, 'her parents very unusually arranged for her to go to Paris to study in the studios there. Later she went to Munich, returning to London at the outbreak of the First World War. Her circle of friends in London included John Ireland and Ethel Walker. She had a long life and a distinguished career, spending much time in France. She died one week before her 100th birthday when still painting. We met in Edinburgh where she and Mac, her husband, had made their home since 1928, the same year that she was 'hung in the centre and on the line' in 1928 at the Paris International; the last year that Degas was its president. He complimented her on her portrait painting, Mrs Mappin. Beatrice and I knew each other for well for over twenty years. She was a constant inspiration to me, both as a person and in her work.'

'Both dear Beatrice and Dr. Sackler must be so proud of you,' Norma told David in a letter in May 2009. 'Their belief and foresight they felt and saw in you, both as a person and your magical talents. Faces In History is now to conclude with the new USA president, Obama – another worldwide achievement… amazing! Heartiest congratulations and may you be blessed with good health and strength to continue your earthly pilgrimage of beautiful and unique artistry in sculpture, especially heads – a lasting tribute to so many rare and wonderful people who have helped to make and fill this troubled world with faith, hope and charity.'

★

In a 2014 catalogue for David Cregeen: His Work by Lois Katz, Norma is especially mentioned. It reads: 'Early in his career Cregeen met one of this country's leading contraltos of the past fifty years, Norma Procter, when both were taking part in The Mannanan Festival of The Arts in the Isle of Man. Well-known through the great concert halls of Europe for her rendition of oratorios under the leading conductors of the day and on the stage for her beautiful interpretation of Gluck's Orfeo. Cregeen stresses her features and strong presence as reminders of her remarkable vocal authority and purity of line.'

An elderly friend of David's, who was helping with the material for this latest publication, went onto correspond with Norma. He wrote asking her to sign a programme from a 1971 Prom Norma sang in and said: 'It is wonderful to be in touch with you in this way! You must have been asked for your autograph countless times, but perhaps not almost 40 years after the event and by a nonagenarian (I am 94). For all that, it might have been yesterday because of your singing.'[187]

Norma replied: 'What a wonderful surprise… literally enclosing that beloved programme of the Mahler 3 Prom! My heartfelt thanks and almost disbelief that you still have that actual programme of 40 years ago! I'm amazed that anyone remembers, especially when I read your remarkable age – 94! I am now 81! I so loved making Mahler's deeply moving and magical music with Bernard Haitink and have many special memories. He was very humble, deeply intuitive, and spiritual – soul to soul – but with a Mahler twinkle when needed. Now – so very important – I must especially praise the wonderful new catalogue. I was greatly surprised and deeply touched that this ole gal was humbly included – thank you for your generous words.

'David and I go back a long way – to a Messiah performance in the beautiful church in the Isle of Man when afterwards in the vestry, I was astounded he asked if he could create my head! In fact, so shattered that I just very rudely laughed in total disbelief. For his sins, he then moved to London and he began one of his most difficult creations (!!) at his studio, then in Roupell Street. We have remained on special artistic wavelengths of love and understanding ever since.'[188]

The bond between Norma and David remained strong. In a handwritten dedication in the front of a catalogue for an exhibition, David wrote: 'To Dearest Norma… someone whose voice is a constant inspiration – I shall never forget the wonder of seeing and hearing on the Isle of Man in 1981.' In pencil, Norma added later, comically: '20 yrs ago!! Help!!!' They corresponded as frequently as possible, David often writing from his studio in Turkey. 'I have a recording of the Coronation Mass (Deutsche Grammophone) with you on it,' he said in a letter dated December 1987. 'I play it so often here in Turkey and think of that first meeting. In your performances you brought a touch of the divine into people's lives and with your recordings, you still do. No one's voice moves me so very profoundly as yours does.'

In later years, a decline in Norma's mobility meant she could not attend events as she once used to. David invited her to an exhibition in July 2006. 'Sadly, my mobility problems make it impossible to be there, but my spirit will be floating for sure,' she told him. 'I purposely haven't been in touch knowing how busy you've been. In your last letter, you'd had the first sitting with Camilla [Duchess of Cornwall]. All went well as the head is included in your view list for July. So sorry not to be there but hope you have a wonderful and memorable evening.'[189]

⋆

Was David Cregeen – an artist of high profile in his own right – ever fazed by the equally high status of some of his sitters? No. For him, it was always a question of the work and doing his best.

'Certainly, it felt like an honour, requiring all the abilities I had,' he said, 'but I was never really fazed. There were certain moments when I would be particularly conscious of who my sitter was but the challenge that any serious artist must feel is always the work and to do it to the best of one's ability.'

'Amazed at including ole Norm in such a distinguished army of worldly notables,'[190] Norma once wrote, of being in his stable. And as for David, the feeling is mutual.

'I have a huge debt to Norma,' he said. 'At the beginning of one's career, to meet somebody of that calibre and who is so unpretentious with that, but professional, is priceless. She was all those things for me from the moment we met, and I learned a great deal from her. She had an aura of both elegance and professionalism. It was wonderful to study her. Her personality was so forceful, very intense. I think that's why she had such an extraordinary voice, because it came from the depths of her being. She absolutely felt what she was singing. And here's another parallel with my working on a sculpture: which is that until I feel it within me, it's not done. Norma didn't suffer fools gladly, and her self-discipline was phenomenal. That's something that really struck me when I was working with Ballet Rambert, too, which I also spoke with Norma about.

'Her voice was truly remarkable, and a very English voice if you see what I mean. She was – is – the antithesis of the materialistic world and celebrity culture, a very rare person. Some people at her level, of her status, assume a certain grandness. But she was so utterly human in the best sense of the word. Her life was about her art, and she commanded that with a deep spiritual conviction which was really very wonderful to meet.

'She very kindly left her edition of my head of her to me and it has been sitting near my computer these last few months. The second caste which she gave to her friends at Sharrow Bay is now also with me. It has a lightly different patination and is tilted forward slightly, as though she is about to speak. I plan to give one of the heads for permanent display to a suitable location.'

★

From his principal studio and home in southern Turkey, David Cregeen works and exhibits internationally, particularly in New York and London.

He has received correspondence from figures in the musical world about Norma, including Jonathan Groves, the son of the conductor Sir Charles

Groves. 'The major years of his [Sir Charles] career, from the 1950s to the 1980s, happened to coincide with when the great Norma Procter was in her prime, and I can attest that she was one of my father's favourite singers,' he wrote. 'The oratorio repertoire featured very strongly in Sir Charles's programme planning and I can well remember the countless occasions when Norma worked with him in this context – he could always rely on her to give the finest possible performance. He was also a passionate advocate of the music of Gustav Mahler, before his music enjoyed the popularity it enjoys today (indeed, he was the first conductor to conduct a complete cycle of the Mahler symphonies), and Norma was always his first choice for those works of Mahler (especially the second, third, and eighth symphonies) that call for a contralto soloist.'

The English baritone Graham Trew, MVO, declared: 'Norma Procter possessed one of the finest voices of her generation and was the first choice of conductors such as Sir Malcolm Sargent and composers including Benjamin Britten, who wrote parts specifically for her voice. Norma Procter's recordings of the Spring Symphony by Britten and the Messiah by Handel remain definitive.'

And Roger White, CBE, chief executive of Aldeburgh Music, said: 'Norma Procter was invited to perform at the festival regularly in the 1950s and 1960s by our founder, Benjamin Britten, who wrote parts specifically for her. She was considered to be one of the foremost contraltos following the Second World War. Following her retirement from public performances, she continued to dedicate her time to helping the next generations of singers through her teaching and adjudication.'

There is no doubt, said David Cregeen, that Norma's voice is one of the great English voices of the 20th century. 'She was a person of integrity,' he said. 'I was fortunate to have met her at a time when I was new to my career and she was a great support. She was a deeply spiritual woman and that is still there for us to experience in her recordings – as it was for me when I heard her first heard her at the cathedral in Douglas in 1981.'

Chapter 12: Last Performance

Meeting David Cregeen was, in Norma's mind, another example of fate bringing her a special friend, and her circle provided much comfort when her mother fell ill and died. According to Norma's diaries, Edith became very poorly on May 9, 1982.

There is a gap until June 8, when Norma comments simply: 'No sleep.' Then, on June 13: 'Mother so v. ill.' Although Norma travelled the world and was away for long periods, she was never once tempted to move from Grimsby, and she was devoted to her mother, 'who was my greatest encouragement and support throughout my career.'[191] 'I was very fortunate in having a wonderful mother who was always there to encourage and understand when many times I faltered. I owe everything to her,' she said.

'I know well the scary feeling of no work for a while. When I began, there were no summer festivals or concerts except for Glyndebourne Chorus and one usually had nothing from May until September or October. My mother used to "keep me", so to speak, and then I'd pay her back when the season began again. I loved to spend!'[192] In truth, they were devoted to each other equally, so it was without hesitation or question that Norma nursed Edith in her final days. By now, Edith was living downstairs at Nor-Dree. She had renal problems and a malformed right knee due to arthritis. 'Worn out!' Norma commented, in her diary of June 15. Edith died of renal failure two days later, at 3am. 'Sat alone with her,' Norma said. 'Shattering experience.'[193]

★

In 1983, Norma made a rare non-singing appearance on camera, as a guest on Yorkshire Televisions' Calendar Tuesday. Presented by Richard Whiteley, it focused on The Great Grimsby Competition for Singers, for which Norma was a juror. The week-long triennial event was established by Norma's friend and accompanist, the well-known pianist Anne Holmes, in memory of the late Alec Redshaw.

'It is a very happy occasion,' Anne told the programme. 'It was a dream to tie the three great loves of Alec's life together rather than have a static memorial. His great loves were adjudicating, young singers and the choir he conducted for 40 years, the Grimsby Philharmonic Society. The dream grew from that – to have a competition for young singers; not one that brought forward just one voice, but all voices. This we did in 1980 and it was such a wonderful, happy, festive feeling that we just had to go on. Alec was very much the driving force of a lot of music that went on in Grimsby. He was active almost to the time of his death. I didn't think it would be any more than perhaps just a one-off. Last time we had a Canadian singer and also an Australian. This year we've got people who've come over from America, New Zealand, Canada, and Australia to sing, so it really is quite tremendous, and I just hope that Alec knows.'

Norma said: 'It's a wonderful idea and I hope that it goes on for a very long time. I hope the competitors realise how fortunate they are to have such a competition and so many opportunities, not only just the prize money but the offers of engagements which is so necessary for a young student, penny-wise, and a chance to literally perform because that's the only way you learn – in performance. We had nothing of this ilk – only just the ordinary competitive festivals. The prizes were a medal, or perhaps just a certificate. Even for those who don't reach the very top four, people are listening and thinking about trying them out. If they don't sing from their heart, then don't bother to sing. This is my feeling. The audience must make contact; the singer must take them way up on cloud nine if it's possible to elate them and make them feel when they leave the concert –"gosh I feel so good, I felt rotten when I came in but by Jove that's done something for me, and that particular singer has done so-and-so for me" – and that's what it's all about.

'It's very tough to begin and make your first move and get into the swim of finding societies who are willing to take on a new, unknown singer. I literally had to go around all the small societies and tiny halls. This [competition] is a wonderful experience because it takes time. You can't go straight up there because you won't stay there otherwise. You need time and experience. Many times, I would go home and burst into tears… still do! My career now is beginning to ebb, shall we say, but there was a time when I had to be booked two or three years in advance. It can be very tiring and also very lonely. You need tremendous stamina and before that, good health. Those are the two main factors. People think it's just a question of opening your mouth, you sing, the sound comes out and there's nothing else to it. There's so much more before that. All the travelling, working, and practising. Really, the last thing you do is sing, by which time you're nearly too tired to be bothered!'

Jury chairman Noel Cox, warden of the Royal College of Music, said: 'I married a fellow student at the Royal Academy who came from Cleethorpes and who in fact was distantly related to Alec, so I've known him as long as Norma has. I've always admired his musicality and the things he did for music in the area. I've adjudicated with Alec in many places; he was a marvellous judge of musicians and would put his finger on the spot, as we say. Alec taught me a lot in the early stages, and one tries to profit from that experience.'

Singing for a living can be gruelling on the body, mind, and spirit. It was around this time that Norma made a conscious decision to slow down; not quite retire, but not take on so much. It was 'a mortal and emotional blow, but one knew it was time to stop,'[194] she said. Instead, she channelled her passion and energy into emerging generations of singers. She gave masterclasses and on August 17, 1984, became a teacher – with Anne Holmes – tutoring private students at Nor-Dree. One thing was certain: she did not miss living out of a suitcase. She was 'basically a very private and shy person, never more than now,' she wrote, 'not at all ambitious and the so-called fame and limelight not my forte, but only the glorious music and its message. [I am] so humbly grateful I was allowed to share such special memories and occasions.'[195]

It was also time for her to enjoy a little freedom. She loved watching Wimbledon and golf on the television, sketching and painting, listening to classical music on the radio and corresponding with friends and acquaintances. She may have slowed down professionally, but her personal standards never slipped: as elegantly dressed as ever, her polished nails were perfect and make-up immaculate, even for her regular trip to Tesco, where she'd secretly burst with pride when shoppers stopped her to reminisce about her career.

Norma was lucky – she had so many special memories. She was thrilled to discover a photograph of herself and Yehudi Menuhin from 1978 in the book The Music of Man, authored by Menuhin and Curtis W Davis. The photograph shows Norma singing the Bach aria Erbarme Dich Mein Gott in the parish church at Saanen, Switzerland, where the Yehudi Menuhin Festival had been held since 1956. In a note in her archive, she recalled: 'I was singing to the most memorable and beautiful violin obligato of my favourite aria from this work. I was suffering from a bad flu virus, tho' said nothing, but had Yehudi's love and support. It was a once-in-a-lifetime experience.' She was very fond of Menuhin. The last time she ever performed the St. Matthew Passion by Bach was with him. 'Bach was indeed blessed when he wrote that glorious and deeply moving work,' she said. 'Listen especially to the contralto aria and orchestral leader violin in the most beautiful aria ever written, Have

Mercy Lord – Peter's outpouring of grief and guilt after denying his Lord. It always moved me to tears.'[196]

★

Norma continued singing publicly, though infrequently. She became a participant in BBC listening panels, giving her opinions on output by the broadcaster. That, alongside teaching and judging, more than occupied her time, and she fitted in treasured trips to Sharrow Bay and Jersey, as well as to London in April 1985 to attend an exhibition of David Cregeen's. Not long after that trip, she came down with a flu attack. Then, in May, she travelled to Jersey to visit Bee and her new husband Jack. 'Dizziness began,' she wrote. 'St. Helier's seafood lunch with Bee and Jack. Very ill.' Then: 'Upset stomach. Bug in the village.'[197] Her much welcomed holiday was ruined by ill health, and on her return was diagnosed with vertigo. She was also at the time of life where the menopause was making her feel unwell. She was prescribed tablets, but the dizziness and nausea refused to go away. On June 10, she was diagnosed with Meniere's disease.

Once again, Norma faced the prospect of having to work while feeling dreadful. She sang in Dudley on July 6: 'Hardly knew how to sing. Giddy and terrible pains in stomach and back.' On the return train home, she was so uncomfortable she couldn't sit properly. Thankfully her ever-faithful brother-in-law, Norman, collected her in the car from Doncaster station. She adored Norman, an RAF man and county tennis player who was always there to help Norma, no matter what time of day or night. She paid privately for a course of physio for her neck, shoulders and back but it was useless. The pain only got worse.

On July 14, she was hurriedly admitted to St. Hugh's Hospital 'for a grim and complete hysterectomy, followed by terrible hormonal problems – back ache and lower spine, and across hysto scar and lower front abdomen. Hot water bottle my greatest comfort and ever since. I've never known such depression and aggression – I'm unable to recognise m'self. Back pain worse since hysterectomy.'[198] She convalesced at Audrey and Norman's house. 'Hellish days!' she exclaimed in her diary of August 5. 'Painful, lonely and fed-up! No energy.' The pain continued into the autumn and winter, and she recorded her feelings in her diary:

October 28: *'What is wrong with me? Feel like hell.'*

November 4: *'Terrible depressions. Don't know how to battle on. Never felt so alone and ill.'*

November 18: *'No improvement. Always weeping. Battling. Feel ghastly suicidal.'*

November 25: *'Hellish depression and desperate. I can't keep battling. So alone. Feel so ill.'*

December 2: *'Don't know how to keep going.'*

December 9: *'Stomach giving me hell.'*

December 20: *'Terrible stomach pains. Stopped all food. Onto milk diet.'*

December 24: *'All Christmas in bed. Terrible stomach pains. Spent alone.'*

★

In April 1986, Peter Pears died aged 75 and was buried next to Benjamin Britten at Aldeburgh's parish church. 'Peter was a very special singer and person,' Norma recalled. 'I always loved being and singing with him. I have many lovely memories.'[199] Another unmistakable voice from Norma's generation of singers was gone. She had so much respect for Peter; he introduced her to Mahler as a teenager, when she heard him sing Das Lied von der Erde with Kathleen Ferrier on the radio in 1947 at the Edinburgh Festival. 'Mahler became and is one of my most loved composers,'[200] she commented. How wonderful she must have thought it, all these years later, to have made Mahler something of a specialism. Throughout her career she recorded Mahler's works with an alto part, including the first ever complete version of Das Klagende Lied.[201] 'He really is an incredible composer with the deepest possible intuitive and emotional heart and soul,'[202] she said.

A few short months later, Norma gave her last ever public performance. It took place in Leatherhead, on September 27. 'Terrible evening,' she wrote. 'Glad to come home and to stop singing.'[203] She launched herself straight into judging the Grimsby Singers competition but felt ill throughout the entire week. By November, she was back in hospital. An endoscopy revealed fifteen polyps in her stomach and bowel. 'After a barium enema, they showed me x-rays and pointed out arthritic signs in lower spine, which I was already aware of, possibly from carrying luggage and lifting my mother, whom I cared for at home,'[204] she said.

Stoic Norma braved more 'ghastly' examinations and had the polyps removed on December 4: 'Terrible night on ward. No private beds. Ghastly old hospital tho' a private patient.' February 1987 saw her undergo a colonoscopy. 'Sheer hell!' she said. 'New equipment. Completely out of control and unable to bear the pain. Swore no one would ever do that to me again.'[205] Unfortunately, she had to have another, but that time it was thankfully under general anaesthetic. A third colonoscopy followed in February 1988. Her diaries and notes are unclear as to what the complaint was here, but in March she wrote: 'Refused to go to London hospital and another colonoscopy without a general. A very frank talk after such previous hell. Three years before next session.'

The year continued with more masterclasses and private tutoring. In October, she contributed to Klever Kaff, a BBC radio programme about Ferrier, hosted by Brian Kay. Naturally, it brought back memories. In correspondence with a magazine journalist writing about Ferrier, Norma vented her feelings about modern musicianship: 'When Kath was alive, there were very few mezzos, and those mostly connected with opera, and we contraltos sang many more religious, scared and spiritual works then as soloists or chorally. Now opera has literally taken over – opera schools, colleges, academies etc. Teachers put opera to the fore and train natural contraltos into mezzos for opera, and often against the natural low vocal cords. Watch the wobblers – mouth, tongue, lips! And we haven't mentioned breathing or breath control. Opera was not Kath's first love – the same for me – she had a rough time at Glyndebourne's first Lucretia. A voice will change if it's being pushed unnaturally out of its bounds.' She added: 'I am sadly constantly asking, "Where have all the contraltos gone???" We're fated, altos, m'thinks!'[206]

It was a justifiable gripe. Corresponding with a friend, later, she confessed: 'Very glad I came into the profession when I did – wouldn't be much point now. Contraltos verboten![207] It makes me very sad. I have nothing against mezzos etc but Bach, Handel, Mahler and all the glorious composers wrote for that special tone/colour. Vast changes and not for the better – so many people complain to me.'[208]

Chapter 13: Alexander

Time marched on and in 1990 she met another of her 'specials.' On Saturday, May 19 she climbed behind the wheel of her beloved Mini and made the short journey to Lincoln, where she was hosting a masterclass. In entered Alexander Anderson-Hall, late and in a rush of noise. Norma's eyes glinted as she appraised him for several seconds. Alexander was mortified. The masterclass was an opportunity he badly wanted, and he was anxious that he'd upset Norma before even meeting her. He need not have worried.

'In my early 20s, I was a pop singer in a band,' he said. 'I was encouraged to enter the Lincoln Music and Drama Festival. I entered a lot of classes and was fortunate to win almost all of them. It was quite something because I'd never won anything in my life! One of the prizes was a masterclass with Norma Procter. This was in 1989. I hadn't heard of her because I was new to that musical world, so bought some CDs and did some research. We were due to begin the masterclass in a Methodist church at 10.30am. The night before, I was performing with the band in Edinburgh and the gig didn't finish until 3am. I drove back to Lincoln through the night – there was no time to sleep – and abandoned my car in an alleyway behind the church. A meet-and-greet with Norma had already taken place with the other students and as I walked in, Norma's back was towards me. I was absolutely terrified because I was late, and I could tell she was an imposing woman. All the other students were standing in front of her. She turned around and smiled, and I melted. She said simply, "You must be Alex." She had a glint in her eyes and I instantly warmed to her. It was wonderful.

'During the breaks in the masterclass, we chatted and there was an immediate connection between us. At one point, it was my turn to sing solo. I will never forget it. She stood very close by; I could see her out of the corner of my eye, but I dared not look directly at her. Suddenly but gently, she touched my cheek to make me lift my face. It was a revelation that I could feel the way I did when I was singing, and make my voice sound so different, so much better. She was a big advocate of not straining the voice. Keeping it natural and free is paramount. The masterclass finale was a concert in the evening. Afterwards, I went to say goodbye to Norma, and she said I was to visit if ever I was local to her and gave me her business card. Soon after, I wrote a thank-you letter, she replied, and that sparked decades of writing to each other, between visits.'

Alexander knew Norma's hometown of Grimsby well. His mother, Margaret Anderson, was a well-known singer in town with her sister June. They performed as The Anderson Sisters and, just like Norma's upbringing, there was always music in the house. Margaret, who encouraged her son to pursue a musical career, took him to singing lessons with a chorister from Lincoln Cathedral, who was excited by his vocal range and potential for opera, although back then opera did not interest Alexander. Replying to his thank-you letter, Norma wrote: 'So very pleased to hear you enjoyed my efforts in the Lincoln masterclass and I hope in some humble way I was able to give some help and guidance. I too enjoyed the day, and especially working with you, though I would have loved more time and to work one-to-one privately, which is my favourite way of trying to teach.'

Norma had spotted his talent and wanted to help, imparting knowledge and advice. 'She was a very warm woman and ours was an extraordinary relationship, mostly long-distance through letters and lasting almost 30 years,' said Alexander, 37 years Norma's junior. 'The age difference meant nothing – we just clicked and our connection spanned generations. She was so protective, supportive, and not at all bullish. She was gentle and understood people very well. Norma learned early on that it's all about the text, delivery and interpretation, and beauty through music. She'd tell me about recordings she made in just one take; it really is amazing how she intuitively understood the pieces she performed. That was a huge part of how she taught. She never came from a stressful point of view – singing was very spiritual for her. She definitely wanted to pass on her knowledge.

'For Norma, music was a gift, a beautiful pure thing, and a part of you – an extension of your true self. She'd tell me that as long as you can stay well and interpret on a personal level, that's all you can do. She would find today's musical world very different I should think! Pop music – the world I was in when we first met – wasn't her world, and she would sometimes shake her head in dismay when I told her about things that had happened. She didn't understand it. Even though she could see opera was my way forward, she never pushed me one way or another. All she was ever about was taking care of the voice and staying healthy. In later years, her letters would almost always include a line about staying safe and healthy.'

Alexander brought out Norma's nurturing nature, and she looked forward to his visits and phone calls. 'She would have cake ready, always buying

Battenburg when she found out it was my favourite,' he recalled. 'She had a little Mini and would pack it full of cakes. I would arrive at, say, eleven in the morning and not leave until six that evening. She was so funny and witty, and told some fantastic stories and anecdotes about her career. She would sometimes play for me on the piano and give me new pieces to learn, passing on everything she knew. There were others she tutored too, with just the same care and attention, and I always felt so lucky that I was one of them.

'Her home was exactly as I'd expected – very smart and with its own music room, of course! I loved being there. There were angels everywhere, in paintings and sculptures. I used to send her lots of angels that I came across on my travels, and an angel-themed calendar every year without fail. She could be quite naughty when she wanted to be – the things this glamorous, very well-known lady sometimes came out with made me laugh. If she didn't like something, she'd shout "Balls to that!" or "Bollo, oh bollo!" She did not suffer fools gladly. Most of the time we had together was spent giggling and laughing. She was like family to me. I had my mum, and Norma was like a surrogate grandmother – but never granny-like in the slightest.

'Her modesty was so strong. She would frequently say that people had forgotten her, forgotten who she was, and it was her own fault for staying in Grimsby. She cared for her parents and her sister, too. But there wasn't the media then that there is now – she travelled by train and boat, for instance. It was a different era. But she was certainly never forgotten. She told me how she always had a suitcase packed, ready to go away at the drop of a hat, but that she loved coming home. Home was very important to her. She'd always say, "It's nice to come home and sit on your own loo". She used to call me her boy. She'd say, "My boy is coming to visit". I know I shared something very special with Norms, and I am very proud of that.'

Her correspondence was packed with advice for the young singer and his burgeoning career. In one of the many letters she wrote to Alexander, she said: 'Well you certainly have a punishing schedule. The travelling used to weary me and the constant companion suitcase! Makes me dizzy now reading of your demands, and total disbelief that I used to live like that m'self!' Alexander said: 'I loved how she talked about Roy [Henderson], Jennie [Jennifer Vyvyan] and Joanie [Joan Sutherland]. That was a big deal for me because she was so famous, and so were they. I remember her telling me how once she flew to Vienna to meet Erich Korngold, who was famous for composing scores for Hollywood movies. I was so impressed. They had booked three or four days for a recording. They did one take and Korngold didn't want to do it again – that's how good she was.

'We talked about a lot of things, like the stresses of being a tenor – who has to do the acrobatic stuff. She used to say that the girls all wanted to be sopranos, but she was really proud of being a contralto because they don't make them anymore. She was very sought after, especially for the sacred pieces she was skilled in. She was much in demand in those circles. But she wasn't really at home on the operatic stage; she was a concert artist and for her, it was about being on your own terms with the audience. She wanted to give herself – not hide behind a character or a costume – which is very noble and simple. In opera, you can't properly take in the audience. In concerts, you get better feedback because you address them personally and check in with them. Norma and her friends all worked together for the same cause – the craft. Musically, she never pushed me. She said I'd instinctively know which road to take, and she was right.'

Norma told him: 'I always had a feeling, way back to the Lincoln masterclass, that opera would eventually become your real forte, whereas I knew at Glyndebourne it would never be mine – too much accent on production for me. Music was my love. I had other opera offers but turned them all down after Orpheus – even Bayreuth! So much more I could say but need a toilet roll – in length!'

'She was a puritan when it came to the arts and liked things to remain beautiful,' Alexander said. 'She did not see the point of crudity or ugliness. Some people may not agree with that, but that was the way she was. I think that came from her spiritual beliefs. She believed she was given a gift and by singing, she was giving back. That was part of her worship. Spirituality poured from her, even when she was aged in her 70s. We would sing Lieder together and she would say, "Try it like this" or "sing the phrase like that" and it would be transformed. She would be at the piano and physically lean back into the phrases. It was wonderful to watch and was clearly a lifetime of loving the music. As a young man starting out in opera, it was amazing.'

Alexander's career took off. After studying at the Royal College of Music, he joined Scottish Opera, debuting on the operatic stage in roles including The Peacock in Param Vir's Broken Strings, Janek in The Makropoulos Case and, rather fittingly, Flavio in Norma. He has performed around the world and was enrolled on an English National Opera programme to hone his skills. 'I always kept in touch with Norms,' he said. 'Her letters were exciting and funny and important to me. We would write silly stuff. She was so unique. If I had a concert, she would know about it and wish me luck. I always wore a white hanky in my top pocket, and she'd say, "Just remember, I am hiding behind your hanky, in your pocket." She also used to say she was a white witch and hovered on a broomstick!

'When I went to America on tour, she sent me little tokens to keep in my pockets, like cherubs and paintings. They weren't just gestures; it was her way of being with me. As time went on, I found it harder to get back to

Grimsby to visit. When I did, parting became more and more difficult for us. She was naturally becoming older and more infirm and would get very upset and angry with herself. My last visit was hard because she couldn't speak for very long, and then she became too ill to write. But I continued to write up until she died. I felt awful. I know no one can live forever but Norms was one of a kind.

'I remember once being in an outdoor restaurant in London, sitting in the sunshine, and my phone rang. It was Norma. She was upset and told me she was ringing to say goodbye, because she knew she would soon find it impossible to talk on the phone. She said she was in a minor key – she always used musical terms to describe her moods – and described how her health was worsening. I sent some flowers and she left me a voicemail message saying how much they had cheered her up. That phone call was the last time we spoke.

'I have had some wonderful singing teachers in my time but there's no one like Norma Procter. Only she could move me. Every now and again I get her voice in my head with a saying or perhaps an anecdote. Even when I'm in a bad mood, she still makes me smile. She was the ultimate glamorous fairy godmother. She was impeccably dressed, with lovely jewellery, and always smelt amazing. Her perfume was gorgeous. And her make-up… her eyebrows were always done, and her lips too. And her posture was perfect – always upright. We had a very special, loving bond. She was amazing, funny, hip, very intuitive and somewhat out of her time, in her own way… a very cool lady!'

Chapter 14: Reflections

Throughout the 1990s, Norma's ill health failed to ease. In June 1991, she noted that she had to take four litres of Golytely, a liquid which readies the system for a colonoscopy; she was battling with Irritable Bowel Syndrome. During 1990 and 1991, she was placed on Estraderm patches ('a great help and improvement,' she noted), and in June 1992, she endured a 'hellish' tooth extraction, having had all of her teeth roots-treated and crowned in 1987. Thankfully, her letter-writing remained as vociferous as ever, offering a unique insight into her retirement.

She wrote regularly to friend and former pupil Alexander Anderson-Hall, updating him on everyday life as well as recalling precious memories. In July 1991, she told him: 'Serenade To Music is a most beautiful piece. My own dear Prof, Roy Henderson, was one of the original soloists. He's 92 years old tomorrow and still as bright as a button and can sing. I keep in touch by pen and phone. He's in London and, of course, retired. He's such a love. I have to confess I go to very few concerts these days, even in GY [Grimsby]. Do hope you enjoy your singing course in Oxford – please give my love to Jane (Manning), we sang together many times, and especially to Pauli (Hamburger), who was my Lieder teacher. I loved working with him, and we shared some lovely and memorable BBC recitals and recordings together. He lost his wife about two years ago, after a long, tragic illness. She was also a very dear person. I don't think he has ever really recovered from that, but courageously keeps on working hard, bless him.'

The following month, she managed a few days of rest at Sharrow Bay, taking a break from tutoring pupils. 'It was wonderful to share so much beauty… surely a corner of Heaven tucked away there,' she noted. 'A favourite spot for well over 35 years now.'[209] In another letter to Alexander, dated October 31, she recollected how much she was expected to learn as a singer. 'One finds all the learning daunting. I still do and know so little,' she said. 'As for French, it wasn't my favourite language and always felt it better in an artist with higher register voices but have learned much more since teaching. I often wish, as with many things, I could sing or have sung more French melodies. If you have recordings of baritone Gerard Souzay, listen to them if only for his native French pronunciation and vocal colouring – very lovely. One can learn much from just listening to his true French accent. German was and is my favourite language. You'll love singing Nacht und Träune, but it needs enormous control in every way, and lovely pianissimo moments.

'I consider myself privileged to have known the musical era I was born into, though I began to see many changes – not always for the better – towards the end of my career. Many things in today's system trouble me, though I know there are perhaps more, or different, opportunities for young singers and musicians. I still cling on tight to my music, though miss my real music-making days, but not present-day travel and my constant companion – a suitcase (packing and unpacking!). Do your best in all things and what is meant will be, though I'm not a complete fatalist. Above all, keep your health – the key to all things, and all professions.' In an aside, she added: 'Oh don't mention Christmas! I still love the real meaning of Christmastide but the commercialised hassle of cards and pressies makes me both sad and mad when compared with days of yore. I expect it will be generally a quiet time with my sister and brother-in-law, and perhaps some of my noisy, young great-nieces and nephews! Oh!!'

These letters to Alexander reveal more than her diaries do, which are, around this time, perfunctory and brief. Even her correspondence in earlier years is not as revealing as that written during her retirement. Not one for talking about her private life or feelings, she felt comfortable confiding in her 'specials'. To Alexander, she spoke often of her health and moods – a side she rarely allowed anyone to see, and Alexander has kindly given permission for the contents of her letters to be published.

In February 1992, she wrote thanking him for a birthday present, a CD of Handel's Alcina that featured Norma and Joan Sutherland. Norma was wary of new technology, especially how it may affect performers' rights. 'I couldn't wait [to open it] until Saturday – still very much a child at heart! I must agree, the reproduction – even after 30 years – is excellent and crystal clear. Amazing!' she said. 'I except it was taken from the Westdeutsche Rundfunk (Köln) master spool – and still can't believe it's all been transferred to CD, but of course, dear Joan is the main reason, I'm sure. Yes, I have seen CDs before, and they are quite something! But I still love my ole cassettes. They are so light and easy to use, especially when travelling as I used to – and much less expensive! I saw a programme on TV t'other night and they [CDs] only cost 69p to press, so someone's making a lot of money somewhere! Certainly not yours truly. There are no royalties in it for me when they're transferred. The prices certainly need to drop. You ask what it's like to see your name on one. I've never really given it much thought, quite frankly – publicity, advertising, the Press, the media (especially today's!) … I have always made little of it. So seldom accurate, or what you wished to be printed, and after beginning in my profession, I avoided it all as much as possible. It was far more important to just get on with my work and job. Nothing I produced was ever good enough – it always had to be better.'

Norma would sometimes write letters in stages, breaking off for teaching or going to the supermarket, and then picking up the pen again later on. They provide an almost running commentary on her days and thoughts. In the same letter to Alexander, she confessed: 'I am very nervous of relationships these days, after many let-downs, and sorry if I gave an impression of desperate loneliness – or worse, self-pity, which I abhor. I just feel a bit cut off up here at times and guess I've always been a loner deep down – apart from my scattered specials. Was half torn I had to go out, as I just switched over to see who was on This Is Your Life and it was a great favourite of mine, George Shearing. At least I heard the beginning and saw his incredible face and smile. To be able to play as he does with such an affliction [Shearing was blind] is quite wonderful. I so love classical jazz pianists. It must be wonderful to just sit down and doodle at the keyboard, improvising ad lib, but in his case, not to be able to see is quite amazing – hence his humility and lovable personality. It is agony to watch the lack of humility and humanity in some artists. I could relate many such stories but prefer to hold on to the memories of those in another orbit who restored my faith in human beings, after being on the receiving end of very hurtful and corrupt treatment. Oscar Peterson is another favourite but totally different, of course. I adore the piano. '10pm. Just come in from teaching and now relaxing, listening to lovely Stella By Starlight, beautifully arranged by Chuck Gerhardt [Charles Gerhardt, the American conductor]. I worked with him many times. He was a love.'

Ever ready with encouragement and love, Norma's bond with Alexander was unshakable. 'What a lovely thought to invite this ole gal for a visit sometime. You really are a love, though the chances of me inflicting m'self upon you are pretty slim these days – but y'never know your bad luck!' she told him. 'I'm just so thrilled everything's working out OK. I said it would, didn't I? The ole witch had one of her strong feelings again. I never seem to stop learning and revising some of my special favourite works and songs. Oh, to be able to sing them as in days of yore but I've had my innings and must be grateful for that, I guess. It just doesn't work when the ole voice no longer obeys as it should. I had a lovely surprise phone call last week – guess who? Charles – Chuck – Gerhardt. I hadn't heard from him for many moons – he's mostly in America these days – and he surprised me with all his clear memories of our super sessions of music-making in the past. I nearly dropped the phone when he said who was speaking. How lovely of him – lucky ole Norm!'[210]

★

There is a saying that retirement is a full-time job, and Norma discovered this in spades: 'Très busy – teaching, and constant learning and prep for a teaching weekend shortly. Shattering how little one knows! Help! Music calleth!'[211] And still, that kernel of self-doubt: 'Niggles and worries never seem to go away, at least in my experience. To keep well and count what blessings you have seems to be the only solution.'[212]

In a way, her constant self-evaluation kept Norma as sharp as a pin. She wrote of refusing to listen to recordings she made. 'I seldom ever listen unless to brush up pre-wise for teaching. It's really too painful to listen, and it would be so different now, were I still able to sing,' she said. 'I well remember our Lady Macbeth sessions with Joe [the composer Joseph Horovitz] and rehearsing firstly at his house. I was very nervous indeed, for a first broadcast of this unknown work to me. Singing music of composers who are no longer with us is difficult enough, to try in vain to do them justice; but literally seeing them at the end of the piano – help! He was most kind and helpful. I have the BBC recording and really enjoyed singing the work eventually.'[213]

She was delighted when Alexander was given the opportunity to listen to Bernard Haitink and Felicity Lott rehearsing. 'Flot [Norma's nickname for Felicity] was just emerging as I was beginning to count my last concerts one by one, so I first met and heard of her at a very difficult time for me,' she said. 'As for Bernard, what a conductor! He was an absolute love to work with, and his Mahler concerts we shared are among my most treasured memories. I was usually in tears at the end, especially in the final orchestral movement of the 3rd Symphony. Goodness knows what he must have thought of me, but so often it was all too much for this ole heart of mine, which just overflowed and is, in fact, doing so as I write and recall those very special occasions. Enough!'

All these memories make up a wealth of information about the music industry during Norma's heyday. But it changed beyond recognition and in her later years, Norma lamented on the effect of time. Alexander asked if she had ever considered writing a memoir. This was her reply: 'I really can't be bothered now. Most people don't remember me anyhow. Goodness, a student was asked about Barbirolli the other day and had no idea who he was, so what chance would I have? Much of it they wouldn't believe, and if I was honest, it could be libellous!' Real life, it seemed, was her most pressing concern: 'My sister is now home from St. Hugh's Hospital and glad to say, making reasonable progress. I have been busy chasing back and forth to the hospital, and now at home, helping where I can betwixt teaching. Must away – my washer's just stopped, so domestic chores call, which I loathe! A necessary evil for this ole gal.' 'It's a real "winter drawers" day again, in spite of the spring flowers trying to cheer us in the gardens, and blossoms on the trees. Everything seems all mixed up, doesn't it?'[214]

Modern life, as it was, was indeed mixed up for Norma. No wonder she took comfort in the warmth of her memories. She recalled with fondness making a recording of The Sea Hawk. 'I was in Copenhagen for concerts when asked to record this very lovely extract/finale from the musical score of the film starring Errol Flynn – quite unbeknown to me!' she wrote. 'A single-line manuscript was air-mailed out to me – I always vetted any new piece before saying yes – and I then recorded with Chuck Gerhardt conducting, and [Eric] Korngold's son, George, producing in London en route home to Grimsby. Imagine my great surprise when I then heard this amazing Mahler/Strauss arrangement which, at times on the LP, I still feel is over-recorded orchestrally against the voice. Huge forces! Choir too, and the text/words are not as clear as I'd wished. We made only two takes, the first being a first rehearsal also! I was all set for hopefully an improved balance in a third take but was told, "That's it! OK! We're finished!". Sadly, I had to let it go and wasn't at all happy with the result, though I loved the piece and loved trying to sing it, the words of which I love, but have no idea who wrote them. You may feel this is a la Hollywood/Warner Bros, but Korngold certainly knew how to write his famous film scores.'[215]

When Alexander mentioned he had met the singer Felicity Palmer, she wrote: 'I sang my almost last concert abroad with her in Switzerland, and during that trip had made up my mind it was time to bid farewell to the concert circuit, though I said nothing to anyone then on the trip. During the past few days, I have been listening to her first major recording of Faure songs when she was still a lovely soprano (now mezzo). I hope she is well and happy – small world. Yes, we did perform in Liverpool – our first meeting, I believe.'

In the same letter, she went on to say: 'Sometimes it's better to be lonely alone than lonely with, m'thinks. It's very hard but sometimes the lesser of two evils. Can't win either way! My sister's improving slow but sure. I did go to the Grimsby Phil concert last Saturday, alone.

'Well m'dear, all the miserable household chores call – food to organise and the unending new scores and revision. I'm always looking, listening and seeking new thoughts and ideas of interpreting these great masters of music and poetry. I saw the final of the Young Musician (BBC2) pianists… I adore the piano, and there was no doubt who should and did win that competition, even though 14 years old! But far more mature than his years. I only hope and pray he's guided to go gently and not pressurised too soon or early. I so often turn to the piano when I want a rest from voices and only wish I'd studied more as a youngster. I can't turn the clock back now!'

★

'It's such a lovely day – a cool coastal breeze – so I have decided to come into the garden for the first time this year, in my corner near the dining room window where I can shelter when the sun becomes too much. I used to be a sun worshipper, but I can only take so much now, and it can be dangerous – as I know to my cost. I'm swotting très hard for a singing weekend.'[216]

Norma's description of a pleasant May day in 1992 paints a wonderful picture but it was music that still truly filled her mind. Of the recordings she made during her career, she told Alexander: 'Frankly, there aren't so many really, and some are now deleted. There used to be a Decca Elijah with Josef Krips; my second recording for that company and generally, so a very young Norm indeed! I was in my early twenties… centuries ago! DDG's Samson, with Karli [Richter] conducting and harpsichord, may still be around. He was one of the most wonderful Bach conductors I worked with, and died all too soon, at 52, some years ago now. He was conductor of the then very famous Münchener Bach Choir and orchestra at the recording. I have many very special musical memories of Munich, I think, my favourite German city. He played and conducted all the Bach works from memory and often from the harpsichord – incredible! When it was first released, it was only available in Germany.

'Good vocal teachers are not always easy to find, and to teach is such a great responsibility. One has to be so careful with a voice – an instrument we cannot see or pick up as other instruments. It's so fragile and mysterious. I can't help wishing that my own Prof was still able to teach. He's 93 in July, bless him – amazing! For me, I was never in doubt. Things were very different in those days. I don't go to many concerts these days, mainly the Grimsby Phil. They gave Carmina Burana (not my favourite work – I'm still not a complete convert – very dangerous vocally at times for the three soloists, though they coped very well). They also gave the first performance of Lincolnshire Voices by William (Bill) Llewellyn, based on Lincolnshire folk songs, for the Phil's 140th anniversary. It was very tricky but lovely tunes well-arranged. A charming work for soprano, tenor, and baritone with two pianos and percussion.

'Otherwise I watch TV concerts and constantly listen in to Radio 3. One has wonderful shots of singers as the cameras zoom in – far more than if in a large concert hall, can't see or too far away, though I realise one misses the actual hall atmosphere. But if it's a good performance, that comes through too. I'm not keen on being out alone at night either (poor ole gal!), at least in wintertime and if parking's difficult.'

She spent June and July working on Berg's Seven Early Songs. 'It's not really my forte but slowly getting there, hopefully. It's interesting to try and understand all the different thinkings of the various composers, although I am still trying to catch up with the old masters. The poems are lovely but I'm such a romantic – I guess I don't really belong in this century, except for mod cons! Some early 20th century composers appeal but it takes me too long to grasp their medium, whereas with something melodic and soulful, the ole gal's wafted off!' she said. 'Big change weather-wise today; really cold after all the lovely sunshine. Wimbledon approaches yet again and I shall try to watch some of the matches. The behaviour on court – as in soccer and sport generally – worries me greatly. What's happening to humanity? The hooligans! The terrorists! Greed for money and all the corruption. Man's humanity to man never fails to shatter and devastate me. Oh, that we had more romantics and sentimentalists. This dear ole world is starved of such necessities. It's time ole Norm came off her soapbox and organised some food!'[217]

Here, she talks of a clear recording Alexander found of Le Laudi, an oratorio by Swiss composer Hermann Suter: 'All I have left is a tattered LP, after trying everywhere to buy a new recording, but it was only distributed in Switzerland as far as I know, and which I transferred to cassette earlier this year, pops, squeaks and all. It was recorded originally in Basler Münster [Basel Minster] – superb to sing in. Suter composed this work for the Basler Gesangverein, of which he was conductor for many years until his death in 1926, two years before this ole gal came upon this planet for everyone's sins! Suter is a kind of Swiss Elgar for me. It's not perhaps the greatest orchestral/choral playing/singing but the dearest people sang and played their hearts out and were so kind to me. Dear conductor [Fritz Münch] – brother of Charles Münch, also a conductor. Strangely enough, the other soloists weren't very keen on the work – tricky at times – but can't think why?! I adore the choral passacaglia, with wonderful moments with the great organ in that beautiful setting.'[218] And here, of singing the Messiah in Leicester: 'I was often with the Leicester Philharmonic over the years at Christmastide – a wonderful time to sing that glorious work and very much the fashion in my day, before carol concerts took over. And then there's the Passion recitals – beautiful. Many people and singers snigger at this work but very few can really sing it. "Tossing it off" won't do!'[219]

By now it was November, and Norma had judged another singing contest. 'The competition went very well,' she reported, 'and we were a happy and supportive jury – one of the best I've known and lots of laughter! It was lovely to link up with some of my old colleagues again, but it was very hectic… over 100 singers from 181 countries! Some lovely music. Alas on the Friday, I was smitten with this wretched flu bug. Since, I've been battling on and loathing the winter which has set in. Me no like! Heaven knows what I have in m'veins but it's not blood – I'm always freezing. It's been so cold and damp here. M'old bones ache!'

The following month, Alexander sent Norma a gift, a recently published book about Kathleen Ferrier. 'I'll at least make a start – am actually sitting in the dentist's waiting room for a check-up, tho' I don't really know where to begin,' her responding letter opened with. 'When I returned from town, there was your parcel awaiting me in the front entrance, all so beautifully wrapped. Oh! What a wonderful surprise when I opened it! I'd heard about Kaff's latest book but just hadn't got around to buying it since the previous Maurice Leonard "Kathleen", which is always by my bedside. Have quickly flicked through the photo pages – lots of new ones – and faces of many of my own special buddies I worked with and loved – alas, no more. The photo taken from a Carlisle recital is exactly as I last remember her singing in Grimsby, including the glorious Brahms Serious Songs. She looked and sang like a dream, and we little realised how very ill she was then. The very last time I saw her was in hospital, and she was so excited she was being allowed home shortly. Must stop – my turn in that wretched chair!' Concluding the letter, she wrote later on: 'Now home again and touch wood, I escaped further treatment. I have an appalling dental history!'[220]

★

In late 1992, Norma's trusted Dr. Mike – who had looked after her since she was a teenager – retired aged 92, and she was put under the care of Dr. John. He sent her to Grimsby's hospital for x-rays on both feet, not that outsiders would have known, of course. 'Pain in right large toe and toes. Osteo-arthritis,' she wrote. 'Ibrufen [Ibuprofen] 200mg tablets to ease pain. Blood and urine checked – all clear, mercifully. Weight approximately 10st 3lb in m'nothings! I have to have a colonoscopy every few years and watch my diet – no alcohol for six years! Bad circulation, especially in the winter. Feet worse in cold weather, naturally.'[221] In October, a delegation from the Wuhan Conservatory of Music, based in China, visited Grimsby and Norma was delighted to meet them, spending time chatting and talking about music.

In March 1993, she complained of 'severe pain in left foot from osteomyelitis. Fused foot operation but weak lower spine. First physio sessions and use of crutches.'[222] On June 22, she had another operation on her foot and went under general anaesthetic to have the plaster changed a few weeks later. The pot was finally removed on September 22nd but by October she was back to using crutches. In November she gave in and bought an orthopaedic chair and mattress.

Her letters to Alexander during 1993 show that, although her health was worsening, she was determined to carry on as usual, by sharing her knowledge and skills with the young singer. 'Gorecki is très interesting… to hear the Polish language – such lovely and brilliant poems, aren't they?' she wrote that February. 'I know how difficult and hard-going this profession can be, and not only in the earlier stages – cold comfort! One needs endless patience, dedication and discipline, and a very great love of your art, singing and music-making… a spiritual depth will always carry you through, tho' it will not be easy. Nothing worthwhile ever is, and there will always be doubtful days. Just let your heart and soul take over and it will automatically shine through in the sound. Soul and sound go hand in hand, and a superb sound without soul means or moves nothing and no one. I remember seeing Ivor Novello in some of his shows. He knew how to write a tune – rare in this age – perhaps sentimental and romantic, but this sad and weary ole world needs lots of that just now, and more love and care.'[223]

In April, Norma made a cassette of William Heddle Nash for Alexander: 'The background noise doesn't worry me because of his unique and glorious soul-sound. What wonderful music-making and special memories. I still love the Velius song – it literally stole my heart, and a glorious accompaniment too. A great lesson just listening to this special sound and very special person. His Gerontius really is too much – wonderful! I shall never forget his kindness. It was a real privilege to have known him and shared his singing/interpretation – so heartfelt – if only for a short while. His son, John Heddle, was equally kind to me in the few concerts we shared together too.'[224] More advice followed in May: 'Don't push your voice. Be gentle and it will gradually obey.' And 'How strange the "to and fro" of musical fashion – composers etc. One minute they're "in" and the next, on the shelf. Until the ole wheel turns full circle again.

In the same letter, she recalled memories of Dame Gwyneth Jones: 'We worked together in the very early days before she really made her name in opera. She had a tough beginning – no pennies. She was a waitress and scrubbed floors to help out. Her first marriage failed (when I knew her), then she blossomed in international opera and met this fabulously wealthy man in Switzerland, married and has a daughter. It was the Bernstein Mahler 8th concert and recordings when we linked up again some moons later. Also, one day in Hamburg when I was having lunch with friends (the last concerts/days of my career), I noticed this handsome, lovely lady walk into the dining room but didn't recognise who it was. She spotted me as I left to collect my coat in the cloakroom, and we had a very quick "hello and goodbye" as she chased after me. I was rushing to get to the airport! Then we linked up again through another musical friend, Jimmy Littlejohn, two or three years ago, though sadly he died very suddenly. She was always very kind to me.'[225]

By August, Alexander had moved to London to further his career. Norma said she knew how lonely the city could be and, expressing sympathy over a relationship break-up, she told him: 'You see why I'm so wary of relationships, except those who have proved themselves against all odds. Joys and sorrows over many years! I saw my super specialist on Wednesday and the x-rays. He allowed me to put two feet on terra firma, which is a great bonus, albeit still in plaster for another month at least. It will take a long time to learn to walk again… m'second or third childhood?! – as the foot is now doubly fused and won't give at all. It took three years last time to master it and the limp… I'm damned if I'll be beaten this time. I'm taking each day by day.'[226]

Norma was delighted when Alexander made it to Grimsby to see her. He must have complimented her beloved Mini during his visit. 'Had to smile at your thoughts of this ole gal whizzing around in m'Mini – poor leg and all, and all drivers skidding out of my way, as they usually do! Pleased I made you laugh when you came, in spite of the shock of this one-legged monster! I'm hobbling onwards,' she wrote. 'No, the pot isn't off yet – Sept 1st, if my super specialist laddie considers ready for what I know will be the next difficult round – trying to learn to walk again with this newly doubly-fused foot. I won't like it without the pot support, but I won't be beaten, and please God, m'guardian angel will still be high. I'll let you know the worst! Have looked for you at any possible Proms on TV but no luck. So glad you're enjoying them. Haydn's Seasons not really well-known to me but you'll love Gundula (Janowitz). She was lovely to work with and a fine singer. We worked together two or three times and she was a love. The last time we met, I was passing through my favourite hotel where I stayed in Munich, unaware she was in the lounge and bless her, she ran forward to greet me. It was so good to see her – and what a voice that was!

'Do hope that gentle inner voice and inspiration will guide you at the right moment, as I'm sure it will. Our patience is constantly being tested isn't it? But perhaps we are better mortals as a result – testing tho' it is at times. Well m'dear, I've really little news and please excuse the late posting of this epistle – but Audrey and I are away until late Tues. No pupils – holidays! – tho' working hard and forever learning and listening, e'en tho' somewhat housebound, but grateful for many blessings. Time I stopped blathering and got me to the Land of Nod – hopefully.'[227] Then: 'You may remember my talking about and showing the cover photo of Dinu Lipatti… have just finished re-recording the enclosed Lipatti programme which I thought you would like to hear – and should hear, m'thinks! I have found this amazing man and unique pianist such a balm and healing these past weeks, and a great challenge too – in that he could produce such deeply moving music-making against such cruel odds – literally tugging your heart strings – and that is what music is all about to this humble ole gal. Such a short life, alas, but what a legacy for us all.

'I only hope you receive similar blessings when listening, and when the struggle seems too great. Dear God, having listened yet again, that Liszt is so beautiful and played like an adoring angel, full of love and passion for his art, and what a composer! Contemporary composers should listen to this melody [Pace Non Trovo] – so simple and glorious… one feels so close to the text and, for me, Lipatti's exquisite playing of the piano arrangement stands out in this glorious and very moving recital, showing how the spirit can conquer all suffering and ills, e'en tho' at considerable cost. This is incredible playing and courage throughout, which deeply inspires me.'[228]

Reading Norma's letters now is the next best thing to having a face-to-face conversation with her. She wrote as she spoke, with typical energy and lyricism, and while she spoke of her foot with humour, it will have caused her pain. On September 9, she said: 'I am seeing at last a specialist for a minor op today, but I will be out of action until very late September at the earliest, so I'm having to rearrange everyone etc, and everything's somewhat vague.' Alexander must have written about a pile of ironing because she replied: 'My heart went out to you with the wretched ironing session. Oh, I'm just not a domesticated bod at all – loathe it! But I like to keep the house in a reasonable state. This house takes some coping with, though I prefer to muddle on my own rather than having help and finding someone who you can trust.

'I'm rolling on, mostly without m'sticks now around the house, and I made my first big trip outside (apart from St. Hugh's Hospital) to the Tesco supermarket to collect groceries. It's quite a walk round and I am grateful for the trolley support, but a welcome bonus to do something for m'self again – almost 12 weeks now, and I hate being trouble. No driving yet – late October – and I'll have to get the clutch released, as it needs a firm, deep push as it is at present and m'ole paw won't want to know. I won't be taking a holiday this year. I have a considerable battle ahead yet and I suspect more physio! I'm quite content to potter around here until this ole paw is stronger.

'Leeds International Piano Competition began this week but sadly no coverage on TV as yet, nor in the Press or on the radio. I have mixed feelings about competitions; it's not always the winner who goes on to really make the grade. It's all a reflection of our current era I guess, but not all pianists can cope with the demanding occasion, and all the media coverage, then to follow the agents, travel, repertoire demands and certainly a lonely life. One needs tremendous physical and mental stamina. I don't think I'd have the courage nor the ability to cope now, but when you're younger one can "jump over the moon".'

December arrived and Norma struggled to prepare for Christmas. This extract from a letter dated December 8 shows just how well-loved she was. 'I'm snowed under with cards and letters,' she complained. 'I'm sure Christmas wasn't meant to be like this. It was all so simple and humble. Nothing special for Christmas – just we three oldies, and Audrey's family on Boxing Day. Just had m'phone bill – wow! I'll have to be more disciplined, though it's my one luxury these days.'

★

The following March, Norma took a much-needed journey to Sharrow Bay to see her good friends Brian and Francis. 'I've been trying to arrange a trip to see my boys in the Lakes, and after much-changed plans for the past weeks, my sister and hubby, Audrey and Norm, were able to drop me off at Scotch Corner en route to their son Paul, in Newcastle. Brian collected me there and took me to their magnificent home and hotel. I haven't seen them for almost three years, so it was wonderful to see them and give them a big hug again,' she wrote. 'We're constantly in touch when we can't actually meet, but much has happened to us all in those three years and it was lovely to catch up on so many things. It's rather hectic there and I've crammed more into the past four days, travel and talk-wise, than all the three years! The weather has been appalling; driving rain and winds. The lake – Ullswater – where the house and hotel stand on its bankside was more like a very wild sea. However, we made it, though the journey home yesterday was really glum, and I was very glad and grateful to reach this apologetic place after all the grandeur, but it's still home. It's very quiet and silent by comparison.

'I hate leaving the place when we're all away together, which is very rare, but my neighbours were watchful and helpful. So, I'm trying to catch up on things and get back to this strange normality. We've been close friends for almost 40 years and time is no longer on our side, so to speak. The boys are now in their 70s. We're all rather ole crocks after various illnesses and still battling, and we manage to laugh at our old age and problems, when compared with our youthful days! How short life really is, though sometimes an hour can seem like years!'[229]

For a time, she was able to forget her aches and pains. There was also a further irritant in her life: she was having terrible trouble with the bespoke shoes she needed to walk properly with. Each pair she ordered never seemed to fit well and it became a constant complaint throughout 1994. In May, she thanked Alexander for a card featuring the Royal College of Music: 'You may think this rather strange, but I had somehow forgotten the actual building and just where it was in relation to the dear Albert Hall – it brought back many memories, of all the Three Choir rehearsals there, usually with the LSO then, also an adjudication date, and many other rehearsals. Memories! Memories! I can always remember thinking during my visits, how dreadful to try and work in this hellish noisy place! I don't expect it's changed one jot. All colleges and academies are the same in my experience, and how grateful I was – and still am – to work privately and in comparative peace.

'Not much news here – things a little quiet. So many of my little flock [her pupils] are ill! Small wonder – everyone trying to do far too much and, it seems, pressurised to the hilt – the worst thing possible for singers/voices. I'm still battling away with these damn expensive so-called "wonder shoes", which have been returned to me again, but once again they haven't got it right – most uncomfortable! This saga began way back in January and they would be ready in three weeks – also three times the original price quoted! It's now months and we're still doing battle. I only have one other pair of shoes that will fit my present manipulated foot, tho' a wardrobe of several lovely pairs of shoes (after I sent a considerable bag-full to Oxfam last year).

'Such a waste and nuisance. I am very reluctant to order any more of these privately made shoes at such an excessively expensive price, and the fact, worse still, that they don't fit properly! Enough! Grrrr! I try so hard not to grumble or complain, but mi' north-country blood rises. It's a miserable, dark, cold day again – just when I thought spring/summer had arrived – and on this coast we're back into winter woollies… if they were ever put away! I so love this beautiful month of May, but it will soon be over and almost half the year! Must stop – and work!'[230]

Her diary of May 21 reads: 'Very ill but did not phone or bother A & N [Audrey and Norman].' Alexander, thinking it may cheer her up, rang Norma and they spoke on the phone for some time. Unable to resist, she wrote a small note: 'Many thanks for your welcome call and sorry I sounded so grim – this Meniere's disease and vertigo really makes me feel desperately dizzy and sick. I am rather surprised it has occurred again, as it's supposedly under control from some years ago. Wot an ole past the sell-by date crock you have for a friend!'[231]

By June, she was 'battling on and hopefully have now got the vertigo under control, and at last getting somewhere with those damn shoes, which have to be completely remade again. Give me strength! A very moving weekend with all the D-Day remembrances and services. Oh, that man would heed the great sacrifices… one feels unworthy for all that they gave for our freedom.'[232] The issue with the custom-made shoes continued into July. She said: 'As for (Mary) Norma Procter, she's still trying to hang in there but them shoes are a total dead loss. I have had to buy some from a local semi-surgical shop this week in Grimsby. I had to see my dear Doc about another problem yesterday and he's very cross about them. He thinks we'd have done better on Freeman Street Market! It was one of those "O for the wings of a dove" days and not much improved today, but there's always tomorrow. It can only get better. I mustn't complain when I see those poor tormented refugees in Rowanda, the little orphan ones especially make my heart ache. What a living hell. I'm busy constantly learning and found some more lovely ballads from many moons ago. It never fails to literally shatter me how little one knows. I'm working again on Schubert's The Shepherd On The Rock, a glorious piece for sop, clarinet and piano, and my beloved Brahms viola songs for contralto – gorgeous! Oh, that this ole gal could make a humble attempt at singing them again. Make the most of every opportunity – it doesn't last long.'[233]

In August that year, Alexander described the backstage goings-on of a production he was singing in. 'Your description of your make-up, costumes, hair-do etc made me think of Un Ballo in Maschera, and we chorus girls as fisherwomen/tarts, as we looked! One of my family completely passed me by backstage – didn't even recognise this ole hag!' she recalled. 'Trying to cope with m'foot and them shoes. Frankly, I don't wear them – I loathe them and they're so uncomfortable and give no support. I had to see my physiotherapist two days ago – another problem. She had other suggestions but I'm reluctant to try any more handmade surgical efforts, and at that price! I just wish we could get it right. One gets fed up with the wasted time and hassle.'[234]

September brought cooler weather: 'It is damn cold here. The first day for some time without the heavens pouring down. The nights are drawing in – winter looms, and Christmas too. The ole family Christmas has gone I guess, and lots of my closest "specials" are very ill or no more, so the wide circle becomes much smaller. I miss my ole specials, who are almost impossible to replace. I'm still clinging on tight to my music, which is really my saviour, and certain friends remaining to cheer me on. Wonder if you watched the Domingo programme last night? Very interesting. Oh, for some of his stamina! I only hope he doesn't push himself too far, especially with the Wagner, which I wouldn't wish to sing even if I could. I'm not mad about the basics of the story. I sincerely hope his voice is still able to go back to the lighter Boheme operas he loves so much. It made me shudder looking at all the people involved behind stage, like masses of ants running around. It brought back too many heartache memories of Covent Garden. He's a very strong man in every way, self-disciplined and very intelligent.'[235]

On November 19, she wrote: 'Had a sad ten days. My dear Doc[236] ill and finally slipped away. The funeral was yesterday. One feels so useless. I haven't any special plans [for Christmas] at all – something I used to look forward to but frankly not anymore. It just seems so wasteful somehow. When I think back to my earlier days, I really can't believe it's the same person. I certainly couldn't chase around like I used to, nor have the inclination! Travel days are over for me and I'm just grateful for what I was allowed to do in past days – and have to cope with my present adagio tempo! Now trying another pair of shoes. They arrived this week after writing a very strong letter to the powers that be over all this past ten months of aggro and trauma. I made some shattering discoveries as to what has been going on from the manager and supervisor of the factory, who have both been very helpful and co-operative. They knew nothing about my patient details etc.' Then: 'I'm battling with a rotten, steaming cold, throat and flu virus, which is rife around here, and many other areas I gather – a real stinger. Thank goodness I'm not singing anymore. Audrey and Norm are not well – what a crew of crocks. I guess we're just getting old.'[237]

In December, Alexander was in Scotland, which prompted more memories from Norma: 'Can imagine Edinburgh and Glasgow just now, especially the former, a city I always loved and spent many Hogmanay/New Year's Day concerts there. Usher Hall – a beloved hall! Messiah midday and then celebrity concerts the same evening, as they were then called. A long day and trying to fit in rehearsals, so no merry making to see in the new year, which frankly has never really interested me. Always a sense of foreboding – now what will this year bring – and still the same today, perhaps even worse. Old age!'[238]

★

Old age was something Norma increasingly referred to as time went on. It clearly did not suit her, and her health remained a constant cross to bear. During 1994, there did not seem to be a time when she wasn't under the weather. That July, she developed an infection, in August she put out her right shoulder and collar bone, and in September she had more x-rays. Norma must have been exhausted – and it wasn't about to get better. In 1995 she suffered from a bad bout of flu, a vertigo attack and tendonitis in her left foot, while still battling with IBS. Her outwardly stoic attitude is a credit. Like her heroine Kathleen Ferrier, only her nearest and dearest knew exactly how much she was suffering. She found solace in their friendships and remained dedicated to writing to Alexander.

In March, at his request, she sent him one of her Prom recordings: 'Well here it is! For y'sins! I send it somewhat hesitantly, as this is not the usual passive singing Norms, but the ole witch on a broomstick with a vengeance! A wonderful piece to sing – or at least try to?! I don't find it easy to listen. It brings back so many memories, and a very memorable evening. A very demanding "scena" and I gave my all, though could I sing it again today? C'est la vie! Suggest you listen without a score. It will all depend on your equipment if the words/text comes through clearly enough – sometimes covered by that large orchestra – tho' I quite expected the Promenaders to catch mi'denture and fillings before the finale and final outburst!'[239]

She valued their strong bond dearly, and in her letters often commented on how she could not understand why he was interested in her. 'Good to talk and to laugh a little, for a change… the ole witch needed it, believe me,' she wrote on February 23. 'May the moon shine lovingly in your dreams.' And this on March 2: 'I still find it both very touching and almost unbelievable your love and interest in this ole has-been. But it's also re-awakened my interests and stimulated my thoughts, past and present, in researching into my beloved music and repertoire. You're even gradually converting my operatic thinking, though my concert work will always be my first love.'

Though Alexander cannot clearly recall their frequent phone calls, he made a determined effort to stay in touch. Grateful Norma would write after the calls to say thank you. 'Just to wish you well and hope you have a lovely weekend after safe journeys up to Bonnie Scotland,' she wrote. 'Also, the Traviata rehearsals gradually take shape and go well too. A nice – and another – challenge for you, and hope you have kind and supportive colleagues. You know I'll be hovering, or in y'top pocket, broomstick and all! Many thanks for our talk tonight. I'm OK – please excuse the minor key somewhat, which is gradually merging into major!'[240] One can imagine Norma picking up her pen as soon as the line was disconnected.

Just over a week later, she wrote: 'You've been much on my mind since we last talked. I've purposely stopped m'self phoning/writing to give you "breathing space" and time to be alone – and not be "smothered" by this ole gal! I've missed you but know we are close in spirit.'[241] The following day, she penned this: 'Hello m'love – unbelievable telepathy! Your lovely card and loving message just arrived, which has really tugged at m'ole heart strings and I couldn't stop it o'er-flowing. No one has ever written to me in this way in connection with Mother's Day celebrations. Bless you for such a wonderful, sensitive, and touching thought – I am completely overwhelmed and hope we'll be friends forever. I'm quite lost for words.'

Norma had highs and lows, and Alexander's kind gesture buoyed her mood. On March 27 she told him: 'It's now 8.30pm and I'm back in the snug in m'dear ole chair, housecoat and slippers! It's lovely and cosy – it's a brass-monkey eve, and there's more snow forecast through the night and tomorrow.

'I may be doing a swap with m'little Mini for a possible automatic Mini Mayfair. It's about the same age as my own but post box red, which I'm not mad about. I just love the blue one I already have. I wouldn't think of changing it, but it might help this crazy old foot, if the exchange offer is a good one. I'll just have to play it by ear and if it's meant to be… Due to see it tomorrow, weather permitting, and if I can cope with an automatic… I'm a clueless clot with cars. I had to give mine the biggest blitz-clean it's ever had. It nearly killed me and m'back! I hadn't realised how tall and big I am, and how small the interior of a Mini is when trying to manoeuvre, especially in the back. My only hope is my guardian angel wasn't taking language or shorthand notes!' A postscript the following day said: 'It's snowing so I have postponed trying out the red Mini until tomorrow, if the weather improves. Damn the weather. I'm very nervous about it all. I don't want to change m' car. Here's hoping for guidance.'

★

As spring rolled on, Alexander was about to take to the stage in La Traviata. Norma searched through her cards and notelets to find one depicting an angel, her favourite icon, to wish him luck. 'Have no idea where I found this card!' she declared. 'The only one (would you give someone your last Rolo??!!) – but seriously, it seemed v. appropriate, a golden star in the azure blue night sky, and inside it the cutest tiny cherub with a lovely facial expression, and ringing a bell – I hope to watch over another rising star, bringing you happiness and every success for your first night of Traviata on May 3, and for your future performances. [I am] hovering v. close, in y'pocket, and again surrounding you with special and constant love, thoughts and blessings. 'I try to learn something new each day; a word, a text, a song, any small or great wonder of this world, but there are so many. If only man would be more aware of the lovely things on this earth.'[242] As ever, she was on hand with professional advice too. Here, she talked about taking vitamins: 'Powdered glucose has often saved m'life. Some singers had enormous steak meals etc, but I couldn't cope just before a performance, nor afterwards. Everyone to their own taste, I guess! Fruit, cheese, boiled eggs, cold meats – a simple light diet usually before a performance for this ole gal, but I always tried to have a good lunch.'[243]

In May, she gifted Alexander a tie: 'I'm sending the enclosed somewhat nervously, not knowing if these are really you, but have always chosen a classic tie design. Sorry not silk, tho' there again I have mixed feelings re: that lovely material – it marks so easily and needs cleaning! Only hope this material ties/knots well and at least it can be washed?! If you "no like" you can always throw/give away. Daren't send another picture/miniature, or any more sounds of this ole gal, as I know you have enough of your own to do battle with just now and need to literally switch off when you've finished rehearsing, prep, and performances. 'Do hope you are feeling much better, tho' this rotten virus lays one v. low vitality-wise afterwards. I haven't phoned purposely so as not to make you talk and irritate the ole chords. How important and literally a lifeline to keep well – for us especially – but with colds and throats, as where other people can sometimes keep going in other professions, we're finished both financially and job-wise until complete recovery.'[244]

Chapter 15: Losing Friends

Norma's heart-warming maternal love for Alexander meant a lot to them both. He kept all of Norma's letters and is happy to share them here, so while other material most likely exists somewhere, it is through these documents that we see intimate pictures of how Norma's retirement played out. 'Another Monday AM! Me no like Mondays. It goes back to my school days, I guess. I loathed it, the beginning of another week, and what will this one bring… still the same feelings. I watched MasterChef yesterday and also enjoyed very much, as always, the Antiques Roadshow, from Wymondham, Norfolk – where one of my singers comes from.'[245]

As well as these more mundane aspects of her life, Norma's nurturing nature compelled her to regularly send music suggestions to Alexander, with the aim of increasing his repertoire. 'Enclosed is Be My Love, which I love so much,' she wrote on July 2. Be My Love was written for the film The Toast of New Orleans. 'You set me off when we stopped talking… I just let rip m'self (neighbours out hopefully!). It's so lovely to sing (in G), but you'll have to decide your key. Think this may be too growly, all those low Bs, tho' just right for this ole gal. I had forgotten dear David Niven was also in the film. Lawd, it makes me feel so ancient – and I am.

'Just watching MasterChef out of my eye-corner, which always fills me with soul-destroying shame when I watch these incredibly talented cooks (mostly amateurs) but I couldn't cope or be bothered with such detail and hard work, to be demolished in a matter of minutes! Though I guess I've never had much encouragement in the past and lived in hotels most of my life, or had hospitality with far better cooks, so I am very nervous about it all – and it always goes wrong whenever I've tried to entertain, so I've given up the ghost! I love good food – or did – but simple fare is my lot today, and all the preparation is too time-consuming. Got a busy-ish week but I shall try to watch some tennis. Just managed to catch Agassi and Wheaton, a really cracking watch! Oh, for some of their stamina – and in such heat!'

Of performance nerves and payment for singers, she said: 'You're beginning to really find out what a costly business this is – and I don't mean penny-wise! Lawd, I used to "die" singing in Grimsby. Grimsby always makes me extra nervous. To say nothing of the post-mortem afterwards, and unable to sleep when the damage was done. Please do think about a proper fee now – and I'm not a money-making ole moo! I know it's not easy in one sense; it was a very long time before I stopped feeling guilty – if ever – about taking or asking for a fee because I was able to sing, which was a God-given gift and lent to me for a short time. It's très tough getting started and when pennies are in short supply, so be brave and don't let them "door-mat" you as they did me. I'm trying not to preach but save you from some of the pitfalls I fell into. At last I've thrown off these hot, tight, heavy shoes and now in m'jamas, listening again to this new-found Scriabin piano concerto. The LP is at least 20 years old and never played until today (schame mich!). It is so beautiful. I needed a rest from voices, and sometimes I feel I love piano the greater of the two. If only I could begin to play like this. Too late now, as with so many things. A very passionate, sensual, and sad composer. He was only 43 years old when he departed this life, but what a legacy. Enclosed is Je te veux, plus m'humble literal translation… a love – almost sexy – love song. I hope you enjoy singing it.'[246]

The following day, she wrote: 'I'm just back from taking the Mini in for its first MOT and servicing. I can't believe it's three years old on Wednesday – but only done something over 2,000 miles. Hopefully, I'll have it back late afternoon. It was very misty early on – sea or tide mist. I know you're saturated with learning but seem to remember you hadn't a copy of Art Thou Troubled? by Handel. This is the highest key I have (F). I know many people around you will say, "Oh, everyone knows it and sings it". Fair enough but it depends on how you sing and colour it, and from your very soul depths. Kath [Ferrier] was the first person I heard sing it, and I was so moved not just by the music, but by the message. I was troubled! I was weary! Like many others in the audience, music brought comfort and joy. She began, as I often did later, with this English version. One is really able to reach out to your audience. In the first aria, which is so important, the message is personal and an intimate bond betwixt you all.

'Now 11.15am – am very hot (who isn't) – but at last, I cleaned my bay windows in what used to be the dining room and my mum's room, which has been taunting me for some time. It was in a state… the worst window in the house, collecting dust from the wind. The nets need washing and ironing, which I loathe. I try to keep up with cleaning this place, but I am not a domestic forte! Just as well I never married, for the other bod's sake! Tho' perhaps I'd never found the right one?? A real partnership might have helped but the fates forbade it, and now I can't be bothered. I still love m'music too much!'[247] Then: 'Just back from my usual Tesco trip, which is my great outing for the week, and damn them, they've moved everything again! Give me strength – literally! So good to have m'little jalopi back again, in spite of being completely cooked! I must sweep and tidy up the garage – another taunting disgrace.'[248]

Norma's mood flagged in the middle of August. She wrote: 'I'm nervous and fearful of relationships; I always have been… a desperately, painfully shy being beneath all my outer shell and camouflage, and never more so than now and my latter years. Having been taken for granted, used and hurt too many times emotionally, I just can't cope anymore, or be bothered. Like a moth who flies too near the candle, I don't want to get my wings burnt again. Although there's still oh so much love to give within me, which I used to pour out into my singing and now lies somewhat nervously dormant, except when occasionally I try to – or am able to – burst into song.'[249]

Norma was outwardly independent and feisty, with no need of romance in her life. Here, the intensely private woman reveals one of the deepest parts of herself, and it is incredibly moving. She channelled her desire for someone to share her life with into singing – and now, her voice had deserted her. Alexander tried to cheer her up by suggesting she still may find that special someone. She replied: 'I've smiled many times since we spoke last and your suggestion that "someone might sweep you off your feet". I can assure you, that's never happened in my whole life and it would have to be someone super-human to do that now at this late stage. I couldn't take on any family of his – for that's where the trouble usually lies, and the red lights start flashing. I guess I just couldn't be bothered and have wasted enough emotion and tears already over the years.'[250]

Norma would not want our sympathy. Long ago, she knowingly chose music over love and, thanks to this personal sacrifice, her glorious voice is recorded in history forever. What this small exchange demonstrates is that she was just as human as the rest of us – only, she had the voice of an angel.

★

'I've just been listening and looking at tonight's Prom, or at least Scriabin's Poem of Ecstasy. I have a cassette of Abbado and the Boston Symphony Orchestra… an extraordinary, mystical, passionate and very difficult piece with an enormous orchestra. But the BBC Symphony Orchestra are doing themselves proud this evening, especially certain solo instrumentalists.' August 1995 and Prom time in the Procter household. 'I must confess that literally seeing it performed has helped my understanding of it a little more. I've still quite a way to go before being finally convinced! It ends on the most incredible and one of the loudest orchestral crescendos imaginable, and the Promenaders doubling the sound with their cheers, yells and applause. Ouch! I then quickly switched over to the remainder of One Foot In The Grave; sublime to the ridiculous! Victor Meldrew is an absolute yell!'

This was written to Alexander on August 29 following one of their long chats on the phone. 'It was really good to talk but please excuse my lack of control moments. You caught me on a very bad day. I try so hard not to let those feelings show but this crazy ole heart of mine just becomes so full at times. 'It's been a strange year. I've lost two of my close friends and confidants, another is very ill and talking is seldom possible. I miss them and their love, total trust and understanding more than words can express, and there's no one to replace them. They were all 25–30 years older than me; proof that age is just a matter of figures. I watched some of the "Don" but couldn't take it! I thought the sets were horrendous, and the costumes grim and useless for such wonderful music – an insult to Mozart! The Telegraph reviewed it as "too clever for its own good". I'm no lover of critics generally but think he's absolutely right, sorry! I wonder what those seats cost?! I missed the overture, which I always loved, but when I think of our sets, costumes and production, Carl Elbert, a great German producer, Rafael [Kubelik] conducting and an amazing cast, how fortunate I was to have been a very small choral part. With such glorious music, either do it justice and do the job properly or don't bother. I can't say I was mad about the singers either, though possibly because they looked such a mess and not what Mozart intended, I'm sure. I've just listened finally to Parkinson's interview on Kenneth Williams. How brilliant he was and what a command of language. I'm very sad he took his own life; what a waste. I still think Parkie is one of the finest interviewers. It's chilly and autumnal today. I'll be glad to snuggle beneath the bedclothes.'

★

That summer, Beryl Jordan, Norma's close friend in Jersey, was battling Parkinson's disease. She'd had it for some time, but her condition was deteriorating. It is unsurprising, then, that the past was on Norma's mind. 'I miss all m'specials scattered far and wide. My life's always been a constant "I miss you" and "hello and goodbyes", so I should be used to it by now. But in these latter years, it has taken on a different and deep poignancy, especially as so many are no more and a permanent "miss you", which as you grow older happens all too frequently,' she wrote.[251] 'I am afraid I never seemed to have much time for books and reading, only music and scores. It was constant learn, learn, learn and memorising, and it hasn't changed much really, although not so pressurised. I was never in the "diva" class, nor wished to be.'

She recalled her first ever recording with Decca: 'I was green with fright. I still feel I must have dreamt my lost past and career. I have the deepest doubts about it all now.' She also remembered performing with Dickie Lewis: '[He] was a fine singer and a great buddy. We had some special times together and sang our last concert (he out of retirement and recovering from a second hip replacement) – some of the Brahms Liebeslieder at Emmie Tillett's (agent) memorial concert at the Wigmore. It was my only concert there and almost my last London effort. He was a big, tall fellow, similar to Peter Pears in build, though had a somewhat sad, complicated personal life marriage-wise, which he confided in this ole gal.' And, to a suggestion from Alexander that she might keep a pet for company, she replied: 'Your tropical fish – thanks for the thought but it's not for me. A number of people have suggested my having a dog, and as much as I love them, they're too great a responsibility, plus there's the emotional heartache when it's time to depart. I've been there and don't want an encore. Emotionally I'm drained these days anyhow.'

One can tell through Norma's tone that she was feeling melancholy. After a page or so, she confessed – there was bad news from Jersey. 'Frankly I'm feeling very sad. Yesterday my dear B's nurse, Hilary, rang in the AM from Jersey to say that Jack, B's husband, who had a biopsy earlier this week, has cancer as feared and has to go to Southampton on Monday – B's 84th birthday of all days – for a month's course of radiotherapy. Hilary, their private nurse but really for B, is taking him. He too is 84. Poor B. She'll be so devastated without him. She's so brave and putting up such a fight against that very cruel and painful Parkinson's disease. I only hope he'll cope with the flight (he's on morphine) and then that rotten treatment. One feels so useless and helpless to do something positive. She can barely speak now, is so very confused and is wheelchair or bedbound. I guess all the strain of B's illness has caught up with him, having had a pacemaker fitted last year and a hip replacement due. Hilary returns to B on Monday eve. She's almost an adopted daughter, though Jack has a daughter and son in Bath and London respectively from a previous marriage. I've been watching this slow, cruel deterioration for some years now and when I think how active and talented they were – she such a lovely looking and wonderful friend and closer than my sister until this last stroke of fate. I fear they will both pine for each other, poor loves. I only hope the good Lord doesn't allow them to suffer too much. They've already had enough.

'I'm surrounded by similar illnesses, especially this year. I've used up my emotions and spare energies but trying to help, listen etc. I know it's all part of this life but it's not always easy to accept. At least the sun is shining, which helps to cheer, and I had a lovely letter from one of my young singers. They all pour out their problems and worries… there must be something astray with m'face! I feel like an agony aunt, not a singing teacher! I'm drained and far too hyper-sensitive, and frankly haven't any spare energy m'self these days. I'm just an old misfit crock but battle on, though I wonder what for? Only the good Lord knows – for I don't! I'm ready for m'bath and bed, and hopefully to slip into oblivion. I'm pooped for all the wrong reasons.'

Two days on, she was in a more cheerful frame of mind: 'I'm grateful for another peaceful night's sleep. The sun is shining but it's chilly. I didn't go out yesterday. It was raining and I just needed to be quiet. I'm thrilled we've won the Ryder Cup… my golfing idol, Seve Ballesteros, is no longer able to make his body obey him. He played a great part in encouraging his team and in certain shots. There's a wonderful tribute to him in the Daily Telegraph this AM and rightly so. We have some fine players, but no one has that special, undefinable character which he has. It comes from the soul, I'm sure. I first became hooked on golf – and him in particular – after my hysterectomy, when I had to rest, although I still don't understand all the golfing terms and scoring. It is generally a quiet, relaxing game, but also frustrating to watch. He was in his heyday then, and wonderful to behold.'[252]

That year, Norma took a break from being on the jury of a singing competition in Grimsby and instead watched in the audience. 'I hate the clocks going back, and dark and early nights,' she wrote on October 22, in a somewhat disjointed letter to Alexander. 'Woe betide those who push their luck too far with me. I just can't be bothered, and life is too short, I fear, for disharmony. It makes me very sad. It's a lovely autumn day. I have tried to scoop up the damn leaves but m'ole bones have also said, "Enough's enough, Norm". I've had my flu jab. The Grimsby singing competition was very interesting and it was good to see some of my old jury colleagues again, and also to sit in the audience and really concentrate on every move of the singers and accompanists without having to write constructive crits, perhaps just at the very moment when something special or important happens. But I did make my own brief notes. As in 1992 on the jury, one despairs for approximately the first two or three days but eventually some real talent did appear, including a talented and lovely German tenor, one Dutch sop and a special 20-year-old British accompanist (no wonder I feel so ancient!). I found I chose the same finalists as the jury, though we did not exchange comments as it's not allowed. I didn't attend every session – hadn't time, and ghastly parking at the town hall.'

More bad news arrived from Jersey in December. Bee's husband, Jack, died. It was a devastating end to 1995, and 1996 began gloomily. 'It's a typical January – dark, grey, foggy, raining and cold,' she reported. The weather caused a pipe to burst at Nor-Dree. It leaked water everywhere, damaging the bay windows in both the music room and dining room. For a time, the water supply was cut off too. Worse still, Norma's dear friend Beryl's health was worsening. 'Sorry and sad to say B's husband Jack died on 20th December, so near Christmas, and because of the holiday period and so many other deaths, the funeral could not be until next Monday,' she wrote on January 6. 'Poor B is so confused but Hilary is wonderful to her. It's very difficult to accept but one can only hope he's now at peace and no longer in pain. I must stop getting into the minor key. Let's hope 1996 begins to improve and back into the major key.'

'I had the bay window installed yesterday. Chaos everywhere, and I'm trying to clear up all the mess and moving everything back again but had to get help moving the ole Joanna,' she said, a few weeks later. 'Where does all the clobber come from, though 40 years is a long time. I'm telling myself it's worth it, but not the bill.'[253] She marked her birthday on February 15, and afterwards sent a thank-you card to Alexander: 'Thanks for your remembrance of this ole gal as she journeys forward into yet another year. I had a happy and chaotic day midst new floorboards needed, carpet problems, blitzing the house. People and friends are far too kind. I'm throwing out lots of things and giving to charity shops when possible. I must stop collecting things!'[254]

Maintenance work on her home continued, much to her chagrin. Floorboards were replaced in preparation for a new window: 'Covered in dust, inside and out, after sweeping up and more floorboards in the dining room. I must've swallowed masses of dust – fool me not to have worn a mask… wot a mess, and y'know how I love such chaos! The new uPVC bay window is due to be banged in on March 4th, I hope. And after some more painting (alas, not oils!), lugging furniture and dragging up the ancient carpet after finally finding a suitable replacement to incorporate the crazy and mixed colour scheme, it's yet to be fitted. Norm's allergic to workmen (most of 'em!). I'm well past such capers but it has to be done. I'm busy practising and transposing betwixt the dust, dust sheets and banging (sends me silly!). Oh, to be young again – but no going back for me.'

Alexander was still in Scotland, and he must have mentioned trying out one of the country's national dishes, for she added: 'I've never tasted haggis, nor wished to… small wonder with those ingredients, and five hours of steaming time! It reminds me of my mother steaming all her masses of homemade Christmas puds. It was like being in a sauna. No wonder I don't enjoy cooking.' 'I seem to be getting nowhere fast,' she complained on March 6. 'Super but costly windows have been installed in the lounge, but it hasn't stopped the condensation, which has made me hopping mad. I've had to invest in a dehumidifier, which I suggest they include in their contract! It's a complete mystery to me. None of my friends have had this problem. Now I wait with certain anxiety should this dining room effort react the same? Heaven help 'em if it does! Everywhere looks as though a bomb's hit it – again! There's a pile of clearing up to be done, but the curtains are ready, washed and ironed, to hang – me with 'em! I still have considerable painting to do – walls, skirting boards etc – and the central heating is to be put back, if m'plumber remembers to come. I always have to double remind him... having been brought up to obey the clock all my life, I find it difficult to understand people who don't keep appointments on time, unless it's an emergency or whatever. This lot arrived two hours late with no explanation or apology. I was disciplined. Thank God we're all gifted in different ways – I should go bonkers doing their job.'

★

Tragically, Beryl Jordan caught pneumonia and died on March 16. Norma wrote to Alexander on March 27. 'B died at 2.05pm, as I'd begun teaching... a very wonderful and treasured friend of more than 40 years, who certainly didn't deserve a cruel, heartless, sad and tragic end to her special and goodly life,' she said. 'I try to hold onto the happy memories and wonderful laughter we shared – our music and artistic wavelengths, not to mention all the men/male problems we suffered and endured! Dear B was finally laid to rest in peace yesterday at 9.45am.' She'd also heard from Francis Coulson, her friend at Sharrow Bay. 'Francis just phoned – another casualty. He was in hospital all yesterday for the removal of terrible facial blotches due to taking damnable steroids for a leg muscle problem. I'm beset with so many sick and dying folk, and weary of being unable to do anything positive.'

★

The remainder of the spring was spent enduring house repairs, and Norma's frustration is clear. 'At last – a few moments betwixt the continued chaos in this place!' she wrote on April 4. 'Gradually we are getting there. Finished the bathroom this week and found two slow leaks in the kitchen and the "glory hole" above the large snug cupboard. Meantime, there are many more cupboards and drawers grinning at me and taunting me until they are cleared of debris. Grrr! I was wide awake at 6am, m'little grey cells churning over so many things.' And this in May: 'Another hectic week but my bedroom's completed thank God, and me with it, and the bank balance! Now to slowly finish off sorting out the remaining cupboards and drawers, plus my evening dresses. I won't be needing those anymore! I have given away all of my lovely fashion shoes now. I can't ever wear them with this paw. I must confess, some of these decisions aren't easy but I have had to be ruthless, which really isn't me at all. As you grow older, material things become less and less important. Good health and friends take first place, and I cling on tight to my music, which has always been a balm and saviour.'[255]

Summer followed, and in September Norma was saddened by the deaths of some of her contemporaries. 'I watched one of the Edinburgh Nights programmes but dropped off and forced m'self to watch the remaining clips of other festival offerings, including sculpture. I was very bored and horrified at what I saw. Enough, save to say I don't belong in what seems to be an ugly and evil era we're passing through,' she said.[256] 'I'm still hanging together, though bits keep falling off and wearing out. I was very sad to read dear Rafael [Kubelik] had left us recently. He was such a wonderful man and musician, of great integrity, courage, and humility. I wrote to Elsie (Morison that was), his wife, immediately. I didn't know he'd endured a long illness, bless him; another of the greats in my life no more, from way back from my Glyndebourne Chorus days in Edinburgh in the 1940s.

'Then, earlier this week, Ljuba Welitisch, 83 years, a memorable sop, again of Glyndebourne days, and also Sylvia Fischer, a sop too. I'm so glad I came into this profession when I did, for I would think even harder and longer than I did then, although I am still deeply in love with my music. I have just had the most wonderful laugh in weeks watching Parkinson's interview repeats with dear Les Dawson. I loved him – and still do. He was truly brilliant and unique, and a mean pianist and musician. The tears rolled down my cheeks for the right reasons – for a change. Another great in his field gone. Must stop. This week I've suddenly had a backlog pile of letters and bills, all winking at me for attention.'

This missive followed in October: 'Hooray! A day at last which actually belongs to me, without counting all the usual interruptions. Last night m'gardener laddie rang – could he come in later today, so more interruptions! However, the garden does need finally finishing off before real winter sets in; this and perhaps one more session, weather permitting, will hopefully do the trick.' Of Christmas, she said: 'I don't feel like decorating. The real simple faith and belief of Christmas is still deeply within me, but I am sick of all the razzmatazz. It's only one day really – such a fuss! As for New Year, I really loathe it and always have (though a real Scot would kill me for such a remark!). I used to love to dance, though it's years since I was on a dance floor! Many years ago in Barcelona, I was taken to a flamenco show and enjoyed it. I like my beloved ballet.

'Glad you're enjoying your leather coat. I tried some on when in London many moons ago, a black one, but the smell of the leather was so strong for me, so I decided against it. No offence but it always reminds me of the Gestapo coats they wore, or punk rockers. Blue denims have the same effect on me too, though I love the colour. Suede too was once a great rage but again, I didn't get involved as they marked so easily. A fur coat was my luxury and bought for warmth and protection against the continental winters.

'I've been watching Sir Simon Rattle's programme on Channel 4, hoping to find a greater understanding of what some of the 20th century composers are trying to tell us. He's clever and has interesting thoughts but I'm no further forward with understanding their complex writings and ugly harmonies. Press on Norm!'[257] December arrived soon enough – 'Just finished between 70 and 80 Christmas cards, and more to do – and letters. Give me strength!'[258] – and Norma ploughed on, passing on her knowledge to the pupils she taught.

The new year of 1997 dawned cold and grey, and prompted Norma to contemplate one of her most-performed works – the Messiah – with a tinge of melancholy. 'After this recent brass-monkey blast, I know I should have been a door-mouse and hibernated for the winter,' she said.[259] 'It's still a wonderful work, dear ole Messiah, and in spite of everyone thinking they know it backwards – which we don't. It's a very difficult work to really sing and project. I've given up long ago trying to fathom the real meaning of happiness. Define it if you can, being such an elusive, complicated mixture of bitter-sweet emotions, and usually lasts for fleeting moments. But one holds on tight to special memories of yesteryears and grateful blessings of the present day too.'

She spent that winter and spring busy working on some rare, unusual French composers and their melodies for her pupils. 'I find I'm much slower these days, mentally and vocally, but I try to battle on, L plates and all,' she admitted.[260] And life carried on, as it does. In May she told Alexander: 'Have nearly phoned a number of times but didn't really know when it's convenient? I should hate to intrude, especially during a snogging session! (Oh my God, what's that?!!). Little to report here – plenty of unnecessary problems, which weary this ole gal. I wish I'd never heard of uPCV windows and condensation! Grrr!'[261] And this in June: 'I have just awakened from a two-hour "drop off" in the land of nod, and it's only 3.45pm! I had a bad night so have relished a lovely, peaceful escape, tho' somewhat guiltily as it's such a perfect summer's day. One should be outside lapping up the sunshine 'midst a glorious heavenly blue and white skyline. However, the sun's not for this ole gal and I'm so grateful for the balm of sleep I was obviously needing.'[262]

★

In February 1998, in what was Brian Sack and Francis Coulson's 50th year running the hotel at Sharrow Bay, Francis died aged 78. A few days after his funeral at Carlisle Cathedral, at which the actor Tom Courtenay gave a reading, Brian went into hospital but thankfully recovered.

Professionally, interest in Norma's career remained. Dr. John Ketteringham, a Lincoln-based author, contacted Norma while researching his book, Lincolnshire Women. He was keen to include her in the book and wrote requesting a meeting, and information about Norma's early singing and her parents, as well as reminiscences about people she worked with and favourite venues and roles. Her reply, dated February 17, 1998, said: "Believe me, I am nowhere near ready to let you have possible details – so much mulling around in my head and still somewhat daunted about who or what to include – without causing offence to those who was/will be unable to be mentioned. Leave it with me – tho' humbly honoured to be included in this book – writing about myself and my career is really not m'forte, sorry!! But will try to make some humble offering. I note on your list I'm down as opera singer – could that be concert singer please – as opera was not my first love, believe me."

The first edition of Lincolnshire Women, in which Norma was duly included, was published in November that year; the second of Dr. Ketteringham's Lincolnshire People series. She appeared alongside other county notables including writers, actresses, religious martyrs, and sporting greats. In it, she recalled her childhood, and how her career began and grew, paying tribute to people such as Prof and Alec Redshaw. She told how, after embarking on studying musicianship and piano with Alec, she eventually moved onto German Lieder with Hans Oppenheim and, later, Paul Hamburger. 'Any success I have had is due to all these teachers,' she told Dr. Ketteringham. 'My beloved Prof, as he became, is now in his 99th year and still as bright as a button mentally, tho' with physical problems, whom I phone regularly. Hans 'Oppie' worked with me until his death, and it was later in my career with Paul we made many memorable BBC recordings together, when he was chief accompanist for Radio 3. He was wonderful to work with too, and we still keep in touch to this day.'

She went on to explain how she progressed: 'Very slowly, after hours of learning and memorising (Prof insisted on the latter whenever possible for complete freedom and total communication with an audience singing from the heart and depth of one's soul which I always loved to do when the music and text permitted), gradually I became known and in demand all over the UK at all the leading festivals with all the great British orchestras, choirs and wonderful conductors and the, even greater surprise, travelling throughout Europe which I loved so much. Out to Israel an amazing tour, and also South

America. Sadly I am unable to give more details of the many memorable concerts and wonderful musicians and people I met in Germany, Spain, France, Portugal, Norway, Sweden, Denmark, Finland, Holland, Belgium, Austria and Luxembourg, but I am so humbly grateful I was allowed to share such special memories and occasions. I must not forget another surprise and grateful honour when I was made an Honorary Member of the Royal Academy of Music in 1974, and way back in the late 1960s when Alec Redshaw asked me to become president of the Grimsby Philharmonic Society, which I gratefully accepted – tho' in name only; I was too busy travelling, and had no desire ever to become involved in committee meetings and so on.'

Making these handwritten notes for Dr. Ketteringham was, for Norma, a welcome trip to her beloved past and there is no doubt that her vast archive will have aided her. 'I am truly humbly honoured and grateful to have been included in this Lincolnshire book but must confess to considerable heartache and headache trying to give but a very brief outline and impossible precis of a thirty-five year singing career into such a short chapter,' she concluded in her letter to him. 'I should like to end by thanking the countless number of people who have helped me. It would be impossible to mention them all individually – but I am humbly grateful to my family, teachers and many friends – and any success I have today – they are very much part of it all.'

★

Norma continued to write to Alexander Anderson-Hall, but not as frequently. She worried over her friend Brian Sack, after the death of his partner Francis, at Sharrow Bay. She cared deeply about the pair who had given her much-needed respite and a retreat from her hectic career. In September, she wrote: 'Apart from a few days in August, it's been a grim summer. My garden has never been so full of weeds. I tried to see Brian at the Lakes, but he's been busy with the various demands since Francis died, keeping Sharrow going and constant streams of people. When I could find a time, as always, it was impossible for him, but we keep in constant touch by phone. He's had a helluva year and it's not over yet but has coped wonderfully well and is a good example to us all. It's tough going and this being their 50th anniversary for Sharrow. Wish we lived nearer.'[263] She travelled to Sharrow Bay the following month, and it was a momentous occasion. 'Sang with Brio and a solo carol. First time in public for 15 years,' she noted in her diary.[264] This was all she wrote about it; one can only imagine how emotional she felt.

★

It had been another tough year, yet there were moments of light: 'I had some lovely songs and ballads sent to me by a dear elderly lady in Bristol who conducted a ladies' choir there. She gave me a first chance, thousands of years ago, deputising for dear Gladys Ripley when she was ill, and we've always kept in touch. Some precious pieces and wonderful neglected songs which I doubt are even archived. Bless her, the nerves of her ears have gone, and she can no longer hear music – only a mass of distorted sounds. What a torment, poor love. She and her elderly companion are poorly. Oh, old age makes me so sad, tho' mentally she's amazing. What an atrocious year it's been – rain, rain never-ending, though we have to count our blessings compared with the flood areas. It must be absolute hell – all that water raging around one and through the house. What a terrible trauma trying to clear it up and all one's special possessions ruined or washed away.'[265]

The new year of 1999 arrived, and Norma continued to be beset with health issues. Her correspondence with Alexander is mostly made up of reminiscences of her career. 'The key to it all,' she said in May, 'is to be fit and well, which certainly wasn't always my good fortune, but I learned many lessons from that – and the most important priorities in life.' She spoke of performing in France: 'I sang in Paris four times but never had the opportunity to explore. I must confess, it was not one of my favourite cities. In fact, whenever I touched down on French soil, there were always problems.' And of the health of her brother-in-law: 'Norm has been far from well since his cataract op, though the eye has made good progress. But there's been a build-up of one or two things and last Friday, April 23rd, he suffered a minor stroke. Mercifully, he was at home – 11.30pm. I have been trying to help Audrey when possible. He's remained at home, but it's been all go – memories of caring for my mother, though she was downstairs by then.

'He's doing reasonably well, providing he's not too impatient to be over-venturesome! He'll be a long time – three months before trying to drive, golf etc. A real test on patience. Audrey's weary and not too well herself. We're all in the Crock Club. I'm weary too, and also tried to cope with some spring cleaning. M'bones are killing me. There's too much to cope with and I'm so damn slow these days. All this, not to mention the terrible doom and gloom of the past two weeks around the world. It's as if the devil himself has taken over.'[266] Later on, she wrote: 'Audrey and Norman battle on. He was 78 last Monday and we all agree we don't like being in the 70s club. I'm recovering from the flu. I went for my flu jab and within less than a week, I was smitten, having been cold and flu-free for 18 months.'[267]

★

On July 4, 1999, Prof celebrated his 100th birthday. Prof had difficulty hearing, but Norma persisted, often phoning Ivor Newton House, in Bromley, where he lived – a benevolent home dedicated to caring for retired musicians. He would sometimes sing a bar or two to her down the line. A letter from his son, the Rev Canon Alastair Roy Henderson, said: 'He does appreciate your calls, though we all find it quite a job to make him hear. He will economise on his batteries so that they are often on their last legs. But in all other respects he is in very good form for one so old, and they do look after him very well. Apparently, Flora Kent, who used to accompany him in the studio at Belsize Park, is to go there for a break this summer and may go there as a resident later. Of course, Flora never stops talking, but Dad is fond of her, and I know he will be pleased to feel she is satisfactorily settled.'[268]

The milestone birthday was celebrated by the release of an album, called Roy Henderson: Centenary Recital. Norma sent a gift and received this response from his daughter Shirley: 'He can't write, bless him, but Dad wants to thank you for your lovely cards and messages for his great day, and for the well thought out ties, which certainly lift his wardrobe to a new high. It was a terrific day, and we were so thankful he was well enough to enjoy every minute. All the family were there – 38 of us, from 78 down to three months – and he sat on the terrace like the Pope, receiving congratulations and dispensing blessings to the high and lowly.'

Just eight months later, on March 16, 2000, Prof died. Norma immediately wrote to his son. 'Thank you so much for your call this morning,' she penned. 'You have all been so much in my thoughts, and thank God it was peaceful, though a very difficult and emotional parting – such one I experienced alone after long nursing my dear mother.' The memorial service was conducted by his granddaughter, the Rev Debbie Dewes, at Christ Church Chorleywood. Prof's son sent a copy of a family newsletter to Norma, in which she was credited as one of his star pupils. It read: 'I think he felt that his greatest gift was as a singing teacher. He was pleased to have lived in three centuries, having been born in 1899. I am left with very happy memories of a father whose Christian faith, character and example have meant so much to me in my life.' A subsequent reply from Shirley read: 'I know you were thinking of us on Monday and I hope… you feel in some way a part of the farewell. There was an overwhelming sense of love and tenderness all the way through. I know how much you loved Dad and that he is bound up with your past – "threaded through" – and I know you will have sadness as you come to terms with the loss. Have faith – he is in what a friend of mine calls the concert hall of God. It's a wonderful thought.'

Chapter 16: Abe and Ike Rediscovered

The new millennium ('What a rip-off!' were her only thoughts[269]) came and went without consequence and with little to report. In April 2001, she complained to Alexander of the cold weather causing havoc in her garden: 'Don't talk about gardens. Mine is in chaos! Patiently waiting for Rob, a super gardener, but constantly held up by rain. I got up at 7am, ever hopeful, for 8am but it was cancelled again. My one hope and joy – my beloved magnolia tree – is in full bloom and somehow survived the frosts. Gorgeous to behold, as if Our Lord is in the garden.'[270]

May brought exciting news, which she was keen to impart. 'I thought you might like to share in a little history making,' she wrote. 'Approximately two years ago, after the release of Jennie (Vyvyan) and my joint CD, as Decca were delving into their archives, I was given courage to ask was there by any miraculous possibility of finding a recording of Ben's Canticle II, Abraham and Isaac, I made with him and Peter at the Decca Abbey Road studios? After considerable contacts with past and present Decca staff, and more archive delving, to my utter amazement and disbelief, the master tape was found – although Decca had no idea it was there at all. They were as surprised and shattered as this ole gal at such a find and very kindly sent me a private CD for me to hear before it was finally put together and released this month. Hope doth spring eternal and this is perfect living proof – never give up hoping. And after 44 years… I still can't believe it.

'Faith, Hope and Charity, the last of my beloved Brahms Serious Songs, have been constant companions throughout most of my life and career. I am reminded of an elderly lady of long ago, who always said, "Everything comes to him who knoweth how to wait". Now I wait to be clobbered by the critics! This miracle find is one of Ben's loveliest and simple works which I so loved performing with Peter – in recitals too. It's only a short work, approximately 20 minutes, and Decca's problem was what to programme it with. Eventually the final CD was made, but perhaps some of the other pieces – later and more complex writings of Ben's – may prove more difficult on the ear!'[271]

In September, Norma suffered a small accident. 'Felt left hip give way climbing onto a chair, cleaning,'[272] she wrote. 'Never been right since – more pain and in the lower spine. X-ray at Grimsby's hospital on November 8. Dr. John reports a deterioration of left hip. Pain worsened and arthritis everywhere – my hands and also right leg, either pulled a tendon or muscle. Groin pain. I walk lopsided and have difficulty getting in and out of the Mini. Long walking is no longer possible. I have difficulty climbing stairs – bending, hoovering, playing piano – everything is an effort. Last week I had great trouble getting out of the bath. I now have a disabled badge.' Determined to soldier on, Norma commissioned more repair work to Nor-Dree. 'I have been up to my eyes with decorators,' she said. 'Three weekends doing the kitchen, snug and cloakroom, plus endless clearing of papers and books, trying to make room for all the never-ending clobber in this place. Arthritis continues to creep. I am sad my dear recording equipment in the music room has given up the ghost. The cassette play/recording button has gone, and parts are obsolete. Buddies are searching the internet but no use... ghastly-looking CD stuff and cassettes are disappearing – crazy!'[273]

New Year's Day 2002 brought bad news. Brian, her good friend from Sharrow Bay, died. And Norma's poor health was not easing. She wrote: 'Pain worse during cold winter months. I'm at St. Hugh's for a hip operation – how long out of action? Will this condition worsen? Still hanging on in Bupa but September will be a new registration and I will be 75. Better to wait or have an op? £7,000 cost if not in Bupa. No driving, walking, bending down. Shoes – need new ones.'[274] In April, she wrote: 'I have often wondered why we want to go abroad – climate of course – but there really are some glorious and unique areas here. Cheltenham and that area bring back lovely memories. There used to be such super shops and real character there, but I expect it's changed from my long-ago travels – as most places. Exeter and Coventry have wonderful cathedrals; very grateful for all those years and glad I'm not travelling now. Devon and Cornwall... lovely countryside, and their dialects. I used to love all the little shops. I've had more bone problems, but my super consultant and physiotherapist have both come to the rescue. One just has to live with being an ole crock.'[275]

Then this, later in the year: 'Sorry I sounded so much in the minor key last time we talked. A bad patch, which keeps recurring, though I have much to be grateful for. Pity one can't call at the corner shop and buy a bag of new bones. M'bed calleth – it's p-----g down again – almost non-stop for the past three days, and brass-monkey temperatures. Dark, early nights; the clocks change on Saturday. Me no like!'[276]

Reminiscing as she did, Norma probably thought she was the only one who remembered her glittering career – but she was wrong. She was far from forgotten in the musical world, and her legacy lived on. A letter from Raymond Leppard arrived via Airmail from Indiana: 'I had such a delightful surprise last evening when a friend played me a lovely recording of Ben's Abraham and Isaac which you made ages ago and has only now been reissued – or even issued – for the first time. I hear of you often from John B [Barbirolli] and think of you and the times we had together. I hope one day we may have a glass of something delicious together but for the moment I wanted to send congratulations on beautiful music-making, and what a stunning piece it is!'

*

February 2003 heralded yet another distressing period. Norma's brother-in-law, Norman, fell desperately ill. Four years before he'd had a stroke and survived. '6am call,' she wrote in her diary of February 17. 'Life support machine. Two litres of fluid removed from lung and heart.' He died exactly a week later. 'Rushed to hospital but too late,' Norma said.[277]

Norman, the former RAF navigator who drove his dear sister-in-law around the country during the height of her career, clocking up hundreds of miles, was gone. In a letter to friend Alexander Anderson-Hall, dated March 25, she revealed how badly the family took his loss. 'Norman was very ill and was rushed into hospital on 4th Feb,' she wrote. 'After a very brave and courageous battle, the cruel like of which I never hope to witness again, he died on the 24th Feb, the funeral on 28th Feb at the Crematorium. Gerontius has never been closer these past weeks. It has been a very sad and difficult time but hopefully we are surmounting the problems and trying to come to terms with this sad loss, Audrey in particular – now living alone – though she has her two sons, grandchildren and many friends, and ole Norm. I had known him for sixty years – just turned 15 years old – when they met on a blind date.'

For as long as her health allowed, Norma continued to hand-write letters to her special ones. 'The internet makes me nervous,' she wrote in her archive, 'and I have never dabbled there. No equipment! Very clever technology but also very dangerous.' In 2003 and 2004, Norma contributed extensively to Britten Pears Arts (then called the Britten-Pears Foundation), donating documents and records of her own observations. She commented on it as a 'deluge' and a 'mighty mass of memorabilia' and was 'somewhat surprised' to find so much herself. 'One cannot put a price on such special memories,' she said, and found a delighted archivist as their recipient.

A letter to Norma from the organisation read: 'It matters so much to touch the hem (only you're much higher up than that!) of the garment in the very few people left who were so closely involved with those inexpressively precious years of music making and giving. Memories are treasures. I think the Norwich Gerontius you recall is the one of which BB [Benjamin Britten] wrote to someone of "a knock-out Gerontius". We played again our 2001 CD of Abe and Ike, from 1955… the thing that struck us was the way your voice blended and entwined flawlessly with Peter's. No wonder you did so much with them. If only that Gerontius were recorded too. I really can't thank you enough. Never think it was a dream, except in the way that Nacht und Traume are the truth. As Aschenbach sings in "Death In Venice" – it is all true.' Norma responded: 'So glad you approved of the 2001 Abe and Ike CD – perhaps my favourite miniature work of Ben's,' praising the 'amazing and unique Ben and Peter library for the world to see and enjoy.'

Meanwhile, Norma was aware of her body slowing down, after years of ill health and the usual aches and strains old age brought. On April 16, 2003, she told Alexander: 'There's been much to do, coping with admin and paperwork, sorting through clothes etc since Norm's left us. Audrey has done very well but I think we're both in post-shock. It seems very strange and we miss him so much, though he couldn't have gone on suffering as he was. I've been blitzing this house too – masses of papers, programmes, clothes to charity shops, cupboards, drawers etc taunting me for moons, but at long last I have been very ruthless and there's still masses more to do. I can hardly be bothered but it must be done – albeit such a slow ole Norms. I am also preparing to cope with a new boiler next week, which I'm really dreading. A good plumber and son, but it's all the prep and cleaning up afterwards… I am allergic to workmen! Something always goes sadly wrong! I'm hoping the Angel Gabriel will be close by again. I'm not moaning – just realistic facts! It's wonderful to have springtime with us… glorious flowers and some blue skies and sunshine.'

Later, in July, she said: 'We are slowly coming to terms with Norm's loss, Audrey especially, but life must go on and regardless, somehow does. I watched the final of the Cardiff Singer of the World, as always with great interest, though they've made changes – and no comment on paper! Also, some of Wimbledon. I love to watch not only their playing skills but character reactions too – always so close to my beloved Kipling poem "If", which sums it all up.'[278] And this, in October: 'It would have been Norm's 82nd birthday today but life goes on, regardless of memories. Don't like the return of winter but we've had a glorious summer. Then Christmas looms!'[279]

In 2004, she celebrated her 76th birthday. "Had a memorable birthday,' she told Alexander. 'Everyone was so kind and thoughtful – truly overwhelmed. Now 76! Help! Really old age! Oh dear! And so damn slow!'[280] In August, she wrote: 'Just heard from musical buddies at Gloucester Three

Choirs, reminding me next month will be the 50th anniversary of my first Three Choirs/Worcester – The Apostles – 1954! I was 26 years old. Help – tho' must confess my ole arthritic bones certainly confirm it. Everything is very different now.'[281] And at Christmas: 'I'm "eating" Christmas cards and still hanging together – arthritically! – but counting many blessings, tho' not in largo tempo.'

Retirement gave her the time for reflection and contemplation, of her life, friends, career and more. Throughout her archive around this time are jottings and notes that must have been made as they occurred to her. 'Watched The Last Night of the Proms,' she told Alexander in September 2005. 'It brought back special memories – 34 years ago, 14th Sept 1974 – of my own humble efforts. How I was given the courage and strength to just walk out there, let alone try to sing! My Prom Angels did it – or was it another dream?! Believe it or not, I began this letter days ago, but I am so low and have constant interruptions. I am still hanging together, but walking is no longer m'forte. Wonder if you were able to watch the return of the Ashes? Never really a cricket fan/gal but just switched on to Trent Bridge to looksee if much had changed from my first encounter there with the man I nearly married! I am an avid cricket fan now and became completely hooked by Freddie Flintoff and all his wonderful team – both teams – admiring their great skills, strength, and camaraderie, especially character-wise. Nuff said Norm – must organise some supper.'[282]

In December that year, she described herself as 'battling on, tho' spinal/bone problems make me a very Largo (tempo) Lass – or an arthritic ole crock! I have difficulties walking and standing, and I'm very grateful for m'walking stick and disability badge. Not moaning – but realistic facts, I fear.'[283] The problems with her bones were painful and incurable, and made her move frustratingly slowly. The new year, 2006, arrived, marking 20 years since Norma's last ever public concert. And time marched ever on. 'I have developed a truly terrible and frustrating memory at times. Enjoying the glorious month of May – "The Month of Mary" – and my own favourite month, m'thinks. We have had some lovely weather, tho' it's pouring again now, but the much-needed beauty of all the powers spring has... May bursts forth, oh so welcome, and we have a blackbird's nest nearby. Just to hear him pouring forth... such soulful sounds of beauty, puts me to shame... what's left of the ole noise-box.'[284]

In July, she wrote to her close friend Marion Thorpe. In 1948 at the Aldeburgh festival, a 21-year-old Marion met and fell in love with the festival's president, the seventh Earl of Harewood. They married and she became chatelaine of Harewood House, hence Norma's reference to it in the letter. They divorced in 1967, and she later married the MP Jeremy Thorpe.

'What a wonderful surprise to hear your voice again this evening,' wrote Norma. 'Thank you so much for your lovely and generous call. It made this ole gal's day. Please forgive my clumsy memory of Harewood – the last thing you wished to be reminded of. Can't think why it poured forth. I loved Harewood – completely overawed by everything and everyone, and constantly pinching myself. Those were very special days. It's lovely we all share the special friendship and talents of dear David [Cregeen, the sculptor]. I know like me he shares the greatest admiration for all your courage throughout many years.'[285]

To February 2007, and: 'I had a memorable day for m'79th year (which should read 179th!) and completely overwhelmed by so many kind and generous remembrances. Certain things remind me of my travels to Israel in August heat; what wonderful and incredible history, biblical locations, but always the dreaded jetlag. South America… heat and horrendous flights. A night flight to Naples, Helsinki in the winter (I couldn't breathe outside!).'[286] She wrote to Alexander on August 6: 'Counting many blessings apart from a flooded rear garden – but such heartache watching all the poor souls in their ruined homes and belongings, living on filthy, hellish water conditions. Global warming apart – why hasn't this Government renewed the old drains and drainage system? This beloved country… I can't believe what is happening to it. I'm still hanging together – just! – but have considerable walking/mobility problems, and never-ending house repairs and replacements. Can't believe my past life ever existed!'

Christmas soon came around again. 'I still love Christmas – at least, the real meaning,' she declared. 'It all began so humbly in a stable, but it drives me silly now. So commercialised. I am no longer able to keep up with it all, especially the cards – I'm eating them!'[287] On December 26, she wrote again to Marion Thorpe, who'd been suffering from ill health herself. She said: 'I knew nothing of your cruel and devastating illness this past summer. I feel so guilty for I would've written long ago but can only hope and pray at least you are beginning to make a real recovery and send special love, hope, thoughts and healing blessings as we approach the new year. Thinking of you and Jeremy with fond love and special memories.'

Norma also wrote a note about the pleasure of singing Bach and Brahms. 'Two of my favourites!' she declared. 'The Brahms really should be "auf Deutsch", as I sang later, but Sir Malcolm wouldn't allow it, as with the Four Serious Songs. Another wonderful text and orchestration – I love the dark-toned music and Sir M's interpretation orchestrally – Goethe at his finest/deep-thinking. This is a vocal score – Novello edition and translation by the Rev W.G. Rothery, and the only recording I have with Sir M of this work. We performed several times – all the Proms – but this is in the vast

Maida Vale BBC studio. A fabulous work which both Sir M and I adored. The Bach – my favourite solo contralto No. 169 – gorgeous text and music, and a super organ obligato – very difficult, especially the very lovely bubbling aria. A dear organist playing on a lovely miniature organ – and very nervous of my moving/bubbly tempo. I eventually got him there (my tempo) by the Da Capo of the aria. Bravo for him! Then the beautiful orchestral aria which followed. Lovely people to work with. I sometimes feel the words are slightly lost acoustically, in this lovely but vast church in Gouda – yes, the Dutch cheese town! Clever Johann Sebastian! What a privilege it was to try and sing these amazing works. Special days and special memories – and my only proof it wasn't just a dream.'

★

By now, Norma's archive was a large mass of programmes, records, certificates, notes and more. She wrote about how she first heard Paul Robeson singing There Is A Green Hill Far Away on an old 78 [rpm] record and described it as 'wonderful – glorious sound!' She went on to sing it herself aged about 16 in Mill Road choir concerts and at other churches, in F Minor/Major. 'Be sincere in whatever you are singing – love, hate, passion, joy, grief – you must mean every word you sing and feel and project this in your voice and facial expression,' she said. 'It's so important to an audience.'

She speaks here on an aria in Bach's Mass In B Minor: 'This is an appallingly difficult aria because it just flows on and on. It's a real test in breath control and trying to find contrast in dynamic and vocal colour. It follows the beautiful Passion music and is immediately before the wonderful Et Resurrexit, so this is really a prayer of absolute faith and belief, with the lovely oboe obligato.' And here, a note she attached to a postcard, with dried palm leaves attached from Madrid: 'A crucifixion painting from a fan in Niesbaden in the Fifties, and sprigs of palm always given to me on Palm Sunday morning in Madrid when we sang our final performance of three concerts (Friday, Saturday evening and Palm Sunday at 11am), which became a yearly Easter pilgrimage in Spain, including Barcelona, throughout the Fifties, Sixties and Seventies. They were very special occasions, with Argenta and Rafael Frühbeck de Bourgos.'

It seems that Norma was trying to empty her thoughts and memories onto paper before she lost hold of them. Perhaps her beloved angels were guiding her.

★

Norma's diaries from 2008 to 2011 are absent from her archive, though she doubtless kept them. During this time, thankfully, correspondence fills in some of the gaps. 'It's been a very long and bitterly cold winter here, which still exists, tho' sunshine today! What is that??' she told Alexander brightly, on April 21, 2008. 'I'm battling on – oh so slowly – in total disbelief of my own past life and travels. I turned down a Far East tour, including Australia and New Zealand, because of the long flights everywhere, demanding solo recitals and concerts, and receptions on arrival day before concerts – cocktail affairs, no way! – not for Norms, travelling alone. Far too far away.' And this in July: 'The world and our dear country are midst vast changes which trouble me greatly. I battle on but walking and being on m'feet [is hard]. I'm just an arthritic ole crock! I teach very occasionally; fingers and feet no longer obey, nor m'little grey cells.

'I enjoyed watching Wimbledon and the final – I was a wreck! Federer is still the man and player for me. Nadal is very clever and cunning! He's the king of violation time, especially against Roger. From the first time I watched them play, I've shouted at the TV and refs! I try to make time to watch and marvel at such incredible strength and mobility. I see the Proms began on Friday and watch when possible. I'm very concerned for dearest Joan [Sutherland], who has broken both legs whilst picking flowers in her Swiss garden. Doubly cruel, for last year she had two new knees. She was always so wonderful to me, especially with my bone problems which began way back in 1961/2. Strange, last week I had to re-check dates in old diaries and found by chance our first meeting/concert together in Brecon Cathedral and so began many special memories – musical, personal and laughter. She's 81 years old now, bless her.'[288]

Norma also began exchanging letters with David Whittaker, of the Kathleen Ferrier Society, in 2009 until 2012, displaying her terrific sense of humour and honesty from the off. 'Norma, that's m'name, or Norm, or Mary, mi' first name, which now has to be used for official papers etc,' she told him in one of her first letters. 'There are others, but I'll spare you!!?? Unfortunately, I have difficult mobility problems – walking and travelling is no longer my forte – I'm now 81 years old!! … Time waits for no man! I have just seen the final part of Songs of Praise from my beloved Southwark Cathedral, and suddenly many memories came flooding forth. I will write again when my ole memory bank is also less arthritic!'[289] David's correspondence prompted her to examine the older documents in her archive, looking for information about her dearest KK to help the society. It was around now that she began adding to – sometimes writing over – old diary entries and notes.

In September 2009 she told Alexander: 'I have recently had to check through my old diaries and papers since 1948! Just beyond belief what I used to do and where I found the energy. But years do make a difference, believe me. We've had a very mixed summer weather-wise but loathe to see the nights drawing in. I only go out when I have to. M'little 17-year-old Mini has been rebuilt but driving is also a problem. Norms needs rebuilding too! I am very sad at what is happening to this beloved country of ours – September 3, 1939 (I was 11 years old!) – wasn't that enough? How the music industry has changed too. No contraltos needed anymore. I was told recently someone asked for a CD of beloved KK in Glasgow and the shop assistant said "who – never heard of 'er". Unbelievable! I've had boiler and washer/dryer problems, and the plumber is waiting in the wings. Wot price peace?!?'[290]

And this, also to Alexander, over December 3 and 4: 'Many thanks for your letter, which made me dizzy trying to keep up with your tempo… into so many orbits! Oh, for a quarter of that strength. I'm afraid "langsam" [German for 'slow'] is my second name. So very slow, especially walking with m'ole stick, including in Adagio brain/mind. But we plod onwards! You write from a wonderful three weeks in France. My singing visits to France/Paris were usually very mixed – somewhat minor key-ish – and sadly, I never had time to explore as in other European countries, like Germany, Spain, and Switzerland. I sometimes wonder if I dreamt it all. Truly! French is not really my favourite language… I sang only a few songs and had to hurriedly learn Les Noces by Stravinsky, which should have been Handel, in the first Jordanian Festival but was cancelled. War broke out and we had to do Les Noces in dear Madrid – but Norms no like! My nephew Paul, in Newcastle, now has the most gorgeous Airedale puppy, Holly. She's about 16 months old and occasionally visits and has completely stolen m'ole heart. She's just adorable and full of mischief. We all had Airedales when children.'

In 2010, she told David Whittaker: 'Please forgive m'terrible scribble – it's m'very wandering pen. Am losing control?! No excuses but must confess my memory (it used to be a bit considerable) this past year keeps on letting me down, and at that time, various sad/difficult emotional problems beset me. I'll spare you the details. I'm so slow and hopelessly behind this year!'[291] To Alexander, she said May was turning out to be a lovely month, with the 'sun shining, blue skies and beautiful blossoms everywhere'. 'Oh dear! I've done it again – so very sorry to have misplaced your birthday!' she continued. 'I have eight b-days in May and my mind/memory is really playing every forgetful trick possible, all 82 years of 'em. Can't remember names, where I've left things… guess I've exhausted m'memory bank from past years, which used to be m'forte – and I don't like it! I'm so slow… my dear specialist plus all x-rays, MRI scans etc… since nothing can be done for m'ole spine and bone problems – just painkillers – but they don't help! Can't believe I was

33 years old when all this began – and still driving everyone mental!! Very grateful still for my wicked sense of humour. Love ole Norms – your unique name, no one else has called me so, tho' perhaps many other variations – best not printed!!!'[292]

★

On October 10, 2010, Dame Joan Sutherland died aged 83 in Switzerland. The Australian-born soprano achieved international fame almost overnight when she appeared as Lucia in a new production of Donizetti's Lucia di Lammermoor at Covent Garden in February 1959. This fame came after years of hard work and dedication; she had actually made her Covent Garden debut in 1952 in the role of First Lady in Die Zauberflote. A singer from childhood, her career spanned four decades. She had been ill for some time, something Norma worried over. A note from her husband Richard, written on October 2 – just seven days before she died, read: 'Dear Norma, how lovely of you to remember my birthday – I can now say I am in my ninth decade! It's a long time since we saw each other but, in some ways, it is as yesterday. I will never forget your lovely voice and your beautiful face. Joan is sadly very ill – not in much pain but no strength left. She can't stand and spends much of her time in bed, sleeping a lot. She sends you much love – I send you mine. So lovely to hear from you.'

Norma replied: 'I'm so sad and concerned to hear of beloved Joan's heartache problems. The last news I had she was improving, bless her – after such an unbelievably cruel double twist of fate [Norma is referring to Joan breaking both her legs], and for you, the family, the other Norm [Norman Ayrton] and special close friends having to be "watchers". Please give her my dearest love and special strength. I couldn't be closer in spirit… and my own osteoarthritic spine, legs and bones… she was always so wonderful to me from our first meeting – Adam was just months old. I then met you and you kindly took me to Covent Garden to see her worldwide incredible success as Lucia Di Lammermoor. Then followed our very special shock Alcina in Koln! Norm, stop! Forgive my ole memory running away with me. As you said, it feels like yesterday but it's 54 years ago!'

Tucked inside the cover of a boxed Lucia LP was this small, handwritten note from Norma: 'I have just seen the TV news and am completely shattered. La Stupenda to the last. Words are so very difficult to express my deepest feelings, but I hope praying hands will perhaps speak for me. I had no idea she had become so seriously ill, bless her, until Ric sent a thank-you letter for his 80th birthday card – he too now joining the 80s club. I wrote back immediately but the six o'clock TV news announced the terrible news. That heavenly choir will have gone up a magnificent tone since she joined them. I still have the wonderful boxed Lucia she so generously sent me in early 1962 when I was unable to walk and was bed-ridden.'

Norman Ayrton, the long-serving head of the London Academy of Music and Dramatic Art, was Joan's acting coach. He wrote to Norma in the days after Joan's death to express his grief. 'It was a great blow and I still can't quite get my head round the fact that she is no longer there,' he said. 'Every day I find myself saying, "I must remember to tell Joan" and then realise that I can't. We had talked on the telephone about a week before she died and happily, we had a wonderful week together back in July, when the weather was glorious, and we were able to eat out of doors every single day. I made her favourite summer pudding and although she was in a wheelchair, she enjoyed herself. But I feared for the end of summer – and I was right. She suddenly went downhill fast.

'I was able to get over to Switzerland for the funeral, which was simple and private and no press, thank goodness. Adam and her grandson came from Australia and it was just family and very close friends. It is going to take us all a while to fully realise that she has gone but how lucky we are to live in the age of technology, as we have videos and DVDs and many CDs and tapes of her, so we can never really lose her. She is always here! I am still staggering on and managing to teach three days a week, which keeps my brain ticking over, and this coming week I'm going to Paris to do a masterclass with young singers, which will be tiring but fun. I could do with a new pair of legs as walking is no longer the pleasure that it used to be, but I mustn't grumble.'

Norma was too ill to attend Joan's memorial service at Westminster Abbey the following February, so a friend forwarded her a programme. Conducted by The Very Reverend Dr John Hall, Dean of Westminster, the service was sung by the choir of Westminster Abbey and two of Joan's recordings were played. The Prince of Wales, representing the Queen and Prince Philip, was among the attendees, and the address was given by Sir John Tooley, who was the general director of the Royal Opera House between 1970 and 1988. Norma noted: 'I would dearly loved to have shared this honour. I haven't travelled to London since 1992!' A note sent from Richard afterwards read: 'I'm so sorry you couldn't get to the abbey. It was an unforgettable and moving service. I'm sure you were there in spirit. I so appreciate your lovely words. I hope we may yet meet again. We are both getting up there! Do look after yourself.'

Norman Ayrton provided Norma with the details she so wanted to hear: 'It was really wonderful! I'm sure Joan would be very pleased at such a moving and beautifully organised tribute. I found myself sitting next to Felicity Lott, which was nice. Everybody who had known or worked with Joan seemed to be there – it was absolutely packed. So, I saw a lot of old friends and colleagues. The most moving moment was Joan singing Let The Bright Seraphim while her grandson Vanya walked very slowly the entire length of the aisle by himself carrying a cushion with all her various orders and medals on it and gave it to the Dean at the altar steps, who placed it on the altar. I believe that yesterday Richard had to go to Buckingham Palace to personally return her Order of Merit to the Queen. Prince Charles kept a very low profile and slipped into a private pew with no ceremony. The abbey is such a wonderful setting for such a ceremony, especially with the whole orchestra from the Royal Opera House and the choir. One will never forget it! It was a remarkable day and a precious memory to add to all the others. Hope this helps to put you in the picture.'

By now, Norma was 83 years old. Thanking Alexander Anderson-Hall for a birthday card, she wrote: 'I am still feeling very sad about Joan. She was so wonderful to me, both in our early careers, but she was La Stupenda. I saw the thanksgiving service at Westminster Abbey for her, and I received a loving invitation, but I was sadly unable to go/accept due to mobility problems. I have since received the order of service. It must have been achingly beautiful – but I was there in spirit. Bless her.'[293]

*

Meanwhile, she continued to correspond with David Whittaker from the Kathleen Ferrier Society. They had struck up a friendship through letters. 'Please excuse this delayed reply – but am so painfully slow, and trying to keep up with letters etc,' she wrote. 'I think folk are expecting me to pop m'clogs. I am in the midst of sorting out masses of my own papers and piles of music scores, cassettes, recordings, LPs etc. What to do with them? I'm trying to catch today's post but having constant interruptions.

'My 87-year-old sister Audrey is battling heart-wise too – doubt if I'll make it! Audrey is also living alone. Her RAF F/Lt ex-navigator husband Norman died eight and a half years ago. Two married sons and families. She had a lovely soprano voice – we used to sing duets. As for Christmas, the real meaning of love, I dread it now – all those cards to write! Most of the family away this year – still just take it easy, tho' sadly no vino allowed by medics for many moons! Perhaps Christmas Day with Audrey – all a bit chaotic this year!'[294]

In early 2012, she told how she'd received an interview request from writer Paul Campion, the author of Ferrier: A Career Recorded. 'Think it will be a written work but to include a CD of the interviews, and he wants to come up to GY [Grimsby] and talk to ole Norm, the CD machine giving a far clearer recording than by phone,' she wrote. 'I'm amazed – having to trail all that way up here. I'm troubled a bit too – speaking and interviews are not my forte.' The interview duly took place on February 28 and afterwards, she told David: 'How I wish I could have travelled to London and so save Paul a dreary trail up to Grimsby – no through trains – there used to be four daily in my beginning days. M'bones are under the rail lines and I'm troubled hospitality wise. Paul was very kind and helpful. This very modern recording equipment… he phoned and said it just hadn't recorded for some reason, but I felt it was me! Lovely to be asked but I prefer to write. I have his wonderful book – incredible detail.'

That year, Royal Mail produced a stamp of Kathleen Ferrier in its Eminent Britons series: 'She looks – that unique expression, just as she did when I asked for her autograph and she changed my life, bless her. Bravo!'[295] On April 22, Norma wrote a card to Ferrier on what would have been her 100th birthday. It was inscribed with the verse 'Love like you have nothing to lose and live like there is no tomorrow'. In it, she wrote: 'Beloved Kathleen, Kath, Kaff, KK – where ere ye be? A very special happy birthday/100th to you, and heartfelt gratitude for you, your heavenly voice and beauty in sound and soul, and wondrous laughter, smiles and caring. Thanks be to God. I found this card by chance and thought it belonged to you – the deep quotation.'

Although her health was worse than ever – she had to sell her beloved Mini because she could no longer manage driving – she maintained her correspondence with David. 'I have always loved and found strength in Durer's Praying Hands,' she told him. 'I loved to sketch and paint. I enclose a small copy. Keep it in your pocket and may its angels bring you healing blessings where ere ye be. I have such slow bones and brains! I can't keep up with everyone and everything. So glad more Kaff recordings have been found, tho' not surprised, especially the beloved Brahms Four Serious Songs, which she loved so much, and with John Newmark. Sadly, our paths never crossed but I always felt there was a very close wavelength betwixt him and Kaff. The voice is an incredible human vocal instrument. Not one you pick up and play – for me, it could only be God's creation. I am very humbly still covered in those never-ending L-plates. I was and am always deeply critical of my singing, and it's not just the vocal sounds – one needs to be very strong physically and one needs the deepest intuition of what the composer, poet, conductor, accompanist, or producer feels or demands. Enough! One could go on and on about this God-given blessing and mystery.'[296]

In September 2012, she wrote of having a bad attack of Meniere's disease and vertigo, the latter being one of the symptoms of the condition. She also reported suffering from rhinitis. 'Wot an old wreck!!!' she declared. 'I have had two minor strokes and have difficulty writing. Scuse! M'right hand no longer obeys.' Her diary of September 9 reads: 'Rheumatoid arthritis/ hips and spine/ osteomyelitis/ Meniere's/ vertigo/ Parkinson's.' That December, she began taking three tablets a day for Parkinson's disease – the same illness which took her beloved Beryl. And soon, she would stop writing.

Her diaries for 2013 to 2015 are sporadic. For 2013, she noted:

> ***March 7:*** *'Parkinson's paralysis of muscles and mind.'*
>
> ***March 26:*** *'Hospital. Long assessment. Very weary.'*
>
> ***April 20:*** *'1948 Southwark YouTube!!!'*
>
> ***July 21:*** *'To bed. Nasty paralysis.'*
>
> ***September 16:*** *'Bad fall 3am.'*

This fall resulted in the paralysis of her legs and spine, and a 'terrible invasion of people' into her home.[297] By people, she meant carers, and although she knew they were there to help her, it was a huge breach of her privacy. Despite everything, she was still attempting to live her way. In January 2015, she had a pancreatic cyst. It is a poignant diary; all year she felt unwell and called Parkinson's 'hellish'.[298]

It was her final diary.

ABOVE: Norma's family home in Scartho, Grimsby. A note on the rear says 'Father, who built it, made us leave in panic! We were heartbroken to leave.'

LEFT: Edith and John Procter's wedding day.

BELOW: Audrey and Norma as children. Norma noted she was 'very nervous of the cameraman under a black hood! Nervous little hand on Audrey's knee.'

ABOVE: Young Norma with her father in Skegness

RIGHT: Norma as a child. She loathed swimming.

BELOW RIGHT: Audrey and Norma, the singing sisters from Scartho. 'Grief!' wrote Norma, 'I was in trouble again! I had poured a bottle of Brilliantine on my head just before the photographer arrived. Help, my mother was furious!! Mischief! A Brilliantined Norm, who was also losing all her milk teeth – goofy!' Photo courtesy of Norma's family.

ABOVE LEFT: Norma, Sir Hugh Robertson and Nita Garrod at the Cleethorpes Festival, the last one before the Second World War. Norma was 11. ABOVE RIGHT: Norma's second prize medal from the 1935 Cleethorpes Musical Festival. BELOW: The programme of Handel's Messiah at Mill Road Church, Cleethorpes, in 1946; Norma's first Messiah, aged 18. RIGHT: Norma aged 13, pictured here after winning at her last ever Grimsby Festival.

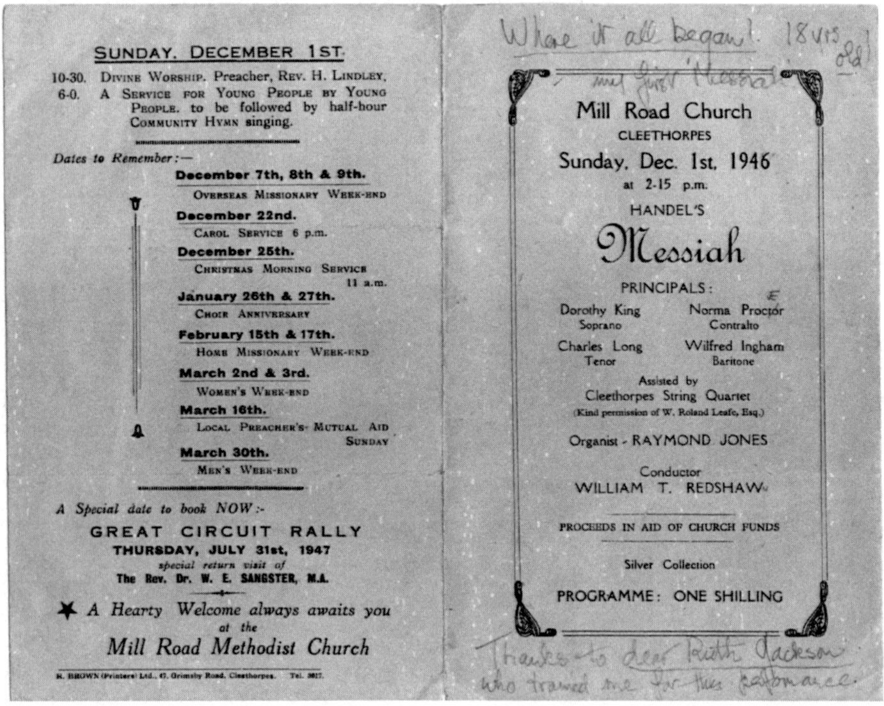

SUNDAY, DECEMBER 1ST.

10-30. DIVINE WORSHIP. Preacher, REV. H. LINDLEY.
6-0. A SERVICE FOR YOUNG PEOPLE BY YOUNG PEOPLE, to be followed by half-hour COMMUNITY HYMN singing.

Dates to Remember:—

December 7th, 8th & 9th.
OVERSEAS MISSIONARY WEEK-END
December 22nd.
CAROL SERVICE 6 p.m.
December 25th.
CHRISTMAS MORNING SERVICE 11 a.m.
January 26th & 27th.
CHOIR ANNIVERSARY
February 15th & 17th.
HOME MISSIONARY WEEK-END
March 2nd & 3rd.
WOMEN'S WEEK-END
March 16th.
LOCAL PREACHER'S MUTUAL AID SUNDAY
March 30th.
MEN'S WEEK-END

A Special date to book NOW:-
GREAT CIRCUIT RALLY
THURSDAY, JULY 31st, 1947
special return visit of
The Rev. Dr. W. E. SANGSTER, M.A.

★ A Hearty Welcome always awaits you at the
Mill Road Methodist Church

H. BROWN (Printers) Ltd., 47, Grimsby Road, Cleethorpes. Tel. 3817.

Where it all began! 18 yrs old!
my first 'Messiah'

Mill Road Church
CLEETHORPES
Sunday, Dec. 1st, 1946
at 2-15 p.m.
HANDEL'S
Messiah

PRINCIPALS:

Dorothy King, Soprano — Norma Proctor (E), Contralto
Charles Long, Tenor — Wilfred Ingham, Baritone

Assisted by
Cleethorpes String Quartet
(Kind permission of W. Roland Leafe, Esq.)

Organist - RAYMOND JONES

Conductor
WILLIAM T. REDSHAW

PROCEEDS IN AID OF CHURCH FUNDS

Silver Collection

PROGRAMME: ONE SHILLING

Thanks to dear Ruth Jackson who trained me for this performance.

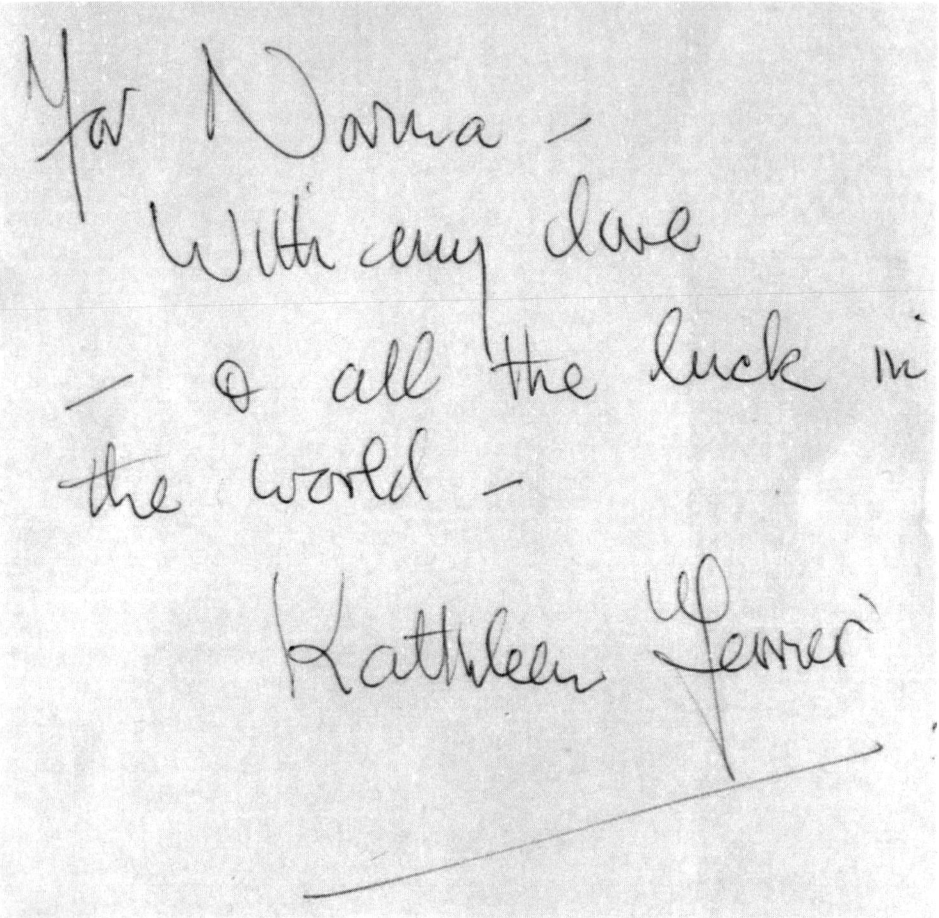
For Norma –
With every love
– & all the luck in
the world –
Kathleen Ferrier

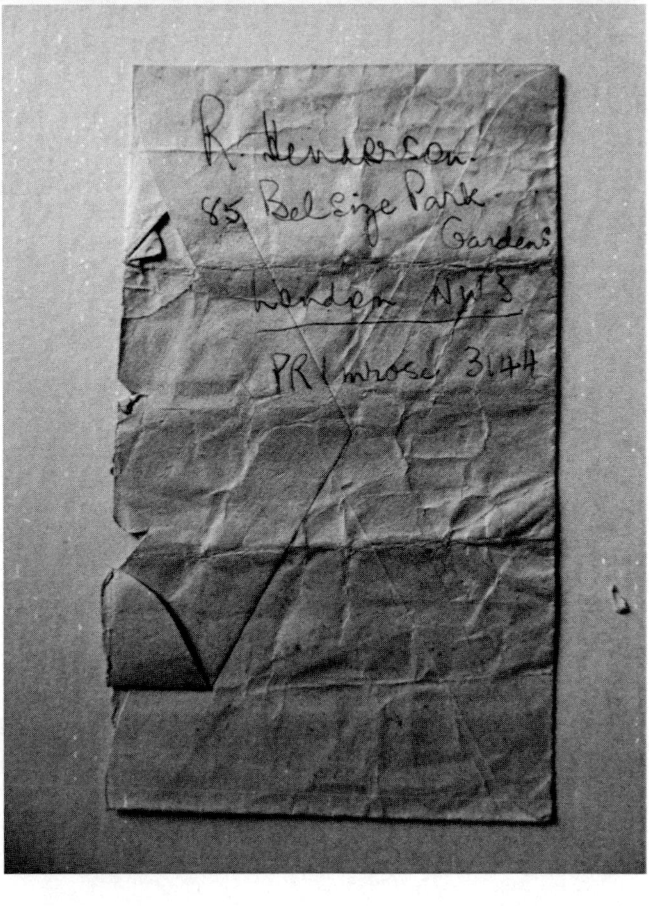

ABOVE LEFT: Kathleen Ferrier's autograph for Norma.

BELOW LEFT: Kathleen Ferrier. Photo courtesy of the Ferrier family.

ABOVE AND RIGHT: The envelope Kathleen Ferrier used to pass Roy Henderson's address onto Norma, after a Messiah at Mill Road on December 1 1946.

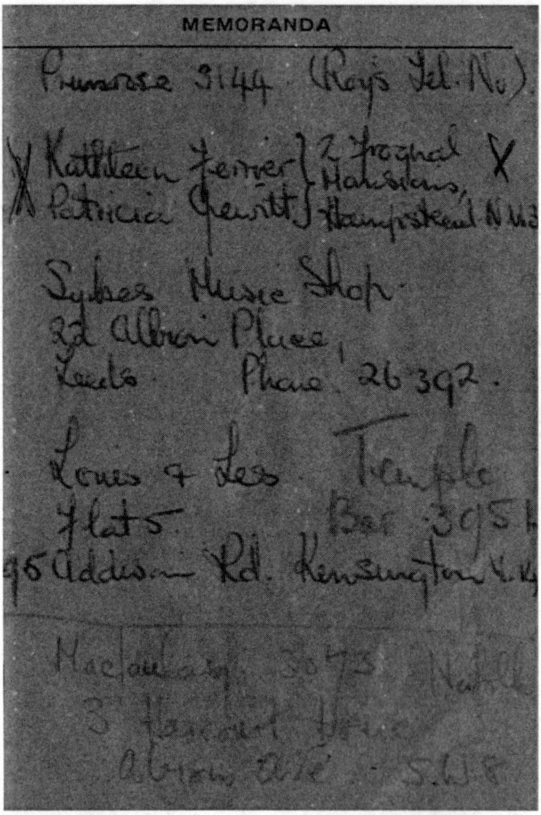

MEMORANDA

Primrose 3144 (Roy's Tel. No).

Kathleen Ferrier } 2 Frognal
Patricia } Mansions,
Hampstead NW3

Sykes Music Shop.
2d Albion Place,
Leeds. Phone 26392.

Temple
Flat 5 Bar 3951
95 Addison Rd. Kensington W14

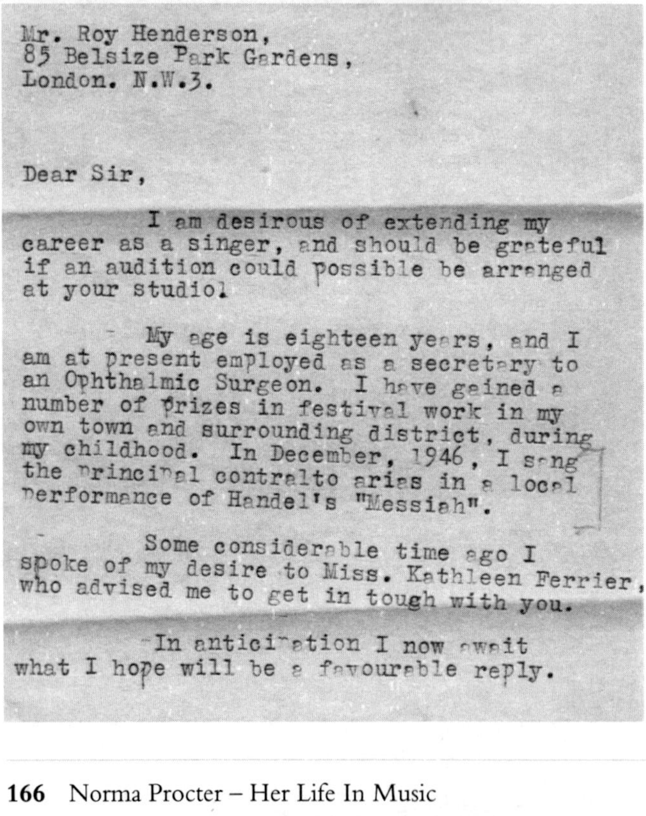

Mr. Roy Henderson,
85 Belsize Park Gardens,
London. N.W.3.

Dear Sir,

I am desirous of extending my career as a singer, and should be grateful if an audition could possible be arranged at your studio!

My age is eighteen years, and I am at present employed as a secretary to an Ophthalmic Surgeon. I have gained a number of prizes in festival work in my own town and surrounding district, during my childhood. In December, 1946, I sang the principal contralto arias in a local performance of Handel's "Messiah".

Some considerable time ago I spoke of my desire to Miss. Kathleen Ferrier, who advised me to get in tough with you.

In anticipation I now await what I hope will be a favourable reply.

ABOVE LEFT: A page from Norma's 1948 diary, containing Roy Henderson's and Kathleen Ferrier's contact details.

ABOVE RIGHT: A young Alec Redshaw. Photo courtesy of Grimsby Philharmonic Society.

LEFT: Norma's letter to Roy Henderson, asking for lessons.

Lincs. Owner Hopes To Win Grand National

THAT he might one day run a horse in the Grand National has been an ambition cherished by Mr. John Procter, of the Lord Nelson Hotel, Brigg, since he was a telegraph messenger boy in Crimsby.

This was realised a few weeks ago, when he bought the Irish 'chaser, Sheila's Cottage. Now he has reasons for being hopeful of winning this great race.

Although he has been interested in racing for many years, it was only three years ago that Mr. Procter first became an owner and he has done very well up to now.

Proud of his humble parentage—he was running errands for half-a-crown a week at 10 years of age—Mr. Procter now has what is perhaps the largest fish-curing business in Britain, in addition to being a trawler owner, a hotel pro-

ABOVE: The February 9, 1948, edition of the Lincolnshire Echo, about Sheila's Cottage.
BELOW: Sheila's Cottage. The photograph is signed in pen by Norma's father, John, and reads 'Lots of love, Daddy.'

ABOVE: Roy Henderson. Photo courtesy of the Ferrier family.

BELOW: Norma (on the right, second row down, two from right) with the Glyndebourne Opera in Edinburgh, 1948. This is scene two from Cosi Fan Tutte.

1948.

Glyndebourne Here—Chorus Ready

Some of the chorus of the Glyndebourne Opera Company in a rehearsal study at the King's Theatre, Edinburgh, to-day. ("Dispatch" picture.)

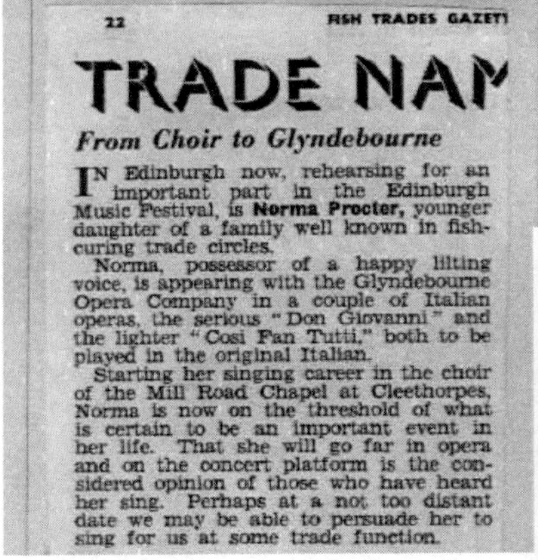

22 FISH TRADES GAZETT

TRADE NAM

From Choir to Glyndebourne

IN Edinburgh now, rehearsing for an important part in the Edinburgh Music Festival, is **Norma Procter,** younger daughter of a family well known in fish-curing trade circles.

Norma, possessor of a happy lilting voice, is appearing with the Glyndebourne Opera Company in a couple of Italian operas, the serious "Don Giovanni" and the lighter "Cosi Fan Tutti," both to be played in the original Italian.

Starting her singing career in the choir of the Mill Road Chapel at Cleethorpes, Norma is now on the threshold of what is certain to be an important event in her life. That she will go far in opera and on the concert platform is the considered opinion of those who have heard her sing. Perhaps at a not too distant date we may be able to persuade her to sing for us at some trade function.

ABOVE: The Fish Trades Gazette, 1948.

RIGHT: Norma performing at the Fish Trades Concert, taken by Ronald Stilling.

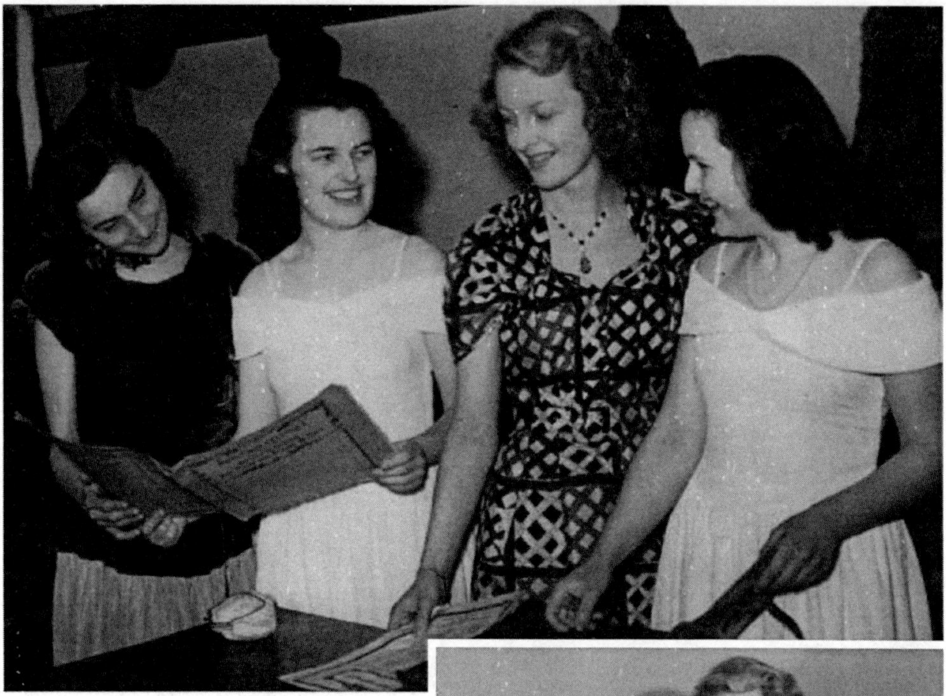

ABOVE: Norma (second right) when she performed in Bach's St. John Passion with the Nottingham Oriana Choir and the Eastwood Male Voice Choir in 1949.

LEFT: A rare photograph of Norma in Southwark Cathedral in 1948, making her London debut.

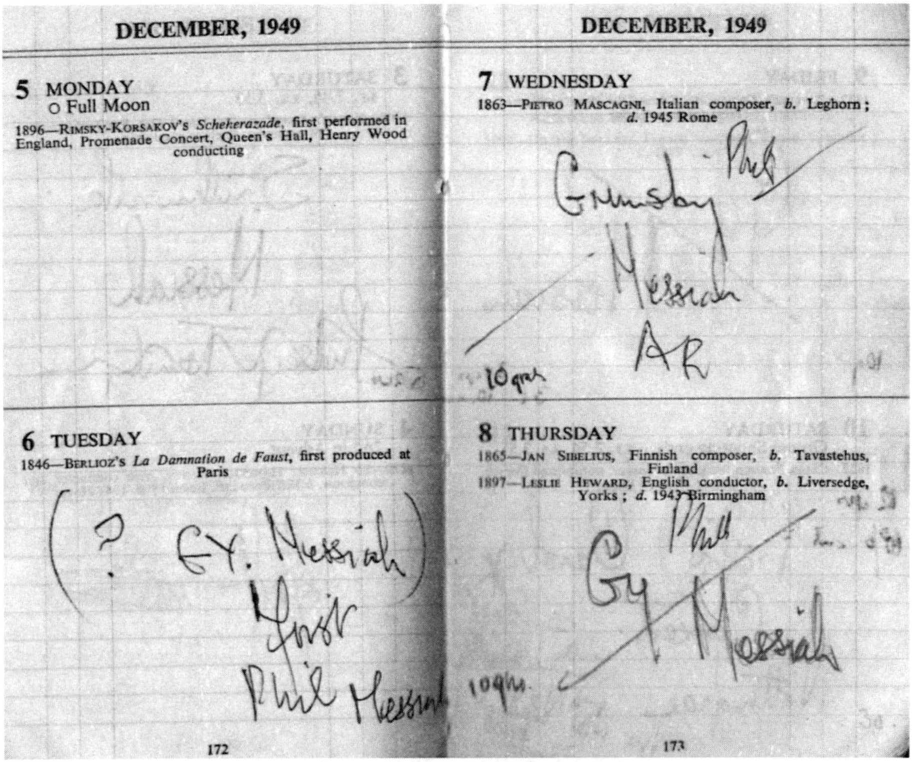

DECEMBER, 1949

5 MONDAY
○ Full Moon
1896—RIMSKY-KORSAKOV'S *Scheherazade*, first performed in England, Promenade Concert, Queen's Hall, Henry Wood conducting

6 TUESDAY
1846—BERLIOZ'S *La Damnation de Faust*, first produced at Paris

(? GY. Messiah)
Phil Messiah 10gns.

172

DECEMBER, 1949

7 WEDNESDAY
1863—PIETRO MASCAGNI, Italian composer, *b.* Leghorn; *d.* 1945 Rome

Grimsby Phil
Messiah
AR
10gns

8 THURSDAY
1865—JAN SIBELIUS, Finnish composer, *b.* Tavastehus, Finland
1897—LESLIE HEWARD, English conductor, *b.* Liversedge, Yorks; *d.* 1943 Birmingham

Phil
Gy Messiah

173

ABOVE: Norma's 1949 diary noting December Messiah performances in Grimsby. LEFT: Cutting a cake for Norma's 21st birthday. 'Was I ever as slim as that – 18 inch waist – help! And now...!!!' she wrote on the rear. BELOW: Roy Henderson conducting a Christmas concert with his Nottingham Oriana Choir at the Central Hall in the city on December 10, 1949. Norma and tenor Heddle Nash are sitting at the top left of the photograph near the organ.

ABOVE LEFT: Norma, pictured with whom is thought to be Mitch, her one-time fiancé.

ABOVE RIGHT: A portrait of Alec Redshaw, taken in the early 1950s by Sid Burton.

RIGHT: A studio portrait of Norma, taken by Sid Burton, Grimsby.

FAR RIGHT: The programme from Norma's first ever recital in Grimsby, at the Central Hall in 1954.

GRIMSBY PHILHARMONIC SOCIETY

present a

SONG RECITAL

by

NORMA PROCTER

(CONTRALTO)

accompanied by

ALEC REDSHAW

CENTRAL HALL
DUNCOMBE STREET
GRIMSBY

THURSDAY
4th MARCH
1954

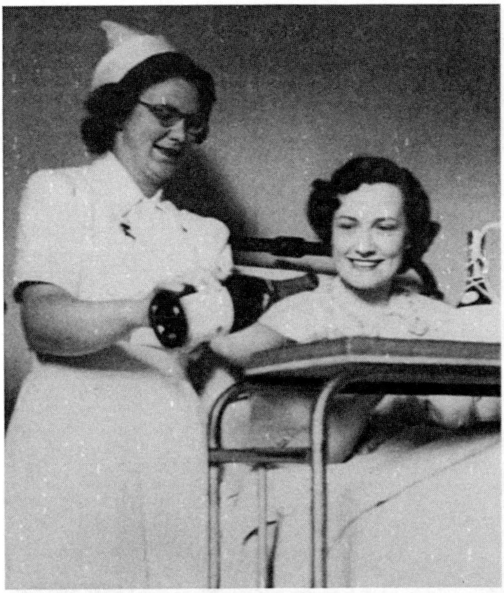

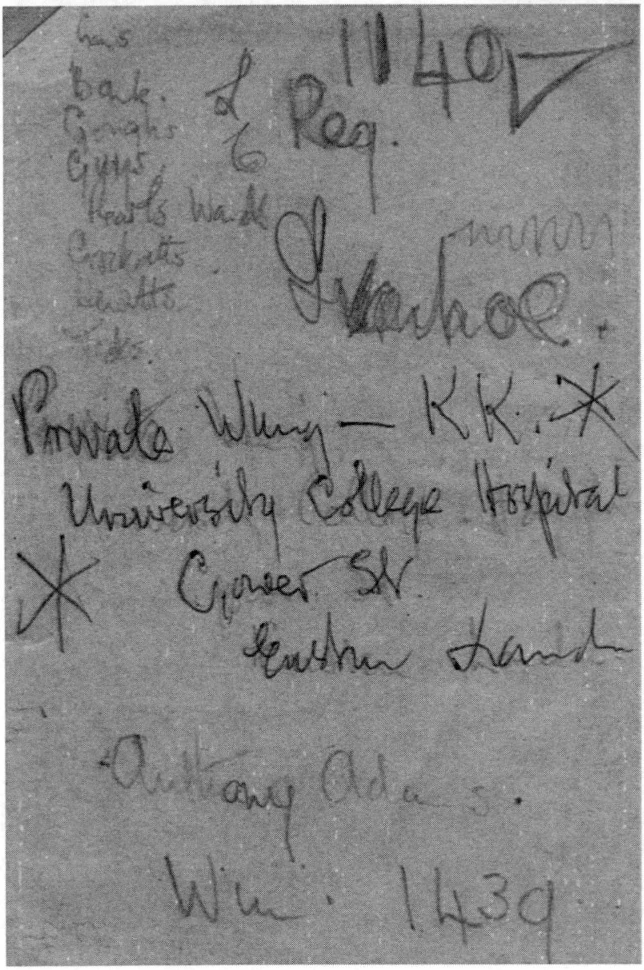

FAR LEFT: Norma in the early 1950s. 'Pink tulle dress which I embroidered.'

ABOVE LEFT: Kathleen Ferrier with her nurse, Bernie, at University College Hospital. Picture kindly provided by Kathleen Hopcroft.

ABOVE RIGHT: Norma on the front cover of Record News magazine, in April 1954.

LEFT: A note in Norma's 1953 diary about Kathleen Ferrier's private hospital room.

ABOVE: Norma's first Three Choirs concert, performing The Apostles, Elgar and the Messiah, in Worcester in 1954. She was 26 years old. This was taken after The Apostles concert.

FAR LEFT: *A portrait taken by Brendan Kerney, dated Sept 10 1954.*

LEFT: *An advert from the 1950s for Norma's Decca recordings.*

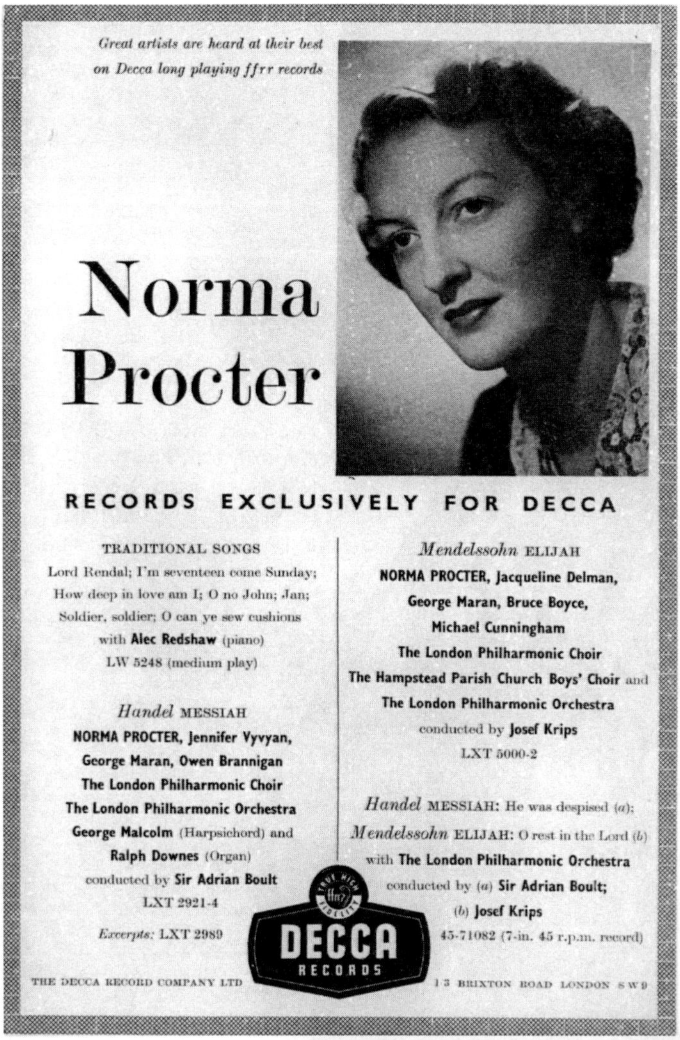

FAR LEFT: *Norma on holiday in Jersey.*

RIGHT: *Norma and Beryl Jordan, who designed her gowns, relaxing on holiday.*

Traditional songs
DECCA
RECORDS
LW 5248
LORD RENDAL
I'M SEVENTEEN COME SUNDAY
HOW DEEP IN LOVE AM I
O NO JOHN!
JAN
SOLDIER, SOLDIER
O CAN YE SEW CUSHIONS?
NORMA PROCTER
(Contralto)
with ALEC REDSHAW
(Piano)
DECCA MEDIUM PLAY 33⅓ R.P.M. MICROGROOVE FULL FREQUENCY RANGE RECORDING

ABOVE LEFT: The artwork for the Decca recording of Traditional Songs by Norma and Alec Redshaw. BELOW LEFT: Norma and Francis Coulson, from Sharrow Bay, enjoying the Lakes. ABOVE: A performance of Merrie England, by Edward German, at Fomby Hall in Atherton, Manchester, in 1955. BELOW: A performance of the Messiah in Grimsby. Alec Redshaw is third from left. Courtesy of the Grimsby Telegraph.

LEFT: Antwerp, 1956. Norma talking to HRH King Baudouin of Belgium. Norma said he was a lovely, gentle and shy man. She performed Bach's Mass in B Minor.

BELOW: Norma at an annual dinner of Hull Choral Union. She was guest speaker.

ABOVE: Norma singing during Elsie Balmond's concert in Bristol on February 7, 1959. The photograph appeared in Evening World. BELOW: Norma signing the mayoral visitors' book in Grimsby, on the morning of an evening recital with Alec Redshaw. Courtesy of the Grimsby Telegraph.

LEFT: In Guernsey during the summer of 1957, for a Gerontius concert. ABOVE: The Jersey Gleemen Annual Celebrity Concert at the Opera House on April 9 1959. The rear reads 'To dear Norma, wishing you good health and good fortune always, George.' BELOW: Alec Redshaw and Norma before their second recital in Grimsby.

ABOVE LEFT: Norma holidaying in Positano, Italy in 1958.

BELOW LEFT: Relaxing after a concert in Newcastle in the late 1950s.

ABOVE RIGHT: Audrey and Norma in the late 1950s.

RIGHT: Benjamin Britten and Peter Pears visiting Grimsby Town Hall and signing the visitors' book. Courtesy of the Grimsby Telegraph.

BELOW RIGHT: Benjamin Britten and Peter Pears with Norma and Alec Redshaw at Grimsby Town Hall. Courtesy of the Grimsby Telegraph.

LEFT: *Dancing with her father, John Procter.*

ABOVE: *On holiday in Jersey.*

ABOVE RIGHT: *'My little mum outside the music room.' Norma's mother, Edith.*

RIGHT: *'Nicky Noo and his Auntie Moo!' Norma with her nephew Nick.*

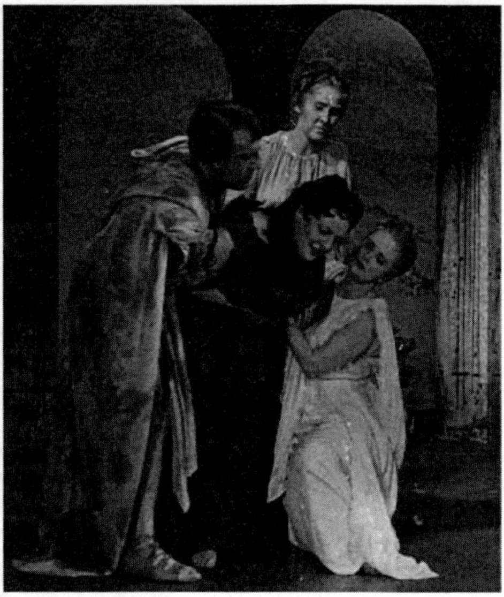

ABOVE LEFT: Norma's very well-used score of The Rape of Lucretia, used for her performances at the Aldeburgh Festival on June 20, 1959 and June 18–20, 1960. She also sang Lucretia for BBC radio on June 30, 1959.

ABOVE: The final scene of Lucretia, 'having stabbed m'self!' noted Norma, in Aldeburgh in 1959. This uncredited photograph was stored in Norma's archive.

LEFT: Norma as Lucretia at Aldeburgh in 1959. She was 31 years old and this was her first operatic appearance. This uncredited photograph was stored in Norma's archive.

NORMA PROCTOR A SUCCESS AS ORPHEUS

Norma Proctor, who made her Covent Garden debut on Monday last, when she sang the title-rôle of Gluck's "Orpheus".

GLUCK'S "Orpheus," not seen in London since the memorable Kathleen Ferrier performances in 1953, was revived at the Royal Opera House on Monday evening in a "revised" production. The producer, Colin Graham, devised some effective groupings for the large chorus, which were enhanced by Sophie Fedorovitch's beautiful

"ORPHEUS"

Opera by Gluck, with words by Raniero de Calzabigi, in an English version by the Rev. J. Troutbeck.

Revised version by the Covent Garden Opera Company at the Royal Opera House, with costumes by Sophie Fedorovitch and choreography by Kenneth MacMillan. Conducted by Louis de Froment.

Orpheus	Norma Proctor
Amor	Jennifer Eddy
Euridice	Elsie Morison
Blessed Spirits	Jeannette Sinclair, Anne Heaton, Alexander Bennett

Directed by Colin Graham.

costumes. The simple setting, now with no distracting giant harps or other impedimenta, was adequate for the purpose, with the lighting conveying all the necessary changes of place and mood.

Kenneth MacMillan devised the choreography, strikingly good in the dances for the Blessed Spirits, where Anne Heaton and Alexander Bennett conveyed the mood of the music with considerable feeling.

Norma Proctor was making her Covent Garden début as Orpheus and, judging from the ovation she received at the end, there was no doubt of her success. Her voice has a rich, even timbre in all registers, except for a slight deterioration of quality on the highest notes. During the first act her grief was under control and her performance lacked real dramatic bite. In the later scenes, however, her singing grew in emotional intensity until the climax was reached with a truly superb "Che farò" in the last act.

EURIDICE

The sprightly Amor was Jennifer Eddy, singing clearly and with authority. Jeannette Sinclair, heard all-too-briefly as a Blessed Spirit, also formed part of the choreographic pattern and blended well with the dancers. Euridice was sung by Elsie Morison with passion and feeling, making a positive character of this comparatively small rôle.

Another debut was that of the conductor, Louis de Froment, who drew some silken string tone from the orchestra. His control was firm and brought out all the light and shade of the clear-textured score. The chorus sang and played its important rôle magnificently, providing a strong foundation for the performance.

The complete success of this opera, however, depends ultimately on the singer of the title rôle, and so the Covent Garden Opera can congratulate themselves on having found a worthy successor to the past exponents of this rôle, making this both a welcome and a successful revival.

D.E.B.

ABOVE: A review of Orhpeus in The Stage, published January 19, 1961. Note the error in the spelling of Norma's surname; this happened regularly in the media. ABOVE RIGHT: The front cover of Music and Musicians magazine, dated January 1961, featuring Norma as Orpheus. RIGHT: At the Ulm Festival, 1961. 'V ill with flu virus'

LEFT: Norma at Aldeburgh for Lucretia with a friend, Viola.

BELOW LEFT: Norma and Peter Pears, taken on June 29th 1961.

BELOW: Norma in 1962 in St. Hugh's with her nephew Nick. She notes on the rear that 'he was terrified of the nuns and sisters in their white habits! In his lovely blue and black suit and hat – dear little love!' Photo courtesy of Norma's family.

ABOVE RIGHT: An advert for a concert in Grimsby in 1961. Courtesy of Central Hall.

RIGHT: April 1962 in Cannock, visiting her friends Sue and Ron.

ABOVE: Norma with Walter Midgley, Canadian Lois Marshall and American William Warfield in a dressing room at the Albert Hall. Norma noted 'William telling a wonderful joke!'.
BELOW LEFT: Norma rehearsing Mary of Magdala with John Carol Case and Sir Arthur Bliss at Worcester Cathedral as part of the 1963 Three Choirs Festival. 'No scores allowed!' wrote Norma. 'Lovely work which sadly wasn't accepted as it should have been.'

BELOW LEFT: Norma with Alec Redshaw at a recital in Grimsby at the Technical College in 1965, It had been postponed from the autumn of 1964. Norma notes 'I was v. ill'.

ABOVE RIGHT: Norma in the gown she designed to perform Mary of Magdala, by Sir Arthur Bliss, at the Worcester Three Choirs. The photograph was taken in Roy and Sue's back garden in Cannock. Norma sang in the work's first performance in Worcester Cathedral on September 2, 1963 with the City of Birmingham Symphony Orchestra and baritone soloist John Carol-Case. The work was recorded, and a CD made. Norma repeated the performance on October 31, 1963, at Birmingham Town Hall.

RIGHT: November 1960, pictured with Edinburgh Choral president Mr. Burgan. Norma performed Gerontius.

BELOW RIGHT: Norma in an evening gown designed by Colin Beck of Bond Street. In the back garden of Sue and Ron's home behind Cannock Bank.

RIGHT: The 20th Festival de Lyon, which ran from June 15 to July 9, 1965. The Symphony Radio Orchestra and Frankfurt Singakademie Choir, under the direction of conductor Ljubomir Romansky. Norma is with Lothar Ostenburg.

ABOVE LEFT: In Tel Aviv as part of a tour of Israel with Josef Krips in 1964. BELOW LEFT: A rehearsal dated July 2, 1965, marked by Norma in German as 'Generalprobe', in Lyon for the Hindemeth Requiem. ABOVE: Rehearsing in Brussels for the Ansbach Bach Festival. BELOW: A performance of the Messiah at Grimsby Central Hall in 1965. Norma has noted on the rear, 'v ill.' Her sister Audrey is in the third row from the back, three along. Courtesy of the Grimsby Telegraph.

LEFT: Norma at Haddo House, Aberdeen. ABOVE LEFT: Performing the Messiah on June 27, 1972. ABOVE RIGHT: A recital in Barcelona on October 20, 1971, with Miguel Zanetti. BELOW: Norma performing two Georg Philipp Telemann arias during a Bach recital in Heilsbronn, probably at Heilsbronn Abbey, on July 19, 1967, with the Collegium Musicum des Westdeutsche Rundfunk (WDR).

ABOVE: Norma was on the jury of the Franco Vinas competition in Barcelona. She paid 40 pesetas for this photograph of the jury and singers, which was taken on November 21, 1973.

BELOW: An uncredited photograph marked as being in Barcelona.

ABOVE LEFT: An uncredited photograph marked as being in Barcelona.

ABOVE RIGHT: Norma in 1973 at St. Michael's Church, Luxembourg.

RIGHT: Alec Redshaw in later years, courtesy of The Everyman Club of Great Grimsby.

ABOVE LEFT: An uncredited photograph marked 'Barcelona – Samson Handel.'

LEFT: Norma talking to Rafael Fruhbeck de Bourgo in the dressing room at Teatro Real Theatre, Madrid.

BELOW: Relaxing off-stage in Madrid, where Norma was performing in the St. Matthew's Passion.

Above Left: The sculpture of Norma by David Cregeen. Courtesy of Ed Wolkey.

Above Right: HRH Princess Margaritta of Romania, The Rt Hon. Jeremy Thorpe and the then director of Save the Children at the opening of the Humanism in Contemporary British Sculpture exhibition at the Royal Festival Hall in 1985. Courtesy of David Cregeen.

Right: Norma and the international sculptor David Cregeen beside the sculpture The Chosen Maiden, inspired by Ballet Rambert's revival of The Right of Spring. London 1985. Courtesy of David Cregeen.

Below Right: David Cregeen with Marion Thorpe, at the Thorpe's London home in 1993. Courtesy of Ed Wolkey.

ABOVE: Norma was a special guest at a literary luncheon in Grimsby in June 1989. Courtesy of the Grimsby Telegraph. BELOW LEFT: Ros Marba conducting Mahler's 2nd Symphony in Barcelona. BELOW RIGHT: Alexander Anderson-Hall at the start of his operatic career. ABOVE RIGHT: Brian Sack (left) and Francis Coulson with Norma in 1969 at Sharrow Bay. ABOVE FAR RIGHT: Norma in 2014, aged 86, in her music room at Nor-Dree. The caption reads 'Little Mia.' RIGHT: Norma with Prof Yang Jin Lan (right) and a young soprano at a luncheon marking a visit to the UK by a delegation from the Wuhan Conservatory of Music, China, in 1992.

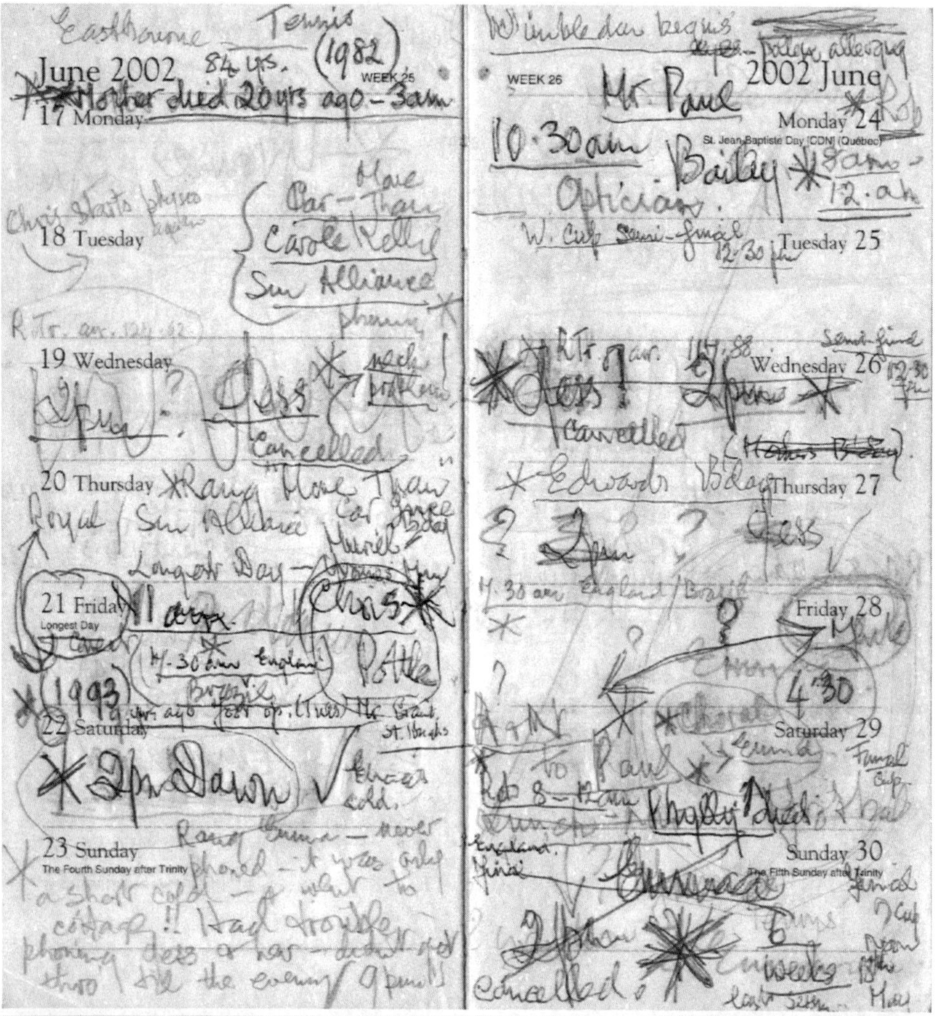
Eastbourne Tennis
June 2002 84 yrs. (1982) WEEK 25
Mother died 20 yrs ago – 3am
17 Monday
18 Tuesday
Carole Kelly
Sun Alliance
19 Wednesday
Cancelled
20 Thursday
Royal / Sun Alliance
Longest Day
21 Friday
Longest Day
11.30 am England
Brazil
(1993)
22 Saturday
2pm Dawn
23 Sunday
The Fourth Sunday after Trinity
Wimbledon begins
WEEK 26 Mr. Paul 2002 June
Monday 24
10.30 am
St. Jean Baptiste Day [CDN] (Québec)
Bailey
Opticians.
12.a.m
W. Cup Semi-final 12.30 pm
Tuesday 25
Semi-final
Wednesday 26
Cancelled
Edwards Bday
Thursday 27
11.30 am England / Brazil
Friday 28
4.30
Saturday 29
Sunday 30
The Fifth Sunday after Trinity
Cancelled

Death of singer Norma Procter

BY VINCENT McDONAGH
Reporter

NORMA Procter, the Cleethorpes-born girl who went onto become one of England's finest classical singers, has died at the age of 89.

A contralto, she was blessed with a rich, warm voice that was in constant demand at home and across the world.

She was not only up there with the best, but worked with the very best including Leonard Bernstein who wrote the score for the Broadway musical (and later hit film) West Side Story, Britain's Sir Malcolm Sargent and the French musical maestro Pierre Boulez.

She also rubbed shoulders with operatic legends like Maria Callas and Dame Joan Sutherland, and was a close friend of Kathleen Ferrier, another great English contralto.

Her talent brought her engagements at such prestige events as The Last Night of the Proms and the Vienna New Year's Day concert.

Yet despite her fame – it reached its peak in the years after the Second World War – she never lost a deep affection for the town of her birth, regularly returning home after major events wherever they happened to be.

Norma Procter pictured at the height of her fame.

Born Mary Norma Procter on February 15, 1928, she was one of two daughters to John and Edith Procter.

Her fish merchant father found brief fame himself when his horse, Sheila's Cottage, won the 1948 Grand National.

Both girls showed musical talent from an early age; her sister Clarice Audrey was a member of the Grimsby Philharmonic Orchestra. But it soon became clear that Norma had an exceptional voice.

After leaving Cleethorpes Girls Grammar School, she studied with Roy Henderson, the well-known baritone and music teacher, and with Grimsby's Alec Redshaw.

Norma became well known for her oratorio and recital work, but also performed in opera, making her debut at the Royal Opera House, Covent Garden, in 1961 as Gluck's Orpheus.

Earlier she sang Lucretia in The Rape of Lucretia for Sir Benjamin Britten at the 1958 Aldeburgh Festival and became particularly well known for recording virtually every work by Gustav Mahler.

Her popularity with the record buying public was sealed when she made a particularly lovely recording of Blow The Wind Southerly, the Tyneside song about a girl wishing for her sailor boyfriend's safe passage home. It had echoes of the perils faced by the fishermen from her own port.

Honoured by the Royal Academy of Music in 1974, her many other recordings included Handel's Alcina with Dame Joan Sutherland.

Norma never married, but remained close to her Cleethorpes family throughout her life especially her sister who married Lincolnshire tennis champion Norman Haste. They had two sons, James and Norman.

James told the Chronicle: "My aunt loved Cleethorpes and refused to permanently move away from the town. Her most beloved possessions were her piano and the radio."

After retiring, she taught singing and music locally.

Norma Procter belonged to a Grimsby and Cleethorpes generation which produced a rich seam of artistic and sporting talent, the like of which has never been equalled since.

Names such as Dame Janet Baker, one of the world's leading mezzo-sopranos, actors Patrick Wymark, Patricia Hodge and John Hurt, Freddie Frith the world motorcycle champion and Channel swimmer Brenda Fisher.

Her funeral service will be held at Grimsby Crematorium on Friday, May 19, at 3.40pm.

RICHARD BONYNGE

Les Avants
2.10.10

Dear Norma,

How lovely of you to remember my birthday — I can now say I am in my ninth decade!

It's a long time since we saw each other but in some ways it is as yesterday. I will never forget your lovely voice & your beautiful face.

Joan is sadly very ill — not in much pain but no strength left. She can't stand & spends most of her time in bed, sleeping a lot. She sends you much love — I send you mine.

So lovely to hear from you.

Rick

ABOVE LEFT: A page from Norma's 2002 diary.

LEFT: Norma's friends at the Musicians' Chapel service in London. L–R: Mike and Dawn Stewart, Paul and Kath Hopcroft, David Whittaker, David Cregeen and Ed Wolkey.

ABOVE: An article in the Cleethorpes Chronicle.

RIGHT: A note from Richard 'Rick' Bonynge to Norma dated October 2, 2010 about Joan Sutherland.

an
England
CARROLL LEVIS FILM DISCOVERIES
SONG
polyphonia sacra
Gabriel Fauré
20 MÉLODIES
WALK
MY LOVE
ARIAS

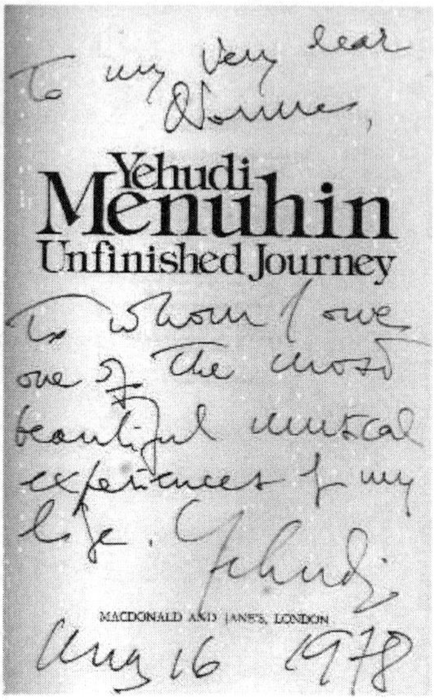
To my very dear
Norma,
Yehudi
Menuhin
Unfinished Journey
To whom I owe
one of the most
beautiful musical
experiences of my
life. Yehudi
MACDONALD AND JANE'S, LONDON
Aug 16 1978

ABOVE FAR LEFT: A small selection of the many programmes and scores from Norma's archives.

ABOVE LEFT: Yehudi Menuhin's dedication to Norma inside his autobiography.

BELOW LEFT: Dawn Stewart, who took possession of Norma's archive, on stage at Grimsby's Central Hall. This is the view Norma would have seen when she performed there.

ABOVE RIGHT: A signed photograph from Prof, Roy Henderson, to Norma, stored in her archive.

RIGHT: A signed postcard from Spanish cellist, conductor and composer Pablo Casals in Norma's archive.

ABOVE: Norma's friends studying the archives at Britten Pears Arts.

BELOW: A snapshot of Norma's archive on display at Britten Pears Arts.

RIGHT: Norma Procter, contralto, 1928–2017.

Chapter 17: Tributes

Mary Norma Procter, daughter of John and Edith, sister of Audrey, famous contralto, and friend to many, died on May 2, 2017.

For the last five years of her life, she battled acute Parkinson's disease. Fans from all over the world regularly sent bouquets of flowers and cards to Nor-Dree, despite Norma being too ill to respond.

She died in Grimsby's Diana, Princess of Wales Hospital from the effects of the disease, aged 89 – five months after 92-year-old Audrey passed away following a short illness. A funeral was held at Grimsby Crematorium on May 19, at which her own recording of Rule, Britannia! was played. Her ashes were scattered privately at a location precious to her.

'As boys, Paul and I only really became aware that our Auntie Norma was a successful singer when we were around six and ten years old respectively,' recalled Nick Haste, Norma's nephew. 'I loved her very much. She was a humble woman and dedicated to her career but loved coming home – it's what kept her feet on the ground.'

Nick lives in Grimsby, while his brother Paul, has lived in Newcastle for 37 years. 'In later life,' Nick said, 'Norma grew reclusive and did not confide much with the family. She had us but chose not to seek our help in private matters. She had always been a strong-minded and proud person. I hope this serves as a plea to people to engage in conversation with their loved ones when the going gets tough.

'I believe it's because she was so intensely private that Norma got little recognition in the latter years of her life – she never put herself about. It was her choice, at the end of the day, but she would remark on how other singers were always in the headlines and loved to be in the limelight. I guess she was affected greatly by the bad press her father attracted. It is just so very hard to accept, as she had such a brilliant career. To this day, nothing much is said of her. In this modern age, a lot more would have been made of her, had she had that life and career again.'

Nick paid tribute to his mum, Norma's sister Audrey, and his partner, Ingrid Stevens, who both looked after Norma in her older age. 'When she became ill, my mum did so much for her that we had to stop her so she could rest herself. It was so sad to see Norma deteriorate so badly, but she had the love of her remaining family to her dying day.'

Ingrid told the Grimsby Telegraph at the time of Norma's death: 'She was always elegantly spoken and dressed. Her house is full of music and she kept all of her gowns from the concerts. She would meet people in the supermarket who remembered her, and she was always receiving flowers from fans of her music.'

★

'True contraltos are very rare indeed these days,' commented one reader of The Times, upon the publication of Norma's obituary. 'Norma Procter was the greatest of her time. Some of my best memories of concert-going are associated with her. In its lower reaches her voice was of the richest. Her warm and humorous personality was evident the moment she made her entrance. She came after Ferrier and in various ways surpassed her – witness her recording of Blow The Wind Southerly. The beauty of her singing is said to have reduced at least one famous conductor to tears. We can be thankful that she lives on in her recordings.'

Visitors to international cultural website slippedisc.com were similarly saddened by the news. 'She was a wonderful Angel in Gerontius,' wrote one. Another said: 'Norma Procter was one of the first professional singers whom I heard live, in Messiah in Reading Town Hall, with a very young Heather Harper. I was entranced by her gorgeous contralto voice and, I have to admit, her regally stunning good looks. Perhaps it was her misfortune to be performing at the end of Kathleen Ferrier's career and the rise of Janet Baker's. Nevertheless, her extant recordings speak for themselves.' Another recalled: 'I watched Norma Procter give a Lieder masterclass at the RNCM *[Royal Northern College of Music]* many years ago. She was indeed magnificently well dressed (highly polished red nail varnish and high heels) and I can remember the Head of Vocal Studies fretting because she had left him in charge of her rather splendid coat. Clearly a lovely lady who exuded 'presence' even when not singing. She had such a fine contralto voice and was a truly sensitive singer. I am so sorry to hear that Parkinson's came on in later years because she had a razor-sharp mind and I know that she was a very helpful singing teacher to many for a number of years.'

Norma's obituary in the Daily Telegraph recalled: 'In 1974 she sang Rule, Britannia! at Last Night of the Proms, the last of 27 appearances there stretching back over two decades. That concert took place weeks before the second General Election of the year and Charles Groves, the conductor, used his speech to emphasise the importance of music and the arts in a civilised society. Describing Norma Procter, the critic Edward Greenfield wrote that "looking more than ever like Britannia herself with golden hair flowing, with eyes wide and with brow unfurrowed, she sang with a power and beauty that had us realising afresh that… the Proms remain the greatest annual music festival in the world".'

⋆

Former broadcaster Clive Champney and his wife Jo formed a friendship with Norma at Sharrow Bay. For many years he was the voice of Border Television, and trained many presenters including Anna Ford, Fiona Bruce, and Richard Madeley.

Clive, who was known as Mash, admired Norma as a singer, and Kathleen Ferrier too. He passed away in 2019. In correspondence, he said: 'Norma is such a wonderful person and has been a true friend for quite a few years. By coincidence, the first weekend I met Jo all those years ago in London, we went to the Messiah at the RAH and the contralto was a certain Norma Procter. That goes back to 1957! I do wish she would accept that she was a star among singers and gave pleasure to hundreds of thousands – indeed, millions if we include her recordings over many years.'

The feeling was mutual. Norma often spoke of Mash and Jo with great fondness. For a brief while, Clive was custodian of the second caste of Norma's head, sculpted by David Creegen. In correspondence with the artist after the head was returned to him, Clive said: 'I get a nice warm feeling that beloved Norm is back where she belongs though I don't deny that I miss her. And as for shedding tears, hearing her Bach and Mahler… I've done my share of that! I remember Sir Thomas Allen saying she had the finest breath control of any singer he'd ever heard. Listen to the final "grief" in the Adrian Boult Messiah – "A man of sorrows and acquainted with gri-e-e-eff". You find yourself wanting to breathe for her!'

Such was his enthusiasm that Clive would wax lyrical about singers he enjoyed, and he inspired a friend, David Percival, to explore Norma's work. David then wrote a 'fan' letter to Norma. The correspondence, particularly because of its conversational tone, must have delighted her. David described how he and Clive would nod politely at each other in the supermarket before eventually speaking: 'We would smile a greeting, then after a period of natural middle-class English reserve, we would hazard remarks about the weather, and the rising prices of the shop. After another decent interval, we began talking of the things that interested us and our backgrounds. I was quite clear from the beginning that I was going to like Clive very much, and you were to become part of the seal on the friendship. One day we got talking about music. I had just discovered the voice of the late Mark Reizen. I hope you know the voice. I feel you must.

'Anyway, I then introduced Clive to him, and he too agreed his was an extraordinary talent. Once we were on a firm basis of mutual admiration, Clive asked me round to the house. He had just then moved to the rather puzzlingly named village of Aglionby. I live about 10 miles away. And what should have pride of place in the music room – there is certainly a grand piano there that he frequently tortures into melody, but a bust of you. I will not pretend that you were then more than a name to me from that most illustrious period of recent musical history. But just as my enthusiasm for Reizen fired me, so he was fired by love and devotion to you. I am pleased for my sake to say I am now feeling the same enthusiasm. He has done me a CD of you singing arias from Messiah and The Constant Nymph. Both quite wonderful. So, I am now numbered, very humbly, amongst your fans.

'Talking of music is difficult for most people. The vocabulary is not precise, and it is difficult to make yourself clear a lot of the time. But one thing of which I am sure is that some voices, and only the finest, have a timbre so ravishing that when you hear them perform a certain song or aira, you know at the time that no one can ever sing it better. It is the feeling of the moment and it is the only measurement that I can make of a great voice. I felt that it is true of you in the performances mentioned. So, let us congratulate ourselves in having such a delightful friend in Clive, who can communicate his enthusiasm to the extent of firing me to write to you. I have never written fan mail in my life before. It is a pleasant feeling.'

After Norma died, Clive wrote: 'I have many cassettes she did specially for me. I had only to say that I'd love to hear her sing, for example, None But The Lonely Heart, and it would arrive a few days later… darling lady.'[299] And: 'I don't hear well on the phone [so] we spoke seldom in the later years. Our time spent together at Sharrow with Brian and Francis are treasured memories. I miss her so much.'[300]

★

Kath Hopcroft, Kathleen Ferrier's goddaughter and treasurer of the Kathleen Ferrier Society, lives in Stafford with her husband Paul. Her father, Harry Vincent, was a leading figure in the musical life of North Staffordshire during the 1930s to the 1950s. At the outbreak of the Second World War, Harry – a bass soloist and choir leader – complained to the Government about entertainment and concerts being cancelled, maintaining 'if ever people needed entertainment, it is now'. The Council for the Encouragement of

Music (CEMA) was formed in 1940 and he was asked to become the honorary music organiser of the Midlands. It was through CEMA that he made friends with Kathleen Ferrier, and Kath was named after her.

'As a child I had always heard my father speak of Norma Procter with great fondness and admiration,' said Kath, 'so I had always assumed he knew her personally. I now know this was not so, but he would have heard Norma and been told about her by his many friends in the music industry, so when I became more involved with the Kathleen Ferrier Society, Norma's was a name I already held in high regard and for a long time it had been my intention to get in touch with her. In fact, Norma rang me and so began regular phone calls. She often said how she wished I had contacted her sooner and she had known me when she was fitter, and before the onset of her debilitating illnesses. From those first telephone exchanges, little did I know we would become such good friends and, as well as sharing a love for Kathleen, have a similar sense of humour and opinions on things in general. We both had arthritis and Norma would know instantly if I was suffering that day. She said she could hear it in my voice.

'As I got to know her better, she told me about the osteomyelitis affecting her foot and ankle, and that when she came to resume her career after taking months off, how difficult it had been to walk and then stand on stage for long periods. One had to admire her courage and stoicism. She said she had become very arthritic, which is one of the reasons it took so long to diagnose Parkinson's disease. That diagnosis had been a bitter pill to swallow. She read up about the disease and was frustrated to be told that there was no respite. In later years, writing became impossible and the telephone was her lifeline to keep in touch with her many friends.

'As the disease progressed, calls became less frequent and sometimes it was heart-breaking to hear how difficult it was for her to talk. When I asked about the pain, she always made light of it. She hated having to accept help and have carers. Typically, Norma, although frustrated at never being quite sure what time help would arrive, felt sympathy for her carers and how much they had to do within unobtainable time limits. I could empathise with Norma. My mother had received care at home and always felt her house was no longer her home with all these strangers coming and going – something Norma would often echo. But no matter what, we always managed to have a laugh and hopefully bring a little cheer to her day.

'Long before Norma's singing career had been contemplated, she had admired Kathleen Ferrier. She loved her voice and stage presence and said her interpretation of He Was Despised from the Messiah was unforgettable. Norma first went with her mother to see Kathleen in concerts in Grimsby and, Norma then being about 15 years old, met her a few times. Kathleen had a good memory for faces and was well known for seeking out the waitress in the cafe, or the usher or caretaker from a previous visit to a hall and asking if they were better, or how the family were getting on. To Kathleen, the "ordinary" person was as important as the most influential and it was probably one of the reasons she was so admired for.

'The kindness and practical help shown to Norma from Kathleen was not unusual, but to be given this by one of your idols was enormous to the young Norma. For a singer of Kathleen's stature and at the height of her fame, to support Norma at her London debut meant the world. Norma remained a true fan all her life. She bought Kathleen's recordings and books about her and kept newspaper clippings. She often said, "She is here beside me now"; in every room of Norma's home, there was either a recording, photograph or book, or the treasured envelope on which Kathleen wrote Roy Henderson's address.

'One of Norma's singing pupils always sent her a red rose on Kathleen's birthday – Norma's love and respect for KK was well known among her inner circle. I would always receive a phone call from Norma on Kathleen's birthday or the anniversary of her death, initially speaking of Kathleen before expanding to day-to-day things, or what was happening in the world. Norma, who like Kathleen was a good pianist, would never have dreamed of copying her. She admired and respected her too much, although it had amazed Norma that Kathleen had given such encouragement to another contralto.

'Kathleen was like that. She was not possessive about her career, and Kathleen always appreciated the people who helped her along the way. She never forgot them. Norma knew this and it strengthened her admiration. As Norma's own career progressed, she soon realised what a hard profession it was, and not everyone was as supportive and encouraging as Kathleen had been to her. On reading a book based on Kathleen's diaries, Norma was astounded by her busy schedule. As a fellow professional, she was in awe of her workload and the amount of learning that had to be done. We often talked about this and both said it was as if Kathleen knew she only had a short career and needed to do and learn as much as she could. She respected Kathleen's rapport with her audience and that she had time for that 15-year-old girl in Grimsby, and later the effort she had made to lend support to a young singer, despite her own busy schedule.

'We can imagine how Norma felt when, soon after Kathleen's death, she was asked to record Messiah with Sir Adrian Boult, a recording that had long been earmarked for Kathleen but had been unable to progress with because of her illness. Norma was understandably nervous. She said she felt overawed and somewhat guilty.

'It was the same when Norma played Orpheus in the 1961 production at the Royal Opera House. She was given the same robes to wear as Kathleen had worn back in February 1953 on the fateful night that became Kathleen's last public appearance. She told me no matter how sad she was at the loss of Kathleen, she had to put that aside, channel positivity and do her very best for her. She truly felt that Kathleen was there with her on stage. Norma was very self-depreciating, never thinking she was good enough to follow in her beloved idol's footsteps. She was never one to say anything bad about anyone, but she did say that when she recorded the Messiah for Sir Adrian Boult and Abraham and Isaac for Benjamin Britten, she felt very uncomfortable and thought both men were wishing it was Kathleen making the recordings.

'Norma's life revolved around music. She loved listening to programmes such as The Proms, after which she would telephone and enthuse about a pianist or piece of work. I loved to talk to her about her 27 Proms appearances and once details of them became available online, I printed them off and sent them to her. She said they brought back many memories, mostly good but some not so. Always discreet, no matter how hard I tried, Norma would never say anything bad about anyone. Similarly, with the Cardiff Singer of the World on television, she relished the opportunity to actually watch young singers at the beginning of their careers. She loved it and always bemoaned that there was not enough classical music on the television. How I miss these chats.

'It was as I sat on a train coming home from a glorious week in Cardiff for the 2017 competition when an air of melancholy suddenly surrounded me. This time I would not be phoning dear Norm to tell her about my week and hear her take on the entrants, their programme, the judges, and guests. Her telephone conversations always ended with, "Sending you an angel." Norma was a great believer in angels and she always said she felt KK, as she always referred to Kathleen, had sent me – KH – to her. I feel very privileged to have known her and how I miss her, dear Norm.'

★

'Like ships that pass in the night, people meet for a short time and as often as not move on; so it was with my friendship with Norma, who was and will remain a very special lady indeed.'

So recalls David Whittaker, also from the Kathleen Ferrier Society and with whom Norma corresponded. He said: 'Norma was a singer, a good one too, a contralto and a rare voice these days. She freely admitted to having sung in many – if not most – of the great English cathedrals and minsters. She was an enviable interpreter of the works of Britten, Mahler, Handel, Bach and Mendelssohn, a glorious angel in Gerontius and some of her recordings, most of which she was personally rather critical of, are wonderful to listen to. Would it be right to say she was probably one of the last of the "old brigade" of singers and, by saying that, one of the first of the "new"?

'From her photographs, we can see Norma was a strikingly good-looking woman too, tall, handsome, bonny you might say, always beautifully dressed, looking marvellous in front of an audience or, according to her friends, just out shopping. She had presence. However, out of the spotlight, until she knew us better, we found her somewhat shy, reserved even, with a positive horror of indiscretion but, once the ice was broken, there was that marvellous sense of humour and a great wit. All this said, at the end of the day, we only knew her for the smallest part of her long life; the tip of the iceberg, one might say, which is a contradiction as you cannot have a warm iceberg?

'Around 2009, a few friends, also members of the Kathleen Ferrier Society, decided we should try to compile a chronology of Ferrier's professional career – only ten years long and no time at all, but then we realised what a huge task we had given ourselves. Rather like Norma, the redoubtable Kathleen had quite a work ethic, so what began as a good idea turned itself into an almost never-ending challenge. We began our task by collating as much information and personal data as we could from the Ferrier Archive at the Blackburn Museum, such as old newspaper clippings, reviews, and recollections, often second-hand. We quickly realised it would be wiser still to contact the fabled few who had actually known, or better yet, sung with her. Fifty-odd years after her death, the numbers had naturally dwindled.

'Then, out of the blue someone suggested Norma Procter and with a little trepidation, we contacted her and thankfully we seemed to have found an angel. The formality quickly disappeared. She gave us her time and memories via lovely letters, all about "our Kathleen", a lady she knew and very much admired, the person who had helped and advised her at the beginning of her career. With the same kindness and great tact Ferrier had shown her, the new girl, Norma shared with us her precious memories, coupled with marvellous and valuable chronological information. I think she knew we were sincere, so she never pushed and unless asked she rarely offered advice. Her letters were just "her" – Norma spoke as she found and this came across clearly; always discreet, warm, kind, tactful and, when the occasion called for it, tongue-in-cheek.

'Sadly, we never actually met but for a time she became a friend and, at the end of her long and illustrious career and life, she gave us her gentle help. As the time passed and illness made writing difficult, we spoke on the telephone. Her wry observations and great sense of the absurd came through like marvellous flashes of light. We knew her for such a short time in her life and the friendships of her musician colleagues and mentors throughout her career were of much greater importance. We were the little bit tacked on at the end, an afterthought perhaps, but no worse for that.

'When she succumbed to her final illness and died, two "Ferrier friends" [David, along with Kathleen Hopcroft] made the journey to Grimsby to say our prayers and goodbyes. Back to Gerontius and Norma and her precious angel that, incidentally, she insisted always guarded her. I think the Angel's journey with the soul of Gerontius, from his earthly deathbed via trials and tribulations to its goal, Heaven itself, turned itself into Norma's last journey. She was a very special lady and that rarest of things – a contralto. What a voice. Thank goodness we can listen to her recordings and remember her with great fondness.'

Chapter 18: Dawn

Until now, the custodian of Norma's archive was Dawn Stewart, who first met Norma decades ago, as pupil and tutor. Friendship blossomed, and the pair were as close as family in the end.

Following her death, Dawn advised Norma's solicitor of the national importance of the material Norma amassed during her lifetime and was given permission to remove it for safe keeping. She visited Nor-Dree on a sunny day, and spent a few hours looking through the massive archive. 'It was overwhelming,' she said, 'in so many ways. Not only was there so much – even though I visited her on many occasions, I never really thought about how much she had actually kept – but there was Norma's glaring absence. She was gone, and it really hit me then.'

Once home, Dawn found herself surrounded by boxes brimming with documents, papers, letters and more. At first, she didn't know where to start, but then began ordering them by year. This was a precious gift – and one which kept on giving. 'I'd pull out a programme or a score, open it and there would be little notes of Norma's, or comments. It was just wonderful. It was as if she was speaking to me. Her diaries were particularly fascinating. Obviously, I only knew her in later life, and although we spoke many times about her career, reading her diaries from the very beginnings of her career was fantastic. I spent hours poring over them, and it was a moving experience. I just knew she'd be looking down on me with a big smile. She was so humble and hardly ever acknowledged the contribution she made to music, but she was also very proud of her achievements. I know, deep down, she would be so pleased about this book.'

Born Dawn Stocks in 1955 in Waddingham, near Brigg, the family soon moved to Gainsborough and then Great Coates, near Grimsby, at the age of four, where she has lived ever since. Her father, Rowland, was the village's police officer and they lived in the police house. Her mother, Jean, still does and Dawn and Mike's home is next door. 'I always showed a talent for singing,' she said. 'When I was 12, my headmaster suggested that I take a teacher, after having heard me at assemblies and in the school choir. It was always about music. When careers officers came to see us, I told them I wanted to be in music, but they said try typing instead!'

Undeterred, in 1969 Dawn sought out the expertise of well-known singer Vera Burton. Vera had recently returned from New Zealand, where she had worked professionally and formed a successful opera company. Like Norma, she had been taught by Roy Henderson, and was friends with Isobel Baillie.

'She accepted me for lessons and that's how my career began,' Dawn continued. 'Vera was a lovely, wonderful person, very caring, and she took her time over lessons. We worked so hard. I am a soprano but didn't know it then, at 12, and it took a few years as my voice was still maturing. She also tutored me in piano and the theory of music. I initially took on small engagements. The first was at a winter meeting of the Women's Institute at St. Giles Church Hall, Scartho, and I sang the Virgin Slumber Song by Max Reger. I was fourteen years old, and it felt lovely – I knew I was in the right place. I remember being a little bit nervous but got over it as soon as I began to sing. Vera would sit in the audience of those first concerts, making notes on posture and so on. The idea was I was working towards being a professional.

'Throughout my teens, I competed in competitions all over the country, and took on paid and charity engagements. I'd receive £5 or a voucher, or sometimes flowers. I didn't think about the money side too much. Then, at fifteen, I started giving singing and piano lessons myself. My first pupil was Tracy Eastwell, who lived like me in Great Coates. She was aged eight or nine at the time. I remember it well. She passed her grade one piano lesson in December 1974, and later moved to Australia. Quite a few of my pupils since have gone on to study music at Oxford and Cambridge, and in London. I've taught hundreds of people over the years.'

By the age of 21, Dawn had passed every exam possible in singing and piano with the Royal School Of Music: 'Vera and I worked very hard at our weekly lessons, at her home in Queens Parade, Cleethorpes. She continued teaching me until she was well into her 70s, and then she became ill and stopped teaching. She suggested Dame Isobel Baillie for me. Vera was very much family to me. We would have afternoon tea in her music room and walk around her garden. We both loved flowers. She was a very big part of my life. She died in her late 80s. I am eternally grateful to her and still miss her to this day,'

Scotland-born Baillie's career spanned the golden days of music-making in the 1920s and 1930s, when conductors such as Beecham, Sargent and Hamilton Harty – who gave her her first break – were famous names. In 1933, she became the first performer from Britain to sing in California's iconic Hollywood Bowl and she was one of the original singers in Serenade To

Music by Vaughan Williams.[301] Dawn applied to audition for Baillie and within days her request was granted. Dawn travelled to the Manchester School of Music on April 27, performing before Dame Isobel, the school's Professor of Singing, and principal John Grierson. She passed the audition and returned on May 24 for her first lesson, armed with a list of every song she'd already learned. Lessons followed after that until 1985. 'I travelled to Manchester once a month, sometimes more often, and a lesson lasted 40 minutes,' Dawn recalled. 'Dame Isobel was always impeccably dressed, with a hat and feathers and plumes. She would sit on a stool without a back to it, and her posture was perfect. She had presence. She would sing with me sometimes, and her voice was so beautiful.'

Like Norma, Dawn made comprehensive notes about each lesson. On July 27, 1979, she detailed how Dame Isobel was back from visiting her daughter in Florida. 'She signed her Anthology of Song folder at the end of my lesson,' wrote Dawn. 'She is going to write to me when she is lecturing in the Lincolnshire area and hopes I may go along with her. This has been one of my happiest and most memorable lessons.' On November 15, she noted: 'Mr Grierson asked me to sing the first phrase of Come Unto Him again. He said it was very good, and if I think of the pure tone I produced, I "would not go far wrong". I thanked him for the compliment.'

All the while, Dawn continued to teach pupils herself, as well as perform professionally at home and abroad, receiving favourable reviews in the Press for her 'sweet, clear voice'. Dawn's notes reveal how pleased Dame Isobel was every time another engagement was secured, and the pair would immediately set to work on planning the programmes. Ida McColgan was Dawn's usual accompanist, and the pair bonded onstage and off. Their performances often included amusing anecdotes, such as when Ida accompanied Dawn on a tiny keyboard at an open-air concert, and an ancient pipe organ at RAF Scampton. 'Dawn's father used to arrange concerts,' Ida would tell their rapt audiences. 'One such concert was to raise money to erect a radio mast at Caistor. Unfortunately, the church at Great Coates did not have a piano, so Dawn's father arranged for a local farmer to transport one on the back of a tractor and trailer. As it travelled through the village, there was the Rector, the Reverend Norman Lancaster, of St. Nicolas Church, perched on a bale of hay, playing it!'

While Dame Isobel was often described by Dawn in her diaries as 'radiant' and 'on fine form', throughout Dawn's time at the school, Dame Isobel experienced periods of ill health. Dawn noted on April 9, 1981: 'Dame Isobel looked very radiant and sat in the corner of the music room. A picture in my memory forever. I said how well she looked, and she said she was feeling so much better after being ill.' And this, on September 10 of the same year:

'Dame Isobel looked rather pale and had lost weight (she only weighs eight stone). She remains very busy teaching in London and Manchester and giving lectures. She is, by what I could gather, writing a book[302] and giving an interview in London.'

In October 1982, Baillie gave an evening talk about her life at the United Reformed Church in Grimsby. Her fee was £200, and tickets were the bargain price of £2.50. Grimsby, of course, was well-known to the singer and Grimsby knew her. No doubt many in the audience recalled the performance of Messiah many years before when the soprano became ill mid-concert, and Vera Burton stepped in. Dame Isobel never forgot that kindness. Vera went on to establish the Cleethorpes Ladies' Choir and Baillie, then aged 79, appeared as guest soloist at its first annual concert in 1974.

Frank Whitmarsh, writing in the Grimsby Evening Telegraph of the talk, said: 'A legend for most of my lifetime has been Dame Isobel Baillie, recognised as one of the finest sopranos of the past 60 years. If only, I remember thinking, if only I had heard her sing! Well now I have. She sang at Grimsby United Reformed Church on Saturday evening – and an audience of more than 100 sat there enthralled by this frail-looking little old lady in her late eighties. Only four songs, it is true, as a flavouring, so to speak to her talk about her life. As you might expect, the voice is faded, a shadow of what it once must have been. Yet the technique was still there, the effortless breathing, the control, even the authority, and there too were some astonishingly clear and carrying high notes. It was an experience to hear her.'

Meanwhile for Dawn, training continued in earnest. For her lesson on February 24, 1983, she wrote: 'Top notes not far enough to the front of the mouth. Do not point the chin out when opening the mouth. Push the breath out from the stomach muscles and make the tummy hard. I sang four times before it was right.' And here, on May 26, she noted: 'Dame Isobel was ill and so my lesson was cancelled. She had been taken ill in London and had to have blood transfusions.'

Dame Isobel Baillie died following a short illness on September 25, 1983, in Withington Hospital, Manchester, aged 88. A memorial fund for singers was set up in her name. Only a few weeks before, she'd rejected an offer to retire in luxury in Florida with her daughter Nancy. She'd told a local newspaper in Manchester: 'I could sit in a chair in the sun and be waited on hand and foot – but I don't want to.' In her lifetime, she sang Messiah more than 1,000 times.[303]

Dawn continued lessons with John Grierson until 1985, when she took a break from tuition. She resumed with Grierson in 1990 and by the summer of 1995 had found a second tutor closer to home – a certain Norma Procter. Coincidentally, Dawn's mother, Jean, attended the private St. Giles School, in Scartho, with Norma and Audrey. Norma and Jean were born in the same year. 'I clearly remember Audrey accompanying Norma on the piano,' Jean recalled. 'We would have been about five years old at the time.' Later, Dawn and Jean avidly followed Norma's career, going to concerts and meeting her backstage, so the Procter name was very familiar to Dawn.

'We would often see Audrey in Marks & Spencer, and she'd say that Norma was on the skid pad,' recalled Dawn. 'She meant Norma was flying off somewhere or another.' Later in life, another coincidence occurred; Dawn's uncle, Ken, was admitted to hospital and ended up in the next bed to Norma's father. 'He was a nice, cheerful chap. He would lose his tablets, drop them on the floor, and Uncle Ken would get out of bed to help him.'

Dawn's first lesson with Norma took place on July 18, 1995, at the house of accompanist Anne Holmes. Dawn's diary reads: 'I met with Norma, as she wishes me to call her. I just had that feeling that all would be okay, and it was! We chatted like old friends, and found we had many friends in common. The nicest thing was when Norma asked me about dear Bella (Baillie). I have to start deeper breathing again and to hold the bridge of my nose and feel the vibrations. Norma reckons I will get the top notes as pure as ever.' After a while, the lessons took place at Nor-Dree, with Norma at the piano. Dawn recalled: 'Norma was pleased I'd been with Isobel Baillie. She told me how she remembered driving along Cleethorpes promenade with her father in his Rolls Royce, listening to her [Baillie] on the radio. She was his favourite singer.'

During their careers, Norma and Dame Isobel clashed, though later became friends. 'Baillie was older than her,' Dawn explained, 'and sang with Kathleen Ferrier a lot. Isobel wrongly thought that Norma was copying Kathleen. Their voices were so similar, and both had trained with Roy Henderson, so it is hardly surprising that they sounded alike. With a piece like Messiah, for example, Norma's breathing, pauses, and diction was identical to Ferrier's, so Baillie took umbrage with Norma, and she did not like the way she dressed sometimes – and would tell her so. Once Norma was wearing a black gown and Isobel sharply told her to put some lace over the neckline because her cleavage was too much on display. Also, after Kathleen died, Norma took over her engagements and Isobel found that difficult. Later, mid-way through Norma's own career, when she would have been aged in her 40s, they became friends. Norma said they were both outspoken women, and what with Norma being a single woman, she would always stick up for herself.'

Slotted into the diary almost immediately after Dawn's first lesson is a photocopied letter from Norma, reciting an Indian poet. Receiving a missive from Norma, as we know, was a sign of approval. The pair soon developed a friendship so close they may well have been family. Norma enjoyed reminiscing, and Dawn loved hearing the stories she told. 'Roy Henderson, she said, was a wonderful teacher who worked her hard, very hard,' said Dawn. 'He wouldn't take any nonsense, and it was all about the breath and diction. I have the same birthday as Roy, July 4, and Norma liked that. We talked a lot about her career and experiences. It was lovely, hearing these little snippets of her life. Before performing, for example, she would sit in a quiet place and just be quiet. It was her way of preparing for a concert. She wasn't really like a teacher. I would book an hour but would end up staying for two or three, talking about music. She only ever came to my house once, in her beloved Mini. She wanted to see the location and where I practised, so she could visualise me at home herself. That might seem a little strange, but it was because she was so very connected to people. We listened to music together, her own recordings and those of others. We'd sit on the settee in her music room and I'd hold her hand, and she'd say, "Isn't it beautiful, dear" and she'd talk me through the piece, and we would just be in another world, listening. We also loved poetry; we had shared passions. She also talked about people in the industry we both knew, and people I admired, and she would show me her diaries and pictures. She'd go into the snug and out would come photographs or little notes. I loved it and thought it was wonderful. She had so many memories and could recall with precision what she sang and where. She was told by Roy Henderson to sing in Grimsby every five years because of the publicity. She was hounded by the Press. They would wait outside halls with their flash bulbs, and she hated it.

'The fame aspect of what she did never appealed to her. She was happiest at home in Nor-Dree. It was all part and parcel of her caring nature. For instance, her mother Edith died in 1982 and had been quite ill. Norma sat with her night after night and nursed her. She was very interested in medicine, in fact, her first job of course being in medicine. She would have been a nurse if she hadn't gone into singing. She loved red wine and coffee, and gardening and flowers. And she was quite superstitious. Once she met an astrologer and had a chart done, which was permanently on display in her music room. She believed that you did the rounds in life, and if you didn't do well, you'd come back again to have another go. She used to say, "I want to leave this orbit". She didn't want to come back again, because she thought she'd learned enough from this world and had done her bit.'

Norma's deeply held religious beliefs – 'Francesco d'Assisi – a favourite saint of mine,'[304] she once said in correspondence – continued to remain important. 'She couldn't have done the works she did without being religious,' said Dawn. 'She would be drained after singing because she had a strong spiritual connection, and believed her voice was a God-given gift. And she passed her spiritual conviction on to the listener, you see. She would always say people had auras, and that she could see them. Mine, she said, was blue, just like hers, and that represented calmness and openness. She was a very rare person.'

In 2001, Dawn released her first CD, accompanied by John Grierson, entitled Dawn Stocks – Soprano, and ever-supportive Norma was thrilled. 'She was so generous in that respect. She could have said, "well I'm not bothered with that, I'm too busy with my own career" – but she didn't. She would encourage other people along the way. That's such a giving spirit and a big heart.' And in 2009, when Dawn married her husband Mike, Norma sat at the front of the church with Dawn's mother: 'We stood next to her as we sang Jerusalem, and I could hear her lovely rich contralto voice. Tears were streaming down her face. It was lovely. She was wearing a beautifully embroidered jacket and black skirt. She used to say I was the daughter she never had, and I used to call her my second mother. I sent her Mother's Day cards and address them to Mum Mark 2. We used to laugh about that. When she was poorly with Parkinson's I was the only one, really, allowed to go in the house beyond her family. She wanted people to remember her how she used to be. I would sometimes knock on the door without arranging anything, and she would always answer. My husband Mike would drive me to her house and would take a newspaper to read – he was never invited in!

'She endured the symptoms for quite a few years. She knew there was something wrong when her hand began to shake. I went to hospital with her for consultant appointments and scans and so on. She would get quite cross sometimes, because often the staff spoke to me instead of her. She'd say, "We are here for me – you speak to me!" A symptom of Parkinson's is emotional changes. She felt things deeply anyway, and when this increased through the disease, her shaking got worse whenever she felt emotional. It was hard because there was little I could do to help her. At first it was difficult because there was no record of her years of previous health issues. She told them about everything but because there wasn't any proof, at first it was hard to get the message across – very frustrating. She was put on tablets and had regular physio sessions, and as time wore on, she became bent over. She'd say, "I'm like an old crone!" but she could still sing, right to the end.

'Once in 2016 she had a fall and had to go for respite at Beacon House care home, in Cleethorpes, for about six weeks because she couldn't cope on her own. She took large photographs of herself that she showed to fellow residents. While she was there, admirers sent her flowers and cards. She went home and did amazingly well but continued to have falls. Once, we were passing her house on the way to an event and we saw an ambulance outside her house. I went inside to find her being attended to by two paramedics.

She was very surprised and pleased to see me. I often checked up on her. She was very brave to live on her own as she did. She had carers and family help, naturally, but she liked her own company. She'd travelled the world and done what she'd wanted to do and was very happy being at home. During this time, she had most definitely gone back over her archive, making new and additional notes. The quality of her handwriting is different on the later notes, less firm and shakier.

'I last saw her about two weeks before she died. Even then, she always got ready for the day and put make-up on. Every day. By that time, her symptoms had worsened, and she would often become agitated. She couldn't swallow very well, so couldn't talk long on the telephone and that, of course, was her lifeline. I'd popped round, like I'd normally do, and there was no sign or indication that the end was nigh. After that, I didn't know she'd been taken into hospital. Her family called to tell me she had died. It was very sad, and for some time I felt quite alone. It was the end of an era. I still have her music and the memories, but the absence was strange at first.

'Not many people attended the funeral service, I suppose because she was of an age where many of her friends had already gone before her. Her coffin entered to one of her own recordings, Rule, Britannia! from Proms Night, and she left to the sound of her beloved Kathleen Ferrier. I was telling my husband about a wreath from the Kathleen Ferrier Society and how Norma would have been so pleased when a lady standing beside me introduced herself as Kath Hopcroft and her companion as David Whittaker, both from the society, and that she had sent the wreath. Kath had travelled from Staffordshire and David from Dorset that very day. I invited them back for refreshments and they stayed with us until after 7pm. We have been friends ever since.'

Dawn, her husband, and friend Sue Shaw were granted access to Norma's home on the instruction of her solicitor to remove all music, books and letters connected to her musical life for safe keeping.

'It was very peculiar,' Dawn said. 'On the one hand, I felt very comfortable because I so familiar with her home, but she'd gone – although I felt her presence everywhere. I could still smell her perfume. It was almost overwhelming. There were boxes in every room, and every cupboard was full of material. We filled three cars and a trailer, and that was probably not even a third of what was there. I hadn't realised exactly how much of a hoarder she was. Every part of the house was full. I'd never been upstairs, and before we left, I went into each and every room to say goodbye. I went back into her bedroom and Gus, a teddy bear she adored and named after Gustav Mahler, was sitting in a chair. He was gifted to her by her friend Clive Champney.[305] I can't remember seeing him there when I'd been in the room previously, and that was strange. She loved Gus and would take him upstairs when she went to sleep. I like to think she was with me then, and I'm sure she's pleased that he now lives in my own music room.

'We stored it in our garage, conservatory and front room, and it took about two years to sift through everything. Every piece of paper was a revelation, and it was wonderful. It wasn't until we delved into it that we realised what a treasure trove it was. I used every spare moment I had to sort it, and it was as if I was rediscovering her from a different angle. It was an absolute joy – I am very pleased she was a hoarder! I came across a letter from the then-named Britten Pears Foundation. Norma had been in contact with the foundation, and so I decided that everything should go to them. She has left a truly fantastic archive of national importance.'

Dawn no longer sings professionally but continues to teach piano and vocals. 'Norma was a large part of my own successes, and took great pleasure in them, and now I enjoy passing on the knowledge I gained from my teachers to the next generation. Through future singers, Norma's expertise will live on. She was a true force of nature – you'd absolutely know when she walked in a room. She was always so glamorous and impeccably dressed. You certainly knew you were in her presence, even on the phone… when she answered the phone in that deep voice, you knew it was her. Even right at the end. This was her, naturally. She never tried to cultivate it or present an alter-ego. She was born to sing. Thank goodness she chose to follow singing. If she hadn't, there would have been something missing – for her and for music.'

Chapter 19: Legacy

Norma Procter lives on in many ways, from the beautiful music she created to the records she left behind, and in the hearts of her family and friends.

During her professional lifetime, she amassed a repertoire of more than 200 works, from oratorio and arias to Lieder and folk songs. Her recordings include Messiah; Elijah; Mahler's 2nd, 3rd and 8th Symphonies; Das Klagende Lied; Hartmann 1st Symphony; Malcolm Williamson Julius Caesar Jones; Nicholas Maw's Scenes and Arias; Herman Suter's Le Laudi di San Francesco d'Assisi; BBC Last Night of the Proms; Prelude recording – Brahms, Mahler, Ballads; and Handel's Alcina. It is an impressive legacy from a unique era in music and, as well as leaving us her voice, her meticulous archive – on which this book is based – is now being preserved.

The collection is vast. There are hundreds of scores, often annotated with hand-written notes or instructions. There are scraps of paper containing her thoughts, correspondence with eminent composers and singers, contracts, and documents. Her diaries demonstrate just how punishing schedules were on singers of the day and reveal the 'behind the scenes' ups and downs of a professional life in music. According to the mentions in the diaries, her tally of Messiahs was 332 – and it's likely there were more she didn't bother noting down.

Among the famous photographers who captured Norma's image was Houston Rogers, whose prestigious archive is now housed with the V&A, and copies of those photos are now carefully stored and cared for within her archive at Red House, in Aldeburgh, once the home of Benjamin Britten and Peter Pears, and now home to Britten Pears Arts.

One such annotated score is to Gluck's Orpheus. Inside, she wrote: 'This was the score sent to me from Covent Garden, which I'd fully memorised to begin rehearsals, but arrived to find they had changed most of the text! I had to re-learn the whole opera completely. Grr! And that was only the beginning! I had been promised to choose my dates at Covent Garden –

when less pressurised betwixt concerts – but was given no choice, rehearsing all through December, the busiest month and constant concerts and travelling pre-Christmas time. Horrendous!'

She will forever be remembered in the memories of her family and friends: those who knew her best. In 2016, a group of supporters had nominated Norma for recognition in the Queen's Honours. Although the nomination was unsuccessful, the sentiment expressed here by Jonathan Groves, the son and manager of the late Sir Charles Groves CBE, in his part of the nomination, is eternal. He told how his father's conducting career coincided with Norma's. 'I can attest to the fact that she was always one of my father's favourite singers,' he wrote. 'I can well remember the countless occasions when Norma Procter worked with him and the fact he could always rely on her to give the finest possible performance.'

Norma considered her voice a gift. Giving was in her nature, so it was no surprise that, in her will, she left the Kathleen Ferrier Society Bursary for Young Singers £500. As a mark of respect to Norma and to celebrate her gratitude to Ferrier, the Norma Procter Song Prize was created. The 2018 winner was Laurence Kilsby, from the Royal College of Music. The following year, Molly Beere, from the Royal Welsh College of Music, won with her unaccompanied Jonathan Dove's My Love is Mine. This additional prize to the bursary is a mark of recognition for young singers today – something Norma would be very proud of.

Her dedication to her hometown was as equally significant as her devotion to music. That she refused to move to London, despite it being an advisable career move, is proof alone. She was instrumental in organising the country's first ever all-Britten concert in Grimsby and was always very happy performing before home crowds. She was president, though in name only, of the Grimsby Philharmonic Society since Alec Redshaw asked her in the 1960s up to 2012 – a devoted tenure.

★

On April 23, 2019, a small circle gathered in London to witness Norma Procter officially entered in the Book of Remembrance at The Musicians' Chapel.

It is a fitting location for a fitting honour. The chapel is housed within the Church of the Holy Sepulchre, opposite the Old Bailey, home to the tomb of Sir Henry Wood who died in 1944, having conducted Promenade concerts for 50 years.[306] It also stores a host of other musical treasures, including an embroidered kneeler in memory of Kathleen Ferrier. The Book of Remembrance is displayed in a glass case against the west wall of the chapel and contains the names of more than 2,000 professional musicians, preserved in a mighty roll call of people privileged to have made music their career.

A commemoration service of thanksgiving is held annually. The service in which Norma's name was inscribed was conducted by the church's rector, The Reverend David Ingall, a moving ceremony accompanied by a Queen Anne Evensong of the early 1700s, sung by the choir of Gonville and Caius College, Cambridge.

Norma was represented by Dawn and Mike Stewart, Kath and Paul Hopcroft, David Whittaker, David Creegen and Ed Wolkey, and this writer, Lucy Wood.

Many fond memories were exchanged during the warm spring day. Dawn said: 'I was so proud of her. It was a wonderfully poignant service, and to hear Norma's name mentioned was very moving. I'm so glad she had friends present to honour her. I have no doubt that she would have loved it.'

*

Two months on, in June 2019, Norma's friends journeyed to Suffolk to personally hand over her archive to Britten Pears Arts.

Here, David Whittaker recounts the day: 'The Britten-Pears archive is built within the extensive grounds of the Red House, which was the home of both Britten and Pears. The house has an exhibition area and studios abutting it which, latterly, Pears taught in. Britten had a studio set high up overlooking the grounds. Both these rooms, especially the teaching area, contain valuable items, paintings, sculptures, and musical instruments, all of which were the property of the composer and are still used today. As well as a visitor centre and an exhibition area, the buildings are still a working, evolving environment, and visitors arrive from all over the world. The archive building itself is set back a little way from the house and contains a working area for a number of archivists.

'The actual archive was principally built to maintain and safely conserve an enormous collection of unique items, so it is elevated high up within the main frame of the building. The likelihood of flooding was remote, but this was taken into consideration. Naturally, security is considered most important, so the rooms are completely secure, and temperature and humidity controlled. It is, in short, a state-of-the-art facility containing a considerable amount of historic, not to say, priceless items not only pertaining to Britten and Pears but to a number of people associated with them. There is a safe in which are stored Britten's original musical scores, which were presented to the nation in lieu of death duties, deposited with the British Library, faithfully copied and then, in an unprecedented move, re-presented back to Britten Pears Arts for safe-keeping within the collection and in perpetuity.

'Norma's archive was wheeled into the building where the archivist had, in her honour, laid out a small exhibition of items of interest relating to her, Britten and Pears. Then the incoming archive was examined and re-boxed in appropriately marked grey containers ready to be conserved, catalogued and cross referenced by the archivists. At last the material relating to the great singer's long life and career will be cared for, preserved and made available for research by a team of world-class specialists.'

Judith Ratcliffe, archivist at Britten Pears Arts, worked with Dawn to curate the collection, which added to a number of other significant female collaborators of Britten's, such as Imogen Holst, Nancy Evans and Joan Cross.

'Norma Procter's papers are a wonderful mixture of the professional and the personal,' said Judith. 'It includes the usual type of material collected by a singer, documenting her successful singing career in detail. Unusually, however, Procter has annotated many items at later dates, with her memories and thoughts. Her annotations provide useful context and additional information but, more interestingly, a closer insight into Procter as a person, her personality, and opinions.

'This mixture of personal and professional is perhaps best illustrated in her treasured and well-worn copy of Handel's oratorio The Messiah found among her papers. It is evident that this volume, a gift from her mother, meant a lot to Procter.

'Procter's numerous lively, vivid and characterful annotations are a delight to read and make the reader feel closer to her. Her voice speaks out to the researcher as in an oral history interview – her comments giving a more personal insight into her story. Her papers sit well among the archives of others with whom she performed and recorded. Britten's work was a collaborative process involving librettists, producers, designers, conductors, singers, and instrumentalists. Procter's strong links with Britten and his network of collaborating artists are evident.

'Acquiring the papers of Britten's artistic associates is important as they enhance the Britten story as well as provide research materials into these creators and performers themselves and their important place in the British music scene of the 20th century.'

★

The last words must, of course, go to Norma, and so to a poem she wrote in her twilight years.

It is elegant and poignant, and sad too, as it was penned when her health was failing. Yet it remains honest to who she was: a true, passionate woman with a strong world view. It is reproduced here exactly as she typed it.

Look beyond her melancholy and Norma Procter – our lyrical, artistic, warm, funny and caring Norm – is eternally present.

My Weary Life (1989 – May onwards)

This weary world's become too big for me –
Nay, I am <u>too small</u> –
To battle with its griefs, its torments, sufferings – & all.

A world of such great beauty –
But clouded by power, greed, money & sin –
Of illness & heartache – so desperate within.

One counts <u>many</u> blessings – laughter and my welcome, wicked sense of humour!
For <u>special</u> friends – most scattered far & wide,
But they & closest family cannot heal <u>deep</u> wounds here inside.

Unbearable loneliness – my constant companion for so many years
When all I've longed for?? – a <u>kind</u> man's loving care
To replace my ever flowing tears (tho' no children I fear).

For marriage & career have been Fate's 'Forbidden Fruit'
Having seen so many heart aching failures before and after "I will"
Also lacking the stamina to combine both skills to fulful.

My music & message – perhaps my greatest joy and solace*
(It seems my lover too) – but for all my years of dedication)
devotion)
Now even it rejects me too/through.

* The love of my life.

My life seems totally wasted –
When compared with good days of <u>old</u>
I've tried so hard with my teaching & even being bold
But I – the insecure, shy, isolated misfit – no one wants to know.

To be born at all was certainly not <u>my</u> choice,
Nor even indeed to be blessed with my voice –
Tho' I've tried with all my love & might
To use God's gift for His delight –
But these last ten years – & more –
Have been my loneliest/battle and sadness) is for sure.
grief)

And frankly, what I've had to offer –
Doesn't seem important to me,
Dogged by illness, two faced people and constant jealousy.

In this present academic system – so anti to my own,
No longer produces singers who sing from their hearts – just throats,
And who seldom <u>more</u> an audience – which is what singing is all about
But stand like blocks of marble – often copy bound throughout.

My demands are great – of that I know –
But was taught & disappointed so
Being hyper sensitive – tho' not clever – since a small child,
Living & singing from deepest emotions inside –
Some bringing joy – but more bringing woe –
And always to project – facially – my heart's deepest flow
From the pain/joy literally felt – to my audiences below.

I miss being unable to sing as in the days of yore –
More than words can express – or my heart endure,
When one's voice literally 'dies' – a very painful mortal blow,
Tho' not the dreaded nervous fears – fought all through my career
Nor present-day travelling – my suitcase always in arrears!

There is so much upon this Earth one cannot understand –
And perhaps my real work has yet to begin in another 'far off land'
For my trust in people was never so low –
Nor my depression & depending sorrow.

These words are not self-pity – of which I abhor –
But facts & reality – not meaning to bore –
From a once young, positive, out-going, laughing me –
To now – a private façade – & unhappy 'loner' I be.

Perhaps my greatest heartache & insecurity –
Stems from a very unhappy childhood,
With bitter battles betwixt my parents & their families –
All preaching their so called goodness to God? –
Until my parents finally parted for good.

Tho' I have always loved & felt Angels nigh me –
As when singing Gerontius – & one day when it's 'time'
My Guardian Angel will quietly be by me –
And gently lead me onwards – as Mahler (Wagner) wrote†
Hopefully to an eternal, loving life sublime.

My one prayer too – that meanwhile perhaps I may find
The most elusive thing on earth
And that is possible peace of mind –
Which has eluded me from birth.

But the second of Brahms 'Serious Songs' –
Whose text from the Apochrypha be –
Explains its great wisdom & true answer for me –
"Yea, he that is not – is better dead or living –
For he doth not know of the evil
That is wrought forever – on earth"
And this I would have chosen – rather than my birth.

Meantime, as the last song says – Cor. I. XIII
I cling to my quiet personal faith –
In deepest love & hope – that one day I shall know –
PEACE & accept/understand all things here below –
But – please God – I ask – never to return – e'en so.
Perhaps my greatest grief of all on earth
And the most difficult to understand –

† (Urlicht 2nd Symphony, Der Engel – Wiesendonk Lieder) Wagner.

Is 'man's inhumanity to man' –
The daily worldly tragedies continually occur,
Tho' life's too short for such despair,
We've lost our neighbourly love & caring,
Our spirit, standards & priorities & discipline
Which won for us the World War II
Oh – that we could renew that love
And message from above-below.

Author's Afterword

'A blackbird is singing his little heart out at this moment! It's a glorious sound and makes one feel très humble regarding one's own noise-box.' This little line from a letter to one of Norma's 'specials' may at first seem inconsequential. For me, as the author of this book, it sums up everything I have come to know and love about a woman I shall, devastatingly, never meet.

Imagine the thrill at getting the phone call. 'Would you be interested in writing a book about the life of Norma Procter? We have quite a few boxes of material for you to look at…' Would I?! I don't think a second passed between the offer and my answer. I grew up knowing Norma's name (in fact, I went to school opposite her house, Nor-Dree, and my uncle was her postman) – a hugely talented artist who contributed to putting our shared hometown on the musical map. But that was all: she was a name and a voice only.

My delight on first viewing the archive was akin to being in a sweet shop as a child. I did not know which box to open first… that was, until Dawn – the wonder that she is – explained she had carefully ordered everything in chronological order, highlighting particularly important artefacts with brightly-coloured sticky notes. That first day (and those that followed) was this writer's dream.

Spending many hours poring over Norma's treasures has been a joy. Each time I looked inside an envelope or opened a new piece of paper, the same thrill overcame me – what would I discover next? What a privilege to come across a dashed line here or there, which revealed so much about her personality. I soon became used to her handwriting (at the top of one letter to a friend, for example, she wrote: 'Brace yourself! Hope you can decipher?') and as I spent time with her archive, it felt as if she was with me, so alive were her notes and scribbles, written in what I imagine was precisely her tone of voice, and the sort of words she'd have used aloud. Every so often, I would experience a shiver and feel Norma at my shoulder. A pencilled note in the front of a programme from a concert in 1970 ended like this: 'Everyone totally overwhelmed. Norm'. That tiny addition of 'Norm', and similar others I came across, often made me feel like she was reaching out through time to speak to me directly, as I wrote. It is a comforting thought.

Because, you see, Norma was a contradiction. She was humble and loving, fiercely loyal to her special ones, a self-confessed home bird and intensely shy of publicity. Yet she was also a magnificent voice, a force of nature, a woman who stood no nonsense in her professional and personal life. A stage presence that demanded to be noticed.

Why Norma would never fully admit to her terrific talent is because of exactly that reason: off-stage, she was one of the most unassuming people one could wish to meet. 'I always hear m'self with very different ears – I am highly critical!' she noted once. 'I was never good enough or worthy of the composer or poet. If I dare listen to m'self, I'd be horrified and hyper-critical as always.'

Humble, certainly, and private – fiercely so. 'I have always purposely avoided any contact with the Press or given interviews – not my forte,' she wrote. In later years, a friend recalled: 'The internet was a thing she regarded with the deepest suspicion. The internet, according to her, was rather impertinent. It rather broke the bounds of the inherent privacy that was part of her nature.' So, it was with caution and a certain amount of trepidation that I embarked on this project. 'Some years ago,' says a note on a single piece of paper in Norma's archive, 'I actually wrote my own biography and memoirs. Only two writers showed interest – no publishers – so I have no wish to repeat such a demanding, expensive and extremely time-consuming heart and headache experience again.'

So, she had a go herself – and who better – at documenting her life. The manuscript, I understand, has been lost to the passage of time. One can only wonder what treasures (and juicy gossip!) it contained. I cannot help but wonder what Norma would make of this book. An envelope she had kept contained a request, dated 1998, from a company asking to write Norma's biography. Her kind but firm rejection letter was also in the pile. It read: 'Your proposal is much appreciated but I have always been a very private person during the whole of my career and life. Sorry, but I am not sufficiently interested to accept your offer.' Then, a footnote: 'What people do not know of my past and present life – they can discover the other side of the tomb – Anon!!' With this footnote, a wave of relief washed over me; I like to think this is Norma giving us all permission to learn about her fascinating life.

And what a life it was. We are honoured to have been with her through thick and thin.

Health problems she hid from the world with admirable fortitude. 'My mother wore a thigh-length calliper for some years and then used a walking frame. No operations,' Norma wrote in a document about her medical history. 'My father had sciatic nerve problems for two-thirds of his life and wore a knee-length calliper. Perhaps I inherited their genes.' She realised, very quickly, to look after herself as best she could. 'I quickly learned too that good health was the key to everything, and without it I could do nothing,' she told the author of Lincolnshire Women, the late Dr. John R. Ketteringham.

And then there was her crippling self-doubt, amplified, it seemed, in later years. It was this ever-present humility which, I believe, made her the first-class artist she was. That, and her ability to touch the heart – not only with singing. The sadness she felt at having never married, or being blessed with children, runs very deeply throughout the notes and correspondence she left behind. It is heart-breaking, of course it is, to read the poem My Weary Life. But, as she quite rightly points out within the text, it was not an exercise in self-pity. It was the truth – a simple, honest truth – and Norma's nature meant she did not think twice about telling it.

We have, too, journeyed with her through happier times, and shared in her amazing successes. Her unadulterated joy from the glory and power of music is as breath-taking as her voice. Reading her diaries was like being on a fairground ride: dizzying and breathless, her professional stamina extraordinary. Then there is her wicked sense of humour, that shone so strongly during my research. 'Hope your letter turns up – spit and all!' she wrote to a correspondent, just one of many humorous missives.

I never met Norma. She died some months before I embarked on this wonderful project. It will remain, for me, a significant regret. Yet I feel that I know her. Her small notes, her little asides… as I read her diaries, I heard her speaking in my mind. Such a strong, talented, rare, and courageous woman I can only wish to be. I hope, from t'other side of the tomb, as she'd say, that Norma is pleased with my effort. How I would have loved to have heard her say: 'Yes m'dear, you've caught me perfectly.' I can only hope this book does this wonderfully warm, generous, dedicated, and talented woman justice.

Lucy Wood is a writer, journalist and public relations specialist. She lives in Lincolnshire. Her previous books are: The Grimsby Book of Days; Blonde In Deep Water – Brenda Fisher: The Story of a Channel Swimmer; and The Little Book of Lincolnshire.

Thanks: Dawn and Mike Stewart, for giving me this opportunity, their endless hospitality, and Dawn's keen eye for detail; Norma Procter's family; Kathleen Hopcroft, David Whittaker and the Kathleen Ferrier Society – their help is immeasurable; Linda Roberts and the Grimsby Telegraph; Alexander Anderson-Hall; David Cregeen, for devoting precious time to collaborate on his chapter; Judith Ratcliffe and Britten Pears Arts – thank you Judith for answering my many questions; Tim Leadbetter and the Everyman Club of Great Grimsby; Carol Foster and the Grimsby Philharmonic Society; Claire Wollington; Angie Burnett and the Grimsby Central Hall; David M. Heather; and my family.

Procter's Diaries

In Norma's twilight years, she read her diaries as others read books, making notes of her memories. Because she occasionally rewrote entries, etching over the original writing, there are some discrepancies with dates and details. She also sometimes wrote in German. Here are selections from each available year. The diaries from 2008 to 2011 are lost, and entries became sparse as she grew older. As with the main text, notes with [...] are the author's additions.

1948

Friday, January 9: Met Frank! / Mitch.

Saturday, February 7: Black Dyke concert (Central Hall).

Monday, March 8: Masonic dinner (Field House). What a racket! Ghastly affair. I loathed it. Father turned up out of the blue. More embarrassment.

Friday, March 19: Saw Grimsby Telegraph photo and first news of father's horse – terrible shock.

Saturday, March 20: Grand National. What a dreadful shock – knew nothing about it. So ashamed and full of heartache and grief.

Monday, March 21: Mother insisted we went to Mill Road. Arrived late – bus late – to be greeted by coughs and nudges, and whole congregation focused on me! I managed the first hymn but in the second, There Is A Green Hill, I burst into tears and ran out of the church and broke m'heart in the Sunday school hall. So ashamed and grief-stricken.

Friday, May 14: Snogger home. Wizard!

Saturday, May 22: Mitchell's away – America.

Tuesday, May 27: Wingham's Memorial concert (Central Hall). Campeys and Janet Baker.

Wednesday, June 23: London/Profs. Sang to Kath.

Wednesday, July 28: Snogger – Bury!

Monday, August 2 and Tuesday, August 3: London. Glyndebourne rehearsals begin. Victoria 8.45am. Rehearsal 10.15am.

Sunday, August 8: Kingsway Hall am. City Temple/Weatherhead pm.

Monday, August 23: Glyndebourne performances commence. King's Theatre, Edinburgh.

Tuesday, August 24: Snogger home in Grimsby.

Thursday, August 26: Mum and Podge to Ed.

Wednesday, September 29: Sang at re-opening of Mill Road.

Saturday, October 2: Frank's birthday.

Saturday, October 9: London debut. Messiah (Southwark). Ena Mitchell very kind. 11am rehearsal. Kath came – what a thrill! And Paddy.

Friday, October 29: 11.20am half term lesson. Snog home!

Thursday, November 4: Roy's cancelled – cold and throat.

Thursday, November 11: Grandpa Hockney's birthday.

Friday, November 12: Dad's birthday.

Monday, November 15: Connaught Rooms 6.30–7pm (wizard show).

Sunday, November 28: York (Messiah). Paddy sop soloist.

Thursday, December 2: Rotherham Messiah.

Saturday, December 4: Grimsby Messiah.

Sunday, December 5: George Street (Messiah).

Sunday, December 19: Halifax (Ebenezer Messiah).

1949

Thursday, January 6: Prof's. £5.

Sunday, January 9: Our first anniversary!

Friday, January 28: Truro Messiah. Isobel Baillie was very rude.

Saturday, January 29: Return fare £5. Lesson 2 10 6. Taxis/tubes 7. Meals 12 6.

Thursday, February 10: Railway concert – Central Hall.

Monday, February 14: Val to Snog.

Tuesday, February 15: My 21st – crumbs! Ill with flu. Father arrived after absence with Uncle Bert – tears!

Saturday, February 19: Nottingham St. John Passion. Prof conducting. Felt and looked terrible after flu.

Thursday, February 24: Prof's. Sang to Kath. She'd had lunch with Prof.

Friday, March 25: Prof's. Paddy met me and stayed at Kath's. Met Win Ferrier and dear Pop Ferrier.

Monday, March 28: London and home. Food poisoning.

Friday, April 1: Easter vac. Snogger home. Prof's.

Saturday, April 2: Wigan Merrie England cancelled – fire!

Thursday, April 7: Worksop orchestral concert. Fare 1 10.

Friday, April 15: Letchworth Messiah.

Wednesday, April 27: Prof's. Stayed at Kath's with Paddy and Pop. She was wonderful. She'd returned from the continent. Troubled – not fair for me to be here. She and Paddy waved me off from Frognal Mansions 28th am. I was staying in Lewes – Stabat Mater.

Monday, May 2: Mitch home for interview! Whee!

Thursday, May 5: Mitch back again! Prof's. Mr. Miller specialist.

Tuesday, June 14: Podge and Norm married! Wot a day. Father in a terrible state.

Monday, July 25: Glyndebourne.

Wednesday, August 10: To Edinburgh. Glyndebourne Chorus.

Monday, August 22: Performances commence.

Tuesday, August 23: Mitch to Edin. Whoopee!!

Thursday, August 25: Mum too – yarwhoo!

Saturday, September 10: Final performance.

Sunday, September 11: Return to Grimsby – whoopee!

Wednesday, September 14: Chris's wedding. Bridesmaid fourth time!

Tuesday, October 18: Elijah Letchworth.

Saturday, November 12: Hull Male Choir – Owen Brannigan.

Sunday, November 20: Uttoxeter Messiah.

Wednesday, November 30: Wesley (York) Messiah. Met Paddy.

Saturday, December 3: Southwark Messiah.

Tuesday, December 6: Grimsby Messiah – first Phil Messiah.

Wednesday, December 7: Grimsby Messiah. Phil. AR.

Thursday, December 8 and Friday, December 9: Grimsby Messiah.

Saturday, December 10: Prof's carol concert, Nottingham. First concert with Heddle Nash. He was so kind.

Tuesday, December 13: Huddersfield Messiah.

Saturday, December 17: Wigan Messiah.

Sunday, December 18: Chesterfield Messiah.

Wednesday, December 21 and Wednesday, December 28: Birmingham Messiah.

1950

Sunday, January 1: Bournemouth – afternoon and evening Messiahs. Prof conducted. Elsie Suddaby, Peter Pears, Harvey Allen.

Wednesday, January 18: Castleford Elijah.

Thursday, January 26 to January 29: Truro – Elijah.

Monday, January 30: Newquay Elijah.

Sunday, March 19: Pontefract concert. Cheque.

Thursday, March 23: Prof's last Central Hall concert Grimsby. Staying with us.

Thursday, March 30: Halifax Madrigal concert.

Saturday, April 1: Matthew Passion Nottingham. Prof conducting.

Wednesday, October 25: Castleford Messiah. Norm's birthday.

Friday, October 27: Faust. Royal Theatre. Heddle/AR conducting.

Wednesday, November 1: Twickenham. Serious Songs.

Thursday, November 2: Northampton Messiah.

Saturday, November 18: Wigan – Merrie England.

Wednesday, November 29: Letchworth Xmas Oratorio and miscellaneous.

Saturday, December 2: Prescott Messiah.

Thursday, December 7 and Friday, December 8: Grimsby Messiahs.

Sunday, December 10: Liverpool Messiah. Afternoon.

Tuesday, December 12: Huddersfield Messiah.

Thursday, December 14: Uttoxeter Bach concert.

Saturday, December 16: Croydon concert.

Wednesday, December 20: Birmingham Messiah.

Saturday, December 23: Liverpool Messiah evening.

Saturday, December 30: Birmingham Messiah.

1951

Tuesday, January 9: Three years not out! German.

Sunday, January 14: Pontefract recital.

Friday, January 26: Truro Messiah. Isobel Baillie was horrible to me, as she had been to Kath. Prof warned me.

Saturday, January 27: Home again. So pleased with me they sent an extra £10 – I was amazed! They were disgusted with I. Baillie.

Saturday, February 17: Poole recital.

Sunday, February 18: Bournemouth municipal concert.

Friday, February 23: Cowden recital.

Wednesday, March 7: Letchworth Messiah.

Saturday, March 17: Nottingham Messiah.

Thursday, March 22: Truro.

Friday, March 23: Light of Life and misc. Cambourne.

Saturday, March 31: St. Helen's Messiah.

Thursday, April 12: Barton Ladies Choir concert. Eileen – lovely accompanist.

Wednesday, April 18: Southwark Cathedral concert.

Wednesday, May 9: Elijah Worksop.

Thursday, May 10: Huddersfield nursing concert.

Friday, May 25: Retford orchestral concert.

Friday, July 6: Bungay Merrie England. Fayre £2 2s.

Friday, August 10: Swanage.

Tuesday, August 28: London rehearsal.

Tuesday, September 25: Birmingham.

Saturday, September 29: Letchworth orchestral concert.

Tuesday, October 2: Bantock's BBC Omar Khayyam. Town Hall. Birmingham. Rehearsal 2.30.

Sunday, October 14: Eastwood male voice concert. £1 fare.

Saturday, November 3: Sheffield Elijah. 2–5 rehearsal. 7pm perf. Fare 18–6. Hotel 1 17 6. Tips and taxi: 10.

Wednesday, November 7: Castleford Messiah. 3.30 rehearsal.

Wednesday, November 21: Liverpool Messiah. 3pm rehearsal. Central Hall. Jennie.

Sunday, November 25: Northampton.

Wednesday, November 28: York Messiah. Wesley. Paddy sop.

Saturday, December 1: Hornsea recital. Sat bots 11.5 12.5. Sun bots 10.25 11.55.

Thursday, December 6: Elijah – Rawsworth nr Sheffield.

Sunday, December 9: Dewsbury Messiah. 3pm rehearsal.

Thursday, December 13: Stoke On Trent.

Saturday, December 15: Liverpool Xmas orat.

Sunday, December 16: 2.30–5.30–7.30 Messiah.

Tuesday, December 18: Morley Leeds Messiah.

Sunday, December 30: Liverpool Welsh choral Messiah.

1952

Wednesday, January 2: Lincoln Cathedral Messiah.

Thursday, January 10: Newquay.

Friday, January 11: Truro.

Wednesday, January 30: Stabat Mater. Birmingham.

Thursday, February 7: Birmingham choral cancelled.

Tuesday, February 26: Pontefract choral soc.

Friday, March 7: Uttoxeter Messiah.

Tuesday, March 11: Newquay Messiah.

Tuesday, March 18: Ibbs & Tillett. Bournemouth rehearsal.

Sunday, March 23: Swanage.

Thursday, March 27: Judas Maccabeus Hull Choral.

Sunday, March 30: B Minor. Bournemouth.

Tuesday, April 1: Lincoln concert.

Saturday, April 5: Stabat Mater Nottingham.

Sunday, April 27: Mansfield.

Saturday, May 3: Hull.

Thursday, July 31: Derby.

Friday, August 8: Swanage.

Monday, August 18: Bath.

Saturday, August 23: Southampton.

Tuesday, August 30: Flicks 3.45pm.

Sunday, October 12: Church Gresley. Burton On Trent.

Friday, October 31: Milngavie recital.

Saturday, November 8: Stamford Stabat Mater.

Wednesday, November 12: Bangor.

Saturday, November 15: Wigan Messiah.

Wednesday, November 19: Atherton Messiah.

Saturday, November 22: Hull male voice concert.

Monday, December 1: Chapel Town nr Sheffield.

Tuesday, December 4 and Wednesday, December 5: Grimsby Messiahs.

Saturday, December 6: Nottingham carol concert. Prof conducting. Noel Cox accompanist. Heddle.

Sunday, December 7: Huddersfield Messiah in its entirety. Afternoon and evening. Hotel.

Tuesday, December 9: Dewsbury Messiah. Town Hall.

Wednesday, December 10: Stoke On Trent Messiah.

Thursday, December 11: Birmingham choral.

Saturday, December 13: Nottingham.

Sunday, December 14: Mansfield carol concert.

Tuesday, December 16: Rotherham Elijah.

Wednesday, December 17: Twickenham carol concert.

Thursday, December 18: Hull choral Messiah.

Saturday, December 20: Coventry Messiah.

Saturday, December 28: Bournemouth Messiah.

Wednesday, December 31: Lincoln Xmas oratorio.

1953

Saturday, January 3: Liverpool Phil Messiah. L'pool Central 11.11.

Sunday, January 4: Halle Manchester.

Sunday, January 25: Pontefract Elijah 2.30pm. 10.30 rehearsal.

Wednesday, January 28: 2pm Prof. 4 yds white taffeta. 6 yds white tulle.

Friday, January 30: Truro Messiah. Isobel Baillie v. rude.

Monday, February 9: Dad in nursing home.

Thursday, February 12: Louth recital cancelled – flood.

Saturday, February 21: Birmingham Elijah. Choral union.

Thursday, February 26: Academy of Music 9.20.

Friday, February 27: Glasgow Phil. 2 groups of 34. Rehearsal 11am.

Thursday, March 12: Grimsby Phil. St. Matthew Passion. Black lace gown from Jackie Delmans – lovely.

Friday, March 13: Recital Brigg.

Saturday, March 28: Bristol Stabat Mater.

Sunday, March 29: Mahler Albert Hall.

Friday, April 3: Westminster Messiah.

Wednesday, April 5: Dorking Messiah. Vaughan Williams conducting – first meeting.

Thursday, April 16: Lesson AM. Mum coming down.

Thursday, April 30: Uttoxeter misc.

Friday, May 1: Goldsmith Choral Union Messiah. Festival Hall rehearsal.

Wednesday, May 6: Buckley. Merrie England.

Saturday, May 9: Croydon B Minor. 11.30 Civic Hall.

Tuesday, June 2: Westminster Abbey.

Thursday, June 18: White shirt. Blouse. RAF shirt. White separate (Dad's shirt). Myla nightie.

Wednesday, June 24: Messiah Festival Hall.

Saturday, July 4: Prof's birthday celebration. Teatime train to London. Westminster Abbey rehearsal. Abbey still decorated with Coronation mantle.

Monday, July 6: Westminster Abbey Messiah.

Wednesday, October 7: Wakefield misc.

Thursday, October 8: Kath died. Winnie Osborne told me after the Denis Matthews recital at the Central Hall. Broken heart.

Friday, October 9: Accrington recital.

Wednesday, October 21: Elijah Birmingham.

Saturday, October 24: Bishop Stortford concert.

Wednesday, October 28: Merrie England Atherton.

Saturday, October 31: Westminster Central Hall.

Friday, November 6: Worcester Apostles.

Sunday, November 8: York Messiah.

Tuesday, November 24: To London. Southwark. Kath's service. On my own.

Thursday, November 26: Doncaster Priory Messiah.

Wednesday, December 2: Reading Messiah.

Thursday, December 3 and Friday, December 4: Grimsby Phil Messiahs.

Saturday, December 5: Liverpool Phil Messiah.

Wednesday, December 9: Minehead Messiah.

Thursday, December 10: Hanley Stoke On Trent Messiah.

Friday, December 11: Uttoxeter. 3pm rehearsal. 7.15pm perform.

Saturday, December 12: Coventry Messiah. Central Hall.

Sunday, December 13: Festival Hall Messiah.

Wednesday, December 16: Birmingham Messiah.

Thursday, December 17 and Friday, December 18: Huddersfield Messiah.

Saturday, December 19: Liverpool Messiah.

Thursday, December 24: Peter Pears and Ben asked me to learn Lucretia.

Tuesday, December 29: Birmingham Messiah.

Wednesday, December 30: Lincoln Cathedral.

1954

Sunday, January 3: Bournemouth Messiah. Prof conducting.

Monday, January 4: Kingsway Hall. 2pm. He Was Despised. First Decca/Boult Messiah recording. Jenny expected – not me – difficult atmosphere and shattering experience.

Thursday, January 7: Kingsway Hall 6pm.

Saturday, January 9: Liverpool Welsh Messiah.

Wednesday, January 20: Mozart Requiem Mass. First Albert Hall. Last for Keith Faulkner, bass.

Thursday, January 21: Broadcast Maida Vale.

Wednesday, February 3: Ben and Peter.

Thursday, February 11: Nottingham Music Club.

Thursday, February 18: Birmingham Mass In C. Harrison. So difficult.

Friday, February 19: Uttoxeter recital.

Sunday, February 28: Stabat Mater (English). Pontefract.

Thursday, March 4: Grimsby Phil recital. AR. Pale blue water silk gown with Elizabethan collar decorated with pearls.

Friday, March 12: Stabat Mater. 7pm. Bradford. St. George's Hall. 2.30pm rehearsal. Duke St. entrance.

Friday, March 19: Bristol concert. Dear Elsie Balmond conducing ladies choir. Poor Gladys Ripley ill.

Tuesday, March 23: Messiah. Albert Hall.

Saturday, April 3: Concert Todmorden.

Wednesday, April 7: Reading. St. Matthew.

Thursday, April 8: First live recital. Studio II.

Saturday, April 10: Requiem Mass Mozart. St. Alban.

Sunday, April 11: Sutton Coldfield recital.

Friday, April 16: Wembley Messiah.

Wednesday, May 12: Elijah. Luton Parish Church.

Saturday, May 15: The Kingdom, Croydon.

Thursday, May 20: Walsall. My first Dream of Gerontius. St. Paul's Church. Heddle Nash. No score – Heddle said leave them in the vestry. Organ up a semitone. Wunderbar!

Sunday, May 23: VW's Five Tudor Portraits. Albert Hall.

Saturday, May 29: Warwick Messiah. Reg Jacques. 11.30 rehearsal.

Thursday, June 3: Five Tudor Portraits. LPO. 8pm. VW on front row – wonderful man – with Ursula his wife.

Friday, June 4: Choral 9th. LSO. Krips. Terrible temper. Hit John Cruft [LSO oboist].

Friday, June 11: First London Dream of Gerontius. LSO anniversary.

Saturday, June 19: First Aldeburgh festival. St. John Passion. Terrified! Ben and Peter. [Imogen Holst conducting].

Thursday, June 24: Tom Jenkins Scarborough. Brocade.

Sunday, June 27: Halle Choral 9th.

Wednesday, July 7: Eastbourne holiday with Mother.

Tuesday, August 17: First Prom. Mozart's Mass in C Minor. Basil Cameron conducting. Muriel Taylor cello and Margaret Ritchie. All Meggies!

Friday, August 20: Aldeburgh.

Saturday, August 21: Mozart requiem.

Tuesday, August 31: Royal College 4pm. 3 Choir rehearsal.

Sunday, September 5: Worcester. First 3 Choirs. Reception 8.45–11pm Guildhall.

Monday, September 6: Elgar's The Apostles 11am with Bella Baillie. Lunch with Ald. Edwards 1.15.

Tuesday, September 7: Apostles 11.15am and 2.30pm. Buffet lunch at Willcocks.

Wednesday, September 8: Tea with Dean 4.15.

Thursday, September 9: Matthew 11.15–2.30. Lunch with Mayor.

Friday, September 10: Messiah 7pm.

Monday, September 13: Decca Recording Elijah. Krips. Krips rather terrifying but here's hoping.

Tuesday, September 14: Rehearsals. Strict time – not used to it but better today.

Sunday, September 19: Really beginning to enjoy working with Krips.

Monday, September 20: Krips most helpful. I am learning lots.

Tuesday, September 21: Krips calls me Miss Bellini. Prof.

Saturday, September 25: Finished recording. Most exciting sessions.

Sunday, September 26: Decca rehearsals.

Tuesday, September 28: Decca recordings.

Friday, October 1: Worcester recital. David Willcocks. 15gns!

Saturday, October 2: Rehearsal 11.30. Studio I. Maida Vale.

Wednesday, October 27: Elijah Wolverhampton Civic Hall. Not paid.

Friday, October 29: Wembley Messiah.

Sunday, November 7: York Messiah.

Thursday, November 11: Worcester Requiem. David Willcocks.

Saturday, November 13: Todmorden concert.

Friday, November 19: Albert Hall Messiah. Royal Choral.

Saturday, November 20: Westminster Messiah.

Thursday, November 25: Priory Messiah.

Saturday, November 27: Oswestry Messiah. Ena Mitchell v. rude at rehearsal because I had to cancel Carlisle.

Wednesday, December 1: Reading Messiah.

Saturday, December 4: Leicester Messiah.

Sunday, December 5: Nottingham Messiah. New Theatre.

Tuesday, December 7: Skipton Orchestral. Met Liz Harwood in gymslip – played piano to me.

Wednesday, December 8: Huddersfield Messiah.

Saturday, December 11: Coventry Messiah. Rehearsal 3pm.

Sunday, December 12: Dewsbury Messiah. Terrible flu.

Monday, December 13: Leeds Messiah. YSO.

Tuesday, December 14: Glasgow Choral Messiah.

Wednesday, December 15: Bolton Messiah. Victoria Hall.

Thursday, December 16: Messiah Cheltenham.

Friday, December 17: LPO Messiah. Festival Hall.

Sunday, December 19: Pontefract Messiah.

Monday, December 20: Home with terrible flu/pneumonia.

Thursday, December 23: Halifax Messiah cancelled.

1955

Saturday, January 2: Dublin Messiah.

Thursday, January 6: Chester Gate Regents Park. Rehearsal and test. Concert Hall. BBC.

Friday, January 7: Peter's London home. Ben/Peter 3rd prog.

Saturday, January 8: Liverpool Welsh Messiah.

Thursday, January 13: Royal Automobile (Pall Mall). Victor Olaf and Head of Decca.

Friday, January 28: 11am–1pm rehearsal. Studios. LPO Choral 9th.

Monday, January 31: Walsall organ recital.

Friday, February 4: LPO Choral 9th (German).

Saturday, February 5: Croydon Messiah. 4.15 rehearsals.

Sunday, February 13: Judas Mac Oxford Bach Choir 2.45pm. Rehearsal 11am.

Tuesday, February 22: Shrewsbury. AR. Rowston Castle 6.15pm. Recital for the blind – wonderful.

Friday, February 25: Lunch hour prom. Sea Pictures. John Hopkins. 10am rehearsal. Town Hall.

Monday, February 28: Music To Remember. Glasgow 7.30–8.30pm. 2.30 rehearsal. Public concert.

Saturday, March 5: Durham Cathedral. Matthew. 7pm. Rehearsal 10.30am.

Thursday, March 10: Gainsborough. 6th Chandos Anthem. Group of songs.

Saturday, March 12: Newcastle Choral Society. Catch train to York after show and travel to Stockport next day.

Sunday, March 13: New Mills Stockport. Misc and duets with tenor.

Thursday, March 17: Julius Katchen promotion at Selfridges 5–6. 3.40pm Decca.

Friday, March 18: West Acton VW recital. Two groups.

Sunday, March 20: Buxton Gerontius 8pm.

Saturday, March 26: Rugby Gerontius. Grand Hotel acc.

Sunday, March 27: Leyton Gerontius.

Wednesday, March 30: Lincoln Cathedral St. Matthew. 2.15 rehearsal.

Sunday, April 3: RFH. St. John Passion. Reginald Jacques. Prof 10am.

Monday, April 4: 3pm piano rehearsal Boult/Liverpool St. Matthew.

Wednesday, April 6: Grimsby Matthew.

Friday, April 8: Liverpool St. Matthew.

Friday, April 15: Leith Hill Bach Magnificat.

Wednesday, April 20: Sunderland Ladies Choir. Bede Tower, concert hall. Misc.

Wednesday, April 27: Lincoln Gerontius.

Saturday, April 30: Walsall Central Hall Choir. Four groups of three.

Sunday, May 1: Send songs to Holland.

Tuesday, May 3: LSO Choral Festival Hall 8pm.

Thursday, May 5: Decca 2.15pm. Peter for tea.

Saturday, May 7: Gloucester recital. Cathedral.

Saturday, May 14: Kendal Mary Wakefield Festival Messiah. To Sharrow.

Friday, May 20: Holland. First trip abroad and first flight. Rio Grande.

Sunday, May 22: Microphone rehearsal. Rio performance afternoon.

Tuesday, May 24: St. Matthew. V. nervous. Wonderful trip.

Thursday, May 26: 11–12.30 Maida Vale. Prof 5.00.

Friday, May 27: 4–5 Concert Hall. Broadcasting House 7.30–8.30.

Saturday, May 28: Maida Vale. Bruno Walter – incredible man. Absolute love and poppet – so kind but what a genius and humility.

Saturday, May 29: Mozart Requiem. Bruno Walter broadcast RFH. Incredible concert. No scores – memorised. [On the crib sheet she made about her career for the book Lincolnshire Women, she wrote: 'I shall always remember my good fortune and special memories of Bruno Walter's last London concert during my mid-twenties in 1955. He was an elderly man but had the most remarkable face and again amazing eyes, but what a genius and what humility and kindness.']

Tuesday, May 31: Decca folk songs with AR.

Wednesday, June 1: Recording cancelled. Too tired.

Thursday, June 9: Music You Remember. BBC.

Monday, June 20: Bach Cantatas 45 and 129.

Sunday, June 26: Worthing municipal concert 7.30pm. Two groups, one with small orchestra and one with piano.

Wednesday, June 29: Lotte Portman (Bruno Walters' secretary).

Thursday, June 30: Ring Decca.

Wednesday, July 27: League of Pity garden party.

Sunday, August 7: Grand Hotel. BBC concert hall. 7pm rehearsal.

Wednesday, August 17: 3pm Burton photographer.

Monday, August 29: 3 Choir rehearsal. Lennox Berkeley College. 10.30 piano rehearsal Gerontius.

Sunday, September 4: Hereford 3 Choirs.

Tuesday, September 6: 9.50 Teresa rehearsal Cathedral. Lunch with Dean, Mrs. Hedley Burrows.

Wednesday, September 7: Four Hymns. Lunch with Bishop of Hereford, 12 noon, at home.

Friday, September 9: Gerontius.

Wednesday, September 14: Decca Recordings. Messiah and Elijah. Victor Olaf with Decca. Jimmy Walker.

Thursday, September 15: Decca Recordings. With AR. Folk songs finished – hooray!

Friday, September 16: Prom. Choral 9th. Albert Hall. 11.15 rehearsal.

Sunday, September 25: Buxton concert. 5pm rehearsal.

Thursday, September 29: BBC Concert Hall. Brahms Vista songs. Alva Liddel.

Friday, September 30: John Decca Studios. Check re: folk songs recording.

Friday, October 7: Decca A+I. Ben + Peter. 2pm-5pm.

Saturday, October 8: Swindon Male Voice. Central Hall. Misc and alto rhap.

Wednesday, October 12: Merrie England Atherton, Formby Hall.

Friday, October 14: Belfast Phil. Gerontius. Ulster Hall. 11.00 piano rehearsal.

Wednesday, October 19: Middlesbrough. Misc and duets with Webster Booth. Sang Eleanote at rehearsal to me.

Friday, October 21: Grimsby Elijah. Phil. Jackie Delman.

Sunday, October 23: Ben and Peter. Harewoods party. London.

Friday, October 28: Kings Lynn. Lunchtime adults 1pm, children's recital 3.30. Guildhall of St. George. Terrible long sing – 2 recitals. 25gns!

Tuesday, November 1: Henry Wood Soc. Messiah 7.30. Sargent. Albert Hall.

Tuesday, November 8: Messiah. Bach Choir Festival Hall. Rehearsal 10–1pm.

Thursday, November 10: Leicester Music YMCA Hall. Recital with AR. 7.30pm. Very ill – come home with AR and Rolana after recital.

Sunday, November 13: Misc concert. Odeon Cinema. Leeds Girls School 2pm.

Tuesday, November 15: Croydon lunch hour recital. Civic Hall. 1.5pm-1.55pm. 1st watercolour painting by Juliet Pannett, painted/drawn during recital. Paid £5 for it.

Thursday, November 17: International concert, misc. Central Hall.

Saturday, November 19: Westminster Central Hall. Messiah. 5pm rehearsal.

Wednesday, November 23: Scarborough Concertgoers Soc operatic programme. 7.30pm.

Thursday, November 24: Five Tudor Portraits. Halifax. Victoria Hall.

Saturday, November 26: Oswestry Xmas oratorio. Hospitality.

Tuesday, November 29: Dream of Geront. Birmingham Choral Union.

Saturday, December 3: Liverpool Messiah.

Sunday, December 4: Messiah 2.15 with Bella Baillie and Gladys Ripley. Plaza Cinema, mid-day rehearsal.

Wednesday, December 7: Reading Messiah.

Thursday, December 8: Brook Choir Shirehall. Hereford. Misc.

Saturday, December 10: Chelmsford Cathedral. Misc.

Sunday, December 11: Birmingham broadcast recording.

Wednesday, December 14: Bradford Messiah. Old choral, St. George's.

Thursday, December 15: Hull Messiah.

Saturday, December 17: Liverpool Messiah.

Sunday, December 18: LSO Messiah. Performance afternoon. Albert Hall.

Monday, December 19: Birmingham Messiah rehearsal.

Wednesday, December 21: Huddersfield Choral Messiahs.

Thursday, December 22: TV Messiah rehearsals. Sir Malcolm. Blue lace. Jennie, Harvey Webster, Alan Booth. Poor Gladys Ripley died. Very difficult for me to sing. [This performance of Christmas music from Handel's Messiah took place at 9pm at Huddersfield Town Hall. It was conducted by Sir Malcolm Sargent. Jennifer Vyvyan was soprano, Webster Booth tenor and Hervey Alan bass, with Huddersfield Choral Society (chorus-master Herbert Bardgett), the BBC Northern Orchestra led by Reginald Stead, Ernest Cooper on organ].

Tuesday, December 27: Birmingham Messiah.

1956

Sunday, January 1: To Edinburgh.

Monday, January 2: Messiah and evening concert.

Sunday, January 8: Rehearsal Goldsmith Hall. 3.45 and 5pm.

Monday, January 9: Third programme rehearsal. 7pm performance.

Tuesday, January 10: Manchester. St. Teresa. Poems. 6pm rehearsal.

Friday, January 13: Rehearsal – radio. Hilversum.

Tuesday, January 17: Darlington Music Club. AR.

Wednesday, January 18: Stockton Music Club. AR.

Monday, January 23: Music In Miniature (Basil Douglas). Concert Hall. BH.

Friday, January 27: Requiem Mass. Mozart. Sheffield Phil. Grand Hotel.

Friday, February 10: Bristol misc concert.

Wednesday, February 15: Consett Male Voice – misc.

Saturday, February 18: Worcester recital. Cathedral.

Sunday, February 19: Gerontius. Wolverhampton. Arnold Richardson. 3pm rehearsal, 8pm perf.

Tuesday, February 21: Manchester mid-day concert. Teatime train home.

Saturday, February 25: Festival Hall. Mozart Vespers. Haydn 7 Last Words.

Tuesday, March 6: Mansfield recital with AR. Parish Church Hall. Brunts St.

Thursday, March 8: Brigg recital with AR.

Saturday, March 10: Rugby Gerontius.

Sunday, March 11: Northampton 'At Foot of Cross'. Discrak.

Monday, March 12: Misc concert with possible duets with tenor.

Tuesday, March 13: Jennie's birthday. Nice present please.

Thursday, March 15: Gainsborough Soc. Misc.

Tuesday, March 20: B Minor Mass Eton College Hall, Windsor and Eton Choral Society.

Wednesday, March 21: Leicester Gerontius.

Thursday, March 22: Doncaster St. John Passion.

Saturday, March 24: B Minor Mass Nottingham.

Wednesday, March 28: B Minor Mass Leeds Phil.

Friday, March 30: Messiah in full. Albert Hall. Car to take to Wembley Messiah. Crazy – 2 in 1 day! B--- Ibbs & Tillett!

Wednesday, April 4: Birmingham Symphony Choral 9th.

Sunday, April 15: Leeds concert. Queens Hotel. Terrible concert.

Thursday, April 19: Grimsby Alto Rhapsody and Sea Pictures.

Wednesday, April 25: Kidderminster Gerontius.

Saturday, April 28: Fly to Antwerp.

Monday, April 30: Antwerp B Minor. King/Prince in audience. Lovely evening.

Thursday, May 3: Walsall Messiah.

Saturday, May 5: Travel to Brecon. Met Joan Sutherland for the first time. Pooks (Adam), her son, four months old. Wonderful person and singer.

Sunday, May 6: Pergolesi Stabat Mater and misc. Brecon Cathedral, Wales.

Wednesday, May 9: Klagende Lied Chester Gate. 3pm piano rehearsal.

Friday, May 11: Klagende Lied. Civic Theatre.

Sunday, May 13: Das Klagende Lied. Festival Hall.

Tuesday, May 15: Turned down Decca recording with Sir Adrian/LPO, arias, supposed to have been for Kath. Prof disappointed.

Saturday, May 26: B.H. Concert Hall. Swedish Mass.

Wednesday, May 30: Gloucester Cathedral. Alto rhap.

Sunday, June 3: Worthing Municipal concert. Two groups; one with orchestra, one with piano.

Tuesday, June 5: Lincoln Cathedral broadcast. Brahms Serious Songs.

Wednesday, June 6: Leeds lunch hour concert with AR. City Museum, Park Row.

Thursday, June 7: Bradford lunch hour recital with AR.

Wednesday, June 13: LSO Choral 9th. Festival Hall. Krips.

Saturday, June 16: Aldeburgh Festival. Samsa. Jubilee Hall. Adele Leigh.

Saturday, June 30: To Guernsey.

Thursday, August 2: Royal Academy Serious Songs.

Saturday, August 4: BBC Golden Treasury. 9am rehearsal.

Tuesday, August 7: Prom Albert Hall. Sargent. Brahms Serious Songs.

Wednesday, August 29: Royal College. 11.45 Gerontius. Messiah 4.25.

Friday, September 7: Messiah AM.

Friday, September 14: Prom Choral 9th (German).

Thursday, September 20: Porth concert, Wales. Chapel. Male voice choir.

Thursday, October 4: Barton recital with AR. Lecture hall 7.30. Pink/lilac brocade.

Saturday, October 6: Swindon Male Voice Choir. Misc. Goddard Arms. Max Jaffa.

Tuesday, October 9: Driving test. Coo, I made it! What a shock. Bought my first beloved Mini.

Saturday, October 13: Elijah Westminster Choral Society. 7pm. Thalben-Ball organ only – amazing playing.

Sunday, October 14: Bach Mass broadcast. Studio I. Maida Vale.

Wednesday, October 17: Ilkley Music Club. Blue lace. Gerald Moore told jokes in between songs – not my type, too sarcastic. Brian and Francis came.

Sunday, October 21: Wisbech Male Voice Choir.

Tuesday, October 23: Warwick recital with AR.

Thursday, October 25: Derbyshire Federation of W.T. Two or three groups of solos.

Saturday, October 27: Coalville, Belvoir Rd Methodist Church Choir. Misc.

Monday, November 5: Antwerp Messiah. 11am. Opera House.

Wednesday, November 7: Swadlincote Church, Gresley and District Male Voice Choir. Reg Arnold acc. Misc.

Thursday, November 8: Wednesbury, Staffs. Methodist Church Choir. Misc.

Saturday, November 10: Wrexham. Misc and duets with Alexander Young. Grove Park Hall.

Tuesday, November 13: Amsterdam recital. Blue lace. Too tired – bad crit.

Thursday, November 15: Methodist International concert. Westminster Central Hall. Thalben Ball.

Friday, November 16: Lunch at Lord Harewood, London. AR to Hastings.

Saturday, November 17: Groves Methodist Church choir. Messiah. York. Evening dress!

Tuesday, November 20: N. Leeds Music Soc. Recital with AR.

Wednesday, November 21: Bradford Beethoven Mass in D. Sargent. Sir Malcolm v. helpful.

Thursday, November 22: Jennie's Grimsby concert.

Monday, November 26: Perth Music Club with AR. Art gallery.

Thursday, November 29: Royal Choral Beethoven Mass in D. Albert Hall.

Saturday, December 1: Coventry Messiah.

Wednesday, December 5: Reading Messiah.

Thursday, December 6: Grimsby Messiah.

Saturday, December 8: Chester and District Music Soc Messiah. Cathedral 6.30.

Tuesday, December 11: Southampton Choral Union. Guildhall. Messiah.

Wednesday, December 12: Newcastle Messiah.

Thursday, December 13: Hull Messiah.

Sunday, December 16: Messiah LPO Albert Hall. White lace.

Monday, December 17: Leeds Phil. Messiah. Town Hall. Rehearsal 2.0 sharp.

Wednesday, December 19: Blackburn Messiah broadcast.

Sunday, December 23: Messiah. Albert Hall.

1957

Tuesday, January 1: 12 noon Edinburgh Choral. Messiah and concert.

Thursday, January 3: BBC rehearsal. Arias.

Saturday, January 5: Royal Choral Messiah. Albert Hall. Blue lace.

Sunday, January 13: Bournemouth Messiahs afternoon and evening. Black lace and silver brocade.

Thursday, January 17: Newcastle recital with AR.

Monday, January 21: Music Tapestry BBC. 10.20–11pm. 8pm rehearsal.

Tuesday, January 22: Decca 11am-11pm.

Wednesday, January 23: Ben and Peter – Abe and Ike.

Thursday, January 24: Decca recording. Had to wait for Dennis Brain to be released from another recording company to make all three canticles.

Wednesday, January 30: Madrid. First visit to Spain.

Friday, February 1: Elijah in German. Silver brocade. Ataulfo Argenta conductor. He spoke no English, I no Spanish, so between us a little German. We poured our hearts into the music! Wonderful orchestra, choir and all.

Sunday, February 3: Elijah 11am. Black lace.

Tuesday, February 5: Recital British Institute. Lilac brocade.

Friday, February 8: Broadstairs recital with Watson Forbes and John Wills. Lilac brocade. Brahms viola songs.

Thursday, February 21: Llanidloes recital. AR. 25gns each. Three full recitals. Ibbs and Tillett rotten fees!!

Monday, February 25: Decca Abe and Ike official recording date. Abbey Road Studios 11.30am.

Wednesday, February 27: Edinburgh recital. Lunch hour. Royal blue lace.

Friday, March 1: Edinburgh Choral 9th. Usher Hall.

Saturday, March 2: Glasgow Choral 9th. St. Andrews. Red brocade.

Tuesday, March 5: Skipton recital with AR. Emerald green.

Thursday, March 7: Grimsby recital with AR. Mayor and Mayoress 11am. Red brocade. Had terrible throat.

Saturday, March 9: Liverpool Welsh St. Matthews. Sargent. Black lace. Straight out to Denmark. ['A lovely country and people,' she noted in her archives].

Sunday, March 10: Scandinavia two week/10 days recital tour. Copenhagen hotel. Two programmes/two gowns.

Tuesday, March 12: Terrible throat/cough. Hot toddies.

Thursday, March 14: Naestved.

Friday, March 15: Radio recital.

Sunday, March 17: Svendborg. Blue.

Monday, March 18: Odense. Blue.

Wednesday, March 20: Kolding. Pink brocade.

Thursday, March 21: Aabenraa. Pink.

Friday, March 22: Sandenburg. Pink.

Saturday, March 23: Fly home. Arrived in Grimsby and went to Phil concert, Central Hall. Father's bankruptcy. Terrible publicity and trauma.

Tuesday, March 26: Felixstowe recital with AR. Lilac brocade.

Thursday, March 28: 2pm Prof. Home whoopee.

Saturday, March 30: Nottingham St. Matthews. Black velvet.

Tuesday, April 2: Stockton recital with AR. Red brocade.

Friday, April 5: Manchester Halle. Barbirolli.

Sunday, April 7: Bach Choir. St. John Passion. Festival Hall. 10–1 rehearsal.

Monday, April 8: Sir J Barbirolli. 2pm. Regent Sq.

Wednesday, April 10: Plymouth Messiah. Hospitality. White organza.

Friday, April 19: Liverpool Cathedral St. Matthews. Joan Sutherland. Party afterwards at John Barbirolli's. Blue jokes galore!

Thursday, April 25: Gerontius. Bournemouth Winter Gardens. White lace.

Thursday, May 2: Hexham male voice choir. Forum Theatre. Misc. Newcastle hotel.

Sunday, May 5: Northampton B Minor. Afternoon. New Theatre.

Monday, May 6: Beverley St. John recital Festival. AR and me.

Wednesday, May 8: Newtown. The Pavilion. Rehearsal 2pm.

Thursday, May 9: Gerontius with Sir John and Halle. White lace.

Saturday, May 11: Walsall Central Hall. Alto rhap. Lilac brocade. Three groups of songs.

Thursday, May 16: BBC Manchester folk songs with AR. Afternoon rehearsal.

Saturday, May 18: Kendal Messiah. White organza.

Sunday, May 26: Rugby recital with AR. Music To Remember. Sea Pictures.

Wednesday, May 29: Abraham and Isaac. Maida Vale. Ben and Peter. 10.00 rehearsal. Studio 3.

Friday, May 31: 9th Choral. FH. Krips.

Sunday, June 2: Worcester Cathedral centenary service. BBC.

Tuesday, June 4: Birmingham City Choir. Gerontius.

Wednesday, June 5: Edinburgh. Usher Hall. Gerontius. 7.30.

Saturday, June 8: Glasgow St. Andrew's. Gerontius.

Sunday, June 9: Return to Grimsby. Abraham and Isaac broadcast.

Sunday, June 16: Grand Hotel. BBC B.H. 5.30 rehearsal. 7.30–8.30.

Tuesday, June 18: F.H. Mass In D Beethoven.

Thursday, June 20: Norwich Gerontius. St. Andrew's Hall. 7.30pm.

Saturday, June 22: Aldeburgh. St. John Passion. Ben harpsichord.

Thursday, July 4: Guernsey Gerontius.

Friday, July 5: On to Jersey. Met by AR. Met Bee.

Wednesday, July 24: Prof 10am. Rehearsal Brahms Serious Songs. Broke down in tears.

Thursday, July 25: 12 noon Sir Malcolm.

Monday, July 29: Prom concert. Brahms 4 serious songs. 12 noon. Sargent. Unbelievable reception from Promenaders.

Thursday, August 15: Lee Crown in town.

Thursday, August 22: Fly to Spain. Hotel Real. Argenta conducting.

Friday, August 23: First rehearsal. Kim Borg.

Sunday, August 25: Beethoven 9th in German and no copies!

Thursday, August 29: 11.45 Messiah rehearsal Royal College.

Friday, August 30: Music Tapestry BBC.

Tuesday, September 3: Worcester 3 Choirs.

Thursday, September 5: Gerontius 7.30. Bournemouth. Chanelle organza.

Friday, September 6: Messiah 7pm. Silver brocade.

Saturday, September 14: To Torquay. 7am train. Holiday with mother.

Sunday, September 29: Marlborough College recital with AR.

Wednesday, October 2: Rhyl Music Club with AR.

Thursday, October 3: Llandudno Music Club recital with AR. Grand Hotel.

Saturday, October 5: Haddo House Gerontius. Sang to lovely Queen Mother. White lace.

Saturday, October 12: Elijah Central Hall Westminster. Thalben Ball organ only – amazing playing.

Tuesday, October 15: Croydon lunch hour recital with AR. Civic Hall. Royal blue lace.

Monday, October 21: Guernsey recital. Red brocade.

Tuesday, October 22: Jersey.

Sunday, October 27: Marple Arts Group recital with AR.

Sunday, November 10: Ashington Central Hall. Misc. Red brocade.

Monday, November 11 and Tuesday, November 12: Edinburgh.

Wednesday, November 13: Bridge Of Allan recital with AR.

Sunday, November 17: Manchester BBC.

Wednesday, November 20: Leeds Philharmonic. Sargent. Silver lace.

Thursday, November 21: Gerontius. Halifax. Silver lace.

Sunday, November 24: Rugby School Messiah. Afternoon. White lace.

Tuesday, November 26: Messiah. Henry Wood. Albert Hall.

Wednesday, November 27: Gerontius Lincoln Cathedral.

Sunday, December 1: Mansfield Male Voice Choir. Pink brocade.

Thursday, December 5: Oswestry. Samson. Silver lace.

Saturday, December 7: Stretford and District. Manchester Free Trade Hall. Messiah.

Sunday, December 8: LPO Messiah. Festival Hall.

Wednesday, December 11: Bolton Messiah. White lace.

Friday, December 13: Huddersfield Messiah.

Tuesday, December 17: Huddersfield Messiah. Gold brocade.

Thursday, December 19: Blackburn Messiah.

Saturday, December 21: Liverpool Phil Messiah.

Wednesday, December 25: Francis [Coulson] bought me the most beautiful cashmere sweater. First I've had. How sweet, bless him.

Saturday, December 28: Liverpool Messiah. No rehearsal.

1958

Wednesday, January 1: Lincoln Messiah.

Saturday, January 4: Liverpool Messiah.

Friday, January 17: Just about to leave for concert and zip in evening dress broke! Messiah in German. Ataulfo Argenta.

Tuesday, January 21: Recital. Lunch at British Embassy. Argenta to come as a surprise but there was an announcement he had died in a tragic accident. Decided to give the recital as a memorial. [Argenta died on the evening of January 20 at his home in Los Molinos from carbon monoxide inhalation. His last live concerts were the Messiahs with Norma on the 17th and 19th].

Sunday, January 26: BBC Maida Vale.

Monday, January 27: Bach Cantatas BBC.

Thursday, January 30: Clive's concert Grimsby. Piano string broke.

Friday, January 31: 10 Ben and Peter.

Wednesday, February 19: Scarborough Concertgoers Society with AR.

Friday, February 21: Dumfries male voice. Misc. Academy Hall.

Tuesday, February 25: Festival Hall. Beethoven Mass in D. Jacques. 8pm.

Friday, February 28: Bristol Handicapped. Misc. Elsie.

Saturday, March 1: Cannock male voice. Parish Church. Misc.

Tuesday, March 6: St. Andrew's Music Club with AR.

Thursday, March 13: Thick snow at Koln. Landed in Hanover. By train to Cologne.

Friday, March 14: Cologne recital. First public performance for me of Abe and Ike.

Saturday, March 15: Dusseldorf recital with Ben and Peter. Duets, solos, Abe and Ike.

Tuesday, March 18: Liverpool Mass in D Beethoven. Sargent.

Wednesday, March 19: Rhyl pavilion 3pm. Boyd Neal.

Thursday, March 20: Boyd Neal. Wrexham.

Saturday, March 22 and Sunday, March 23: St. Matthew Bach. Jacques.

Tuesday, March 25: Huddersfield. Misc. Red brocade.

Friday, March 28: Belfast. Four Serious Songs. Big sing!

Tuesday, April 1: Shrewsbury. Child Of Our Time. Music Hall, Princes St. Met Michael Tippett. A perfect pet. Black velvet.

Friday, April 4: Liverpool Cathedral. St. Matthew. Black velvet.

Saturday, April 5: Joan and Ric.

Tuesday, April 8: Mitch's wedding. Lovely, bless them both with all happiness. Stayed with AR. Clive Lythgoe's recital. Piano string snapped on platform.

Friday, April 18: Grimsby Phil. Britten concert. Abe and Ike, and folk songs. Ben came. What an evening. Ben at piano. No fee!

Thursday, April 24: Beethoven Choral 9th. English. Birmingham. Lilac brocade. Gave dear old lady a lift from Sheffield Mid to Vic Station. Couldn't let her carry heavy case.

Thursday, May 1: Hexham male voice. Misc with Owen Brannigan.

Saturday, May 3 and Sunday, May 4: King David. BBC Maida Vale.

Friday, May 16: Bach B Minor Mass. Bristol Cathedral.

Sunday, May 18: Halle Manchester. Barbirolli conducting.

Saturday, May 24: Stabat Mater. Wales.

Sunday, June 1: Messiah. Huddersfield Choir. Sargent.

Monday, June 2: Home again. Rehearsal with Krips.

Tuesday, June 3: Choral 9th. Krips.

Friday, June 6: Norwich festival. B Minor Mass.

Tuesday, August 5: Prom. Sir Malcolm. Blue chiffon/lace. Brahms Four Serious Songs.

Sunday, August 31: Spring Symphony. St. Pancras Town Hall.

Friday, September 5: Spring Symphony. Edinburgh Festival. Multi blue chiffon.

Monday, September 8: Three Choirs Hereford.

Tuesday, September 9: Recital Ben and Peter. Shire hall. 2.30pm Abe and Ike/duets/folk songs/lieder.

Thursday, September 11: Gerontius 7.30pm.

Friday, September 12: Messiah 7.30pm.

Friday, September 19: Choral 9th. Prom. Red brocade.

Sunday, October 5: Morecambe Phil Choir. Misc. Afternoon.

Friday, October 10: Leeds Triennial Centenary Festival. Horenstein replaced Klempener, who set fire to himself smoking in bed.

Monday, October 13: Temple Newson rehearsal with B+P. B+P forgot their morning suits!

Tuesday, October 14: Abe and Ike recital. Brian and Francis came.

Friday, October 17: Charpentier BBC Leeds.

Saturday, October 18: Final concert.

Sunday, October 19: Abe and Ike London 6.00–8.00.

Tuesday, October 21: Lords Taverners concert, Royal Albert Hall. Sir John Barb.

Thursday, October 23: Music Tapestry 7–7.30.

Saturday, October 25: To Sharrow.

Monday, October 27: Music In Miniature 2.15pm-2.45.

Saturday, November 1: King's Rhapsody. Singing with mother of Ivor Novello.

Friday, November 28: Kings Lynn festival. Two recitals. Guildhall. 1pm and 3.15pm. Approx. 45 mins. 25gns! Worn out! Miserable Ibbs fees again!

Friday, December 5: Bradford Festival. Messiah. Church soc.

Saturday, December 6: Derby Messiah. 2.45. Queen's Hall Methodist Mission.

Saturday, December 13: Albert Hall 7.30. Jacques carol concert. 3rd part Christmas oratorio.

Monday, December 15: LPO Messiah 7.30pm. RFH.

Tuesday, December 16: Blackburn Messiah.

Wednesday, December 17: Wolverhampton Messiah. Civic Hall.

Saturday, December 20: Liverpool Phil Messiah. 7pm. Purple satin.

Saturday, December 27: Liverpool Phil Messiah. 7pm. White chiffon. To Dundee.

Monday, December 29: Dundee Messiah. Caird Hall.

Tuesday, December 30: To Edinburgh. Black velvet.

1959

Thursday, January 1: Edinburgh Messiah and evening concert.

Friday, January 2: Liverpool Phil Messiah.

Saturday, January 10: Royal Choral Messiah. RAH.

Thursday, January 22: Bangor Music Club festival recital with AR. Cancelled.

Wednesday, January 28: High Wycombe recital. Abbey's School. 7.45.

Friday, January 30: Truro Messiah 6.45pm.

Tuesday, February 3: William Alexander Nevsby. Stenberg. LPO FH 8pm. Sang in Liverpool for Stenberg. Das Lied. [A note made later: 'Very foolishly turned down his Das Lied concert in RFH in 1960 waiting for promised concert of some work by Krips but illness came, and I never made it.']

Thursday, February 12: Clive Lythgoe in Hull. Rach 2nd. Wonderful performance.

Monday, February 16: Path Lab 9.15am.

Saturday, February 21: To Antwerp.

Sunday, February 22: Rehearsal St. John Passion.

Thursday, February 26: Barcelona Messiah.

Tuesday, March 3: Keighley. Misc.

Wednesday, March 4: Women's Soc. Brahms Songs mit violin.

Saturday, March 7: Bristol Choral Soc. Gerontius. R'l 2pm.

Sunday, March 8: Live TV. Brahms. First knew of Sir M's daughter's death and how he wrote the orchestral version as she lay dying.

Friday, March 20: Windsor and Eton Choral Soc. Gerontius. Presented to Queen. Had the most awful large blind boil on my forehead. Looked and felt grim. In a beautiful Chanel satin and beaded dress.

Sunday, March 22: F. Hall. St. John Passion. Jacques 3pm.

Friday, March 27: St. Matthew's. Tobin. F Hall. Black velvet or tulle.

Wednesday, April 1: LPO Gerontius. RFH. Prof at night.

Friday, April 24 and Saturday, April 25: Geneva. Decca. Jimmy Walker. Joan, Anton Dermota, La Suisse Romande Orchestra, Arnsermet conductor. Cuckoo clocks brought back.

Thursday, May 7: Kendal Festival. Handel Foundling Anthem.

Saturday, May 9: Messiah.

Tuesday, May 12: Cologne.

Wednesday, May 13: Fritz is wonderful!

Friday, May 15: Handel's Alcina. Koln radio. Young Spanish sop who didn't know work; Gutov, my German agent, phoned and I suggested Joan. Joan and Ric arrived, to the rescue. Joan sang like a dream. Had to stitch her into dress. Zip gave way!

Saturday, May 23: Walsall. Misc.

Monday, June 1: LSO Choral 9th. English. Krips.

Thursday, June 9: Aldeburgh. Lucretia rehearsals to Sat 13th.

Monday, June 15 and Tuesday, June 16: EMI recordings H'field.

Thursday, June 18: Lucretia dress rehearsal. V nervous. Charles Mackerras shouted at me at the beginning of my first scene due to wrong entrance of another singer. Completely threw me!

Saturday, June 20: Lucretia. 1st performance. Terrified! Still making our costume thru the night!

Wednesday, June 24: Lucretia. 2nd performance.

Saturday, June 27: Purcell. Costume. Evening.

Tuesday, June 30: Lucretia BBC recording.

Saturday, July 18: Lucia (Joan). C Garden.

Friday, July 24: Back from Jersey. Lovely tan!

Saturday, July 25: Proms. 1st night. TV. Sea Pictures. No make-up needed. Sir Malcolm, Cyril Smith, Phyllis Sellick (lovely). Turgoose satin.

Monday, August 10: Sharrow.

Saturday, August 22: Temple Newson. AR recital. Leeds. Multi blue chiffon.

Thursday, September 3: Three Choirs Gerontius. Royal College London.

Friday, September 4: Brahms Serious Songs recording. B'ham.

Monday, September 7: Three Choirs Gloucester. Stayed with a doctor and family. 12.15 rehearsal at cathedral.

Tuesday, September 8: Gerontius. Very ill. Carbuncles/boils on foot burst in concert.

Thursday, September 10: Bournemouth.

Sunday, September 13: Haemorrhage.

Thursday, September 17: To Brussels.

Friday, September 18 and Saturday, September 19: Ghent. Judas Maccabaeus. Alex Gibson.

Thursday, September 24: Fly to Berlin. BEA 480. 9.40 London Airport.

Saturday, September 26: Berlin Festival.

Sunday, September 27: Berlin Festival. Very moving concert. Messiah. We visited Berlin wall. Terrible. Russian guards.

Sunday, October 4: Rawtenstall Picture House. Rossendale Male Voice Choir. Misc and duets.

Wednesday, October 14: Hereford recital. Melville Cook. Red brocade. Piano pedal fell off!

Wednesday, October 21: Caerphilly Orpheus Ladies Choir. Misc. Blue chiffon and red brocade.

Tuesday, October 27: Matley Musical Society. Town Hall. Two groups of songs. Red brocade/black tulle. 'It were worth a bring-and-buy stall to have her' – comment by one of the committee after the concert.

Thursday, October 29: Cologne rehearsals.

Friday, November 6: Bradford Festival Society. Gerontius. White organza. David Willcocks.

Monday, November 16: Antwerp Messiah. White chiffon.

Friday, November 20: Emmie lunch 1pm. [Emmie Tillett, her agent at Ibbs & Tillett].

Wednesday, December 2: Woman's Hour live broadcast. Terrified.

Saturday, December 5: Stretford and District Messiah. Free Trade Hall. Blue lace.

Saturday, December 12: Liverpool Welsh Messiah. White organza.

Tuesday, December 15: Blackburn Messiah. Black tulle.

Wednesday, December 16: Leeds Town Hall. Messiah. Blue lace. Sir M Sargent.

Friday, December 18: Huddersfield Messiah. Black tulle.

Saturday, December 19: Liverpool Phil Messiah. White satin.

Sunday, December 20: Birmingham BBC carols.

Monday, December 21: Huddersfield Messiah. Sir Malcolm Sargent. White satin.

Wednesday, December 30: Liverpool Phil Messiah. White lace.

1960

Friday, January 1: Edinburgh Messiah and evening concert. Black velvet and blue lace.

Saturday, January 2: Liverpool Philharmonic Messiah. Blue lace.

Tuesday, January 12: Cardiff TV. Studio A. Rehearsal 11am.

Wednesday, January 27 to Friday, January 29: BBC rehearsals.

Tuesday, February 2: Royal Festival Hall. Prof. Elderly Kodaly came with v. young wife. The Spinnery.

Friday, February 5: BBC recording.

Wednesday, February 10: Birmingham. Rehearsal 6.30–7.30.

Thursday, February 11: Spring Symphony. Rehearsal 10.15am-1.15. 7.30 concert.

Tuesday, February 15 to Saturday, February 20: Amsterdam concerts.

Sunday, February 21: Return Grimsby. Lucretia BBC.

Tuesday, March 1: Croydon recital with AR.

Wednesday, March 2: Royal Choral Gerontius 7.30pm. Albert Hall. 10am rehearsal.

Saturday, March 5: Sunderland Gerontius. Bishopwearmouth Parish Church.

Thursday, March 24: Great Wyrley near Walsall. Wesley Church Hall. Misc.

Saturday, March 26: Rugby Gerontius.

Saturday, April 9: Bath Choir. St. Matthew's. RFH. 10am rehearsal.

Sunday, April 10: St. Matthew Pasion. RFH. Jacques.

Tuesday, April 12: Manchester. Brahms Vier ernste gesange. Clifton Helliwell.

Wednesday, April 13: Messiah. Hanley.

Friday, April 15: Birmingham Gerontius 3pm.

Sunday, April 17: Aberystwyth refugee concert with Brannie and C. Clements. Gerald Davies.

Tuesday, April 26: RFH. Spring Symphony. Return 4pm Grimsby.

Wednesday, May 4: Beverley recital. Ben and Peter. Becoming more difficult.

Friday, May 6: Haddo House, Aberdeen. Ben and Peter came. Spring Symphony.

Sunday, May 8: Haddo. St. John Passion. Peter Pears (Ben there).

Thursday, May 12: Grimsby recital with AR.

Saturday, May 21: Leeds Temple Newsom. Recital with AR. 7.30pm.

Tuesday, May 24: Lincoln Cathedral refugee recital with AR.

Sunday, May 29 to Tuesday, May 31: To Aldeburgh. Lucretia rehearsals.

Wednesday, June 1: Adrian M such a poppet and to mother too.

Thursday, June 2: Choral 9th. RFH. Krips. Roses/white organza. What a day!

Saturday, June 11: Aldeburgh Festival begins.

Tuesday, June 14: Recital with B & P.

Wednesday, June 15: Lucretia rehearsals.

Saturday, June 18: Lucretia 1st night. V. nervous.

Monday, June 20: Lucretia 2nd performance.

Saturday, June 25: Mendelssohn soiree Aldeburgh. Colin (Graham) always at me!! Never told I was going next day to London clinic for tonsillectomy.

Tuesday, June 28: Op. V. ill. Terrible time. Lost over a stone in weight and pints of blood. Never given a transfusion which I so needed.

Thursday, June 30: Prof came to see me.

Wednesday, July 6: Return home to Grimsby. Wonderful!

Thursday, July 14: Bought Mini. Blue. £650!

Wednesday, July 20 to Wednesday, August 3: Switzerland night flight. Oh! Terrible time in Switzerland. Two weeks of hell!

Friday, August 19: Prof 11am. To Jersey/Bee.

Sunday, September 11: Maida Vale 3.3pm. V. nervous. First real sing since tonsillectomy. Three-month break! Never told anyone.

Tuesday, September 13: Prom alto rhap. Midnight blue satin/Julian's rose. Sir Malcolm was wonderful.

Saturday, September 17: Choral 9th. Ghent, Belgium. Royal Opera House. 8pm.

Wednesday, September 21: Oh what terrible days!!

Tuesday, October 4: Rehearsal Maida Vale.

Wednesday, October 5: Mozart BBC requiem mass. Purple satin. RFH. 8pm.

Thursday, October 6: Madame Baldi Italian lesson.

Saturday, October 8: Raymond *[Leppard]* 11–11.15am. Rehearsal 3pm.

Monday, October 10: Battersea Town Hall. 6.30.

Tuesday, October 11: RFH. 8pm. Monteverdi. Raymond Leppard. Royal blue brocade.

Wednesday, October 12: Middlesbrough Music Society with Bill Herbert. He was having a breakdown.

Thursday, October 13: Sunderland recital AR.

Friday, October 14: South Shields recital with AR.

Thursday, October 20: Cheltenham. Elgar. 4 Sea Pictures. Royal blue brocade.

Friday, October 21: Worcester recital with AR. 7.30.

Thursday, October 27: Hanley Centenary City of Stoke-on-Trent Gerontius. Barbirolli.

Saturday, October 29: Coalville. Belvoir Road Methodist Church Choir. 3 groups. Red brocade.

Sunday, October 30: Wisbech Male Voice. Red brocade.

Tuesday, November 1: Henry Wood Society. Messiah. Sargent. RAH. Silver lamè.

Thursday, November 10: Halifax Choral. The Kingdom. Elgar. Victoria Hall.

Friday, November 11: Mass in D. Huddersfield Choral. Rehearsal 2pm (sleeper). Silver lamè.

Saturday, November 12: Guildford Gerontius 7pm. Tech College Hall. White chiffon.

Wednesday, November 16: Rehearsal to Menuhin's 6.30pm. So nervous.

Friday, November 18: Charity concert. RFH. Yehudi. Peter and Ben. Turquoise satin. Abe and Ike. 11pm. St. George's Hotel. Holland Park.

Sunday, November 20: Spring Symphony recording BBC.

Monday, November 21: Covent Garden photo call in Kath's robe 2.30. Met Jimmy Gibson, chief rèpètiteur; an absolute sod! I hated him.

Tuesday, November 22: Ben's birthday. Spring Symphony recording. Decca. 2.15–5.15. Kingsway Hall.

Friday, December 2: Roxburghe. Gerontius. Edinburgh 7.30. Terrible rehearsal. Scottish Orchestra.

Saturday, December 3: Glasgow 7.30. White satin.

Tuesday, December 6: Orpheus rehearsals Covent Garden begin.

Thursday, December 8: Grimsby Messiah.

Saturday, December 10: Messiah Coventry Central Hall. 3pm rehearsal.

Thursday, December 15: Hull Choral Messiah. Tomato sandwiches. V. ill. Injections. Urticaria.

Saturday, December 17: Swansea Choral Messiah. Dr. gave another adrenalin injection.

Tuesday, December 20: Shrewsbury Christmas oratorios.

Saturday, December 24: Home for Christmas. So ill. Crazy with urticaria. Saw Doc again for double injection – all the time trying to rehearse.

Monday, December 26: Back to London for Orpheus rehearsals. Terrible time with Jimmy – I couldn't do anything right. Broke my spirit.

Tuesday, December 29: Liverpool Messiah 7.30. V. distraught and unhappy at Covent Garden. Talked to Peter Pears.

Saturday, December 31: Liverpool Messiah 7.30.

1961

Sunday, January 1: Music call with de Froment.

Thursday, January 12: Piano dress 10.30–2pm.

Friday, January 13: General dress rehearsal 10.30–2pm. No audience. Terrible media session on stage after performance. Houston Rogers v. kind. He took 'Orpheo' photos.

Monday, January 16: First night Orpheus. Covent Garden BBC. What a ghastly night! I knew I was right and should never have attempted this glorious piece. Wasn't ready for the stage. George Harewood so rude and flaming mad – first on set after curtain calls. I was wrung out and shattered. Perspiration pouring out of me.

Wednesday, January 18: Orpheus. I paid hotel and all expenses. £50 a performance!

Saturday, January 21: Orpheus. Sue and Ron. Podge and Norm.

Tuesday, January 24: Orpheus.

Thursday, January 26: Gastroenteritis.

Friday, January 27: Royal Choral Alto Rhap – Sargent – cancelled. Very ill. Griff bored through my sinus!

Monday, January 30: Orpheus.

Wednesday, February 1: Orpheus.

Friday, February 3: Thank God Cov Garden finished with! Home – hooray! Brought m'little pearl lyre.

Wednesday, February 8: Caerphilly male voice 7pm. Misc and duets with Bob Thomas.

Thursday, February 16: Opera ball.

Wednesday, February 22: Mass In D. BBC. RFH. 8pm.

Thursday, February 23: Record Mass In D.

Thursday, March 2: LPO B Minor Mass. Sir Adrian.

Friday, March 3: Voice/flu problems. Cancelled all concerts until after Easter.

Friday, March 10: Bristol Cathedral alto rhap Mozart requiem. Kodaly.

Saturday, March 25: Rehearsal St. Matthew's 10–1pm. Westminster Cathedral Hall.

Sunday, March 26: St. Matthew 11am and 2.30pm. RFH.

Monday, March 29: Copenhagen. St. John.

Friday, March 31: Royal Choral Messiah (entirety). Wembley Messiah at night. Crazy! Car waiting 5pm to take me to Wembley.

Thursday, April 6: Berlin concert.

Friday, April 14: Bristol Guild of Handicapped. Elsie Balmont. Central Hall. Misc.

Thursday, May 11: Newtown Gerontius. 6.30pm Barbirolli.

Sunday, May 14: Dvorak Requiem.

Tuesday, May 16: To Hanover.

Thursday, May 18: Cologne recital/Bach cantatas.

Wednesday, May 31: To London. Rehearsal Ben and Peter.

Wednesday, June 7: Kings College Chapel, Cambridge. Gerontius. David Gallwer.

Thursday, June 8: Cambridge Gerontius. Private record made. David Willcocks.

Friday, June 9: To London. Covent Garden – Joan – Lucia.

Saturday, June 10: Reginald Jacques. Bach Choir/orchestra. Lunch 12.

Friday, June 16: Royal Marines Church. Deale Brass Band. Gerontius 7.30pm. Dark dress. Lt Col Vivian Dunn – brilliant conductor and brass players. Wonderful and memorable performance. No strings!

Thursday, June 29: Aldeburgh festival concert. 8.15pm.

Tuesday, July 4: Aldeburgh, Venetian music. Prof's birthday.

Sunday, July 9: St. John Passion Aldeburgh.

Saturday, July 15 to Thursday, July 27: Jersey.

Thursday, August 10: Prom Mozart Requiem Mass.

Sunday, August 13: Maida Vale Studio I cantata rehearsal.

Tuesday, August 15: Prom Ben's Cantata Academia.

Monday, August 28: Viola 4pm-ish. Stayed at Red House. Very ill. Gastroenteritis.

Thursday, September 7: Gerontius. 3 Choirs.

Friday, September 8: Messiah Hereford.

Wednesday, September 13: Gerontius. Birmingham Town Hall. Meredith Davies/CBSO.

Thursday, September 14: Travel to Ulm festival, Bavaria. Very ill with flu bug – throat specialist. So ashamed, ill again!

Saturday, September 16: Abe and Ike recital with Ben and Peter.

Sunday, September 17: Bach cantatas Ulm Cathedral.

Thursday, October 12: Choral 9th. FH. Krips.

Saturday, October 14: Swansea Festival. Beethoven Choral 9th. Halle Orch. Dragon's Hotel.

Friday, October 20: St. Mary's College Cheltenham recital with AR.

Thursday, November 2: Grimsby Methodist International concert.

Thursday, November 9: Leicester 5 Tudor Portraits V. Williams. Belmont Hotel.

Wednesday, November 15: Exeter Cathedral Gerontius. Very ill – boils getting worse.

Saturday, November 18: Cold infection.

Tuesday, November 21: Cologne recital.

Friday, November 24: Bremen.

Tuesday, November 28: Brighouse recital with AR. Turquoise. 7.30 Danish Hall.

Thursday, November 30: Shrewsbury recital with AR. Blind society. Turquoise.

Saturday, December 2: Derby Messiah. Queens Hall. 7pm.

Sunday, December 3 to Thursday, December 7: Hanover radio.

Friday, December 8: London. Injection – osteopath.

Saturday, December 9: Coventry Messiah. Sang in agony with left foot. Standing on one leg! V. ill.

Sunday, December 10: Arrived home in agony at 3am with Norm. Crawled on knees upstairs.

Tuesday, December 12: To St. Hugh's *[Hospital].* Ambulance.

Wednesday, December 13: To London. Stock Exchange. 2 groups. Turquoise/aqua.

Thursday, December 14: Blackburn Messiah. Black lace.

Friday, December 15: Huddersfield Messiah. BBC. Sir Malcolm. Black lace.

Saturday, December 16: To Koln. 3pm rehearsal.

Sunday, December 17: Hellish painful days. Foot in heavy plaster.

Monday, December 18: Cologne Christmas oratorio. Israel cancelled.

Wednesday, December 20: Huddersfield Messiah. BBC.

Saturday, December 24: Bethlehem Messiah cancelled. Rigors – very ill.

Tuesday, December 26: Very ill. Terrible.

Wednesday, December 27: Bad rigor.

Thursday, December 28 – Liverpool Philharmonic Messiah cancelled.

Friday, December 29: Hellish pain. Rigors.

Saturday, December 30: Plaster removed. X-ray shows trouble at last. Op for Monday AM after talk with Mr. Holdsworth, Sheffield consultant.

1962

Monday, January 1: Left foot op at St. Hugh's Hospital 8.30am. V. v. ill. What bliss when I came round; that hellish three weeks of pain had stopped, thank God.

Saturday, January 14: Began painting.

Saturday, January 27: Two spasms before 1pm. One at 2.30pm. Slight pain right side 5–5.30.

Wednesday, February 14: Lovely day.

Tuesday, March 6: Op on arm. Local anaesthetic.

Friday, March 23: Into St. Hugh's again. Tablets.

Saturday, March 24: Op left arm. V. sick. Four-hour op!

Tuesday, March 27: Dark days.

Thursday, March 29: Matthew Passion Grimsby cancelled.

Friday, March 30 and Sunday, March 31: Terrible days.

Friday, April 20: Royal Choral Messiah cancelled.

Friday, May 11: Bristol Gerontius cancelled.

Tuesday, May 15: Das Lied Mahler Krips LPO RFH cancelled.

Tuesday, May 22: Sharrow, to the boys' cottage. Still in plaster.

Saturday, May 26: Home again. Plaster off.

Sunday, May 27: First walk, to back door.

Tuesday, May 29: Truro Gerontius cancelled.

Wednesday, June 13: Cambridge Guildhall. Haydn Imperial Mass. Britten Cantata Academia. 8.30pm.

Thursday, June 14: Aldeburgh, Orford Church 5pm. Haydn Mass and cantata.

Saturday, July 21: Mr. Holsworth to Sheffield. Left foot problem. Decided against Russia tour and for half of left big toe to be cut off.

Sunday, July 22: Into St. Hugh's again.

Monday, July 23: Op number 5.

Thursday, August 2: Stitches out.

Sunday, August 26: To Prof's. First lesson.

Sunday, September 2: Walsall Church Civic Service. First public sing. What agonies!

Thursday, September 6 and Friday, September 7: Gloucester Three Choirs. V. ill. Te Deum Messiah.

Tuesday, September 11: Prom rehearsal. Sir M made a wonderful welcome speech for me.

Friday, September 14: Prom concert. Coronation Mass. Mozart Choral 9th. Sir M. Terrible trouble climbing stairs.

Monday, September 17: Russia cancelled.

Wednesday, October 3: BBC Choral 9th.

Wednesday, October 31: BBC Cantata Academia.

Tuesday, November 6: Swadlincote male voice. Misc. Terrible!

Saturday, November 10: Gerontius. Nottingham Albert Hall. Noel.

Wednesday, November 21: Berlin. Bach B Minor.

Tuesday, November 27: TV Huddersfield Songs of Praise.

Friday, November 30: V. ill walking/standing.

Sunday, December 2: BBC Manchester.

Thursday, December 6: Grimsby Messiah.

Saturday, December 8: Chelmsford Messiah.

Thursday, December 13: Hull Messiah.

Friday, December 14: Huddersfield Messiah.

Saturday, December 15: Aylesbury Christmas oratorio. Two groups of two songs.

Monday, December 17: Huddersfield Messiah. White organza. Sir Malcolm sent me back to hotel and home. V. ill.

Wednesday, December 19: Leeds Messiah cancelled.

1963

Tuesday, January 1: Liverpool Philharmonic Messiah. No rehearsal.

Wednesday, January 9: To London. Enchantress rehearsal.

Thursday, January 10: Magdala rehearsal. Prof. Home again.

Thursday, January 24: Bliss The Enchantress. Glasgow. Scottish Orchestra. Studio concert. Stayed with Norman Del Mar – very kind but I was terrible company.

Wednesday, February 6: Spring Symphony. RFH. 8pm.

Saturday, February 9: Malvern alto rhap. NFMS Award.

Friday, March 22: BBC rehearsal alto rhap.

Saturday, March 23: 8.30–10.35 concert. Lovely Dean Dixon, conductor, from Frankfurt. Asked me to sing in Frankfurt but very ill again.

Sunday, March 24: BBC alto rhap Ipswich Cinema. Dean Dixon.

Monday, April 1 and Tuesday, April 2: Messiah recordings. John Pritchard.

Monday, April 8: Fly out to Cologne. Very sad and lonely – could hardly walk.

Wednesday, April 10 to Friday, April 12: St. Matthew's. Gunter Wand conducting.

Wednesday, May 1: Songs of Praise Altringham.

Saturday, May 11: Grays Essex. Thurrock male voice. Alto rhap. Went off feeling very grim.

Tuesday, May 14: To Copenhagen. Radio orchestra.

Friday, May 17: Handel/Samson. Jennie. Home again.

Tuesday, June 4: RFH Choral 9th. Krips.

Thursday, June 6 and Friday, June 7: BBC recording. Bach record.

Thursday, June 20: Happy day.

Tuesday, June 25: Bach Choir Gerontius. Lovely welcome back, bless them. Singing is such a battle; one is always having to sing about the things one is trying to forget or longing for and can't have. But we try to press on. Why? And what for? I don't know but am grateful.

Saturday, June 29: Aldeburgh. Music In England. Victorian ballads. Quite an ordeal but a lovely welcome too.

Wednesday, July 3: Lincoln Cathedral. B Minor Mass.

Tuesday, July 16: Manchester TV.

Sunday, August 11: Penzance Mouse Hole Male Voice Choir. St. John's Hall.

Wednesday, August 14: Prom RAH. Alto rhap. Sir M was wonderful and what a welcome from the Promenaders.

Thursday, August 15: Spring Symphony rehearsal. Ghastly dysentery attack. 4pm train to Grimsby.

Monday, August 19: The Enchantress Prom. RAH. What a day!

Tuesday, August 20: Flew to Edinburgh festival. Spring Symphony.

Monday, August 26: Edinburgh festival recital with Ben and Peter. Abe and Ike. Very ill and low. Afternoon train home.

Friday, August 30: YMCA rehearsal 2–5. Birmingham Three Choirs. Went off feeling like death.

Monday, September 2: Three Choirs. Mary of Magdala. Sir A Bliss.

Wednesday, September 11: Royal College 6.30pm.

Thursday, September 12: Prom. Spring Symphony 11.30 Albert Hall.

Sunday, September 15: Terrible cold.

Friday, September 20: El Pesebre Casals rehearsal.

Sunday, September 29: Casals oratorio.

Wednesday, October 16: Songs of Praise.

Saturday, October 19: Birmingham and District Welsh Society. 7pm. Two groups each half.

Thursday, October 31: Mary of Magdala. Sea Pictures. Birmingham.

Wednesday, November 6: RFH Spring Symphony. BBC.

Tuesday, November 12: Stroud Ladies Choir. Misc.

Wednesday, November 20: Leeds Philharmonic. Alto rhapsody. Beethoven Mass In C.

Saturday, November 23: York Messiah.

Tuesday, November 26: Bishop Auckland.

Saturday, November 30: Zurich Weinachts oratorio. Peter singing, Ben came too and Lou-Lou.

Sunday, December 1: Christmas oratorio. Zurich.

Wednesday, December 4: TV Messiah.

Saturday, December 7: Leicester Messiah.

Thursday, December 12: Blackburn Messiah. Went off feeling ghastly.

Saturday, December 14: Coventry Messiah. Just made this concert.

Friday, December 20: LPO RFH. Messiah.

Saturday, December 28: Liverpool Messiah. BBC.

1964

Thursday, January 2: Liverpool Messiah.

Saturday, January 4: Royal Choral Messiah.

Friday, January 10 and Saturday, January 11: BBC Cantata Academia.

Friday, February 21: Messiah RFH.

Sunday, March 1: Recording.

Monday, March 2: Hanover concert.

Tuesday, March 3: Home again! Hooray! Long day, tired out but home!

Thursday, March 12: Hull Choral Mary of Magdala. Sir Arthur at concert.

Wednesday, March 18: To Town. Spain.

Friday, March 20: St. Matthew's. Madrid. Ruth Margaret Putz sop. First time back after osteomyelitis.

Sunday, March 22: St. Matthew's AM. To Cologne.

Wednesday, March 25 to Friday, March 27: St. Matthew Passion.

Saturday, March 28: Home. Hooray! Feeling lousy.

Saturday, April 4: Wigan. Misc with John Holmes. Felt so ill and dreadful. Almost collapsed on arrival home at front door.

Wednesday, April 29: St. James' Church, Grimsby. Songs of Praise. TV.

Wednesday, May 6: Recording Birmingham. Mahler alto rhapsody.

Sunday, May 10: London. Rehearsal. C Groves. Mahler 8th.

Thursday, May 14: Studio G Lime Grove. TV. Music In Miniature. 10am. 12.30pm. 2pm.

Tuesday, May 26: Gerontius. Stirling.

Friday, May 29: Liverpool Cathedral. Mahler Symphony 8.

Sunday, May 31: BBC Manchester. AR.

Monday, June 8: Grasmere. TV recording. Songs Of Praise.

Saturday, June 13: Leeds recital with AR. Temple Newson 7.30.

Tuesday, June 16: BBC invitation concert. Aldeburgh. Schuman.

Saturday, June 20: Aldeburgh Orpheus. Lovely Joyce Grenfell apologised not to be at my concert in afternoon. Meredith Davies in hellish mood, cruelly rude to me. Joyce G gave a great boost and laughed at him. Wonderful concert at night.

Wednesday, June 24 and Thursday, June 25: TV Gorleston.

Sunday, July 5: Grasmere TV.

Wednesday, July 15: To Israel. Boeing. 11am.

Thursday, July 16: Tel Aviv. Four concerts in Tel Aviv, two in Jerusalem and one in Caesarea.

Monday, July 20: Beethoven Choral 9th. Israel Philharmonic. Josef Krips. Jerusalem judge – can't remember his name – premier judge at Nuremberg Trial – wonderful man. Saw sea scrolls. Visited Holocaust memorial and Academy of Music. Rushed back and late for British Ambassador's lunch.

Wednesday, July 22: Caesarea concert. Amphitheatre – first/opening. Wonderful setting on a perfect open-air moonlit night. Restored by Rothschilds.

Friday, July 24 Saturday, July 25: Tel Aviv concerts.

Wednesday, August 12: Prom. Disaster for me. 11.30am RAH. Bee in town. Found problem after Prom. Deep shock.

Monday, August 24: Prom. Mahler 8th. RAH. Charles Groves. Bee there.

Wednesday, August 26: Sir Stan C. Westminster.

Monday, September 7: Sir Standford. Bed available. Single room. Terrible welcome.

Tuesday, September 8: Op. Norm collected mother. V. ill.

Sunday, September 13: Sir S told bad news.

Thursday, September 24: 1st treatment. Terrible day.

Monday, September 28: Back to town and Westminster. Very lonely days but had to be.

[The diary is crossed out until November 8].

Saturday, November 14: York Messiah. First sing. With Wilfred Brown.

Thursday, November 19: Academy adjudication with Noel. Felt grim.

Saturday, November 21: Neville Male Voice Choir, Co. Durham. Misc.

Friday, November 27: Sir Henry Wood Messiah. RAH. Gold coat and dress.

Wednesday, December 2: Middlesbrough Messiah. Town Hall.

Thursday, December 3: Warrington Messiah. Misc.

Saturday, December 5: Leicester Phil. Messiah. Gold brocade (fitted).

Wednesday, December 9: Bradford Messiah. Gold brocade.

Friday, December 11: Huddersfield Messiah. Gold brocade.

Saturday, December 12: Coventry Messiah. Gold brocade.

Tuesday, December 15: Huddersfield Messiah. TV – Europe. Gold coat and dress.

Wednesday, December 16: Leeds Messiah. Gold brocade.

Thursday, December 17: Messiah Blackburn. Gold brocade.

Saturday, December 19: Liverpool Messiah. Gold coat and dress.

Sunday, December 20: Home. Hooray – Christmas! Sir Malcolm's book arrived. I was in tears, bless him.

Tuesday, December 29: Liverpool Messiah. Sapphire velvet.

Wednesday, December 30: Liverpool Messiah. Quaker. Turquoise silk with sleeves. Joan, Peter, Hervey Alan, and Norm.

1965

Saturday, January 9: Grimsby recital. Everyman.

Thursday, January 21: Songs of Praise. Wales.

Wednesday, January 27: Lincoln Messiah.

Monday, February 1 to Tuesday, February 2: BBC recording.

Wednesday, February 10: Consett. Misc. Duet A Holmes.

Saturday, February 20: Orpheus Birmingham.

Tuesday, February 23 to Sunday, February 28: Madrid. Horenstein – wonderful concerts. Das Lied. 1st class flight home.

Sunday, March 7: Rawtenstall. Misc.

Thursday, March 11: 3rd BBC recording out.

Monday, March 15: York BBC singing contest.

Thursday, March 18: Birmingham Bach Cantata Choral 9th.

Saturday, March 20: Oswestry alto rhap. Two groups. Bach cantata.

Saturday, March 27: Gerontius Leicester.

Thursday, April 1: Hull Gerontius.

Saturday, April 3: Grantham Gerontius. St. Wulfram's Church.

Monday, April 12: To Cologne.

Wednesday, April 14 to Friday, April 16: St. Matthew.

Saturday, April 24: RFH. New Philharmonia. Messiah.

Sunday, May 2: Oxford Gerontius. Afternoon concert.

Monday, May 3 to Friday, May 7: Cologne. Radio Marcello. Wupperstall. B Minor.

Wednesday, May 12: To Newtown festival.

Thursday, May 13: Choral 9th and aria at afternoon concert.

Saturday, May 15: Walsall Town Hall. Gerontius. CBSO.

Thursday, May 20: Messiah recording Kingsway Hall. Sir Malcolm wonderful. 2–5 Readers Digest.

Saturday, June 12: Coventry Gerontius.

Saturday, June 19: Southwell Gerontius. Minster. Sir Adrian.

Monday, June 28: To Frankfurt.

Wednesday, June 30: To Lyon.

Friday, July 2: Hindemeth Requiem. Lyon. Terrible hotel and trip, felt so ill – nausea. Bitten to pieces by midges. Hellish hotel.

Wednesday, July 21: To Munich. Bach cantatas.

Friday, July 22: Lenggries.

Wednesday, July 28 to Tuesday, August 10: To Jersey. Holidays, hooray!

Wednesday, August 18: To Edinburgh. Festival.

Thursday, August 19: AM rehearsal. Piano.

Friday, August 20: Orchestral rehearsal. Mahler 8th.

Sunday, August 22: Mahler 8th.

Friday, September 10: Prom. Choral 9th. RAH. Turquoise.

Tuesday, September 14: German rehearsal. Royal College, London.

Friday, September 17: Liverpool Choral 9th. Turquoise organza.

Saturday, September 25: Brahms viola songs 3pm.

Sunday, October 3: Whitechurch services. Shocking pink/navy silk.

Tuesday, November 2: Leeds. Studio. 2.30.

Thursday, November 4: Derby Choral. Halle Orchestra. Gerontius. King's Hall.

Tuesday, November 9: Copenhagen.

Thursday, November 11: Mozart Requiem. Copenhagen. To Frankfurt.

Saturday, November 13 to Monday, November 15: Frankfurt. Hindemitt Requiem.

Tuesday, November 16: Home. Hooray. Bee 2.30.

Thursday, November 18: Chuck Gerhardt recording. Sea Hawk. 10–1pm. Wonderful.

Friday, November 19: Studio portrait.

Sunday, November 21: Hull. BBC Brahms. Serious Songs. Assembly Hall. Royal blue.

Monday, November 29: BBC London. Viola/Brahms/Purcell.

Saturday, December 4: Leicester Messiah. Royal black/gold.

Thursday, December 9: Hull Messiah. Turquoise.

Saturday, December 11: Derby Messiah. Black/gold.

Tuesday, December 14: Wolverhampton Civic Hall. Messiah.

Thursday, December 16: Blackburn Messiah. Royal blue velvet.

Friday, December 17: Huddersfield Messiah.

Saturday, December 18: Wakefield. Misc. Alto rhap. Royal blue velvet.

Wednesday, December 22: Huddersfield Messiah. White satin.

Friday, January 7: Edinburgh Gerontius. Felt so ill. Gold brocade and coat.

Saturday, January 8: Glasgow. Alex Gibson in rotten mood. Very aggressive.

Saturday, January 15: Grimsby Messiah. White lace and coat. I looked ghastly, like a barrage balloon – so ashamed.

Wednesday, January 19: Beverley Songs of Praise.

Saturday, January 22: Horenstein/Das Lied rehearsals. Church Gerhardt came to listen, but voice (upper register) gone!

Monday, January 24: Felt so grim.

Tuesday, January 25: Das Lied. Horenstein. Odeon Cinema Swiss Cottage.

Wednesday, January 26: Home. Terrible singing. Sang so badly. Couldn't lift m'voice.

Friday, January 28: To town. To Geneva.

Saturday, January 29: 1st rehearsal. Cantatas 45, 80 and 105. Scarlatti recording out.

Monday, January 31: Concert Lausanne. Gold brocade and coat.

Tuesday, February 1: Rehearsal. Jacques.

Wednesday, February 2: Geneva concert.

Thursday, February 3: Rehearsal. Messiah. A bit grim again.

Friday, February 4: Messiah concert. Black velvet and black beading.

Saturday, February 5: Home hooray. Felt rotten.

Sunday, February 13: BBC Concert Hall. Grand Hotel.

Tuesday, February 22: Cardiff. Sea Pictures. Boys came. Terrible Spanish conductor.

Wednesday, March 16: Leeds. Wonderful to see Sir M again after his serious illness.

Tuesday, March 22: Royal Choral. Delius. Mass of Life. White satin beaded black velvet top.

Wednesday, March 23: To Barcelona.

Friday, March 25 and Saturday, March 26: St. M. Black velvet.

Wednesday, March 30: Madrid rehearsal.

Friday, April 1: St. M. Black lace and coat. No rehearsal.

Sunday, April 3: St. M. Black lace and coat. To Dusseldorf.

Monday, April 4: To Cologne. Karl Engel.

Wednesday, April 6: St. M. Black lace and coat.

Thursday, April 7: St. M. Günter Wand, conductor.

Saturday, April 9: Karl Engel rehearsal on an old beer piano in hotel cellar. Koln 3.30pm plane. Home.

Sunday, April 17: Mahler 8th. Princess Margaret in audience. Bernstein. LSO. RAH. Televised broadcast.

Monday, April 18: Recording RCA. Walthamstow Town Hall. Gwyneth Jones, Heather.

Wednesday, April 20: To Hamburg. Arrived very tired but grateful.

Friday, April 22: Hanover recital. Brahms. Viola songs.

Saturday, April 23: LSO Choral 9th. Early plane back. Fleishman manager pleased to see me back.

Sunday, April 24: LSO Choral 9th RFH. Lorin Maazel conducted. He was lovely; sorry no opportunity to work together again. Very like Francis to look at.

Saturday, April 30: Malvern alto rhap. Vivaldi. Short blue lace. Glorious concert.

Thursday, May 5: Newport Male Voice Choir. Misc. King Head Hotel.

Saturday, May 7: Sheffield Choral 9th. Barbirolli. Grand Hotel.

Sunday, May 8: Manchester Choral 9th. Barbirolli.

Friday, May 20: To town. Bee in town. Das Lied. Saw Covent Garden ballet; only rehearsal to watch and listen in stalls with orchestra before first performance on June 25. Disgraceful.

Tuesday, May 24: Berrie requiem.

Wednesday, May 25: Zurich requiem.

Thursday, June 2: London rehearsal. Missa Solemnis. 6–8pm.

Saturday, June 4: Swadlincote West St. Methodist Church. Misc. Accompanist John Wills.

Tuesday, June 7: Missa Solemnis. Rehearsal 6.30–9.30.

Wednesday, June 8: Recording. 7–9.30.

Thursday, June 9: Louth/Grimsby B Minor Mass. Terrible cold and very tired.

Saturday, June 11: Guildford Cathedral. Choral 9th. Deutsch Surrey Phi Society.

Wednesday, June 22: Sing of Cross. BBC.

Saturday, June 25: Das Lied ballet. Covent Garden. Nureyev was superb and so kind to me. Rehearsal 10.30am: no orchestral rehearsal allowed. Terrible! Piano rehearsal only. Swarowsky conducting; very angry. Frankfurt Ballet Orchestra played more wrong notes than I've ever heard in Das Lied.

Sunday, June 26: Birmingham Choral 9th. Town Hall.

Wednesday, June 29 to Friday, July 1: Ballet Das Lied. Covent Garden. Nureyev wonderful.

Tuesday, July 12: To Rotterdam.

Thursday, July 14: Rehearsal 10am. Missa Solemnis.

Friday, July 15: The Hague. NJ died. Heart attack. 19/7 funeral. Terrible heartache/premonition.

Sunday, July 17: St. J Passion. Ben and Peter. Guildhall. Ben conducting. Could hardly sing. Concert nearly broke me.

Wednesday, July 20: St. J Passion broadcast. City of London Festival. BBC. Holborn.

Wednesday, August 3: To Wales. Terrible taxi driver who attacked me.

Thursday, August 4: Mass B Minor. Port Talbot. Royal Hotel.

Saturday, August 6 to Thursday, August 18: Jersey. Wonderful Bee!

Thursday, August 25: To Edinburgh. Mahler 8th.

Monday, August 29: To Hanover.

Tuesday, August 30: Louisenhof.

Wednesday, September 7: Ghent Cathedral Messiah.

Thursday, September 8: Tournai Messiah.

Saturday, September 10: Long Melford. St. John Passion. Afternoon concert. Peter/Ben/Lady Hyde Parker.

Thursday, September 15: Ulm.

Saturday, September 17: St. Matthew Passion. Vergnügte Ruh.

Monday, September 19 and Tuesday, September 20: Messiah recording. Storowski.

Thursday, September 29: Mahler 3rd. Royal Phil. RFH.

Thursday, October 6: Decca recording.

Tuesday, October 11: To Madrid.

Thursday, October 13: Choral 9th. Reopening of Teatro Real. Franco/Juan Carlos, Princess Sofia present.

Saturday, October 15: Madrid. Awful stomach.

Friday, October 21: Dudley. Hugo/Jen. CBSO.

Tuesday, October 25: Decca recording.

Tuesday, November 1: Berlin Phil. Mass.

Monday, November 7: Julius Caesar recording. Kingsway.

Saturday, November 19: Messiah. York Clifton. Rehearsal 2–4pm.

Saturday, November 26 and Sunday, November 27: Back cantatas.

Saturday, December 3: Coventry Messiah. Ron died.

Tuesday, December 6: Dusseldorf Rheinhalle Messiah.

Thursday, December 8: Dusseldorf Messiah.

Friday, December 9: Messiah. Rafael Frühbeck. 8pm.

Thursday, December 15: Blackburn Messiah. Very ill. Terrible flu.

Friday, December 16: To Wuppertal. Travel to Dusseldorf.

Saturday, December 17: Christmas oratorio Deutsch.

Sunday, December 18: Wuppertal Christmas oratorio. Terrible flu. Only just got through concert.

Saturday, December 31: To Glasgow. Messiah rehearsal.

1967

Sunday, January 1: Glasgow Messiah. Black velvet/white mink.

Wednesday, January 4: To Wuppertal.

Friday, January 6: Weinachts oratorio. Bronze/gold coat dress.

Saturday, January 14: Grimsby Messiah. Black velvet/white mink.

Tuesday, January 24: BBC. El Amor Brujo. Red brocade.

Wednesday, January 25: Watford public concert.

Thursday, January 26: Tobin piano rehearsal 11am.

Friday, January 27: Houston Rogers. Sloane Square.

Saturday, January 28: Tobin Messiah. 6pm. Black satin/gold white black coat.

Tuesday, January 31: Hanover B Minor Mass. Black velvet.

Saturday, February 4: Richter B Minor. RAM. Rehearsals.

Sunday, February 5: LPO RFH B Minor concert. Peter sang. 1st Karli concert. Black velvet.

Monday, February 6: Home. Karl very agitated and cross.

Thursday, February 9: Bach cantatas disc recording.

Saturday, February 18: Freiburg. St. John Passion. Karl Egel hateful. Black velvet.

Sunday, February 19: Gastric flu through the night. Oh so ill. St. Johannes; terrible conductor, Karl Egel. Marga Huffgen, German contralto's husband absolute swine at rehearsal in front of choir and orchestra.

Wednesday, February 22: St. Pancras Church. AR. Home 4pm. Felt like death.

Monday, February 27: To Copenhagen.

Tuesday, March 7: To Barcelona.

Friday, March 10: Orpheus. Italian. Gold coat and dress.

Sunday, March 12: Barcelona Orpheus. Gold coat and dress.

Friday, March 17 to Sunday, March 19: Madrid. St. Matthew's. Black lace and purple sash.

Monday, March 20: To Köln.

Wednesday, March 22: St. Matthew's 8pm.

Thursday, March 23: St. Matthew's. Günter Wand conductor.

Friday, March 31: To Bielefeld. Rehearsal 8pm.

Saturday, April 1: Missa Solemnis. Rehearsal with audience.

Sunday, April 2: Bielefeld Missa Solemnis. Black velvet with white mink.

Monday, April 3: To Stuttgart.

Wednesday, April 5: Leonsberg.

Saturday, April 15: Walton Gloria Leeds. Black velvet with mink. Terrible work! Ray a devil!

Thursday, April 20: Mass In D Beethoven. Hull. AR very rude. Black velvet and white mink. Performance almost fell apart. Shattered! I saved the day!

Sunday, April 22: Bath Abbey Gerontius. Gold coat and dress.

Friday, May 26: Monmouth Gerontius. White lace.

Saturday, May 27: To Geneva for the World Peace concert.

Monday, May 29: El Pesebre concert. World Peace Conference, Geneva. Pablo Casals conducting his work. Wonderful ole boy! In Catalan – help! Walter Legge's daughter taught me practically by phone from London.

Wednesday, May 31: To Basel.

Thursday, June 1: International piano rehearsal. Hotel.

Friday, June 2: Basle. Le Laudi. Suter. Beautiful work. Black lace with train. Matre Terra solo. Front filling came out; fixed by dentist. Hans Münch.

Sunday, June 4 to Tuesday, June 6: Basle recording.

Thursday, June 8: To Lausanne.

Sunday, June 11: Bach Magnificat. Lausanne. Black lace. New work.

Monday, June 12: Terra Dei. Concert.

Tuesday, June 13 and Wednesday, June 14: Radio recording.

Saturday, June 24: Llandaff, Cardiff. B Minor. Black lace.

Tuesday, June 27: Würzburg. To Frankfurt. Rafael Kubelik first meeting, and Elsie Morison since Orpheus.

Thursday, June 29: Requiem concert. Black lace. Kubelik's birthday.

Monday, July 3: Liverpool Adelphi. Rehearsals.

Wednesday, July 5: Liverpool Cathedral. AR. Black lace. Haydn's Seven Last Words.

Friday, July 7: Southwell Minster.

Saturday, July 8: Bethlehem Messiah cancelled because of the Jordanian/Israeli war.

Wednesday, July 12: Manchester B Minor. Free Trade. Queens Hotel.

Wednesday, July 19: To Heilsbronn.

Thursday, July 20 and Friday, July 21: Heilsbronn recordings.

Saturday, July 22: St. Johannes Passion. Arnsbach Festival.

Sunday, July 23: Johannes. Black lace.

Tuesday, July 25: Verghute Ruh cantata 170.

Thursday, July 27: Home to Grimsby. Cleaners.

Sunday, July 30 to Saturday, August 12: Dear Bee.

Monday, August 21: Copenhagen recital. Turquoise coat and dress.

Tuesday, August 22: To Madrid.

Wednesday, August 23: To Carmona.

Thursday, August 24: Choral 9th. La Coruna.

Tuesday, August 29: La Coruna. Santander. Choral 9th.

Saturday, September 9: Leeds recital. AR. Temple Newsom.

Saturday, September 16: London. Kodaly rehearsal.

Sunday, September 24 to Monday, October 2: Germany. Kubelik. Charpentier Te Deum. C Major Mass. Beethoven. Henning Schlick (Ansbach). Munich night train. Köln. Missa Solemnis.

Tuesday, October 3: Sir Malcolm died.

Wednesday, October 11: Kodaly. Te Deum.

Wednesday, October 25: Skegness recital cancelled. Flu.

Saturday, October 28: Coventry Cathedral. Richter. B Minor Mass.

Sunday, October 29: Newcastle. City Hall. B Minor. Karli Richter.

Thursday, November 9: Vienna concert. Orftheo. Louis de Frament.

Friday, November 10: Luxembourg.

Wednesday, November 15: London recitals. Ernest Lush very rude. BBC Maida Vale. Wonderful BBC announcer.

Saturday, November 18: York Clifton Messiah.

Thursday, November 23 and Friday, November 24: Gothenburg Messiah.

Saturday, November 25: To Rotterdam.

Tuesday, November 28 and Wednesday, November 29: The Hague. B Minor concerts.

Saturday, December 2: Coventry Messiah. Rehearsal 3pm.

Monday, December 4: BBC recording. Tired out. Michael Head's first broadcast 'The Moonlight'.

Saturday, December 9: London RFH. Mahler 2nd symphony.

Sunday, December 10: Mahler's 2nd. RAH. Kubelik.

Tuesday, December 12: Northwick Christmas music.

Thursday, December 14: Leicester. Carols. 7.15pm.

Saturday, December 16 and Sunday, December 17: Essen. Weinachts oratorios.

Thursday, December 21: Northampton music carol concert. Two groups of three. 7.30pm.

Saturday, December 23: Home. Praise God!!

1968

Thursday, January 4: Royal Choral Messiah. White lace ensemble. RAH.

Friday, January 12 to Sunday, January 14: To Essen. Weinachts oratorio. Royal blue velvet and lace collar.

Monday, January 15: To Berlin.

Saturday, January 27: RFH. Spring Symphony. Rehearsal 10–1pm.

Sunday, January 28: Spring Symphony. Haitink. LPO. 7.30. 10am rehearsal.

Saturday, February 3: Tobin Messiah. RFH. Black velvet, white diamante.

Saturday, February 17 and Sunday, February 18: Johannes Passion. RFH. Karl Richter. Connaught Hotel.

Tuesday, February 20: Recital BBC.

Wednesday, March 6 and Thursday, March 7: To Zurich. St. John Passion. Black velvet. Tonhalle concert.

Saturday, March 9: To Köln. Rehearsal 4pm.

Monday, March 11: Köln concert. Missa Solemnis. Black velvet skirt and white evening crystal/pearl top.

Wednesday, March 20: Newcastle Gerontius. Brian and Francis came – surprise visit.

Friday, March 22: Malvern Gerontius. Stayed at London Airport.

Saturday, March 23: To Rotterdam.

Sunday, March 24: St. Matthew Passion. Black velvet skirt with top with white lace collar and cuffs.

Tuesday, March 26: Rotterdam. St. Matthew. Black lace.

Wednesday, March 27: Barcelona. St. Matthew. Black lace.

Friday, March 29 and Sunday, March 31: St. Matthew concerts.

Monday, April 1: To Madrid.

Thursday, April 4 to Saturday, April 6: Madrid. Rafael Frühbeck. St. Matthew. Black lace.

Monday, April 29: Skarde, Sweden. Terrible journey, thick snow. Johannes Passion.

Wednesday, May 8: Kings Lynn. Alto rhapsody. Red brocade.

Saturday, May 11: Smethick Male Voice Choir. John Heddle Nash. Red brocade.

Monday, May 27: To Nuremberg.

Wednesday, May 29: Public rehearsal. Black lace.

Thursday, May 30: Italian tour. Long and tiring.

Friday, May 31: Trieste.

Saturday, June 1: Ravenna Cathedral.

Sunday, June 2: Verona Cathedral. Enormous journey!

Monday, June 3: L'Aquila, near Rome.

Wednesday, June 5: Ravenna Cathedral. Purple lace.

Thursday, June 6: Bergano.

Friday, June 7: Treviso.

Saturday, June 8: Trento.

Sunday, June 9: Home. Hellish trip.

Saturday, June 15: Flu. Just made it to Glasgow. Ben's Spring Symphony. Blue kaftan.

Wednesday, June 19: B Minor. Westminster Abbey. Purple lace.

Sunday, June 23: Munich. A wonderful trip! Karli. Bach choir. B Minor. Purple lace. Choir fantastic.

Thursday, June 27: Wolverhampton. Blue kaftan. John Heddle Nash.

Tuesday, July 2: Sweden. Göteburg recital. Red brocade.

Wednesday, July 31: Karl's organ recital – fantastic! Liszt fugue on Bach incredible.

Saturday, August 3: Black lace. Karli. Samson. Deutsch. Ottobeuren. The most glorious basilica I've ever seen!

Sunday, August 4: Carlo concert. Very memorable weekend.

Wednesday, August 7: Sappho Songs. Radio 3.

Thursday, August 8: Turquoise kaftan. Spring Symphony Prom.

Sunday, August 11: Penzance Male Voice Choir. Miscellaneous. Red brocade.

Wednesday, August 28: 3 Choirs, Gloucester. Te Deum. Tony Hewitt Jones. Blue kaftan. Choral 9th.

Friday, August 30: Gerontius. Gold coat with mink.

Saturday, September 7: Flanders Festival. Louvain. Missa Solemnis. Black lace.

Sunday, September 8: Home. Orpheus transmission Luxembourg.

Tuesday, September 17: Baden. Hartmann 1st symphony. Very difficult – not v. helpful conductor.

Thursday, September 19: Aribert Reimann piano recording. Lovely lieder.

Friday, September 20: Hartmann symphonies concert. Purple lace.

Friday, September 27: Hanover radio recital.

Monday, October 7: Dusseldorf. Turquoise kaftan.

Saturday, October 19: To Munich.

Sunday, October 20: Samson. DGG recording. Karli.

Thursday, October 24: To Amsterdam.

Friday, October 25: Mass In D. 7.30.

Saturday, October 26: 3pm concert. Black lace. Home 9pm.

Wednesday, October 30: Landstrasse, Amsterdam.

Saturday, November 2: To München. Samson. Deutsche Grammophon recording.

Friday, November 8: Lincoln. Sir Malcolm memorial concert.

Tuesday, November 12: Leeds recital. BBC. Lovely broadcast.

Tuesday, November 19: LPO. RFH. Mahler No.2. Purple velvet. Prince Charles and Princess Anne in audience under cover.

Saturday, November 23: Belshazzar. Charles Farncombe. Elizabeth Hall. Gold coat and dress.

Thursday, November 28: Birmingham Town Hall. Bantock symphony. Sappho cycle. Thick fog.

Saturday, November 30: Coventry Messiah.

Sunday, December 1: Northampton Messiah. Purple velvet.

Friday, December 6: To Basel.

Saturday, December 7 and Sunday, December 8: Messiah. Deutsch. Purple velvet.

Thursday, December 12: Munich weinacht oratorio. Royal blue velvet, lace collar.

Saturday, December 14: Sheffield Messiah. Turquoise kaftan. Charles Groves.

Monday, December 16: BBC Leeds recital.

Tuesday, December 17: Zurich.

Thursday, December 19: Orpheus in German. Very difficult to learn after English. Gold brocade coat and dress/mink.

Friday, December 20: Zurich concert. Carlo.

Tuesday, December 24: Study Nicholas Maws Scenes and Arias. Very difficult piece. No Christmas – or cards written. Too busy learning Mr. Maws' work. Horrible!

Saturday, January 4: Royal Choral Messiah.

Monday, January 6: Recording Nick Maw. Terrible piece! No Christmas learning.

Tuesday, January 7: Home thank God!

Saturday, January 18: To Lisbon. Hotel Miraparque.

Sunday, January 19: Rehearsals. 9pm Rivoli's house.

Monday, January 20: Suitcase broken into and jewellery stolen. Très ill – flu.

Tuesday, January 21 and Wednesday, January 22: Messiah (Lisbon). Gold brocade. Purple velvet.

Thursday, January 23: Berlin cancelled.

Saturday, February 1: Tobin's Messiah. RFH. Purple velvet.

Saturday, February 15: St. Matthew. Richter. Queen Elizabeth Hall.

Sunday, February 16: St. Matthew. LPO. RFH. Richter. Gina black lace.

Tuesday, February 18: Newsham BBC.

Thursday, February 27: To Munich.

Friday, February 28: Kubelik recording.

Saturday, March 1: DGG record. Mahler II.

Tuesday, March 4: Royal Choral. Missa Solemnis. Gold brocade.

Sunday, March 9: To Geneva.

Monday, March 10: 9.15am rehearsals. Hotel de La Paux. To Lausanne 20.00.

Wednesday, March 12: St. John. Lausanne. 20.30 Cathedrale.

Thursday, March 13: Lausanne. Gaheo (jeweller).

Saturday, March 15: To Frankfurt. Park Hotel.

Monday, March 17: Frankfurt. Black lace.

Tuesday, March 18: To Vienna.

Tuesday, March 25: Barcelona. Evening rehearsal. Black velvet and organza.

Thursday, March 27: Concert 9pm. Victoria de los Angeles at concert. Wonderful surprise. Lovely photo taken.

Friday, March 28: Barcelona St. Matthew concert. 9pm.

Sunday, March 30: To Koln.

Wednesday, April 2 to Friday, April 4: St. Matthew.

Monday, April 21: To Goteburg. Black velvet and organza.

Thursday, April 24 and Friday, April 25: St. Matthew concert.

Thursday, May 1: Hexham. Miscellaneous. Alto rhapsody. Kaftan.

Saturday, May 10: Norwich Gerontius. Cathedral. Gold brocade dress and coat (mink cuffs). Mouse at rehearsal! A memorable 'Dream' with Peter Pears. After concert Ben horrible!

Wednesday, May 14: Missa Solemnis. Swansea. Brangywn Hall. Gold brocade.

Friday, May 16: Huddersfield Choral 9th. Liverpool Phil. Charles. Kaftan.

Monday, May 26: Madrid.

Wednesday, May 28: Toledo Cathedral. St. Matthew. Gina lace. 7pm concert.

Friday, June 6: Market Rasen recital. AR. 7.30. Methodist church. Turquoise coat and floral dress. Memorable concert.

Thursday, June 19: To Munich.

Saturday, June 21: Bach cantatas. Black bronze coat and dress.

Sunday, June 22: B Minor Mass. Black satin. Black/white/gold coat.

Monday, June 23: To Amsterdam.

Tuesday, June 24: Gouda.

Thursday, July 24: To Bee. 17.35 Air Terminal.

Thursday, August 14: Mahler 2nd. LPO. Prom. RAH. Haitink. Turquoise gold brocade.

Friday, August 15: Mother in town. Show etc.

Saturday, August 23: Messiah.

Monday, August 25: Mozart Requiem.

Sunday, August 31: Rehearsal. Ray Leppard. Hammersmith. 3.30pm.

Monday, September 8 and Tuesday, September 9: Brussels. Turquoise kaftan.

Sunday, September 14: Rio. Hotel Gloria. Dreadful and cruel behaviour from Gerry and Sheila Armstrong.

Saturday, September 20: Coronation Mass. Black, and blue brooch.

Sunday, September 21: TV Coronation Mass. Turquoise, and gold brooch.

Wednesday, September 24: Terrible difficulty to learn programme for Rosehill.

Saturday, September 27: Rosehill. Ray Leppard. Purcell programme. Blue/black brocade. Brian at concert. So glad to see him and go to Sharrow.

Saturday, October 4: Newcastle Choral 9th. C Groves. Liverpool Phil. Blue/black brocade. Blew the hell out of Sheila Armstrong for Rio behaviour.

Friday, October 10: Record cantatas 2–6pm. St. Andrew's Church, Holborn. Emmie.

Monday, October 13: Paris.

Wednesday, October 15: Mahler II. Cancelled radio recording. Rafael Kubelik ill. Heard Arthur Rubenstein recital and met afterwards. Wonderful concert!

Monday, October 27: Munich Messiah. Deutsch. Purple velvet.

Tuesday, October 28: To Amsterdam.

Friday, October 31 and Saturday, November 1: B Minor.

Friday, November 7: York Minster. Angels Farewell. Alto rhap. Purple velvet.

Tuesday, December 2: Das Lied with Haitink no longer possible. Too high for m'voice. Broken-hearted thanks to treatment, 1964.

Wednesday, December 3: To Lisbon instead.

Thursday, December 4: Les Noces substitute, in French. V difficult to learn.

Friday, December 5: Les Noces. TV.

Saturday, December 6: Les Noces concert. Hotel Tivoli.

Monday, December 8: Les Noces concert. Kaftan.

Friday, December 12: Madrid Elias. Rafael. Philharmonia choir and orchestra. Ice blue.

Saturday, December 13 and Sunday, December 14: Madrid Elias. Wonderful concerts.

Thursday, December 18: N.Sinfonia Messiah. Carlisle Cathedral. Red brocade.

1970

Saturday, January 10: Grimsby Messiah. Blue/black brocade.

Tuesday, January 13: Cantata 170. Bach. Mahler II. Haitink. Shocking pink coat and dress. Long sing! Rotten fee for such a whole evening and sing – Ibbs and Tillett!

Sunday, January 18: To Liverpool.

Tuesday, January 20: Mass of Life. Recording.

Friday, January 30: Mass of Life. Delius. RFH. Black/blue brocade.

Monday, February 9 and Tuesday, February 10: Madrid. Elias. Blue/black brocade.

Friday, February 13: To London.

Saturday, February 14: Mozart Requiem Mass. Black velvet. Karl Richter. Rehearsal 2–5.

Sunday, February 15: Mozart Requiem Mass. RFH. 7.30 concert.

Thursday, February 26: Elgar The Kingdom. Boult. RFH. LPO. Concert 8pm. Wine velvet.

Thursday, March 5: To Munich. 10.30am.

Saturday, March 7: Bach Johannes Passion. Karl Richter.

Thursday, March 12: Stockholm. Foyles theology department.

Friday, March 13: To Sweden. Skovde. Black velvet and organza.

Sunday, March 15: St. Matthew. Deutsch.

Monday, March 16: To San Sebastian.

Wednesday, March 18: To München.

Friday, March 20: St. Matthew.

Sunday, March 22: Karl Richter. Munich. St. Matthew.

Monday, March 23: To Amsterdam.

Sunday, April 12: Solomon. Queen Elizabeth Hall.

Wednesday, April 15: Isle of Man.

Thursday, April 16: Elijah BBC.

Sunday, April 19: Gerontius. Northampton.

Saturday, April 25: Guildford Cathedral. Gerontius. Gold coat and dress.

Tuesday, April 28: BBC Brahms 4 Serious Songs. Glasgow.

Thursday, April 30: B Minor. Hull. AR. 7.30pm. Purple and gold.

Friday, May 1: To Holland. KLM. Very early flight!

Saturday, May 2: Deventer. B Minor. Church 3pm. Black velvet and organza. Princess Beatrix and Prince came. Late plane to town.

Saturday, May 9: Missa Solemnis rehearsal. Aberdeen.

Sunday, May 10: Missa afternoon. Black lace. Home.

Friday, May 15: Bilbao. Missa Solemnis.

Thursday, May 21: To Paris. Royal Choral (strike!).

Friday, May 22: Messiah concert 9pm. Black velvet.

Thursday, June 4: Choral 9th Dusseldorf. Shocking pink coat and dress. Remhalle Park Hotel.

Thursday, June 11: Flu. Leeds cancelled.

Friday, June 19: Zurich. Seven Lost Words. Haydn.

Tuesday, June 24: Munich concert. Mahler 8th. Rafael Kubelik. CD recording.

Thursday, June 25: Flu returned, and terrible worries with recording (top notes).

Friday, June 26: Throat specialist advised not to sing.

Saturday, June 27: DGG recording. Home. Late train.

Tuesday, June 30: Beginning of end with Karl.

Saturday, July 4: DGG Bach cantatas 63 and 64 recording. Karli / Pete Schreier. Terrible recording: hopeless!

Tuesday, July 14: Choral 9th. 10.30–1.00.

Wednesday, July 15: Rehearsal. Horenstein.

Sunday, July 19: Southwell Cathedral. Elgar The Kingdom. Blue/black.

Sunday, July 26 to Wednesday, July 28: To London. Mahler 3rd recording. Fairfield Hall. Jascha Horenstein. Boxed Unicorn recording.

Thursday, July 29 to Saturday, August 8: Jersey.

Saturday, August 15: To La Comina.

Sunday, August 16: Missa Solemnis.

Tuesday, August 18: Choral 9th.

Wednesday, August 19: Très ill. Gastric flu. Came back vomiting and diarrhoea all way back on plane.

Sunday, August 23: Hereford Cathedral. 8pm. Sir Adrian. The Kingdom.

Wednesday, August 26: Prom. VW *[Vaughn Williams]* magnificent.

Saturday, September 5: Durham Cathedral. Missa Solemnis. 7.30.

Thursday, September 17: To London and Amsterdam.

Saturday, September 19: B Minor.

Wednesday, September 30: To Lausanne/Montreux.

Friday, October 2 and Saturday, October 3: Mozart Mass. Kubelik. Munich recording. Blue/black.

Thursday, October 8: To Amsterdam.

Friday, October 9: B Minor.

Sunday, October 18: Choral 9th. Liverpool. Ice blue.

Monday, October 19: Mahler II. Kubelik.

Tuesday, October 20: German tour.

Wednesday, October 21: To The Hague. Choral 9th.

Thursday, October 22: Rotterdam. Mahler III.

Saturday, October 24: Amsterdam Choral 9th.

Sunday, October 25: Brussels Choral 9th. Hotel Bendunat.

Monday, October 26: Antwerp Choral 9th.

Tuesday, October 27: Travel to Paris.

Wednesday, October 28: Mahler II. To Munich.

Friday, October 30: Samson. Barcelona.

Sunday, November 1: Barcelona. Samson auf Deutsch. Home.

Thursday, November 19: Mahler 3rd symphony. LPO. RFH. 8pm. Blue chiffon. Incredible concert with Bernard Haitink. Mentioned in his biography.

Sunday, November 22: Mahler III. LPO. Haitink. BBC radio. Home night train. Boys took me to KX *[King's Cross]*. Overwhelmed by this incredible music and text.

Tuesday, November 24: RFH. Mahler III. LPO. Haitink.

Thursday, November 26: To London and Germany.

Saturday, November 28: Bielefeld Missa. Blue/black.

Sunday, November 29: To Oslo.

Wednesday, December 2: Beethoven festivals everywhere!

Friday, December 4: Oslo. Missa. Blue, black, purple, and gold.

Thursday, December 10: Oslo.

Friday, December 11: To Cologne. Senatshotel.

Saturday, December 12: 10am Haüser – Modelle. Evening Missa rehearsal.

Monday, December 14: Köln 7.30.

Tuesday, December 15: Missa 7.30.

Friday, December 18: Huddersfield Messiah.

Sunday, December 20: Farncombe Messiah.

Wednesday, December 23: Huddersfield Messiah. Red velvet.

1971

Thursday, January 7: Royal Choral Messiah. Red velvet.

Saturday, January 23: Tobin Messiah. RFH. 6pm. Turquoise.

Monday, February 22: To London. Bournemouth.

Wednesday, February 24: Barnstaple. 4 Serious. 3 Sea Pictures.

Thursday, February 25: Swindon Methodist Church. Blue/black brocade.

Friday, February 26: Weymouth 7.30. Pavilion.

Saturday, February 27: To Malmo. Mahler. Kindertotenlieder.

Tuesday, March 2: Kindertotenlieder concert. Blue/black brocade.

Wednesday, March 3: To London.

Wednesday, March 17: To Vienna.

Friday, March 19: Karli ill.

Saturday, March 20 and Sunday, March 21: St. Matthew's. 6.30pm.

Saturday, March 27: Müncher Masterclass. St. John rehearsal. Black lace.

Sunday, March 28: Johanne Passion.

Monday, March 29: Munich.

Tuesday, March 30: To Madrid.

Friday, April 2 to Sunday, April 4: St. Matthew. Madrid.

Tuesday, April 6: Phone bill 58p. To Munich.

Thursday, April 8: St. Matthew 10am. German. Hans-Martin Schneidt conductor.

Friday, April 9: St. Matthew 6pm. Karl Richter v. ill.

Tuesday, April 20: To Munich. Karli v. ill.

Wednesday, April 21 and Thursday, April 22: Elias. Hopeless conducting.

Friday, April 30 to Sunday, May 2: Mahler 8th concerts. Madrid. Gold brocade.

Tuesday, May 11: London rehearsal.

Friday, May 14: Brighton Rodelinda concert 6pm. Blue chiffon.

Sunday, May 16: Brighton 3pm Rodelinda. To London and Munich.

Thursday, May 20: Schuman/Faust. 8pm concert.

Saturday, May 29: Beethoven 9th. Halle. York Minster.

Friday, June 18: Collingham Bridge. Gold or blue chiffon.

Saturday, June 19: Temple Newsam. AR recitals.

Tuesday, June 29: Amsterdam. First concert in the Concertgebouw; replacing alto who was ill. Rushed down with passport; was already in London.

Wednesday, June 30: Concertgebouw. Mahler 8th. Haitink. Alto I. Turquoise dress and coat.

Monday, July 12: RFH concert. C Major Beethoven Mass.

Tuesday, July 20: To London. Sir Arthur 4pm. Marlboro Place.

Wednesday, July 21: Prom rehearsals. Mahler 8th.

Thursday, July 22: 18.30–21.30 Albert Hall.

Friday, July 23: Opening Prom night. Mahler 8th. Gold coat brocade. [In correspondence in July 2010, she wrote: 'Another first night, help! Beloved Mahler's 8th Symphony – incredible, beautiful, heartache, mass writing/composing from his soul.']

Monday, August 2: Prom. The Enchantress. Bliss 80th birthday. 11.15–13hr RAH. Red chiffon.

Tuesday, August 3: Prof phoned at Albert Hall. Should have gone to Sir Arthur's 80th birthday party but didn't, great regret.

Monday, August 16: Mahler 3rd Prom. 7.30pm. LPO. Haitink.

Tuesday, August 17: Picnic Regent's Park.

Thursday, August 19: Spring Symphony Prom.

Friday, August 27: To London. Terrible noisy hotel. Couldn't sleep over traffic lights!

Monday, August 30: Berne concert. Brahms. I wanted to sing in English, but Max Rostal (viola) refused to let me and decided not to sing Sapphische Ode as rehearsed. Not an easy concert/atmosphere. Great surprise to find a v. distinguished face at front of the audience – Rudolph Kempe and wife. Never seen or met before. We all had supper together after the concert.

Saturday, September 11: Louvain Messiahs.

Monday, September 13: Home! Airport 9.10.

Tuesday, September 28: Strasbourg Cathedral. 4.00. 7.40.

Thursday, September 30: Messiah. Velvet tulle. Karli Richter. Fabulous cathedral! The largest – couldn't see the far back of the building.

Friday, October 15: Kindertotenlieder. Black/gold roses. Dieskau ill. Rafael asked me to deputise. Sang badly: top notes.

Tuesday, October 19: To Barcelona. Red chiffon. Recital rehearsal.

Thursday, October 21: To Madrid.

Friday, October 22: Concerts. Mahler II.

Sunday, October 24: 11am Mahler II. To London.

Saturday, October 30: Sea concert Hull. Blue chiffon.

Saturday, November 13: Grimsby Phil. 7 Sea Pictures/ Tony Hewitt Jones. 3 Sea Pictures/ Elgar. Blue and stole.

Thursday, November 18: Mahler 3. Haitink. 8pm. Rehearsal.

Sunday, November 21: Mahler 3rd. Festival Hall. Black and gold roses. Haitink. Home. Boys came and saw me off Kings X.

Saturday, November 27: Weihnactsoratorium. Gold velvet brocade.

Monday, November 29 and Wednesday, December 1: Lausanne weihnactsoratorium. Victoria Hall.

Thursday, December 9: Hull Messiah. Red velvet. Home after concert.

Monday, December 13: Munich.

Friday, December 17: Hague concert.

Sunday, December 19: Amsterdam concert. Haitink.

Wednesday, December 22: Zurich Bach cantata 169. Arias.

Thursday, December 23: Home. Worn out!

1972

Tuesday, January 4: Royal Choral recording. Andrew Davis.

Wednesday, January 5: B Minor. Elizabeth Hall. Red velvet. Orpheus Choir. Duchess of Gloucester.

Tuesday, January 11: To Hanover.

Friday, January 14: Concert. Spring Symphony. Blue/silver and long blue stole.

Saturday, January 15: Home via Frankfurt.

Saturday, January 22: Tobin Messiah. Turquoise/gold brocade. AM rehearsal.

Thursday, January 27: Israel In Egypt. Purple/gold.

Wednesday, February 16: Royal Choral. Gerontius. BBC. Boult. Gold brocade and stole.

Thursday, February 24: To Barcelona. Mahler II.

Saturday, February 26: Concert. Gold roses/black brocade.

Sunday, February 27: Mahler II concert.

Monday, March 6: To Luxembourg direct.

Thursday, March 9: Pierre Cao conductor. Mahler II. Blue/silver stole.

Sunday, March 12: Barcelona.

Monday, March 13: Elijah. New Phil. Purple/gold.

Thursday, March 16: 3.30 Prof. BBC.

Sunday, March 19: V. bad throat.

Monday, March 20: Amsterdam for Hague. Choral 9th.

Wednesday, March 22: Choral 9th. To airport afternoon.

Thursday, March 23: To Madrid. Rehearsal 15.30.

Friday, March 24 to Monday, March 27: St. Matthew's cancelled – laryngitis. No voice – terrible.

Sunday, April 9: To Madrid. Teatro Real.

Friday, April 14: Spring Symphony Belfast.

Tuesday, May 2: Gothenburg. Rehearsals. Shocking pink coat and gold pink dress.

Thursday, May 4 and Friday, May 5: Saloma 8pm.

Saturday, May 6: To Amsterdam.

Monday, May 8: General 9.30. 7.30 orchestral.

Tuesday, May 9: Orph. 8.15pm. In Italian. Gold brocade coat and dress.

Saturday, May 20: Radio 2.15.

Sunday, May 21: Paul Hamburger, Netherall Gardens.

Tuesday, May 23: BBC recital Hamburger.

Thursday, June 1: Rehearsal evening at Red House. Terrible atmosphere with Ben.

Friday, June 2: Schubert. Shocking pink coat and dress.

Saturday, June 3: Joyce Grenfell.

Sunday, June 4: Home/Cambridge.

Monday, June 19: Aldeburgh. Wein und Gesang. Blue chiffon.

Wednesday, June 21: Last Aldeburgh concert. Terrible atmosphere.

Saturday, June 24: To Grenada.

Tuesday, June 27: Messiah Grenada. Blue chiffon.

Thursday, June 29: To Madrid.

Friday, July 28: To Munich.

Sunday, July 30: Ottobeuren. Aft. Israel In Egypt. Black and white water silk taffeta. My last concert with Karli. I felt the atmosphere.

Monday, August 28: To Rome.

Tuesday, September 19: Queen Alexandra.

Thursday, September 21: Windsor rehearsal.

Saturday, September 23: Menuhin. Gold roses and black brocade. Beethoven Mass. St. George's Chapel.

Saturday, October 7: Glasgow City Hall. Choral 9th. Blue chiffon.

Sunday, October 8: Choral 9th. Usher Hall.

Friday, November 3: To Dornstadt.

Sunday, November 5: Mahler 3rd. Blue/black brocade.

1973

Friday, January 12: Sargent Messiah.

Saturday, January 20: Messiah 6pm.

Sunday, January 21: 3.30 Paul Hamburger.

Sunday, February 4: Record 2.30–5.30. Invited audience.

Tuesday, February 6: Gothenburg. Rehearsals 10.30am.

Thursday, February 8: Klagende Lied. 8pm. Gold velvet brocade.

Friday, February 9: To Amsterdam. Wash hair.

Wednesday, February 14: Klagende Lied. Phillip's record – Haitink.

Tuesday, February 20: Liverpool Sinfona Sacra. Adelphi. Gold velvet.

Saturday, February 24: To Lausanne.

Friday, March 9: Ely Cathedral. Mahler 8th. Paid. Red velvet.

Saturday, March 17: Elijah. Coventry Cathedral. BBC live.

Sunday, March 18: Bach choir. David Willcock. Mahler 8th. Wine velvet.

Wednesday, April 4: To Amsterdam.

Saturday, April 7: St. John Passion 20.15. Velvet and organza.

Monday, April 9: Hague. Passion.

Tuesday, April 10: Barcelona.

Thursday, April 12: Valencia concert. Black velvet organza.

Saturday, April 14: St. Matthew. Black velvet.

Thursday, April 19: St. John Passion. Theatre. Black velvet.

Saturday, May 5: Bolton Gerontius. Gold lamè velvet.

Wednesday, May 9: Mahler III. LPO. Krips. Blue diamante collar. BBC concert. RFH.

Friday, May 25: To Madrid. Rehearsals.

Saturday, May 26: Teatro Real 11am.

Sunday, May 27: Toledo Cathedral. Messiah.

Tuesday, May 29: To Rome and Florence. [Of Florence, she wrote the following note: 'I have never seen so many jewelers shops all side by side – one after the other. My eyes were popping with amazement at the beautiful artistic arrangements and designs of such jewels.']

Tuesday, June 19: Berlin. Rehearsal.

Wednesday, June 20: Mahler III concert.

Thursday, June 21: Mahler III Kubelik.

Thursday, June 28: Royal College judging.

Sunday, July 1: Mahler 8th. LSO. Alexandra Palace. Charles Groves.

Friday, September 14: Bach-Verein. Amsterdam.

Sunday, September 23: BBC.

Monday, September 24: Lady Macbeth recording.

Sunday, October 7: BBC Hatfield. 7.30.

Tuesday, November 6: To Bergen, Norway.

Thursday, November 8: Bergen. Alto rhapsody.

Sunday, November 18 to Friday, November 23: Barcelona jury.

Saturday, December 8: Messiah Bridgemarsh.

Monday, December 17 to Sunday, December 23: Amsterdam. Concertgebouw. Haitink. Mahler III concerts.

Friday, January 11: Sir MS cancer [fund] Messiah. 2.30 rehearsal.

Saturday, January 19: Tobin Messiah. 6pm.

Saturday, January 26: Spring Symphony. LPO. Haitink. Croydon, Fairfield Hall. Rehearsal 4.00, concert 8.

Sunday, January 27: RFH. Haitink. Spring Symphony. Rehearsal 10.30. 7.30 concert.

Wednesday, January 30: To Leeds. BBC. 7–9.00.

Thursday, February 7: Into St. Hugh's. Mr. da Costa, lovely man. Terrible pain. Norwich Gerontius cancelled.

Sunday, February 10: Infection. Home again.

Saturday, February 16: Derby recital. Terrible problems singing; couldn't hear!

Wednesday, March 13: To London. Kindertotenlieder. Collect Klagende Lied records.

Thursday, March 28: BBC recording 2.30 to 5pm.

Saturday, March 30: Richmond. 8pm. B Minor. St. John's Church.

Wednesday, April 3: Madrid.

Friday, April 5: St. Matthew. Jennie died.

Sunday, April 7: St. Matthew 11am.

Thursday, April 11: J's funeral, bless her. Black velvet.

Friday, April 12: Royal Choral Messiah. V sad. We *[Norma and Jennifer Vyvyan]* should've been singing together.

Sunday, April 14: Sargent fund Messiah. Fairfield Hall, Croydon.

Wednesday, April 24: Liverpool. St. Matthew in English. Adelphi. A muttering, mumbling mass of two-faced mischief-makers amongst the artists.

Saturday, May 4: Putney Heath. B Minor.

Tuesday, May 7: BBC recording 2.30 to 3.30.

Friday, May 24: To Bonn. Alto I. Mahler 8th. Könningshof Hotel.

Tuesday, May 28: To Köln. Hotel Senats. Day off.

Tuesday, June 4: Jen's memorial.

Sunday, June 16: Frankfurt. Mahler 8th. 11am concert. Royal blue.

Monday, June 17: Concert 20.00. Pale blue chiffon.

Saturday, June 22: B Minor. Lincoln Cathedral. Dr. Philip Marshall.

Tuesday, June 25: To London and Göttingen.

Saturday, June 29: 19.45 concert. Shocking pink coat and dress.

Thursday, July 25: Royal Academy diploma. Hon RAM. Terrifying day, made helpless. Forgot to put scroll on the platform!!!

Saturday, August 10 and Sunday, August 11: Walthamstow 2.30–5.30.

Thursday, August 15: Worcester 2.30 onwards.

Friday, September 6: Rehearsals. London. 17.50 train.

Monday, September 9: Dido Prom. RAH. BBC recording disc made. JB [Janet Baker] Dido! 1.30 rehearsal. Turquoise brocade.

Saturday, September 14: Prom (last night). RAH. 11.30 rehearsal. Royal blue. The most memorable evening and concert.

Thursday, September 26: Mahler II concert. London.

Sunday, October 6 to Tuesday, October 8: St. Hugh's. D & C [dilation and curettage].

Saturday, October 12 and Sunday, October 13: Alto rhap. Newcastle Festival. Cathedral.

Friday, October 18 and Saturday, October 19: Bath Abbey. Fernley Hotel.

Friday, November 1: To Worcester. Gifford Hotel (Mrs. Pickles, reception).

Saturday, November 2: Dream of Gerontius. 3–6.00 rehearsal.

Tuesday, November 5: To Madrid. Brown coat, slacks, black/red cloak, black trouser suit, black/striped dress, jersey, leopard sweater and scarf, mink tie.

Sunday, November 10: Mahler III.

Saturday, November 23: Crawley. Alto rhap (Germain).

Monday, November 25: Mahler 3rd. LPO. RFH. Haitink. Prof 12.15.

Saturday, December 7: Isle of Man Christmas concert. Portland Hotel.

Friday, December 13: To Brussels.

Saturday, December 14: Rehearsal AM. Messiah. Hotel Beethoven.

Sunday, December 15: Messiah. Beethoven Halle. Bonn.

Wednesday, December 18: Brussels Messiah. 15.00. Palais des Beaux Arts.

Friday, December 20: To Zurich.

Saturday, December 21: Salve Regina. 4 Lennox Berkeley songs. Fraumünster.

Sunday, December 22: Concert 20.15. 14.00 Fraumünster. Zurich Chamber Orchestra.

1975

Thursday, January 9: To Berlin.

Saturday, January 11 and Sunday, January 12: Mahler III. 8pm. Hotel Schweizerhof. Royal blue.

Tuesday, January 14: Concert delayed. 3.30.

Saturday, January 18: Tobin Messiah. Concert 6pm.

Wednesday, January 22: Llandaff. BBC recording.

Saturday, March 1: Blackburn. Serenade To Music. Beethoven Choral 9th (English). Rose coat and dress.

Saturday, March 8: Truro Messiah. Blue chiffon.

Friday, March 14: Royal Choral. Missa Solemnis. RFH.

Tuesday, March 25: Messiah. RFH. 7.30.

Wednesday, March 26: Oldham. Messiah. Grand Hotel. John Bethell.

Friday, April 4: Newport. Blue/black brocade. Westgate Hotel.

Sunday, April 13: Sheffield Male Voice. Blue chiffon.

Friday, April 18: St. Matthew Passion. Balbao. Mahler III. Black Gina lace.

Saturday, April 26: Guildford. B Minor Mass. Black embossed velvet and white jacket. Walter Deakin.

Saturday, May 3: Kendal Gerontius. Charles Groves. Gold embossed velvet. Boys came.

Saturday, May 17: Cannock Male Voice. Red brocade.

Saturday, June 1: To The Hague. Park Hotel.

Thursday, June 5: Jephtha. De Duif. Rose coat brocade and dress.

Monday, June 23: Zurich.

Thursday, June 26: Mahler 8th.

Saturday, June 28: Lincoln Cathedral. Gerontius. David Willcock. Gold brocade.

Thursday, July 31: St. Hugh's operation.

Saturday, September 7: Pitlochry recital.

Monday, September 15: To Berlin.

Tuesday, September 16: Rehearsals. Gold brocade.

Thursday, September 18 to Friday, September 19: Berlin Mahler 8th.

Saturday, October 4: Sheffield City Hall. Hallè. Choral 9th. Vivaldi Gloria.

Sunday, October 5: Manchester Free Trade Hall. Rehearsal 3.30pm. 7.30pm concert.

Monday, October 13: Manchester BBC. Kindertotenlieder.

Tuesday, October 14: Recording afternoon, 2.30–5pm. Awful broadcast.

Wednesday, October 29: To Edinburgh. Royal blue or gold brocade.

Thursday, October 30: Elijah rehearsal.

Friday, October 31: Roxburghe Hotel (Mr. Addison, manager). Room 321. Miss Glendenning, housekeeper. Free day.

Saturday, November 1: Usher Hall. Elijah. BBC Scottish Orchestra. 2.30–5.30.

Thursday, November 13: To Stuttgart. Schlossgarten Hotel.

Sunday, November 16: Mahler II. Black lace.

Monday, November 19: Mahler II. Royal blue jersey.

Saturday, November 29: To Roland. London/Salisbury. Treasured weekend but what heartache. Last time together.

Thursday, December 4: Roland's birthday.

Saturday, December 6: Leicester Messiah.

Monday, December 8: Messiah. RAH. 7.45. LPO. John Aldis. Red jersey.

Friday, December 12: Bradford Festival. Messiah. Meredith Davies. Richard Hickox wonderful.

Saturday, December 13: Coventry Messiah.

Sunday, December 14: Messiah. LPO. No rehearsal. Blue jersey.

Thursday, December 18: Bonn. Samson.

1976

Thursday, January 8 and Friday, January 9: Concert. Israel in Aegypten. Red brocade.

Friday, January 16: RFH 2.00–5.30. B Minor rehearsals.

Sunday, January 18: Haitink. B Minor. RFH. Black lace and white lace sleeves.

Saturday, January 24: St. Giles, Barbican 6.30–9.30.

Saturday, February 7: Roland died 5.30am.

Wednesday, February 11: Roland's funeral.

Friday, February 13: Royal Choral. The Kingdom. RFH. Meredith Davies. Royal blue jersey. Alfreda came to dressing room with Madame Armstrong, who literally blew Alfreda to hell just before the concert for giving John Mitch her ex-directory numbers. I could have killed Sheila, treating Alfreda in this way and in front of another contralto. Sheila was intolerable. I said nothing but was boiling with rage. Difficult to sing.

Wednesday, February 18: Croydon Messiah. London Choral Tobin Society.

Saturday, February 21: St. Martin in the Fields Messiah. No rehearsal.

Friday, March 12: 12.15–2pm. Kindertotenlieder BBC.

Saturday, March 13: To Willingham.

Thursday, March 18: To Dumfries.

Tuesday, March 30: BBC concert. Ray Leppard.

Saturday, April 3: St. Teilo Salutacio, Basingstoke.

Wednesday, April 7: To Barcelona. Hotel Colon. Adrian Cuffi agent.

Saturday, April 10 and Sunday, April 12: To Geneva. Hotel Ambassador.

Wednesday, April 14: Kindertotenlieder. Wolfgang Sawallisch. St. Pierre Cathedrale. Wonderful conductor and concert. TV/film.

Saturday, May 8: Guildford Gerontius. Walter Deakin. Rehearsal 2.30.

Saturday, May 22: Ross-on-Wye Choral Society. Harmonie. Messiah.

Friday, June 11 and Saturday, June 12: Le Laudi.

Thursday, June 17: To York. Dean Court Hotel for two nights.

Friday, June 18: Nelson Mass. Haydn. Bach Magnificat concert.

Wednesday, June 23: Göttingen. The Triumph of Time and Truth.

Monday, June 28: Berlin Mahler 8th repeat.

Tuesday, June 29: Holland Festival repeat.

Saturday, July 3: Beverley Minster. Elijah.

Friday, July 30: To Middlesbrough. Ramada Droganara Hotel.

Saturday, July 31: Elijah.

Wednesday, September 1: BBC recording.

Thursday, September 23: Record lieder and Christmas songs.

Saturday, October 9: To Antwerp.

Monday, October 11: Concert. Cantata 76. Magnificat and Bach cantata 169.

Sunday, October 24: Hamburg. B Minor.

Friday, October 29: To Kassel.

Sunday, October 31: Alto rhapsody. Requiem Saint Saens. 16.00 concert.

Saturday, November 20: Chester Gerontius. 7.30 concert.

Sunday, November 28: Northampton Messiah. Corby Hall.

Saturday, December 4: Bradford Messiah.

Saturday, December 11: Sheffield Halle Messiah.

Sunday, December 12: Recording. Readers Digest record.

Friday, December 17: To Milan.

Sunday, December 19: Morning concert. Messiah.

Tuesday, December 28 and Wednesday, December 29: Liverpool Messiahs.

1977

Saturday, January 8: Grimsby Messiah (Phil). Never again! No one else knew but sitting on the Central Hall platform, I decided I couldn't and wouldn't go through such a prelude of anguish or sing in Grimsby again, and never did.

Thursday, January 13: To London. Purple ensemble.

Friday, January 14: Malcolm Sargent Cancer [Fund] Messiah. Concert 7.30. Rehearsal 2.30.

Saturday, January 22: Solihull Messiah. Royal blue.

Sunday, February 6: Jürgen concert.

Sunday, February 13: B Minor. TV. Dreadful concert, hopeless conductor, terrible experience.

Saturday, February 19: Norwich Phil Elijah. St. Andrew's Hall.

Wednesday, February 23: Fairfield. London Choral Society. Messiah. Leon Lovett.

Saturday, February 26: London Oriana Choir. Messiah. Methodist Central Hall, Westminster. V sick. Threw up just before leaving for rehearsal.

Sunday, February 27: Home. Hospital.

Monday, March 21: To Helsinki. Fly out.

Tuesday, March 22: Rehearsal 10am–2.30. Finlandia Hall.

Thursday, March 24: Petite Messe Solenelle. Rossini. Charles Farncombe.

Saturday, March 26: To Hamburg and Berlin.

Sunday, March 27: Jephtha. Berlin rehearsal.

Tuesday, March 29: Jephtha concert 8pm. Purple.

Wednesday, March 30: Rehearsal 4pm. Steinway piano.

Sunday, April 3: To Hamburg.

Monday, April 4: Rehearsal. Claus Bantzer.

Tuesday, April 5: Prof Klaus Vetter. Vocal ensemble. St. Matthaüs.

Wednesday, April 6: To London.

Friday, April 8: Royal Choral Messiah. Black lace, white sleeves.

Sunday, April 24: Aberdeen B Minor.

Sunday, May 1: Gerontius. Northampton. Gold brocade.

Friday, May 6: To Hanover.

Monday, May 9: General rehearsal 10am. Mahler III. Royal blue jersey.

Tuesday, May 10: Mahler III.

Saturday, May 14: Carnock. Miscellaneous. Royal blue jersey. Send music to Boston.

Friday, May 20: Watford Royal Choral. Town Hall. Choral 9th. Red jersey.

Sunday, May 22: Rehearsals piano Coronation Mass anthem.

Monday, May 23: RFH. Royal Choral. Beethoven 9th.

Tuesday, May 24: Harrods. Home.

Saturday, May 28: Hereford Cathedral. Red jersey.

Monday, May 30: To London. Rehearsal. St. Margaret's, Westminster. 7pm.

Wednesday, June 1: RAH. Coronation Mass. Mozart Coronation concert. Rehearsal 10–1.

Sunday, June 5: Jubilee concert. Boston Lions. Royal blue jersey.

Saturday, June 11: Silver Jubilee. Dudley. Sea Concert.

Wednesday, June 22: Liverpool. Mahler 8th. Charles Groves. Rehearsals.

Thursday, June 23: Concert. Anglican Cathedral (not on bridge this time).

Sunday, June 26: To Berlin. B Minor rehearsal.

Tuesday, June 28: Jürgen.

Wednesday, June 29: To München. Purple jersey. Imperial Hotel.

Thursday, June 30: Schliesshein. B Minor.

Friday, July 1: Vierzehnheilegen B Minor.

Sunday, July 3: B Minor.

Monday, July 4: Munich Day. Late train to Salzburg.

Tuesday, July 5: Day at Salzburg. Wonderful.

Thursday, July 14: To Berlin. Navy jersey.

Friday, July 15: Schmelli Songs. Rehearsal 2pm.

Saturday, July 16: Rehearsal B Minor. Schmelli. 6 and 7pm.

Sunday, July 17: B Minor. Matthaus Kirde.

Monday, July 18: Berlin B Minor.

Friday, July 22: To Fishguard Bay.

Saturday, July 23: Missa Solemnis. Mass in C.

Tuesday, July 26: Royal Garden Party. Palace 4pm. Terrible! Bored stiff! Alone all the time.

Wednesday, July 27: Harrods. Home. Podge ill.

Sunday, September 11: Bee to hospital.

Saturday, September 24: Truro Male Voice Choir.

Tuesday, September 27: Midland Hotel. To Manchester.

Wednesday, September 28: Daddy died. Halle Cantata Academia rehearsal.

Thursday, September 29: Concert 7.30.

Saturday, October 1: AR died.

Monday, October 3: Father's funeral. Crematorium. Went alone. Sobbed m'heart out as they sang.

Thursday, October 6: AR funeral. St. James and crematorium. Byron sat in front of me looking desperate. Boys home.

Monday, October 17: Antwerp. B Minor. Purple jersey.

Tuesday, October 18: Antwerp. Rubens Gallery.

Thursday, October 20: Hamburg. Shopping day.

Saturday, October 22: Hamburg. Deutsch Messiah.

Saturday, October 29: W'ton cancer research male voice concert. Red jersey.

Monday, October 31: Child of Our Time disc. Grapefruit spoons.

Thursday, November 3: Harrods spoons? Prof.

Friday, November 18 and Saturday, November 19: T. Messiah. York Minster.

Saturday, November 26: Bradford Jubilee concert. Rehearsal 3–6pm. Red jersey. Victoria Hotel. By car.

Saturday, November 27: Sharrow. Super party.

Monday, November 28: Penrith.

Saturday, December 3: Coventry Messiah.

Saturday, December 10: Leeds Messiah. Royal blue jersey.

Thursday, December 15: Hull Messiah. Alan Spedding. 4pm rehearsal.

Saturday, December 17: Swansea Messiah.

Sunday, December 18: York. TV. Huddersfield Choir Messiah. Stay London, Connaught.

Monday, December 19: Fog. Terrible day. To Zurich.

Wednesday, December 21 and Thursday, December 22: Concert. 20.15.

1978

Thursday, January 12: Saarbrücken. 2.30pm Prof.

Saturday, January 14: Grimsby Messiah. Terrible ordeal. Last time I sang in Grimsby. Mother very ill.

Monday, January 16: Had lunch with Ray after AM concert. 19.30 Mahler III. Ray so good.

Saturday, January 21: Solihull Messiah.

Saturday, January 28 and Sunday, January 29: Mahler III.

Tuesday, January 31: Home via Frankfurt.

Saturday, February 4: Middlesbrough. Choral 9th. Charles G. Serenade to Music.

Tuesday, February 7: To Karlsruhe. Hotel Kaiserhof.

Wednesday, February 8: Concert Mahler III.

Saturday, February 11: To Aberdeen. University.

Sunday, February 12: St. John Passion. 7.45. St. Machar's Cathedral.

Tuesday, February 28: Barcelona. Rehearsal 10pm!

Wednesday, March 1: 5pm rehearsal. Victoria de los Ángeles so lovely and paid me a wonderful compliment with Marian Anderson.

Thursday, March 2: Mozart Coronation Mass concert.

Wednesday, March 8: Piano rehearsal. C Farncombe. Wigmore Hall Studios.

Saturday, March 11: Lancaster University. Messiah. W Shaw. Barbara sang sop.

Thursday, March 16: Rehearsal orchestral. C Farncombe. 6.30–9.30 Wigmore Hall.

Saturday, March 18: RFH. Rehearsal from 1.30pm. Concert 7pm. Handel Opera Society.

Thursday, March 23: Bremen rehearsal.

Friday, March 24: Bach's B Minor.

Saturday, April 1: Bingham Choral. Child of Our Time. Nottingham.

Saturday, April 15: Derby Gerontius. 3pm.

Saturday, May 7: Oldham Elijah. John Bethell. Concert 2.30. Organ only. Royal blue.

Thursday, May 11: Mahler II. RAH. 8pm.

Sunday, May 14: Northampton. The Kingdom. Multi blues.

Friday, May 16: Byron died.

Saturday, July 1: Pudley Town Hall. English Phil Orchestra. Neil Howe.

Saturday, July 8: Canterbury. The Apostles.

Monday, July 17 to Wednesday, July 26: Sharrow.

Saturday, August 12: To Gstaad.

Monday, August 14: V. ill with flu. Full of antibiotics.

Tuesday, August 15: Yehudi and Diana wonderful to me. Gstaad concert.

Saturday, September 2: Isle of Man. Elijah. Royal blue.

Thursday, September 21: To Frankfurt.

Friday, September 22: Choral 9th. Evening rehearsal with orchestra and choir.

Sunday, September 24: 11am concert.

Monday, September 25: 8pm concert.

Tuesday, September 26: To München. Concorde Hotel.

Wednesday, September 27: Half day Salzburg. Beautiful.

Friday, September 29: Munich. Hotel Amba. Last visit to Munich.

Saturday, November 18: English Sinf. Magnificat. Nelson Mass. Nottingham. By car. Rehearsal 3–6pm. George Hotel.

Saturday, November 25: St. Albans Bach Choir. Royal blue. Conductor Stephen Darlington.

Thursday, November 30: Elijah. W. Central Hall. Richard Hickox.

Friday, December 8: Bradford Messiah. 2.30pm. Royal blue.

Sunday, December 10: LPO. Messiah. Henry Wood Hall. 11–1 rehearsal. Broadcast live. Silver grey. Concert 7.30. Albert Hall.

1979

Wednesday, January 17: To Glasgow.

Thursday, January 18: Elijah rehearsal.

Friday, January 19: Roxburghe. Edinburgh concert. Elijah.

Saturday, January 20: Glasgow Elijah.

Saturday, January 27: Leamington. Messiah. Concert 7.00. Multi blues.

Saturday, February 3: Norwich Phil. Dvorak. Stabat Mater. Rehearsal 2.15pm.

Friday, February 23: RAH Messiah. Rehearsal 2.30. English Baroque orchestra and choir. Multi blues. Leon Lovett.

Saturday, March 10: Fly out Lisbon, Portugal. BA 436. Tivoli Hotel. Room 405. Black/white lace. Black/camel.

Wednesday, March 14: Black camel. St. Matthew.

Thursday, March 15: St. Matthew.

Friday, March 16: Madrid. Mozart Requiem Mass. Hotel Emperador.

Saturday, March 24: National Westminster Bank Messiah. Queen Elizabeth Hall. Rehearsal 3pm, concert 7.45pm. Ian Humphries.

Saturday, March 31 and Sunday, April 1: Berlin concerts.

Thursday, April 5: To Geneva.

Friday, April 6: Rehearsal 9.30am. 7.30pm. Black lace.

Saturday, April 7: St. Johannes. 8pm. Lou v cool. Last Swiss concert.

Friday, May 4: To Jersey. Prof AM. Eve flight.

Saturday, May 13: Choral 9th. Northampton.

Saturday, June 16: Southampton. Mozart Requiem. Felicity Lott. Purple.

Saturday, June 23: Tewkesbury Abbey. Gerontius. Graham Mayo. N'ton Phil. Silver grey.

Saturday, June 30: Brierley Hill concert.

Saturday, July 14: Gerontius. Croydon. Terrible nerves! Fairfield Hall. Silver grey. Last Gerontius. [A reader of international cultural website slippedisc.com posted a special memory of this concert on Norma's obituary by the site: 'I had the privilege of driving Miss Proctor [sic] to and from a performance of the Dream of Gerontius in Tewkesbury Abbey. Her singing was so warmly beautiful that evening. It remains one of my most cherished musical experiences.']

Wednesday, September 26: Zion. Messiah 8.30pm.

Saturday, October 6: Isle of Man male voice concert.

Friday, October 12: Norwich Triennial Festival. Mass of Life.

Sunday, October 21: Norwich. Mahler III. 5.30 concert.

Saturday, November 10: Driffield celebrity concert.

Friday, November 16: RFH. Royal Choral. Missa Solmenis.

Wednesday, November 21: Bradford Elijah.

Saturday, December 8: Leicester Messiah.

1980

Friday, January 4 and Saturday, January 5: Liverpool Messiah.

Saturday, January 19: Solihull Messiah.

Sunday, February 10: St. John Passion. Paisley Abbey. Last time I saw Peter Pears.

Sunday, March 10: Leamington. Sea Pictures. Sang so badly!

Tuesday, April 29: Bee in town.

Saturday, May 10: Truro. Miscellaneous.

Tuesday, July 1: Royal Academy recital.

Wednesday, July 2: Adjudicating.

Sunday, November 22: Bolton Messiah.

Saturday, November 29: Coventry Messiah. Purple jersey.

Saturday, December 6 and Sunday, December 7: Halle Messiahs. Sheffield and Manchester.

Saturday, December 13: Portsmouth Messiah.

1981

Monday, January 12: Leeds. TV recording.

Friday, March 13: RAH. Messiah. Leon Lovett.

Saturday, May 9: Solihull Samson.

Monday, May 11: Terrible flu.

Saturday, May 17: B Minor Louth.

Saturday, June 27: Isle of Man Messiah. Rehearsal 11am. Met David Cregeen, sculptor, who asked to sculpt my head!!

Thursday, July 16: Bishop Michael's concert.

Tuesday, July 21: BBC Cardiff.

Saturday, July 25: Elijah. St. David's.

Monday, August 10: BBC listening panel. Paid £325.

Saturday, December 12: Blackburn Messiah.

Saturday, December 19: Crawley Messiah.

1982

Saturday, February 6: Norwich Gerontius cancelled.

Saturday, March 7: David Cregeen sculptor. My head!

Saturday, March 13: Tooth abscess.

Sunday, March 14: Flu.

Saturday, April 3: Leicester Cathedral. B Minor. Grand Hotel. Sang badly.

Saturday, April 17: Llanelli Male Voice Choir.

Sunday, May 9: Mother v.ill.

Tuesday, June 8: No sleep.

Sunday, June 13: Mother so v.ill.

Tuesday, June 15: Worn out!

Thursday, June 17: Mother died 3am. Sat alone with her. Shattering experience.

Wednesday, June 23: Nan's [Norma's mother] funeral.

Saturday, July 3: Dudley Prom.

Sunday, September 19: David and Pat Grimsby. Terrible lunch at ghastly restaurant. V. ashamed!

Thursday, October 21: Solihull. Miscellaneous.

Wednesday, November 17: Emmie's memorial concert. Ghastly party afterwards, except for Prof.

1983

Saturday, February 26: Matlock Victoriana concert.

Saturday, April 30: Jack and Bee's wedding.

Sunday, June 26: Isle of Man recital.

Friday, July 1: Bruckner Te Deum. RFH. Flu.

Saturday, July 2: Dudley Last Night of the Proms.

Sunday, July 31 to Saturday, August 6: Sharrow.

Tuesday, September 27: Leeds. TV.

Sunday, October 2: AR memorial concert.

1984

Monday, April 2: BBC royalties.

Saturday, April 14: Llannelli.

Friday, May 11: Birmingham Town Hall.

Saturday, June 30: Bridgnorth.

Saturday, July 7: Dudley. Goldthorn Hotel.

Saturday, July 28: Dudley peace concert.

Friday, August 17: Teaching began.

Tuesday, September 11: Selfridges 3rd floor.

Tuesday, October 9: Annie's recital lunch hour, Lincoln.

Sunday, November 11: Queen Elizabeth Hall peace concert.

Wednesday, November 14: Barnsley Civic Hall. Queen's Hotel.

Saturday, December 1: West Bromwich, Goldthorn. Peace.

1985

Tuesday, April 23: David Cregeen sculpture exhibition. To London.

Saturday, April 27: Phil concert. Got flu.

Sunday, May 5: Banging on floor next door.

Sunday, May 12: Floor banging next door. Phoned police. Terrible treatment.

Wednesday, May 15: Walsall. Multi-blue. Terrible train journey.

Saturday, May 18: Jersey. Terrible aircraft. No pressurisation.

Thursday, May 23: Dizziness began. St. Helier's seafood lunch. With Bee and Jack. Very ill.

Friday, May 24: Upset stomach. Bug in the village.

Saturday, May 26: Home. Not a well pressurised aircraft. Ears very blocked.

Sunday, June 2: Severe symptoms. Mind wouldn't work. Dizzy. Giddy.

Monday, June 3: Diagnosed vertigo. Dizziness, giddy, nausea, headache.

Tuesday, June 4: Lack of co-ordination. Numbness in joints.

Wednesday, June 5: Blood pressure OK. Terrible lack of sleep.

Wednesday, June 6: Had to continue with tablets. Menopause: sweats. Not enough oestrogen.

Saturday, June 8: Mike increased dose of tablets.

Monday, June 10: Specialist Dr. da Costa most helpful. Meniere's disease diagnosed, plus menopausal problems.

Saturday, June 29: Brigworth. Pale sky blue. Terrible train journey. Hardly knew how to sit.

Saturday, July 6: Dudley. Shocking pink and roses. Very ill. Hardly knew how to sing. Giddy and terrible pains in stomach and back.

Sunday, July 7: Home. Could hardly sit in train. Norman met me at Doncaster.

Sunday, July 14: Into St. Hugh's. Lovely Sister Chappie *[Brenda Chapman]*.

Monday, July 15: Hysterectomy. Terrible pain when I came round. Dr. Muldoon operated. Terrible days.

Wednesday, July 24: To Audrey and Norm.

Monday, August 5: Hellish days! Painful, lonely and fed-up! No energy.

Monday, September 2: Mr. Muldoon. St. Hugh's. 3.45pm.

Tuesday, September 3: Watched dear Steve Ballesteros. Wonderful charismatic creature and brilliant golfer!

Friday, September 13: Das Lied. TV.

Saturday, September 14: Last Night Proms.

Monday, October 28: What is wrong with me? Feel like hell.

Monday, November 4: Terrible depressions. Don't know how to battle on. Never felt so alone and ill.

Monday, November 18: No improvement. Always weeping. Battling. Feeling ghastly suicidal.

Monday, November 25: Hellish depression and desperate. I can't keep battling. So alone. Feel so ill.

Monday, December 2: Don't know how to keep going.

Wednesday, December 4: Dress shop.

Monday, December 9: Stomach giving me hell.

Wednesday, December 11: Went to Dr. John. Terrible stomach pains.

Friday, December 20: Mike called. Terrible stomach pains. Stopped all food. Onto milk diet.

Monday, December 24: All Christmas in bed. Terrible stomach pains. Spent alone.

1986

Friday, January 31: Halifax.

Saturday, March 15: Received bounced cheque.

Tuesday, April 22: Coventry. Terrible concert.

Saturday, July 5: Dudley. Terrible concert. Neil sloshed and very rude. Almost cancelled Leatherhead.

Wednesday, July 23: Royal wedding. Andrew and Fergie. Beautiful gown.

Saturday, September 27: Leatherhead. My very last concert. Terrible evening. Glad to come home and to stop singing.

Sunday, October 5: Grimsby Singers competition begins. Felt very ill.

Thursday, October 9: Competition. Navy dress/mink jacket. Mayoral lunch. Felt terrible through whole competition.

Monday, November 3: Dr. Kahn. Path lab. X-rays.

Tuesday, November 4: Lovely Nurse Smith.

Wednesday, November 5: Endoscopy. Horrible. 15 polyps in stomach.

Monday, November 24: Ghastly examination.

Tuesday, November 25: Dr. Kahn hospital 8.30am. Barium enema. X-ray.

Thursday, December 4: Hospital. Dr. Moss 1pm. Ghastly double enema. Polyps removed. Stayed overnight. Terrible night on ward. No private beds. Ghastly old hospital tho' a private patient.

1987

Saturday, January 31: Halifax. Phil workshop.

Monday, February 9: Dr. Moss colonoscopy 1pm. Sheer hell! New equipment. Completely out of control and unable to bear the pain. Swore no one would ever do that to me again.

Monday, April 13: Colonoscopy with general *[anaesthetic]*.

Friday, May 8: To Manchester. Royal Northern College of Music masterclass. Dreadful day. Terrible masterclass. I was terribly upset by rotten co-adjudicators *[who chose the]* wrong prize-winners.

Friday, July 31: Isle of Man. Plane 4 hours late. Terrible journey.

Saturday, August 1: Classes. Bay View Hotel.

Monday, October 12: Injection from chemist.

Wednesday, October 14: Ring library.

Saturday, October 24: Power failure.

Saturday, December 12: Carol concerts.

1988

Saturday, January 16: Messiah. Grimsby.

Monday, February 1: To Halifax. Isolde's Liebestod. Tristan and Isolde. Liszt Dante Sonata.

Monday, February 22: Colonoscopy. Dr. Moss. With general. Sheer hell again.

Saturday, February 27: Bath Messiah masterclass.

Friday, March 11: Piano tuner 10.30/11am.

Tuesday, March 15: Dr. Moss 2.45. Refused to go to London hospital and another colonoscopy without a general. A very frank talk after such previous hell. Three years before next session.

Friday, March 25: Bee to USA.

Friday, April 8: Grimsby Festival.

Monday, April 11: New pension rate £41.55.

Friday, April 29: To Leicester. Felt really grim.

Saturday, April 30: Leicester masterclass.

Friday, July 29: Radiator leaking in dining room.

Sunday, September 11: To Sharrow.

Sunday, October 9: Klever Kaff BBC Radio 2.

Monday, November 28: Flu. Vicks.

1989

Thursday, January 5: Prof 7.30 Radio 4. V.W.

Thursday, February 28: RAM fellows general meeting.

Tuesday, March 21: Grimsby Festival.

Thursday, June 8: RAM alumni AGM.

Monday, July 17: Gas man 2pm.

Sunday, October 1: Grimsby competition begins.

Friday, October 6: Final night.

1990

Friday, February 16: Bursitis. Mike.

Friday, April 6: Grimsby Festival.

Saturday, May 19: Lincoln masterclass.

Thursday, November 15: Bradley Festival.

Saturday, December 8: Phil carol concerts. Beechams.

Saturday, December 15: Second half-yearly poll tax to be paid.

1991

Friday, February 15: Three years since pension began.

Thursday, March 21: Grimsby Festival.

Tuesday, April 23: Workshop.

Saturday, April 27: Phil concert.

Thursday, June 13: Bacteria drug Golytely. Ghastly four litres. Thought I would blow up! Explode! Dr. Ghandour.

Thursday, October 31: Halloween! Grrrr!

Friday, November 22: Bradley Festival.

1992

Saturday, April 4: Phil concert.

Wednesday, April 8: Grimsby Festival.

Tuesday, June 16: Hellish extraction.

Wednesday, June 17: 10 years since Mother died.

Saturday, September 12: Last Night of Proms.

Saturday, October 10: Phil concert.

Saturday, November 28: Brass workshop.

1993

Saturday, January 23: Viennese concert. Phil.

Monday, March 15: Heddle, Radio 3.

Tuesday, March 30: Grimsby Festival.

Monday, June 28: Cleethorpes Festival.

Tuesday, July 6: 12.30 plaster change. General anaesthetic. St Hugh's.

Tuesday, August 3: Plaster change. Six weeks.

Wednesday, September 22: Pot removed. 13 weeks. X-rays.

Friday, September 24: Ryder Cup. We lost! Super playing.

Tuesday, October 19: Crutches returned. 11.30 x-ray.

Wednesday, November 17: To Scunthorpe. Orthopaedic chair and mattress.

1994

Sunday, January 30: Audrey's 70th birthday. The Stables/lunch.

Monday, February 21: Torville and Dean 8pm. Very unfair result. Disgraceful.

Friday, February 25: Pick up scripts.

Sunday, February 27: Scarborough programme ideas.

Saturday, April 16: Phone day. 01 for all area codes.

Wednesday, April 20: Mr. Grant 11.30 x-ray. New hospital! Bespoke shoes too small.

Saturday, May 21: Dr. Sudip Bhaduri came. Super fellow and so grateful. Very ill but did not phone or bother A & N *[Audrey and Norman]*.

Sunday, May 29: Phoned Prof.

Tuesday, July 26: Infection. Trimethoprim 200mg. 20 tablets twice daily. Ghastly!

Thursday, August 4: Right shoulder/collarbone put out.

Wednesday, September 7: Mr. Grant 11.00 St. Hugh's. 40/80 x-rays.

1995

Monday, January 15: Passport.

Wednesday, February 15: Full moon! Six years since pension began.

Tuesday, April 25: Ginger Rogers died, 83.

Tuesday, May 2: Last Question of Sport.

Friday, May 19: Very ill. Flu.

Sunday, May 21: Vertigo attack.

Friday, June 30: Send Prof's 96th birthday card.

Friday, September 8: Prof BBC Prom. Radio 3.

Thursday, September 14: Permed hair.

Saturday, October 7: Phil Messiah competition concert.

Wednesday, November 1: Winifred Ferrier died, 92 years.

Wednesday, December 20: Bee's Jack died. 6.10pm. I was about to phone them and thought not but Hilary phoned me at 7.40 [with] the sad news. Poor B.

1996

Wednesday, January 31: Window in. PVC.

Saturday, February 3: Condensation began.

Monday, February 12: Bought dehumidifier.

Friday, March 1: Hair permed.

Thursday, March 14: Bee in hospital. Pneumonia.

Saturday, March 16: Dear B died at 2.05pm. First met her at Jersey airport on 5th July 1957, with AR.

Tuesday, March 26: Bee's funeral. Crematorium.

Monday, July 1: Stamps gone up. 1st class 26p, 2nd 20p.

Thursday, August 1: 3.30 Dr. Moss, St. Hugh's.

Tuesday, August 6: Post strike.

Thursday, August 8: Blood test. 10am St. Hugh's.

Tuesday, December 24: Two pints milk.

1997

Wednesday, April 23: Check Boots three-for-two.

Thursday, May 1: Election Day. God guide and help us!

Saturday, May 24: Dr. Moss. St. Hugh's 10am.

Sunday, June 22: Four years since foot op.

Wednesday, July 23: Mr. Grant 11.00. Tendonitis left foot. Cortisone injection.

Saturday, August 2: Colitis began late night.

Sunday, August 3: Car five years old.

Monday, August 11: Rafael Kubelik died.

Tuesday, August 26: Mr. Grant 11.45. No injection or further physio!

Thursday, November 13: Zanussi washer delivered.

1998

Friday, February 20: Boys' 50th year at Sharrow. Francis died 2.20am.

Saturday, February 28: Francis funeral. Carlisle Cathedral. 2pm.

Monday, March 9: Brian into Carlisle hospital.

Wednesday, April 8: Spondylitis. Allergy – red botches face.

Thursday, October 8: Christmas cards ordered.

Thursday, November 5: Bonfire Night. Ugh!

Sunday, November 29: Last night at Sharrow. Sang with Brio and a solo carol. First time in public for 15 years.

Friday, December 18: Smoked salmon AM!

1999

Friday, April 23: Norman's stroke 11.30pm.

Saturday, May 1: Clive *[Champney]* phoned. Very grateful to talk.

Sunday, March 9: Nothing to eat/drink. Dr. John Monday 9.05.

Tuesday, June 15: Dr. Moss St. Hugh's 1pm. Cholesterol.

Sunday, July 4: Prof's 100th birthday.

Saturday, July 31: Sharrow weekend.

Wednesday, August 4: Home. Clive took me/met Audrey and Norman Scotch Corner 11am.

Tuesday, September 14: Boots No.7 powder. 40gm not 50gm, and same price!

Tuesday, October 12: Flu jab. Felt rotten for some days.

Wednesday, October 20: Flu arrived in the night. Felt very ill.

Monday, November 8: Cholesterol 9am. No breakfast.

Monday, November 22: Winter fuel paid at Post Office.

Sunday, December 26: David *[Cregeen]* phoned from Turkey. Just completed head of Pope.

2000

Wednesday, February 16: Clive/Jo's KK rose bush arrived. Overwhelmed when I rang to thank them.

Thursday, March 16: Prof died.

Saturday, April 1: Cloakroom radiator flooded. Nasty shock! Felt so ill.

Tuesday, July 4: Tesco, invisible tape.

Wednesday, August 9: To Sharrow.

Sunday, October 1: Blitzed my bedroom!

2001

Tuesday, March 13: Dr. Moss. 3.30pm. Discharged/phone if need to.

Tuesday, March 20: Piano tuning 9.15am.

Thursday, June 7: Election Day. God help us!

Thursday, September 20: Kitchen decorated.

Sunday, September 30: Snug decorated.

Sunday, October 7: Cloakroom decorated.

Tuesday, December 4: Flu/cold.

2002

Tuesday, January 1: Brian died 8.30.

Saturday, January 12: Brian's funeral. Carlisle Cathedral.

Saturday, February 2: Grimsby Phil's 150th anniversary concert.

Thursday, February 7: Had a strange feeling about Princess Margaret.

Saturday, February 9: Princess Margaret died.

Saturday, March 30: 'No' to shower cubicle.

Tuesday, May 28: Hospital/shoe fitting.

Saturday, August 3: Car 10 years old.

2003

Sunday, February 16: Norman *[brother-in-law]* desperately ill.

Monday, February 17: 6am call. Life support machine. Two litres of fluid removed from lung and heart.

Tuesday, February 18: Very ill and weary. Norm had 1 ½ pints of fluid drained.

Wednesday, February 19: Stayed overnight with Norm.

Sunday, February 23: Saw him in afternoon but should have stayed overnight again.

Monday, February 24: Norm died 2.30am. Rushed to hospital but too late.

Friday, February 28: Norm's funeral. Crematorium 4.20pm.

Thursday, May 29: Norm's ashes scattered.

Friday, August 22: Lovely surprise flowers and card from Brian and Sue in Jersey!

Saturday, September 20: Went to Peter Chapman's home with KK draft.

Thursday, October 16: Watched 1945 war film. Had a good cry. Too much pent-up emotion.

2004

Sunday, April 11: Pauli Hamburger died bless him.

Saturday, September 11: Elsie Kubelik phoned.

Sunday, December 26: Horrendous tsunami.

2005

Wednesday, February 2: Audio repairs not possible.

Saturday, March 2: Daffodils. Wonderful afternoon weather-wise too.

2006

Monday, June 5: Haddock. Defrosted fridge.

Saturday, June 17: Mother died 25 years ago. Alone [at] home 3am. I was 54 years old.

Thursday, August 10: Damp course has gone.

Wednesday, September 27: Las concert 27th September 1986, 20 years ago, Leatherhead. Terrible!

Saturday, October 14: Flu jab.

Friday, November 3: Left arm blew up red and swollen.

Monday, November 6: Flucloxacillin tablets. 4x 500mg.

Thursday, November 28: Christmas cards.

2007

Thursday, June 7: My last physio. Very upset.

Thursday, June 14: Floods.

Sunday, July 8: Men's final Wimbledon. Wonderful Federer.

Sunday, September 30: Terrible flu/cold.

Thursday, October 18: Spring cleaned kitchen/cloakroom/net curtains.

Tuesday, November 13: Michael Wilcox book arrived.

2012

Thursday, February 2: Paul Campion phoned re: KK recording.

Saturday, February 4: Snow.

Tuesday, February 28: Paul Campion interview. 5pm train.

Thursday, April 26: Used new walker. Terrible.

Thursday, June 7: Bees attack garage.

Monday, June 18: Blood test. Mini to be sold.

Thursday, June 21: Blood ok.

Sunday, August 12: Meniere's very bad.

Monday, August 13: Vertigo.

Sunday, August 19: Felt very ill indeed.

Sunday, September 9: Rheumatoid arthritis/ hips and spine /osteomyelitis /Meniere's /vertigo /Parkinson's.

Thursday, October 18: House phone kaput!

Thursday, November 1: Napkin silk.

Saturday, December 8: Endoscopy Hull.

Monday, December 10: First Parkinson tablet of three daily.

Friday, December 21: Audiology hospital.

2013

Thursday, January 3: Zimmer frame. Paralysed.

Thursday, January 31: Wonderful dog film ITV.

Friday, February 22: Pancreas cyst. No op.

Thursday, March 7: Parkinson's paralysis of muscles and mind.

Tuesday, March 26: Hospital. Long assessment. Very weary. Taxi.

Thursday, April 4: Bernard Haitink dementia.

Wednesday, April 17: Maggie Thatcher's funeral. Incredible! Lincolnshire lass.

Tuesday, May 21: Domestos!

Sunday, July 21 – To bed. Nasty paralysis.

Wednesday, August 21: Janet Baker 80th birthday.

Monday, September 16: Bad fall 3am.

Wednesday, September 18: Spine and legs paralysis.

Friday, September 20: Terrible invasion of people!

2014

Sunday, February 16: Turkey stuffing with apple crumble.

Tuesday, December 30: Terrible night. Didn't wake until 7am.

2015

Sunday, January 4: Terrible night.

Wednesday, January 28: Pancreatic cyst. Osteomyelitis.

Sunday, April 12: Very ill again after delayed waking.

Wednesday, April 29: Pain in feet and legs. Paralysed. Breathing problems.

Thursday, September 17: Sciatica.

Wednesday, October 28: Very bad day.

Tuesday, November 24: Bad legs.

Wednesday, November 25: Hellish Parkinson's.

Repertoire and Selected Discography

Oratorio and orchestral works

Bach: St. Matthew Passion (English and German); St. John Passion (English and German); B Minor Mass; Christmas Oratorio; Magnificat; Cantatas 11, 45, 106, 129, 34, 85, 161, 13, 10, 27, 151, 96, 36, 80, 105, 170, 125, 43, 169, 147, 12, 103 and 30. Beethoven: Ninth Symphony (Choral); Massin D (Missa Solemnis); Mass in C Major. Bantock: Omar Khayyam – Sappho Songs. Brahms: Alto Rhapsody; Vier Ernste Gesange. Britten: Abraham and Isaac (2nd Canticle); Spring Symphony; The Rape of Lucretia; Cantata Academica. Bruckner: Te Deum. Caldara: Antifona Seconda (Cantata). Charpentier: Te Deum. Dvorak: Stabat Mater. Elgar: Dream of Gerontius; The Apostles; The Kingdom; Sea Pictures. Gluck: Orhpeus. Handel: Messiah; Judas Maccabeus; Israel in Egypt; Samson; Solomon; Jephtha; Belshazar; Joshua; Sixth Chandos Anthem; Te Deum (Dettingen); Alcina. Hartmanns: Symphony No. 1 (Alto). Haydn: Passion (Seven Last Words). Honneger: King David. Julius Harrison: Mass in C. Kodaly: Te Deum; Harry Janos; Spinnery. Mahler: Symphony No. 2; Symphony No. 3; Das Klagende Lied; Kindertotenlieder; Symphony No. 8. N.Maw: Scenes and Arias. Mendelssohn: Elijah (English and German). Marcello: Deus, Deus. Mozart: Requiem Mass; Mass in C (Coronation Mass); Vesperae de Dominica. Pergolesi: Stabat Mater. Rossini: Petite Messe Solonnelle. Stanford: Stabat Mater. Tippett: A Child of our Time. Scarlatti, A: Infirmata Vulnerata (Cantata); Salve Regina; Il Guiardino di Amore; Il Guiardino di Rose. Schuber: Standchen (with male and female voices). Stravinsky: Les Noces. Vivaldi: Gloria; Stabat Mater. Vaughan Williams: Magnificat; Serenade.

Lieder repertoire

Brahms: Sapphische Ode; An Aoelharfe; Roselein dreie inder Reihe; Der Schnied; Es traumte mir; Die Mainacht; Meine Liebe ist grun; O wusst ich doch; Das Madchen spricht; Von Ewiger Liebe; Vergebliches Standchen; Dein Blaues Auge; O kuhler Wald; Der tod, das ist die kuhle Nacht; Versagen, Auf dem Kirchhofe; Veir Ernste Gesange; Gestillte Sehnsucht and Geistliches Wiegenlied (songs with vida and piano). Mahler: Ich bin den Welt abhanden kommen; Ich atmet einen Linden Duft; Um Mitternacht. Schubert: Heiden Roslein; Dem Unendlichen; Lachen and Wienen; Sehnsucht; Die Forelle; Die Taubenpost; Gretchn am Spinnerade; Im Abendrot; Der Tot und das Madchen; Sei mir Gegrusst; Die Junge Nonne; Du bist die Ruh; An die Musik; Der Musensohn; Nacht und Traume. Schumann: Widrung; Frauenliebe und Leben; Meine Rose; Marienwurmchen; Die Lotesblume; Mondnact; Der Nussbaum; Requiem; Wenn ich fruh in dem Garten geh; Belsazar; Aus den hebraischen Gesange; Hauptmann's Weib; Suleika. Wolf: Vergorgenheit; Ach des Knaben; Herr was Tragt; Jesuskind; Fuhr mich kind; Die du Gott gebarst; Alle ginen Herz zu Ruh; Fussreise; Der Gartner; Das Vaerlassene Magdlein; Gesang Weylas; Bescheidene Liebe; Gebet; Dieihr Schwebet; Heb auf dein blondes Haupt; In dem schatten meiner Locken; Zur Ruh; Anacreons Grab; Auf ein altes Bild.

Modern songs

Aitken and Bridge: Sigh no more ladies; Go not happy day; Easter Hymn; When you are old and Grey; Love went a-riding. Britten: The Birds; The Charm of Lullabies – A Cradle Song, The Highland Balou, Sephestia's Lullaby, A Charm and The Nurse's Song. Delius: Twilight Fancies. Dvorak: Songs my mother taught me; God is my Shepherd; I will sing thee songs of gladness. Elgar: Sea Pictures; Damask Rose. Ivor Gurney and Michael Head: Severn Meadows; Slumber Song of the Madonna; Come take your lute; Loves Lament; Three Mummers; Sweet Chance; The Little Road to Bethlehem. Hamilton Harty, Holst and Howells: The Sea Wrack; The Heart Worships; King David. John Ireland: The Adoration; I have twelve Oxen. Easthope Master: The Holy Child. Maurice Jacobson: Willow Song; A Song for Christmas. Mendelssohn: On wings of songs. Quilter: Weep you no more; June; To Daisies; Dream Valley; It Was a lover and his lass; Love's Philosophy; Blow, blow thou winter wind. Parry: Love is a bable; Armida's Garden. Mary

Plumstead, Graham Peel and Dorothy Parke: The Song of the Cross; The Early Morning; Wee Hughie. Martin Shaw: Cuckoo; I know a bank. Alec Redshaw: Adoration. Stanford: Johneen; The Bold Unbiddable Child; The Monkey's Carol; A Soft Day. David Cleghorn Thomson/Tschaikovsky: The Knight of Bethlehem; None but the weary heart. Vaughan Williams: Silent Moon; The New Ghost; The Water Mill; The Sky above the Roof; Mystical Songs. Warlock: My Own Country; Pretty Ring-Time; Milkmaids; Fair and Time; Sleep. Walton: Under the Greenwood Tree. Healey Willan: Whence come you good shepherd?; Music when soft voices are. Arr Wilson and Maude Valerie White: Come let's be merry; So we'll go no more a-roving.

Folk songs

Arr Bax and Arr Benjamin: O dear, what can the matter be?; Jan. Arr Benjamin Britten: O can ye sew cushions; Orphan and King Henry; Come you not from Newcastle; The Sally Gardens; The Ash Grove; Heigh Ho, Heigh Hi; Waly, Waly; Oliver Cromwell. Arr Herbert Hughes: How deep in Love am I; The Spanish Lady; I have a bonnet; The Lovers Curse; I will walk with my Love; The Stuttering Lovers; I know where I'm going. Arr John Ireland: The Three Ravens. Arr Robertson: The Fidgety Bairn. Arr Alec Redshaw: Golden Slumbers; I'm ow're young; Lord Rendal; Soldier, Soldier; Go down Moses; Steal Away; Peter go on ring dem bells; Nobody Knows the trouble I've seen; I got a robe. Arr Cecil Sharpe: Oh no John!; I'm seventeen come Sunday. Arr Howard Ferguson: The Apron of Flowers. Arr Kodaly: Going to Market.

Songs and arias with orchestra

Lennox Berkeley: Four Poems of St Teresa of Avila. Brahms: Four Serious Songs. Britten: Flower Song (Lucretia). Elgar: Sea Pictures. Gluck: Che Faro (Orpheo). Grieg: Ein Schwan; Ich liebe dich. Handel: Ombra mai fu; I will magnify thee; Dank sei dir Herr (Cantata Stromenti). Vaughan Williams: Mystical Songs. Mahler: Ich bin der Welt abhanden gekonnen; Ich atmet einen Linden Duft; Um Mitternacht. Saint Saens: Softly awakes my heart; O love from thy power. Bach: Bist du beinir.

17th and 18th Century Composers

Caldara: Come faggio di sol. Gluck: Che faro (Orpheo); O del mio dolce ardor. John Pepusch: Cupid bend thy bow. Handel: I will magnify thee; How chang'd the vision; Pack clouds away; Dearest Consort (Cara Sposa); Spring; Like as the lovelorn turtle; Art thou trou led; Come to me soothing sleep; Ombra mai fu; Non lo dirro col labbro; Vorrei vendi carmi del perfido cor (Alcina). Haydn and Pergolesi: She never told her love; Se tu m'ami; My mother bids. Purcell: Dido's farewell; We sing to him; Music for a-while; Hark the echoing air; Come all ye songsters; Fairest Isle; Nymphs and Shepherds; The Knotting Song; Man is for woman made; Mad Bess; The Evening Hymn; Here the dieties approve; Full fathom five. Scarlatti: Le violette.

Selected discography

- Handel's Messiah – London Records, 1954.
- Arias and choruses from Messiah – Decca, 1957.
- Beethoven – Decca, 1960.
- Britten's Spring Symphony – Decca, 1960.
- Auferstehungs-Symphonie and Resurrection – Deutsche Grammophon, 1969.
- Handel with Karl Richter – Archiv Produktion, 1969.
- Scenes and Arias – Argo, 1969.
- Mahler's Symphony No. 3 – Nonesuch Records, 1971.
- Mahler's Das Klagende Lied – Philips, 1973.
- Excerpts from Messiah – Turnabout, 1974.
- Selections from Messiah – Decca, 1976.
- Mahler & English Ballads – Prelude Records Ltd, 1976.
- Highlights from Messiah – Quintessence, 1978.
- Bach – Cantate, 1981.
- Beethoven – Decca, 2009.
- Mendelssohn's Elijah – Ace of Clubs.
- Messiah – Ace of Clubs.
- Benjamin Britten: The Rarities.
- Mahler's 8th Symphony – CBS.
- Bach Cantatas – Barenreiter.
- Williamson's Julius Caesar Jones – Argo.

A Singing Lesson With Prof

In the early 1930s, Norma's beloved singing tutor Roy 'Prof' Henderson was a prominent baritone on the music scene. In two articles, his approach to performance is explained, and demonstrates how he would have taught Norma.

Published in The Stafford Sentinel on October 20, 1933: 'Mr Roy Henderson spent an hour and a half last evening at the Newcastle Clef Club, giving away professional secrets and short cuts to success. He was lecturing, and illustrating the lecture bountifully by song and example, on speech and song, and it was a lecture all too short. Merely to listen to the cadence of his rich speaking voice as he talked, even ignoring the great interest on what he had to say, would have been a treat in itself for anyone who appreciates the art of speech. And when he sang – but there, Roy Henderson's skill and artistry as a singer are too well known to need mention here.

'Mr Henderson led off by saying that he did not wish to talk of those who never felt emotion (he caustically observed that they usually made fifth-rate musical critics) nor to geniuses who were a law unto themselves. The people he wished to talk to were those who had loved and hated, and had had joys and sorrows – people, in short, who could feel emotion.

'He was out, he said, to show the amateur speaker and singer how to "window-dress" his art. If you were a public speaker you were rather shy; if you were a singer, you looked like a stuffed owl on the platform – you did not know what to do with your hands or your feet. Those who spoke or sang from the public platform had various rules, like cricketer's rules for certain types of bowling. Like the cricketer, they did not have to think consciously of the rule, for the rule had been made part of themselves, and they obeyed it naturally.'

Published in The Huddersfield Examiner on March 30, 1935: 'The first rule in both song and speech was to avoid monotony. They needed rise and fall of pitch; they should avoid the monotone – the sort of thing they sometimes heard from clergymen who read the Bible with little variation in pitch, never more than a minor third. "If that is heavenly," said Mr Henderson, "then give me Hell every time. There is sure to be some variation of pitch there!"

'The voice should be melodic in outline, in speech as in song, for the rise and fall in cadence of a sentence altered its meaning. To raise the voice at the end of the sentence suggested a doubt, a question – except, of course, in Wales, where they raised the voice at the end of every sentence. The downward inflection suggested finality. The important word in a sentence was usually the highest in pitch, though on occasion it could be the lowest. Every nation, however, had its problems. There was a certain kind of Scotsman who spoke on one note, but another had quite a musical turn in his speech, as had the Irishman, who said "Aah away to Hell" with such charming infection that one didn't mind. But the Englishman tended to speak within too few notes: to use a wider range did not go with the old school tie.

'Another way to avoid monotony was to vary pace and rhythm. Happiness, for example, was always quick. He quarrelled with contraltos, who took O Thou Tellest Good Tidings in Zion at six in a bar. If he were conducting it would have to go much faster – two in a bar. The contralto singing that aria slowly was not thinking about good tidings, but "what a beautiful voice I've got."

'A third way to avoid monotony was a change in dynamics. He wondered if they really considered why they sang pianissimo or fortissimo? The reason for the one or the other was to be found in the words, not in the music. In song words came first because it was music put to words. "If you sing the words with the meaning of the words, feeling the words, you will not get far wrong".

'The fourth way to avoid monotony was a change of colour in either the speaking or the singing voice. Of all singing instruments, human voice was capable of the greatest change of colour. Anger produced a characteristic colour, and love produced another. Whenever a young man began love he produced his voice on the soft palate.'

References

aintree-grandnational.co.uk/sheilas-cottage
allmusic.com/artist/norma-procter-mn0002184202/biography
bach-cantatas.com/Bio/Procter-Norma.htm
Benjamin Britten, by Michael Wilcox, published 1997 by Absolute Press.
British Newspaper Archive
Daily Telegraph, March 18, 2000
Discogs.com
en.wikipedia.org/wiki/Aldeburgh_Festival
en.wikipedia.org/wiki/Joan_Sutherland
en.wikipedia.org/wiki/Juliet_Pannett
everymanclub.co.uk/history.html
Ferrier: A Career Recorded, by Paul Campion (new edition 2005).
Grimsby Telegraph
Huddersfield Examiner, March 30, 1935: 'Song and Speech: Mr Roy Henderson at the Victoria Hall'
Hull Daily Mail
Independent.co.uk, November 10, 1995: 'Obituary: Winifred Ferrier'
irishtimes.com/culture/how-elwes-met-britten-i-was-a-bit-of-a-thug-but-i-could-sing-1.1609394
Lancashiretelegraph.co.uk
leodis.net/discovery/discovery.asp?page=20031110_356182278&topic=20031110_154781521&subsection=2003128_444774807
Lincolnshire Women by John R. Ketteringham (1998).
mwwf.org.uk/the-history-of-the-festival.html
Philharmony 1852–1977: The Story of 125 Years of Music-Making by the Grimsby Philharmonic Society and its Forebears, told by Alec Redshaw.
Sir John Pritchard: His Life In Music, by Helen Conway (1993).
Sharrow Bay: World famous country house hotel at Ullswater celebrates its 50th anniversary: special supplement, Cumbria Life.
slippedisc.com/2017/05/death-of-an-early-mahler-singer/
Stafford Sentinel, October 20, 1933: 'Roy Henderson On Speech and Song'
The Grand National: The History Of The Aintree Spectacular by Stewart Peters (2005).
The Music of Man, by Yehudi Menuhin and Curtis W Davis (1980).
thetimes.co.uk/article/norma-procter-5z0s2mqrb
telegraph.co.uk/obituaries/2017/05/12/norma-procter-classical-singer-obituary/

Endnotes

1 Letter to Alexander Anderson-Hall (1992).

2 Told to Dawn Stewart.

3 Handwritten submission to a book called Lincolnshire Women, by Dr. John R Ketteringham.

4 ibid.

5 Letter to Alexander Anderson-Hall (2003).

6 Handwritten submission to a book called Lincolnshire Women, by Dr. John R Ketteringham.

7 ibid.

8 ibid.

9 Grimsby Telegraph, Odd Man Out column by Peter Chapman, on the 50th anniversary of Kathleen Ferrier's death.

10 Handwritten submission to a book called Lincolnshire Women, by Dr. John R Ketteringham.

11 Grimsby Telegraph, Odd Man Out column by Peter Chapman, on the 50th anniversary of Kathleen Ferrier's death.

12 Correspondence with the Kathleen Ferrier Society.

13 Handwritten submission to a book called Lincolnshire Women, by Dr. John R Ketteringham.

14 ibid.

15 ibid.

16 Letter to David Cregeen.

17 At the time of the 1901 census. By the 1939 census, John was living at 194 Clee Road with his own family.

18 Lincolnshire Echo, February 1948.

19 ibid.

20 Told to Dawn Stewart.

21 Archive note.

22 John Procter was not the first Grimbarian to experience the thrill of a Grand National success. In 1843, farmer and steeplechase rider William Loft, the second son of Grimsby MP John Henry Loft, purchased the horse Cure All at Horncastle Fair. It ran successfully in Lincoln and William Sterling-Crawford made Loft an offer to lease the horse to run in the upcoming Grand National of 1845. Loft struck a deal, on the proviso that he rode the horse himself. This he did, and duly won the race. Loft died in Grimsby in December 1887. In 1873, Maunsell Richardson, who resided at Healing Manor close by, won the National on Captain James Machell's Disturbance. The following year, he won again on the same owner's Reugny, which had been trained at the nearby village of Limber. According to local archives, the bridle used in the race was given to Tom Sutcliffe, of Stallingborough, who presented it to Mr Cavel Lowish, of Aylesby, who in turn passed it on to Mr W. Forster, of Stonecroft, Barnetby. Its whereabouts after that are unknown.

23 Lincolnshire Echo, November 30, 1948.

24 Sir John Pritchard: His Life In Music, by Helen Conway.

25 Uncredited press cutting in Norma's archive.

26 Letter to Alexander Anderson-Hall (2002).

27 ibid (1994).

28 Letter to Alexander Anderson-Hall (2011).
29 ibid (1992).
30 Notes made for the Kathleen Ferrier Society.
31 ibid.
32 Norma stayed with the agency throughout her entire career.
33 Diary entry (January 26, 1950).
34 ibid (January 27, 1950).
35 Correspondence with the Kathleen Ferrier Society.
36 ibid.
37 ibid.
38 Letter to Alexander Anderson-Hall dated 1991.
39 Correspondence with the Kathleen Ferrier Society.
40 Lincolnshire Women submission.
41 Correspondence with the Kathleen Ferrier Society.
42 ibid.
43 Told to Kathleen Hopcroft.
44 Told to Fiona Clampin.
45 Lincolnshire Women submission.
46 Letter to Alexander Anderson-Hall (1991)
47 The Grimsby Telegraph's Odd Man Out column, by Peter Chapman.
48 Lincolnshire Women submission.
49 Diary entry (June 3, 1954).
50 Norma performed at Aldeburgh in 1954, and from 1956 up to and including 1961, then again in 1963 and 1964.
51 Correspondence with the then-named Britten Pears Foundation.
52 Other singers Henderson taught included Constance Shacklock, Pamela Bowden, Harvey Alan and John Shirley-Quick.
53 Letter to Alexander Anderson-Hall (July 12, 2008).
54 Letter to David Whittaker.
55 Letter to Alexander Anderson-Hall (July 13, 2008).
56 ibid (1993).
57 Named after Clytie Hine Mundy, the renowned Australian soprano and Britten's voice teacher.
58 The festival began in 1885, one of the country's earliest competitive festivals, focusing on choral works. Mary Wakefield was born in Kendal in 1853. She trained with notable singing teachers in London and won the praise of critics but, denied a professional career in singing due to the conventions of the time in which she lived, she formed community choirs and established the festival instead. She died in 1901.
59 Diary entry (May 28, 1955).
60 Other sources say the date was 1957, yet Norma recorded this in her 1955 diary.
61 An entry in Benjamin Britten's diary, kept at Britten Pears Arts.
62 Judith Ratcliffe, from Britten Pears Arts, said: 'The entries that all three of them make in their diaries in 1955 for an appointment with Decca concerning the Canticle is a slight mystery. We hold a Britten discography by Philip Stuart which states that the Canticle recording was made on February 25, 1957 as we know. It gives the location of the recording as West Hampstead Studio 3. Stuart also writes 'Intended as a replacement for the recording with Kathleen Ferrier (unmade owing to her death in 1953) this was to have been coupled with a recording of Canticle III with Dennis Brain, in turn unmade owing in 1955 to his exclusive contract with EMI and then to his death in September 1957.' Perhaps the plan was to record all Canticles in 1955 with arrangements having been made but cancelled due to Brain's contract with EMI.'
63 Letter to David Whittaker, 2011.
64 Diary entry (December 22, 1955).
65 Lincolnshire Women submission.
66 Diary entry (October 9, 1956).
67 ibid (October 17, 1956).
68 ibid (November 13, 1956).
69 ibid (February 1, 1957).
70 ibid (March 23, 1957).
71 ibid (April 19, 1957).

72 Archive note.
73 Diary entry (July 24, 1957).
74 ibid (July 29, 1957).
75 ibid (January 17, 1958).
76 ibid (January 21, 1958).
77 Told to Dawn Stewart. Judith Ratcliffe, from Britten Pears Arts, said: 'Britten did certainly suffer with performance anxiety. He would not eat before a performance but drink Complan instead, presumably to cope with sickness.'
78 Philharmony, by Alec Redshaw.
79 ibid.
80 Archive notes.
81 Norma sang Othniel in Handel's oratorio Joshua on 21 June 1958, with Peter Pears, Jennifer Vyvyan, and Trevor Anthony.
82 Archive notes.
83 Diary entry (May 15, 1959).
84 Wunderlich died aged 35 after falling down a staircase while on a hunting vacation. His shoelaces had not been properly tied.
85 Correspondence with Alexander Anderson-Hall dated February 11, 1992. The letter thanked him for a birthday present of a CD of Handel's Alcina, featuring Norma and Dame Joan Sutherland.
86 Diary entry (June 20, 1959).
87 Lincolnshire Women submission.
88 Archive note.
89 Diary entry (September 8, 1959).
90 ibid (December 2, 1959).
91 Lincolnshire Women submission.
92 ibid.
93 Correspondence with Alexander Anderson-Hall dated September 13–24, 2005.
94 Norma, Ben and Peter also performed a recital with oboist Haakon Stotijn, and Norma performed in a Mendelsohn Soiree with the English Opera Group, devised by Paul Dehn and produced by Colin Graham.
95 Correspondence with the then named Britten-Pears Foundation.
96 Diary entry (June 28, 1960).
97 Medical note.
98 Diary entry (July 20, 1960).
99 ibid (September 11, 1960).
100 ibid (September 13, 1960).
101 ibid (November 16, 1960).
102 Archive note.
103 Diary entry (November 21, 1960).
104 ibid (December 24, 1960).
105 ibid (December 26, 1960).
106 Archive note.
107 Diary entry (January 13, 1961).
108 Lincolnshire Women submission.
109 This delightful comment was made at a performance in Matley, on October 27, 1959. She performed two groups of songs for the town's musical society at the town hall, and the remark was made by a member of the society's committee after the concert. Norma recorded it in her diary
110 Diary entry (February 2, 1961).
111 A note in the back of her 1960 diary.
112 Diary entry (September 14, 1961).
113 ibid (December 9 & 10, 1961).
114 ibid (December 13, 1961).
115 ibid (December 17, 1961).
116 ibid (December 30, 1961).
117 Medical note.
118 Diary entry (January 1, 1962).
119 ibid (March 27, 1962).
120 ibid (July 21, 1962).
121 ibid (September 2, 1962).
122 ibid (September 11, 1962).
123 ibid (September 14, 1962).
124 Lincolnshire Women submission.
125 Philharmony, by Alec Redshaw.
126 ibid.
127 Diary entry (January 24, 1963).
128 ibid (April 8, 1963).
129 ibid (June 25, 1963).
130 ibid (June 29, 1963).
131 ibid (August 15, 1963).
132 ibid (August 19, 1963).
133 ibid (August 26, 1963).
134 ibid (August 30, 1963).
135 ibid (March 28, 1964).
136 Most likely her sister, Audrey.

137 Diary entry (August 12, 1964).
138 ibid (September 28, 1964).
139 ibid (January 7, 1966).
140 ibid (January 15, 1966).
141 Philharmony, by Alec Redshaw.
142 Diary entry (February 3, 1966).
143 ibid (April 15, 1966).
144 ibid (May 20, 1966).
145 Lincolnshire Women submission.
146 Diary entry (July 17, 1966).
147 ibid (October 15, 1966).
148 Philharmony, by Alec Redshaw.
149 ibid.
150 Letter to Alexander Anderson-Hall dated September 6, 1966.
151 Diary entry (June 10, 1968).
152 ibid (June 23, 1968).
153 Archive notes.
154 Diary entry (December 19, 1968).
155 ibid (December 24, 1968).
156 ibid (January 20, 1969).
157 Correspondence to the then named Britten-Pears Foundation.
158 Archive notes.
159 ibid.
160 ibid.
161 Diary entry (June 25, 1970).
162 ibid (June 30 & July 4, 1970).
163 ibid (August 19, 1970).
164 ibid (August 26, 1970).
165 Archive notes.
166 Diary entry (August 30, 1971).
167 ibid (September 30, 1971).
168 Diary entries (March 24–27, 1972).
169 While writing to Hamburger's son, Peter, following his death in 2004 aged 83.
170 That February, Norma was admitted into St. Hugh's Hospital, Grimsby, in terrible pain with an infection that affected her hearing.
171 Letter to Alexander Anderson-Hall (March 2, 1994).
172 ibid (1997).
173 Archive notes.
174 Lincolnshire Women submission.
175 Letter to Alexander Anderson-Hall (September 13–24, 2005).
176 Medical note.
177 Diary entry (November 7, 1974).
178 Archive notes.
179 Warwick and Warwickshire Advertiser, May 18, 1956.
180 Diary entry (July 26, 1977).
181 ibid (October 3, 1977).
182 Told to Dawn Stewart.
183 Norma talking in 1983 on Yorkshire Televisions' Calendar Tuesday.
184 Letter to Alexander Anderson-Hall (February 18, 2002).
185 A note to the then named Britten-Pears Foundation.
186 Archive notes.
187 Letter from Malcolm McQueen dated August 25, 2009.
188 Letter to Malcolm McQueen, dated August 27, 2009.
189 Letter to David Cregeen, dated June 29, 2006.
190 Archive notes.
191 Lincolnshire Women submission.
192 Letter to Alexander Anderson-Hall (December 7, 1994).
193 Diary entry (June 17, 1982).
194 Lincolnshire Women submission.
195 ibid.
196 Letter to David Whittaker (2012).
197 Diary entry (May 18, 1985).
198 Medical notes in Norma's archive.
199 Letter to Alexander Anderson-Hall (October 2, 1991).
200 Lincolnshire Women submission.
201 According to the Bach Cantatas website.
202 Notes in Norma's archive.
203 Diary entry (September 27, 1986).
204 Medical notes in Norma's archive.
205 Diary entry (February 9, 1987).
206 Letters to David Whittaker (2010).
207 German for 'forbidden'.
208 Letter to Alexander Anderson-Hall (2011).
209 ibid (August 13, 1991).
210 ibid (February 26, 1992).
211 ibid (May 18, 1992).
212 ibid (April 23, 1992).
213 ibid (March 18, 1992).

214 Letter to Alexander Anderson-Hall (March 25, 1992).
215 ibid (April 9, 1992).
216 ibid (May 25, 1992).
217 ibid (June 19, 1992).
218 ibid (October 2, 1992).
219 ibid (November 17, 1992).
220 ibid (December 16, 1992).
221 Medical notes.
222 ibid.
223 Letter to Alexander Anderson-Hall (February 21, 1993).
224 ibid (April 9, 1993).
225 ibid (May 1, 1993).
226 ibid (August 7, 1993).
227 ibid (August 22, 1993).
228 ibid (August 24, 1993).
229 ibid (April 1, 1994).
230 ibid (May 20, 1994).
231 ibid (May 22, 1994).
232 ibid (June 6, 1994).
233 ibid (July 27, 1994).
234 ibid (August 10, 1994).
235 ibid (September 17, 1994).
236 It is assumed Norma is speaking of Dr. Mike, her retired GP.
237 Letter to Alexander Anderson-Hall (October 9 and 10, 1994).
238 ibid (December 7, 1994).
239 ibid (February 21, 1995).
240 ibid (March 14, 1995).
241 ibid (March 23, 1995).
242 ibid (April 23, 1995).
243 ibid (April 25, 1995).
244 ibid (May 21 and 22, 1995).
245 ibid (May 1, 1995).
246 ibid (July 30, 1995).
247 ibid (July 31, 1995).
248 ibid (August 1, 1995).
249 ibid (August 15, 1995).
250 ibid (August 17, 1995).
251 ibid (September 23, 1995).
252 ibid (September 25, 1995).
253 ibid (February, 1, 1996).
254 ibid (February 18, 1996).
255 ibid (May 10, 1996).
256 ibid (September 6, 1996).
257 ibid (October 20, 1996).
258 Letter to Alexander Anderson-Hall (December 1, 1996).
259 ibid (January 12 and 13, 1997).
260 ibid (February 22, 1997).
261 ibid (May 18, 1997).
262 ibid (June 8, 1997).
263 ibid (September 3 and 4, 1997).
264 Diary entry (November 29, 1998).
265 Letter to Alexander Anderson-Hall (November 1 and 2, 1998.
266 ibid (May 2, 1999).
267 ibid (October 30 and 31, 1999).
268 Typewritten from Budleigh Salterton, Devon, on July 30, 1997.
269 Letter to Alexander Anderson-Hall (October 30 and 31, 1999).
270 ibid (April 28, 2001).
271 ibid (May 22, 2001).
272 Medical note.
273 Letter to Alexander Anderson-Hall (October 27, 2001).
274 Medical note.
275 Letter to Alexander Anderson-Hall (April 27, 2002).
276 ibid (October 21, 2002).
277 Diary entry (February 24, 2003).
278 Letter to Alexander Anderson-Hall (July 7 and 8, 2003).
279 ibid (October 25, 2003).
280 ibid (February 20, 2004).
281 ibid (August 14, 2004).
282 ibid (September 13–24, 2005).
283 ibid (December 7, 2005).
284 ibid (May 20–21, 2006).
285 ibid (July 13, 2006).
286 ibid (February 20, 2007).
287 ibid (December 1, 2007).
288 ibid (July 12 and 13, 2008).
289 Letters to David Whittaker (various dates).
290 Letter to Alexander Anderson-Hall (September 7, 2009).
291 Letter to David Whittaker (2009).
292 Letter to Alexander Anderson-Hall (May 30, 2010).
293 ibid (February 20, 2011).
294 Letter to David Whittaker (2010).
295 ibid (2011).

296 Letter to David Whittaker (2012).
297 Diary entry (September 20, 2013).
298 ibid (November 25, 2015).
299 Correspondence to David Cregeen.
300 Correspondence to Kathleen Hopcroft.
301 See https://en.wikipedia.org/wiki/Isobel_Baillie.
302 Never Sing Louder Than Lovely, published in 1982.
303 See https://en.wikipedia.org/wiki/Isobel_Baillie.
304 Letter to Alexander Anderson-Hall (May 30, 2010).
305 Underneath the window of her music room at Nor-Dree, Norma grew the Kathleen Ferrier rose, a gift from her friends Clive and Jo Champney.
306 See www.musicianschapel.org.uk/history.